Studies in Church History

39

THE CHURCH AND MARY

THE CHURCH AND MARY

PAPERS READ AT
THE 2001 SUMMER MEETING AND
THE 2002 WINTER MEETING OF
THE ECCLESIASTICAL HISTORY SOCIETY

EDITED BY

R.N. SWANSON

PUBLISHED FOR
THE ECCLESIASTICAL HISTORY SOCIETY
BY
THE BOYDELL PRESS
2004

First published 2004

A publication of the Ecclesiastical History Society
in association with The Boydell Press
an imprint of Boydell & Brewer Ltd
PO Box 9, Woodbridge, Suffolk IP12 3DF, UK
and of Boydell & Brewer Inc.
668 Mt Hope Avenue, Rochester, NY 14620, USA
website: www.boydellandbrewer.com

ISBN 0 9546809 0 1

ISSN 0424–2084

A catalogue record for this book is available
from the British Library

Library of Congress Cataloging-in-Publication Data
The church and Mary / edited by R. N. Swanson.
   p. cm. – (Studies in church history, ISSN 0424–2084 ; 39)
ISBN 0–9546809–0–1 (hardback : alk. paper)
1. Mary, Blessed Virgin, Saint. 2. Church history. I. Swanson,
R. N. (Robert Norman) II. Title III. Series.
BT603.C57 2004
232.91–dc22   2004018495

Details of previous volumes are available from Boydell & Brewer Ltd

This book is printed on acid-free paper

Typeset by Pru Harrison, Hacheston, Suffolk
Printed in Great Britain by
Cromwell Press, Trowbridge, Wiltshire

CONTENTS

PREFACE

'The Church and Mary' was proposed by Professor Henry Mayr-Harting as the theme for the conferences of the Ecclesiastical History Society held under his presidency at University College, Chester, in July 2001, and at the Institute of Historical Research in London in January 2002. This volume offers a selection of the diverse and stimulating approaches to the theme which were presented at those sessions. The seven main papers delivered at the conferences are included, with a selection of the communications offered at the Chester meeting. As ever, the selection process to determine the final contents of the volume proved extremely difficult; I am grateful to all those who commented on texts and so helped ease the task.

The Society is grateful to University College, Chester, for accommodating the summer conference. Particular thanks are due to John Doran for his work in ensuring that a pleasant time was had by all, even if the weather was not what it might have been. Thanks are also due to the Institute of Historical Research in London and its staff for accommodating the January meeting and ensuring that the day ran smoothly.

* * *

This is my final volume as editor of *Studies in Church History*. I wish to express my thanks to all the authors who have tolerated my interventions over the years, and the delays which have occurred more often than desirable – especially with this particular volume. I am particularly grateful to Meg Davies for her smooth handling of the copy-editing, all too often at short notice, and to all at Boydell & Brewer who have made the processing of these volumes run relatively smoothly, especially Vanda Andrews, Pru Harrison, and Caroline Palmer. With volume 40, *Studies in Church History* has already moved into a new era. I have passed the torch to Jeremy Gregory and Kate Cooper with some regret, for I shall definitely miss the stimulation of dealing with the wide range of contributions in the volumes . . . and with the contributors to them.

Robert Swanson

CONTRIBUTORS

Henry MAYR-HARTING (*President*)
Regius Professor Emeritus of Ecclesiastical History, University of Oxford

Jane BAUN
Fellow of Greyfriars Hall, Oxford, and Visiting Research Fellow, King's College London

Walter BERSCHIN
Director of the Seminar für Lateinisches Philologie des Mittelalters und der Neuzeit, Ruprecht-Karls-Universität Heidelberg

Sarah Jane BOSS
Director of the Centre for Marian Studies, University of Wales, Lampeter

Averil CAMERON
Warden of Keble College, Oxford

Kate COOPER
Senior Lecturer in Ecclesiastical History, University of Manchester

Mary B. CUNNINGHAM
Research Fellow, University of Birmingham

Nancy M. de FLON
Director of Parish Faith Formation, Diocese of Ogdensburg, New York

Carol Marie ENGELHARDT
Associate Professor of History, Wright State University

Thomas S. FREEMAN
Research Associate, The British Academy John Foxe Project, University of Sheffield

Jane GARNETT
Fellow and Tutor in History, Wadham College, Oxford

Sean GILL
Senior Lecturer in Theology and Religious Studies, University of Bristol

Joan GREATREX
Senior Member, Robinson College, Cambridge

Bridget HEAL
Lecturer in Modern History, University of St Andrews
Trevor JOHNSON
Lecturer in History, University of the West of England
Kallirroe LINARDOU
Research Student, University of Birmingham
Iona MCCLEERY
Lecturer in Medieval History, University of Edinburgh
Diarmaid MAcCULLOCH
Professor of the History of the Church and Fellow of St Cross
College, University of Oxford
Jeremy MORRIS
Dean and Fellow of Trinity Hall, Cambridge
W.B. PATTERSON
Francis S. Houghteling Professor of History, University of the
South
Patrick PRESTON
Research Fellow in Church History, University College,
Chichester
Richard PRICE
Lecturer in Church History, Heythrop College, University of
London
Gervase ROSSER
Fellow and Tutor in History, St Catherine's College, Oxford
David SKINNER
Fellow of Magdalen College, Oxford
Nicholas VINCENT
Professor of Medieval History, University of East Anglia
William WIZEMAN, SJ
Assistant Professor of Theology, Fordham University
A.D. WRIGHT
Reader in Ecclesiastical History, University of Leeds
D.F. WRIGHT
Emeritus Professor of Patristic and Reformed Christianity,
University of Edinburgh
Marta Camilla WRIGHT

ABBREVIATIONS

Abbreviated titles are adopted within each paper after the first full citation. Unless otherwise indicated, the place of publication for monographs is London. The following abbreviations are used for texts and periodicals cited frequently in the volume:

ACO	E. Schwartz, ed., *Acta Conciliorum Oecumenicorum* (Strasbourg and Berlin, 1914–40)
ActaSS	*Acta sanctorum*, ed. J. Bolland and G. Henschen (Antwerp, etc., 1643–)
BAV	Vatican City, Bibliotheca Apostolica Vaticana
BIHR	*Bulletin of the Institute of Historical Research* (London, 1923–86)
BL	London, British Library
BN	Paris, Bibliothèque Nationale
Bodley	Oxford, Bodleian Library
CathHR	*Catholic Historical Review* (Washington, DC, 1915–)
CChr	Corpus Christianorum (Turnhout, 1953–)
CChr.CM	Corpus Christianorum, continuatio medievalis (1966–)
CChr.SL	Corpus Christianorum, series Latina (1953–)
ChH	*Church History* (New York/Chicago, 1932–)
CUL	Cambridge University Library
EHR	*English Historical Review* (London, 1886–)
Holum	Kenneth G. Holum, *Theodosian Empresses: Women and Imperial Dominion in Late Antiquity* (Berkeley, CA, and London, 1982)
JBS	*Journal of British Studies* (Hartford, CT, 1961–)
JEH	*Journal of Ecclesiastical History* (Cambridge, 1950–)
JThS	*Journal of Theological Studies* (London, 1899–)
Limberis	Vasiliki Limberis, *Divine Heiress. The Virgin Mary and the Creation of Christian Constantinople* (London, 1994)
MGH	Monumenta Germaniae Historica inde ab a. 500 usque ad a. 1500, ed. G. H. Pertz *et al.* (Hanover, Berlin, etc., 1826–)
P&P	*Past and Present: A Journal of Scientific History* (London/Oxford, 1952–)

PG	*Patrologia Graeca*, ed. J. P. Migne, 161 vols (Paris, 1857–66)
PL	*Patrologia Latina*, ed. J. P. Migne, 217 vols + 4 index vols (Paris, 1841–61)
PS	Parker Society (Cambridge, 1841–55)
RS	Rerum Brittanicarum medii aevi scriptores, 99 vols (London, 1858–1911) = Rolls Series
SCH	*Studies in Church History* (London/Oxford/Woodbridge, 1964–)
SCH.S	Studies in Church History: Subsidia (Oxford/Woodbridge, 1978–)
Speculum	*Speculum: A Journal of Medieval Studies* (Cambridge, MA, 1925–)
Vassilaki	Maria Vassilaki, ed., *Mother of God: Representations of the Virgin in Byzantine Art* (Milan and Athens, 2000)

INTRODUCTION

The subject of Mary is a perennially topical one in Christian history, not least because Mary is one of only two people besides Jesus mentioned in the Apostles' Creed. In recent decades Mary has been especially topical for two quite different but equally powerful reasons. First, she has become a major figure in the whole ecumenical movement, not least because the Second Vatican Council, by a happy inspiration, chose to treat her primarily as an image of the Church in its large-thinking Constitution on that theme. Recently, in his sermon before the Queen as reported in the *Times* of 14 January 2002, Cardinal Cormac Murphy-O'Connor spoke about Mary, basing his sermon on the story of the Wedding at Cana. He pointed out that the principal guest there had been not Jesus, but his mother; and he then went on to stress those attitudes to Mary which were shared by Christians of all denominations. With further regard to ecumenism, only in the previous year to this sermon, namely 2001, had John Macquarrie's masterly *Mary for All Christians* (1990) gone into a new edition. Second, Mary is a topical figure because so much fine scholarship has recently been devoted to her, for example the great sweep of Jaroslav Pelikan's *Mary through the Centuries: Her Place in the History of Culture* (1996); the fascinating ethnographical study by Thomas Tweed, *Our Lady of the Exile* (1997); the sensitive discussions in Ruth Harris, *Lourdes* (1999); Sarah Jane Boss, *Empress and Handmaid: on Nature and Gender in the Cult of the Virgin Mary* (2000); D.A. Brading, *Mexican Phoenix, Our Lady of Guadalupe: Image and Tradition across Five Centuries* (2001); the publications of the *Ecumenical Society of the Blessed Virgin Mary*, many of the highest scholarly value; and much else besides.

One of the advantages of the theme of Mary for the Ecclesiastical History Society's summer and winter conferences in 2001–2 was that while on the one hand it was a more precisely focused theme than most which have been adopted, on the other hand it offered enormous inter-disciplinary scope. Theology, liturgy, art, musicology, gender studies, literature, social anthropology, and straight history, all play their part in the papers of this volume. Moreover, I think the members of the Society would have said, to a person, *vive la différence!* They were more than happy on one and the same day to consider the niceties of the Latin with which Mary was honoured in the Middle Ages, and the way she provided a localist identity – almost an alternative source of authority to the mainline political – in Genoa of more modern centuries; as happy to listen to what could be adduced about Mary from the government records of King Henry III, as to a paper about the amount of musical organization trained on Marian music at the time when the Reformation was about to break on England.

One could have envisaged that the theme of Mary would lend itself not only to inter-disciplinary papers, which it did handsomely, but also to world-wide studies. But there, notwithstanding a good paper on Ethiopia, one has to admit that this volume is on the whole Euro- and Anglo-centric. Whatever the explanation for this, it is certainly not lack of appreciation of the recent achievements in American Mariology. On the other hand, a certain anxiety of mine when proposing the theme, that it would leave the early modernists with relatively little to say, has proved happily and completely unfounded. The seven or eight papers on that period in this volume will surely come to be seen as of central importance in the discussion of how Mary figured in its confessionalism, and thus in the discussion of the nature of those confessions themselves. I believe and hope also that the cluster of papers on Late Antique and Byzantine religious culture will likewise be seen as important in that field, albeit more obviously a fruitful area of Marian study than is the early modern period.

Finally, when one thinks of Marina Warner's hard-hitting and highly stimulating book, *Alone of All Her Sex*, it can scarcely be doubted that, besides being an object of devotion to many, Mary will always be a subject of lively debate, particularly as an image of womanhood, or rather the various images of womanhood which have been made of her.

Henry Mayr-Harting

THE CULT OF THE VIRGIN IN LATE ANTIQUITY: RELIGIOUS DEVELOPMENT AND MYTH-MAKING

by AVERIL CAMERON

IT is sometimes both necessary and useful to go backwards in history, to disentangle an earlier development not by the usual method of piecing together the contemporary evidence but by approaching it through the eyes of later generations. This is certainly true of the present subject. We can say with confidence that late antiquity, especially the period from the fifth century onwards, marked the formative stage in the growth of cult and veneration offered to Mary. Yet one of the most striking experiences in any attempt to disentangle this development is the gradual recognition of exactly how much of our understanding has been shaped by later ideas, wishes, and religious agendas. Investigation of this subject entails the attempt to deal with many texts which are in themselves extremely hard to date; and indeed some of the 'evidence' itself, at least the written evidence, turns out to consist of a tangle of later legend passing for history – so much so in fact that I am considerably less certain about the subject now than when I originally wrote about it over twenty years ago.[1]

This is undoubtedly due to what has been a remarkable upsurge of interest in the topic of Mary in Late Antiquity and in the East. The important exhibition of icons of the Virgin mounted by the Benaki Museum in Athens in late 2000, with its accompanying catalogue and associated conference, is just one example of this interest. Although the

---

[1] Averil Cameron, 'The Theotokos in sixth-century Constantinople: a city finds its symbol', *JThS*, n.s. 29 (1978), 79–108; 'The Virgin's robe: an episode in the history of early seventh-century Constantinople', *Byzantion*, 49 (1979), 42–56. See also 'Images of authority: elites and icons in late-sixth century Byzantium', *P&P*, 84 (Aug. 1979), 3–35 and 'The language of images; icons and Christian representation', *SCH*, 28 (1992), 1–42. There is a substantial more recent bibliography. See for instance the essays in Vassilaki (the catalogue to the exhibition of icons of the Virgin at the Benaki Museum, Athens), and the further collection, Maria Vassilaki, ed., *Images of the Mother of God: Perceptions of the Theotokos in Byzantium* (Aldershot, 2004). See also Jaroslav Pelikan, *Mary Through the Centuries. Her Place in History and Culture* (New Haven, CT, and London, 1996); Luigi Gambero S.M., *Mary and the Fathers of the Church. The Blessed Virgin Mary in Patristic Thought*, Eng. trans. by Thomas Buffer (San Francisco, 1999); Limberis; M. O'Carroll, ed., *Theotokos. A Theological Encyclopaedia* (Wilmington, DA, 1982). There is also much useful material in the collection of translations and commentaries on later Marian homilies by Brian E. Daley, S.J., *On the Dormition of Mary. Early Patristic Homilies* (Crestwood, NY, 1998).

interest has been by no means limited to art historians,[2] it is a notable feature of some recent art-historical writing on the Virgin that it has been contextualized within a fresh and detailed analysis of the textual tradition, and this has provided a powerful extra tool for historians and philologists.[3] In addition, given the nature of our evidence for the cultural history of Late Antiquity and Byzantium, and the importance of visual representation within that culture, any account of the developing cult of the Virgin must utilize many different kinds of evidence – textual, visual, liturgical, theological. We shall see that part of the story of increased devotional attention to the Virgin in Late Antiquity and beyond is the story of the very characteristically Late Antique and Byzantine combination of fascination and unease in the matter of the representation of the divine.[4] The story must be approached from within the context of the ever-growing legends and tales which attempted to concretize and fill out the disappointing lack of detail provided by the history of earlier centuries.

It is easy enough to identify some key moments and firm points, especially during the fifth century. One is provided by the Council of Ephesus in 431, the third Ecumenical Council, when the title of Theotokos was formally endorsed. Another is the building of S. Maria Maggiore in Rome by Sixtus III a few years later, the first great Marian church now surviving, and a magnificent testimonial to the impact of the Council. A formal iconographic vocabulary had to be found for the decoration of so public a monument, and Mary famously appears in the scene of the Annunciation in the mosaics on the church's triumphal arch dressed as a dignified Roman matron; in the scene of the Adoration of the Magi, while she wears a veil and not a jewelled headdress or diadem, the Child is seated on a jewelled throne beside her.[5] Other

---

[2] Cf. N. Tsironis, 'The lament of the Virgin Mary from Romanos the Melode to George of Nicomedia' (University of London, Ph.D. thesis, 1998).

[3] A particularly rich example, highly relevant to my subject, is the recent article by Annemarie Weyl Carr, 'Threads of authority: the Virgin Mary's veil in the Middle Ages', in Stewart Gordon, ed., *Robes and Honor. The Medieval World of Investiture* (New York, 2001), 59–94.

[4] For an interesting discussion of these difficulties with regard to the representation of angels, see Glenn Peers, *Subtle Bodies. Representing Angels in Byzantium* (Berkeley and Los Angeles, CA, 2001). The Virgin shared in the difficulties felt about the proper visual representation of Christ and the angels during Iconoclasm.

[5] For the latter, see Jás Elsner, *Imperial Rome and Christian Triumph. The Art of the Roman Empire AD 100–450* (Oxford, 1998), pl. 153 (at 228); for the former, A. Grabar, *Byzantium: From the Death of Theodosius to the Rise of Islam* (1966), pl. 161. For the Virgin in early apse mosaics see C. Ihm, *Die Programme der christliche Apsismalerei vom vierten Jahrhundert bis zur*

notable points are the recognition of a feast of the Assumption by the end of the sixth century, and the fabled intervention of the Virgin to save Constantinople from defeat in the siege mounted by the Avars and Persians in 626.[6] Representations of the Virgin in visual art increased during the sixth and seventh centuries. From this period dates the beautiful icon of the Virgin with angels and military saints from St Catherine's monastery at Sinai, and Rome still possesses several important early images of her.[7] No such images have survived from Constantinople from this time, but in the sixth- and seventh-century east the Virgin and Child appears in surviving ivory diptychs, and in apse mosaics and frescoes, and the literary sources tell us of more images that have since been lost.[8] A story describing the beginning of Byzantine iconoclasm in the early eighth century has an icon of the Virgin from Lydda which was thrown into the sea for safety by the Patriarch Germanos. It reached Rome, having sailed up the Tiber in a standing position, and later returned to Constantinople to safety later and was deposited in the church of the Virgin known as Chalkoprateia.[9] Again in the eighth century comes the

---

Mitte des achten Jahrhunderts (Wiesbaden, 1960), emphasising an imperial model; J.-M. Spieser, 'The representation of Christ in the apses of early Christian churches', *Gesta*, 37 (1998), 63–73.

[6] See Cameron, 'The Theotokos'; J. Howard-Johnston, 'The siege of Constantinople in 626', in Cyril Mango and Gilbert Dagron, with the assistance of Geoffrey Greatrex, eds, *Constantinople and its Hinterland* (Aldershot, 1995), 131–42. Bissera V. Penchera, following Leslie Brubaker, argues that the association of icons of the Virgin with Constantinople post-dates Iconoclasm: 'The supernatural protector of Constantinople: the Virgin and her icons in the tradition of the Avar siege', *Byzantine and Modern Greek Studies*, 26 (2002), 2–41. However, the role ascribed to the Virgin in 626 does not depend only on the evidence of icons; cf. P. Speck, 'The Virgin's help for Constantinople', ibid., 27 (2003), 266–71.

[7] For the Roman icons of the Virgin see H. Belting, *Likeness and Presence. A History of the Image before the Era of Art* (Chicago, 1994); M. Andaloro, 'L'icona cristiana e gli artisti', in S. Ensoli and E. La Rocca, eds, *Aurea Roma. Dalla città pagana alla città cristiana* (Rome, 2000), 416–24; Charles Barber, 'Early representations of the Mother of God', in Vassilaki, 243–61.

[8] For some examples see Cameron, 'The language of images'.

[9] Cf. E. von Dobschütz, 'Maria Rhomaia', *Byzantinische Zeitschrift*, 12 (1903), 173–214; also idem, *Christusbilder. Untersuchungen zur christlichen Legende*, Texte und Untersuchungen, 18 (Leipzig, 1899), Beilage VI B. A similar story is told of a Christ icon in the *Letter of the Three Patriarchs*, on which see C. Walter, 'Iconographical considerations', in J.A. Munitiz, J. Chrysostomides, E. Harvalia-Crook and C. Dendrinos, *The Letter of the Three Patriarchs to Emperor Theophilos and Related Texts* (Camberley, 1997), li–lxxviii, at lxi–lxiii. Such stories of the miraculous feats of icons during the Iconoclast period took shape in the late ninth century after the ending of the controversy in 843, a period of intense *post hoc* justification of images and their cult; similarly the idea of the dedication of Constantinople to the Virgin belongs to the period after the Russian siege in 860: see C. Angelidi, *Pulcheria. La castità al potere (c. 399–c. 455)* (Milan, 1996), 134.

first mention of a wonder-working icon of the Virgin painted by St Luke in the work of the Greek writer, Andrew of Crete;[10] this too is told in the context of the defence of icon-veneration against the iconoclasts.

Late though it might seem, this was a period when both the cult of the Virgin and her representation in visual art were still in the process of formation. One problem lies in the skew of the evidence. In the fifth century episodes, the evidence relating to the Virgin is often tangled up with the doctrinal controversies surrounding the Council of Ephesus and the person of the Empress Pulcheria. Much of the evidence also comes from Constantinople, where the Virgin came to enjoy a special role. In later periods the Virgin's story was often told in the context of the defence of images, especially miraculous images of the Virgin herself. Not infrequently, these tales had the hidden agenda of demonstrating the triumph of orthodoxy over a stereotyped Judaism. From the ninth century onwards, after the ending of iconoclasm, the Virgin truly came into her own in the Greek east, and especially in Constantinople. The regular processional liturgies associated with her icon in the Middle Byzantine period, and the different conditions of the Palaeologan period, encouraged the production of new versions of her early cult, but by then history had frequently been replaced by legends and pseudo-history, written down long after the event. This is particularly true when we come to consider the early churches, relics, and

[10] See Belting, *Likeness and Presence*, 57; cf. Andrew of Crete, *PG* 97, col. 1304 B–C. Walter, 'Iconographical considerations', lv–lvi, rightly casts doubt on the story cited in the early fourteenth century by Nicephorus Callistus Xanthopoulos, *PG* 86.1, col. 165A, which envisaged this icon's existence in the fifth century and attributed its acquisition to Eudocia; see also R.J. Wolff, 'Footnote to an incident of the Latin occupation of Constantinople: the church and icon of the Hodegetria', *Traditio*, 6 (1948), 319–28, and Angelidi, *Pulcheria*, 80–1. For wonder-working icons see also J. Munitiz, 'Wonder-working icons in the letter to Theophilus', in L. Garland, ed., *Conformity and Non-conformity in Byzantium:, Papers given to the 8th Conference of the Australian Association of Byzantine Studies, University of New England, Australia, July 1993, Byzantinische Forschungen,* 24 (Amsterdam, 1997), 115–23, and Marie-France Auzépy, 'L'Évolution de l'attitude face au miracle à Byzance (VIIe–IXe siècle)', in *Miracles, prodiges et merveilles au Moyen Âge: XXVe Congrès, Société des historiens médiévistes de l'enseignement supérieur public* (Paris, 1995), 31–46. It was one of the aims of the iconophiles at II Nicaea (787) to demonstrate that icons did indeed work miracles: ibid., 43. Andrew of Crete in the eighth century also composed four homilies on the Virgin: *PG* 97, cols 801–87, on which see C. Angelidi, 'Homilies on the nativity of the Theotokos', in S. Kaklamanes, A. Markopoulos and I. Mavromatis, eds, *Enthymesis. Festschrift N.M. Panagiotakis* (Heraklion, 2000), 1–11 (in Greek) and further for Mariology in Andrew of Crete, Mary Cunningham, 'Andrew of Crete: a high-style preacher of the eighth century', in Mary B. Cunningham and Pauline Allen, eds, *Preacher and Audience. Studies in Early Christian and Byzantine Homilies* (Leiden, 1998), 267–91.

images of the Virgin: earlier stories were reworked in much later periods, and earlier texts recirculated in versions interpolated with passages claiming a probably anachronistic role for religious images. Together they provided an ever-more embellished history of the Virgin's legendary protection of Constantinople.

By the Middle Byzantine period, when the veneration of the Virgin was firmly established in the public life of Constantinople, it was even claimed that the city had been dedicated to her by Constantine.[11] An event referred to as 'the usual miracle' regularly occurred on Fridays at the church of the Virgin at Blachernai. In late Byzantium, the icon of the Virgin known as the Hodegetria was formally carried out of the Hodegoi monastery in procession. It is this icon, believed to have been painted by St Luke, which is anachronistically shown in a fifteenth-century icon in the British Museum depicting in a formalized scene with the imperial personages of the day the official ending of iconoclasm, or 'triumph of Orthodoxy', in the ninth century.[12]

* * *

This article will focus first on the crucial period from the late fourth and early fifth centuries onwards which does mark one of these crucial stages. It is also necessary to ask what constitutes a 'cult'. What are the markers by which such a development can be recognized? Here we encounter a puzzling feature, for it seems that the Virgin was rather slow to share in the manifestations which can be traced for other cults in this period. For example, the cult of Thecla, the virgin heroine of the apocryphal *Acts of Paul and Thecla*, had clearly become well established already in the fourth century, when her shrine at Seleucia (Silifke) in Asia Minor was visited by the pilgrim Egeria in the 380s.[13] The

---

[11] See Cyril Mango, 'Constantinople as Theotokoupolis', in Vassilaki, 17–25, at 23–4; the best overall account of much of the ground covered in this paper is given by Angelidi, *Pulcheria*. For Pulcheria see also the article by Kate Cooper, below, pp. 39–51

[12] On the Hodegetria see several essays in Vassilaki, esp. C. Angelidi and T. Papamastorakis, 'The veneration of the Virgin Hodegetria and the Hodegon monastery', ibid., 373–85. The processions and rituals connected with the Hodegetria belong to the thirteenth century and later: see C. Angelidi, 'Un texte patriographique et édifiant: le 'discours narratif' sur les Hodègoi', *Revue des études byzantines*, 52 (1994), 113–49. For the British Museum Triumph of Orthodoxy icon see David Buckton, ed., *Byzantium. Treasures of Byzantine Art and Culture* (1994), no. 140 (129–30).

[13] For the cult of Thecla see Stephen Davis, *The Cult of St. Thecla* (Oxford, 2001), who surveys the plentiful contemporary textual and material evidence, which provides a striking contrast to the evidence for a cult of Mary in the same period.

evidence suggests that Thecla was a more popular, and perhaps more accessible, object of devotion than Mary during the early period, with all the accoutrements of cult – at least one major pilgrimage site,[14] depictions in visual art and on pilgrim souvenirs, and a fifth-century *Life and Miracles* collection.[15] The development of the Virgin's cult must also be seen in the context of others which are more clearly and conventionally visible: for example Menas in Egypt and Artemius and Cosmas and Damian in Constantinople.[16] The Virgin's healing shrine at Pege, outside the Theodosian walls of Constantinople, is attributed to Justinian by Procopius,[17] though later generations projected this too back to the reign of Leo I; however it did not reach its height until later in the Byzantine period.

I am suggesting that the Virgin's cult started rather slowly, and for different reasons, in comparison with the cults of saints in Late Antiquity, for which we have far better evidence. From another perspective, it may seem surprising that it had not come much earlier. 400 years seems rather a long time to wait. A brief indication of the background in the preceding centuries may therefore be useful, as we seek to answer this question.[18]

Despite the interest taken in Mary by such second-century writers as Justin and Irenaeus and their construction of her as the counterpart to or second Eve, and despite the apocryphal writing about her infancy and childhood known as the *Protevangelium of James*,[19] traces of a real cult of the Virgin before the late fourth century are sparse or non-existent. We should probably leave aside the claim made in Epiphanius of Salamis's list of heresies that there was an obscure group of women, the

---

[14] Davis argues for a major shrine of Thecla at Mareotis in Egypt, west of Alexandria, in addition to the main complex at Seleucia. She was depicted in Egypt at least from the fourth century on, and her cult later spread to many other Mediterranean centres.

[15] See G. Dagron, ed., *Vie et miracles de Sainte Thècle* (Brussels, 1978).

[16] See P. Maraval, *Lieux saints et pèlerinages d'Orient. Histoire et géographie des origines à la conquête arabe* (Paris, 1985).

[17] *De aedificiis*, I.3.6–8.

[18] See my 'The early cult of the Virgin', in Vassilaki, 3–15; also Raymond Brown et al., eds., *Mary in the New Testament* (London, 1978).

[19] For the latter see James K. Elliott, *The Apocryphal New Testament* (Oxford, 1993); E. de Strycker, *La Forme la plus ancienne du Protévangile de Jacques*, Subsidia Hagiographica, 33 (Brussels, 1961). The *Gospel of Thomas* fills out the 'missing' years of the childhood of Jesus in much the same way. The sinlessness of Mary was argued to have cancelled the shame brought on women by the sin of Eve, which had led to the curse of sexuality: Mary was the type of obedience against Eve's disobedience. For a brief exposition see Elizabeth A. Clark, *Women in the Early Church* (Wilmington, DA, 1983), ch. 1, citing Irenaeus, *Adversus haereseis*, 3.22.4.

Collyridians, who particularly venerated her: though feminist and
Marian scholars have wanted to make much of this claim, Epiphanius is
the only early heresiologist to name the 'Collyridians', and later refer-
ences seem to derive from him, rather than having independent worth.[20]
However, we begin to hear more about her by the late fourth century.
This increased attention can be observed not only in Christological but
also in ascetic contexts, for instance in the intense interest of such writers
as Jerome in the physical details of the birth of Christ. Not only was
Mary the touchstone and guarantor of the two natures of Christ in the
Incarnation; she was also now the type of virginity and ascetic virtue, and
as such she is praised by such writers as Cyril of Jerusalem, Ambrose, and
Augustine. For Ambrose, for example, author of treatises on virginity, on
virgins, and on the dedication of a consecrated virgin, and a writer who
makes many references to Mary in his other works, the Virgin is an
example for all virgins, truly the Mother of God and also the type of the
Church.[21] Later in his life he addressed the contemporary debate about
Mary's perpetual virginity, which he passionately defended. It symbolized for him not only the true nature of Christ, but also the purity of the
Church and the ideal of virginity which he energetically promoted.[22]
Nevertheless this does not add up to cult. None of the Constantinian
churches or their successors in the fourth century was yet dedicated to
the Virgin.[23] Depictions of her in catacomb art or sarcophagi are relatively few, being generally confined to Nativity scenes or the adoration
of the Magi (as indeed they are in S. Maria Maggiore).[24] Nevertheless, the
fourth-century Fathers, not least Ephrem the Syrian,[25] can be seen to

[20] *Panarion*, 59, discussed e.g. by M.P. Carroll, *The Cult of the Virgin Mary* (Princeton, NJ,
1986), 42–8; S. Benko, *The Virgin Goddess: Studies in the Pagan and Christian Roots of Mariology*
(Leiden, 1993), 170–95.
[21] See Peter Brown, *The Body and Society. Men, Women and Sexual Renunciation in Early
Christianity* (New York, 1988), 351–2.
[22] Ibid., 357; cf. 359–62 on the differing views held e.g. by Jovinian.
[23] For discussion of the earliest Constantinopolitan churches to the Virgin see Mango,
'Constantinople as Theotokoupolis', 17–19. Good discussion also in Angelidi, *Pulcheria*,
123–4. *Pace* Holum, 164 n.90, the cathedral church of the Virgin at Ephesus is now dated to
c.500; an earlier church had apparently been converted from the Hadrianic Olympieion; see
S. Karwiese, 'The church of Mary and the temple of Hadrian Olympius', in H. Koester, ed.,
Ephesos. Metropolis of Asia, Harvard Theological Studies, 41 (Valley Forge, PA, 1995), 311–19.
[24] Adoration of the Magi: catacomb of Priscilla, late third century; catacomb of SS Mark
and Marcellian, fourth century: see Thomas F. Mathews, *The Clash of Gods. A Reinterpretation
of Early Christian Art*, rev. edn (Princeton, NJ, 1999), 82–3. Nativity: Rome, fourth century,
ibid., 48–9; flight into Egypt: sarcophagus at Istanbul, fifth-sixth century, ibid. 45.
[25] For brief discussion see Cameron, 'Early cult'; for Ephrem, see Gambero, *Mary and the
Fathers*, 108–19.

have been developing an increasingly important role for Mary both in Scriptural exegesis and in their understanding of the importance of virginity as an ideal, and this deepening understanding of Mary, which led naturally to veneration of her as a person, is part of the background for the Council of Ephesus.

* * *

The status of Mary was not an issue debated at the Council of Nicaea in 325 or that of Constantinople in 381. However, by the early fifth century things had changed. Christological debate had advanced to the stage when it was now quite natural that the argument at and before the Council of Ephesus of AD 431 should have centred on this issue.[26] The Council confirmed Mary's title as Theotokos, literally 'she who gave birth to God', a term used in distinction to 'Christotokos', 'she who gave birth to Christ', as signifying beyond doubt the divine nature. The title Theotokos, denied to Mary by Nestorius (Patriarch of Constantinople since 428), but granted by the Council, did not come from nowhere. The contemporary church historian Socrates defends it by referring to earlier precedent, citing Eusebius of Caesarea,[27] and it had been used by some writers for at least a century.[28] Now its justification was famously upheld by Cyril of Alexandria against Nestorius. A previous Council held in Rome in 430 had already pronounced against Nestorius and Cyril sent legates to anathematize him; he was formally deposed by the Ecumenical Council convened at Ephesus in 431, and Mary was recognized as Theotokos.[29]

The events surrounding the Council of Ephesus and its aftermath were undoubtedly critical for the development of the cult of the Virgin. A homily preached in Constantinople at Christmas just before the Council (in fact one of several dating from this heated time), suggests

---

[26] Though some inevitably reduced it to a clash of personalities: see below.

[27] Socrates, *Historia ecclasiastica*, VII.23.

[28] See Nicholas F. Constas, ' "Weaving the body of God": Proclus of Constantinople, the Theotokos and the loom of the flesh', *Journal of Early Christian Studies*, 3 (1995), 169–94, at 174 n.21.

[29] Cyril: J.A. McGuckin, *St Cyril of Alexandria, the Christological Controversy: its History, Theology and Texts* (Leiden, 1994). For a recent brief account see Pauline Allen, 'The definition and enforcement of orthodoxy', in Averil Cameron, Bryan Ward-Perkins, and Michael Whitby, eds, *The Cambridge Ancient History, XIV, Late Antiquity: Empire and Successors A.D. 425–600* (Cambridge, 2000), 811–34, at 811–12. The many personal and other agendas of these few years are brought out by Constas, 'Weaving the body of God', 173; and see his *Proclus of Constantinople and the Cult of the Virgin in Late Antiquity* (Leiden, 2003).

that a language of cult was by now developing.[30] It also helped to inflame feelings on the topic, which were already running high. The homily took to unprecedented heights the imagery and typology of Mary presaged in the writings of Ephrem and others, and it set a pattern for all later homiletic on the subject. The theme of Mary as the new Eve was expanded by drawing on a mass of other Biblical images: Mary as the ark, the ladder of Jacob, the fleece of Gideon, the Red Sea, the temple of Solomon, the unopened gate, the jar filled with manna, and many others. However, biblical language represented only one type of imagery; the language used in the homily ranged more widely, for instance using a striking imagery of weaving, whereby the Virgin's womb was likened to a workshop containing the loom on which the flesh of God is woven.[31]

What was at stake at the Council of Ephesus? As with any question of religious change or formulation, this question can be answered in a number of ways. One theme was the rivalry between Nestorius and Cyril of Alexandria. The Council led to the condemnation of Nestorius, who was subsequently to give his name to those who emphasised the humanity rather than the divinity in the nature of Christ. At a deeper level the Council can be regarded as a stage, and a very important one, in the Christological arguments extending from the fourth to the ninth centuries. Peter Brown has recently suggested that the 'rise' of the Virgin in the fifth century was as guarantor of 'the solidarity between man and God' of which contemporaries wanted to feel reassured.[32] But can it also be read as indicative of personal devotion to the Virgin on the part of the advocates of the Theotokos title?

Here we encounter the role of the Empress Pulcheria, the most prominent of the pious sisters of the Emperor Theodosius II. And here

[30] Commonly cited accounts are Holum, 137–41, and Limberis. For the view that the Council of Ephesus was not concerned with Mary as such, but with doctrinal Christology, the Theotokos title being connected with kenotic theology, see Benko, *The Virgin Goddess*, 250–1, 253–9. Nevertheless there seems already to have been at least one feast of the Virgin: M. Jugie, 'Homélies mariales byzantines: textes grecs édités et traduits en latin, II', *Patrologia Orientalis*, 19 (Paris, 1926), 297–309.

[31] This homily became famous and was much quoted in later contexts: see Constas, 'Weaving the body of God', 175 n.24; imagery: 176–88. Constas wants to connect the loom image with Pulcheria's weaving: 188–90. In modern literature this homily has become widely known through Constas's article, but in fact it was only one of several; see also Leena Mari Peltomaa, *The Image of the Virgin in the Akathistos Hymn* (Leiden, 2001), 101–12; Holum, 139–41; and below.

[32] See Peter Brown, *Poverty and Leadership in the Later Roman Empire*, The Menahem Stern Jerusalem Lectures (Hannover, NH, 2002), 104–6, at 105.

we get into difficulties. Recent scholarship and the sources alike (though the latter are in fact very mixed)[33] lay much emphasis on Pulcheria, and some of this story seems to present her as dedicated to the cult of the Virgin, or even as modelling herself upon her.[34] When Theodosius died in 450 Pulcheria succeeded as Empress (and married, for legitimacy and respectability). She was highly instrumental in calling and organizing the Council of Chalcedon, which claimed to settle the question of the two natures of Christ. Was the cult of the Virgin taken up as a model by empresses, not only Pulcheria, but also some of her successors? I have suggested as much myself, or at least made the point that that is how empresses might be perceived or represented by others.[35] But here we need to be a little cautious.[36] Byzantine empresses are the subject of much attention from scholars at the moment. Until very recently there was no single book on Byzantine empresses: there are now no fewer than four.[37] In such an atmosphere it is tempting to jump to conclusions. Certainly Pulcheria was involved, and took sides, in the issues surrounding the Theotokos title. But the contemporary church historian Socrates writing in the decade after the Council does not give her any special role in this, and his contemporary Sozomen's eulogistic account, which admittedly ends in AD 425, does not link Pulcheria with Mary.[38] As a much-publicized pious virgin at that time, she may well have taken Mary as her model, as some sources seem to claim. Certainly it was predictable that some enthusiasts should

[33] This is noted by Liz James, *Empresses and Power in Early Byzantium* (Leicester, 2001), e.g. 18, 66–8.

[34] The present enthusiasm for Pulcheria derives in the main from Holum, who is followed by Limberis. For a more sceptical view see below, with Angelidi, *Pulcheria* and Peltomaa, *Image of the Virgin*, e.g. at 51 n.10, 57 n.53, 111, 113.

[35] This is suggested by the sixth-century poet Corippus of Sophia, wife of Justin II: see Averil Cameron, 'The Empress Sophia', *Byzantion*, 45 (1975), 4–21, at 12–13.

[36] James, *Empresses and Power*, 143, notes the lack of explicit evidence for the assumption that empresses modelled themselves upon the figure of Mary.

[37] See Lynda Garland, *Byzantine Empresses. Women and Power in Byzantium, AD 527–1204* (London, 1999), and Barbara Hill, *Imperial Women in Byzantium, 1025–1204. Power, Patronage and Ideology* (London, 1999). For this period see James, *Empresses and Power*, with her article 'Goddess, whore, wife or slave: will the real Byzantine empress please stand up?', in Anne J. Duggan, ed., *Queens and Queenship in Medieval Europe* (Woodbridge, 1997), 123–40; also L. Brubaker, 'Memories of Helena: patterns of imperial matronage in the fourth and fifth centuries', in L. James, ed., *Women, Men and Eunuchs. Gender in Byzantium* (Aldershot, 1997), 52–75. Judith Herrin, *Women in Purple* (2001), covers three eighth- and ninth-century imperial women, beginning with Irene.

[38] Socrates, *Historia ecclesiastica*, VII.2,3; Sozomen, *Historia ecclesiastica*, IX.1, 10.

paint her in these colours, and several contemporaries certainly did so;[39] the truth about her own beliefs is of course harder to establish.[40]

Much later, it was claimed that Pulcheria was responsible for building some or all of three main Marian churches in Constantinople, and for bringing to the capital the robe and girdle of the Virgin.[41] However no contemporary evidence associates her with these, and the Hodegoi church, eponymous home of the Hodegetria icon of the Virgin, is not in fact attested before the ninth century. The evidence for the other two, the Blachernai and the Chalkoprateia, is also later, indeed very much later.[42] One must allow for the accretion of tradition, the later desire to claim ancient origins for contemporary institutions, and the loss of soundly based historical memory. Other late sources ascribe the same initiatives to Verina, the wife of Leo I, also fifth-century but a little later,[43] or to Eudocia, the wife of Pulcheria's brother Theodosius. I tend to agree with the scepticism of Cyril Mango on this point, and indeed Christine Angelidi has put forward a persuasive trajectory for the growth of Marian legend in Constantinople and for the gradually increasing association with it of the Empress Pulcheria. According to this not only the many aspects of the Virgin's role in Constantinople but also many of the earlier stories of the alleged involvement in it of Pulcheria, the virginal and orthodox Empress, were imaginative developments of the post-iconoclastic period and the very different conditions of late Byzantium.

The finding stories of the Virgin's robe and girdle are similarly later and equally legendary in nature. It is usually better not to pry too closely into the exact mechanism by which a relic was 'discovered' or

[39] Especially Atticus, successor of John Chrysostom as Patriarch of Constantinople in 404, who urged the model on her: see Constas, 'Weaving the body of God', 171–3 with refs.

[40] For Pulcheria's supposed devotion to the Virgin see Holum, 145–6, 157 (followed by most recent writers); Limberis, 54–61; also the article by Kate Cooper elsewhere in this volume. James, *Empresses and Power*, 14, 39, 150, is more cautious. Limberis, 59, claims that 'as a young woman Pulcheria had taken the Virgin Theotokos as the model for her life'.

[41] Other religious patronage is also attributed to Pulcheria. For Pulcheria as the subject of the translation of relics represented in the variously dated Trier ivory see L. Brubaker, 'The Chalke gate, the construction of the past and the Trier ivory', *Byzantine and Modern Greek Studies*, 23 (1999), 258–85, at 271–7, with earlier bibliography. Brubaker accepts the subject as the translation of the relics of St Stephen to Constantinople in AD 421 but dates the ivory itself to the ninth century.

[42] See Cyril Mango, 'The origins of the Blachernai shrine at Constantinople', *Acta XIII Congressus Internationalis Archaeologicae Christianae*, 2 (Vatican City and Split, 1998), 61–76; Angelidi, *Pulcheria*, 73–4, 83.

[43] See on Verina James, 'Goddess, whore, wife or slave', 33–4.

brought to the particular place where it was later venerated. However, the robe or veil of the Virgin (often, though not always, referred to as her *maphorion*) features in a contemporary account of its miraculous intervention in saving the city from outside attack in 619 or the early 620s, when its arrival in Constantinople is attributed to the reign of Leo I and Verina, that is, later in the fifth century than Pulcheria.[44] The acquisition of the robe, supposedly from Jerusalem, points to a date for the Blachernai church, where it was kept in a special chapel. At least by the sixth century, then, this was associated with this Emperor and Empress. In contrast, the Virgin's girdle does not appear in texts before the eighth century.[45] To anyone familiar with the process by which legends of this kind attached to relics, icons, or indeed monuments, grew more elaborate and changed in detail with the centuries, there is nothing surprising about all this, nor does it require an ultra-sceptical disposition to appreciate what has happened.

As for Pulcheria and the events surrounding the Council of Ephesus, Kate Cooper and Elizabeth James have also pointed out how much of a standard trope it is in texts of this period to personalize, and to put the responsibility for events good and bad onto a woman, especially an empress.[46] Pulcheria is a victim of this tendency. It is clear that Pulcheria's support was highly desirable, and as I have suggested, several protagonists, including Cyril, manifestly went to considerable lengths to claim that they had it.[47] An imperial ally was a much sought-after commodity, and as a dedicated virgin Pulcheria was too precious an asset not to try to use her in the course of a contest over the status of Mary. What she thought herself is another matter. We may reasonably believe that she was an enthusiast for the Cyrillian position against Nestorius, but the spread of the cult of the Virgin needs wider explanations than the personal motivation of the central actors. Insofar as we can discover her personal role, Pulcheria is a classic example of

[44] Cf. Cameron, 'The Virgin's robe'. For the texts see A. Wenger, *L'Assomption de la Très Sainte Vierge dans la tradition byzantine du VIe au Ve siècle*, Archives de l'Orient chrétien, 5 (Paris, 1955), with discussion.

[45] See Mango, 'Constantinople as Theotokoupolis', 19, with n.19. There was more than one girdle in existence at later dates, one of which Westminster Abbey claimed to possess and which was highly regarded in late medieval England: see N. Vincent, *Holy Blood. King Henry III and the Westminster Blood Relic* (Cambridge, 2001), 169–70, with instructive comments on other relics of the Virgin, e.g. at 40–2.

[46] Kate Cooper, 'Contesting the Nativity: wives, virgins and Pulcheria's *imitatio Mariae*', *Scottish Journal of Religious Studies*, 19 (1998), 31–43; see James, *Empresses and Power*, 18–19, 67.

[47] See Holum, 134, 137, 159.

someone who was carried along by other contemporary forces. Quite independently of her support, these were already encouraging the development of a definite cult of the Virgin. In the same way, enthusiasts for the Theotokos theology rather naturally held up Mary as a model for women.[48] Ambrose and others had done so already. But now, as it were, others jumped onto the bandwagon, composing homilies in praise of Mary.[49] Thus the rhetoric of the contemporary controversy naturally and seamlessly fed into the encouragement of a cult.

Another question is commonly asked in relation to the development of the Virgin's cult in this period, namely, how far is it carrying over into Christianity of the characteristics of pagan female goddesses, and did it take off for this reason?[50] Of course it would be surprising if Mary did not take on some of the characteristics of existing female deities. It is, for example, often hard to know whether contemporary Egyptian images of a nursing mother figure refer to Isis or to the Virgin and Child.[51] Some might think it not accidental that Mary was designated Theotokos in the city of the virgin goddess Artemis/Diana, or that contemporary sources should hint at a female following for her in that city.[52] One can equally see in her later role as the protectress of Constantinople and in its associated language traces of a kind of city deity, Pallas Athena or Tyche.[53] Nevertheless, I would prefer to emphasise particularity, especially in the presence of such a huge quantity of theological debate relating to her role. My answer to the question of pagan syncretism would be that no religious development of such importance can be explained in simple or monocausal terms. Like all such major changes, the development that we are tracing came when it did because many different, even contradictory, factors converged. Pagan syncretism may have played a part, but in my view it was a minor one; competition would be a better model. In either case we lack explicit evidence.

Similarly, the idea that the Virgin's cult appealed particularly to

---

[48] So Atticus of Constantinople: Holum, 139–40.

[49] E.g. Atticus, Proclus, Theodotus of Ancyra: Holum, 139–41, with refs.

[50] See Benko, *The Virgin Goddess*, esp. ch. 6, 'From devotion to doctrine'. Benko sees Mary's Christological role as developing out of 'popular, emotional piety' (203), and implausibly connects the *Protevangelium* with the cult of Cybele.

[51] For an example see Elsner, *Imperial Rome and Christian Triumph*, pl. 147, p. 221.

[52] Artemis is also regarded in the texts as a pagan competitor of Thecla at Seleucia: Davis, *Cult of St. Thecla*, 44. However, this element of competition is not made explicit in the case of the Virgin.

[53] See Limberis, 124–42.

women seems to me, like the parallel argument that icons also appealed especially to women worshippers, a largely unproven hypothesis, against which one can produce many examples in the sources of men who were equally devoted to her.[54] As for empresses, it was of course natural to associate them with the cult of the Virgin Mother, but their patronage was more widely spread than this suggests, and for every empress for whom there seems to be such evidence, there are others for whom no special connection is attested. Again, I think we have to look more widely for explanations, and also to look for more complex ones.

* * *

Finally, did the cult of the Virgin take root because it was expressive of a 'feminine principle', in a Jungian sense, or because of some unstoppable tendency to encompass the idea of the female within Christianity? Such again has been argued by some scholars, not in my view convincingly, at least not as a single explanation.[55]

I would still want to argue therefore that the cult of the Virgin, with special churches dedicated to her, images of various kinds, and indications of liturgical feasts and active religious expression, grew naturally with and out of the self-definition of the Church and formulation of doctrine after the Council of Nicaea, and in the context of intense debate about both virginity and Christology which gathered momentum in the late fourth century. But no religious development is simple, and many factors have to conspire before it can become truly successful.

The late fourth, and especially the fifth, centuries also saw an increasing taste for relics, not least to deposit in the grand new churches being built in nearly every city. Like that of her son, the Virgin's body itself was in contention. She had left no remains, and as happened in the case of the Gospel silence about her infancy and childhood, the puzzle was solved by recourse to the fertile imagination of pious people and expressed in apocryphal writings in several languages from the late fourth or fifth centuries, before any liturgical feast of the Assumption or Dormition had been formally established.[56] After Ephesus, such was

[54] Virgin and women: e.g., J. Herrin, 'The imperial feminine in Byzantium', *P&P*, 169 (Nov. 2000), 3–35, at 4–5, with bibliography; Herrin also associates the cult of the Virgin with an appropriation of the role of female deities and with Byzantine empresses.

[55] See Carroll, *The Cult of the Virgin Mary*.

[56] The source for the Emperor Maurice's regularization in the late sixth century is late: Nicephorus Callistus, *Historia ecclesiastica*, 17.28, who despite the dating in fact puts it in the context of the reign of Justinian. However, the belief itself was already well established, and a homily by Theoteknos of Livias on the Assumption probably dates from the sixth century.

the desire to fill those empty churches that pseudo-relics were produced – her girdle and her robe or veil, or perhaps only the latter at this period. They were later joined by her spindle, and by the alleged swaddling clothes of Christ. Later generations familiar with the Virgin's robe and girdle as special treasures of Constantinople set about giving them a history. It was natural enough to ascribe their acquisition, like the three Constantinopolitan churches famous for their Marian connections, to Pulcheria, or to Eudocia, or Verina. But again we must be cautious about the stories. Not only are the 'finding' stories themselves of much later date; but also, the evidence for the history of early Byzantine monuments in Constantinople is notoriously tangled and liable to embroidery or fabrication. In particular, the history of the famous Hodegetria icon so often described in later Byzantine sources was told in different ways and in fact inserted into the already late accounts of the fifth-century churches.

Yet even if a cautious approach is needed to the tangled source material, it is clear enough that the Virgin's importance in Christian religious life was steadily increasing during the fifth century. That at least we can accept, again even if there happens to be a concentration in the written evidence on the city of Constantinople.

In the Avar attack on Constantinople in 619 or the early 620s the Virgin's robe was brought out and used as a talisman. In the Persian and Avar siege of 626 and the Arab and Russian sieges of the following centuries she was regarded as the saviour of the city by her intercession and her active role in the fighting.[57] But by then the Virgin's power and protection were fully established. Episodes from her life were told in the Akathistos hymn, whose origin recent scholarship places not long after the Council of Ephesus.[58] It was revivified after the city's escape

The apocryphal accounts of the Dormition, a group of texts often referred to as the *Transitus Mariae*, go back to the fifth or early sixth centuries; see M. van Esbroek, 'Les Textes littéraires sur l'assomption avant le Xe siècle', in *Les Actes apocryphes des Apôtres: Christianisme et monde païen* (Geneva, 1981) [= M. van Esbroek, *Aux origines de la Dormition de la Vierge* (London, 1995), I], and cf. below, n.75. However in the late seventh century the Jerusalem pilgrim Arculf was reported to have visited the church of Mary, where he saw her empty tomb, but had nothing to say of a bodily assumption: Adomnan, *De locis sanctis*, ed. L. Bieler, CCSL, 175 (Turnhout, 1965), 195.

57 This is clear in the three contemporary accounts: the homily of Theodore Synkellos, the *Chronicon Paschale*, and the poems of George of Pisidia, though despite Cameron, 'Theotokos', 79, 97, and cf. idem, 'Elites and icons', 20–4, the identity of the icon or icons deployed during the siege is not so certain. Some accounts envisage an *acheiropoietos* icon of Christ being carried round the walls: see Mango, 'Constantinople as Theotokoupolis', 21–2.

58 So Peltomaa, *Image of the Virgin*, 113–14.

from siege in 626 and turned into a victory hymn; much later, again in the late Byzantine period, it was attached to a Lenten liturgical context.[59] Again the Virgin was transformed: she had become a warrior, allegedly herself fighting alongside the Byzantines as they engaged with the Persians in the waters of the Golden Horn, and addressed in pane-gyrical poetry as a 'general'. Different again, in the *kontakia* of Romanos in the sixth century she had appeared as the lamenting mother over the body of her son, although the motherly Virgin full of tenderness, like the Russian Virgin of Vladimir, was an iconographic development yet to come.

As I would see it, then, the cult of the Virgin was a product of Late Antiquity, and received a great impetus from the development of Christianity in the post-Constantinian period.[60] As noted, none of the Constantinian foundations thought to give a place to Mary herself, unless one counts the Constantinian church of the Nativity at Beth-lehem.[61] Nor were there Marian churches as yet in Rome.[62] This is a development which we can perceive only fitfully and dimly. There is no clear thread or authoritative account on which to rely. In such a situation the historian must fall back on an intuition, which depends heavily on scraps of evidence, surviving without any rational reason, and from different parts of the empire.

One of the most difficult tasks is that of disentangling the history of the various feasts of the Virgin. Even for the 'official' adoption of the Assumption on 15 August, we have only scanty testimony, and it would be rash to imagine that it was everywhere standardized from then on.[63] Earlier practice varied from place to place, and while there seems to have been an earlier feast of Mary kept before Christmas, the regular calendar of Marian feasts was still a long time ahead. There is isolated evidence for regular processions already taking place in Constantinople in the sixth century, and for the keeping of the Annunciation or Nativity of the Virgin.[64] Later Byzantine churches often had a cycle of

[59] Angelidi, 'Un texte patriographique', 127–8.

[60] So Mango, 'Constantinople as Theotokoupolis'.

[61] See Herrin, 'The imperial feminine in Byzantium', 12.

[62] Apart from S. Maria Maggiore (fifth century), the notable Marian churches known from the seventh–eighth centuries are S. Maria Antiqua, S. Maria ad Martyres and S. Maria in Trastevere; see Barber, 'Early representations'.

[63] For the complex origins of Marian feasts see also van Esbroek, *Aux origines*.

[64] M. Jugie, *La Mort et l'assomption de la Sainte Vierge. Étude historico-doctrinale*, Studi e Testi, 114 (Vatican City, 1944), 82; *Chronicon Paschale*, 373. Possible sixth-century proces-sions: Angelidi, *Pulcheria*, 127–8.

frescoes based on the life of the Virgin, drawn from the stanzas of the Akathistos hymn and ultimately from the apocryphal *Protevangelium*; but again, in Late Antiquity, this was still in the future.

How does one identify the growth of a cult? In this case, as I noted, we have no contemporary source which can helpfully set it out for us. We are therefore left to find signs here and there for ourselves. In the case of the Virgin, the kind of evidence that is plentiful for the cult of Thecla from the fourth and fifth centuries tends not to be found until the late sixth and seventh.[65] One such type of evidence is the appearance in contemporary texts of stories about the Virgin, usually associating her with miraculous interventions, some of which are attached to tales about her icons. These stories are also uncommon until the later part of the period, although Sozomen, writing already in the 440s, reports appearances of a mysterious power, identified with the Virgin, which cured people of ailments in association with a particular church in Constantinople.[66] Tales begin to increase in frequency by the late sixth and seventh centuries, when (as in Sozomen also) she often appears as a mysterious lady who confounds a Jew or an iconoclast.[67] Then as now, apparitions of the Virgin served useful political and ideological agendas.[68] Finally, in this list of indicators, there are casual references in the sources to images of the Virgin either owned by individuals or venerated by them in churches.

Another marker is of course provided by visual art. We rarely know anything explicit about the reasons for patronage in this period, and must make our own deductions from what has survived. However, here too depictions of the Virgin in various media – ivory, panel-painting, frescoes, textiles, mosaics – increase in frequency, particularly from the

---

[65] Barber, 'Early representations', 256 and n.16, makes a similar point, observing that while in the absence of relics icons serve as evidence, ampullae and cloths brought from sites associated with relics of the Theotokos 'would have' been good indicators. However, for 'private' evidence see H. Maguire, 'The cult of the Mother of God in private', in Vassilaki, 279–89.

[66] Sozomen, *Historia ecclesiastica*, VII.5.1–4, cited by Mango, 'Constantinople as Theotokoupolis', 17.

[67] Having become the symbol of orthodoxy the Virgin was strikingly often linked in early Byzantine texts with the theme of the discomfiture of the Jews: see Stephen J. Shoemaker, ' "Let us go and burn her body": the image of the Jews in the early Dormition traditions', *Church History*, 68 (1999), 775–823; idem, *Ancient Traditions of the Virgin Mary's Dormition and Assumption* (Oxford, 2002).

[68] For example, the numerous 'weeping Madonnas' in modern Italy have typically been associated with the Catholic Right, or with areas of social deprivation (*Times*, 3 Feb. 2000).

later sixth century onwards.[69] One question is, how often does she appear alone, without the Child? In other words, is this growing popularity of images of the Virgin about her own personal cult, or is it rather about Christology? Is it justified to speak of 'devotion to the Virgin' if her appearance in iconographic schemes is primarily connected with the continuing and intense debate about the natures of Christ?

Not being an art historian, I would find it difficult to answer these questions. But certainly in many of the images of this pre-iconoclastic period she is shown in highly formal guise, seated on a throne and flanked by angels and military saints, as at Sinai, standing with archangels as at Kiti in Cyprus or in Rome at Trastevere, or seated on a more or less imperial throne as on an ivory from Syria.[70] Even if she wears a simple veil instead of the jewelled dress in the S. Maria Maggiore mosaics, she usually nevertheless conveys a grave regal and formal message, the message of incarnational doctrine.[71]

Recent scholarship has suggested that Mary's depiction in Byzantine art becomes maternal and tender only after the ending of iconoclasm in the ninth century,[72] and this suggests that her role continued to be closely linked with Christological issues.[73] Yet it would be a mistake to be too firmly wedded to this schema. Much of the evidence necessarily used in this paper, especially the art-historical evidence, has been, if not 'official', at least as it were top-down, the product of elite patronage. However, large numbers of lead seals of the early Byzantine period,

---

[69] Leslie Brubaker sees the 'rise of icons' as a seventh-century phenomenon, e.g. 'Icons before Iconoclasm?', in *Morfologie sociali e culturali in Europa fra tarda antichità e alto medioevo*, 2 vols, Settimane di studio del Centro italiano di studi sull'alto medioevo, 45 (Spoleto, 1998), 1215–54.

[70] See for some of this material Barber, 'Early representations'; also Cameron, 'Language of images'.

[71] Herrin, 'The imperial feminine', 15–19, argues for a contrast between representations: a 'humble' eastern Virgin and a queenly western one. However, John of Damascus, for example, continues to refer to the Virgin as *basilis*: see *Dormition*, I.2, in P. Voulet, ed. and trans., *S. Jean Damascène. Homélies sur la Nativité et la Dormition*, Sources chrétiennes, 80 (Paris, 1961), 83. For references to the earlier discussion of the 'Maria regina' theme see V. Pace, 'Between east and west', in Vassilaki, 425–32, at 425. I am not convinced either of the strength of the east-west contrast or of the strong definition of the imperial Virgin type. Benko, *The Virgin Goddess*, 135, is right to say that the idea of Mary as Queen of Heaven is medieval, not early.

[72] See Iole Kalavrezou, 'Images of the mother: when the Virgin Mary became the Meter Theou', *Dumbarton Oaks Papers*, 44 (1990), 165–72.

[73] Angelidi, *Pulcheria*, 138, similarly emphasises the Christological element, while claiming that in the ninth century the Virgin acquired 'una nuova fisionomia'; cf. 121: 'durante la prima metà del V secolo la questione mariana non era stata ancora risolta'.

used by officials at many different levels to seal the countless documents which were part of their trade, show a simple depiction of Virgin and Child with the message 'Theotoke, help [me]'. Is this evidence 'official' or does it indicate personal cult? From the sixth century onwards rings, brooches, bracelets, and even silks and tapestries used for clothing, frequently bore depictions of the Virgin. Her aid was evoked by the use of amulets, especially in relation to conception or childbirth. Similarly, homilies[74] and religious poetry in the form of hymns present a Virgin who is emotional and very human in her feelings. There was a continuing and strong tradition of Marian poetry in Syriac in the centuries after Ephrem, for example in the homilies of Jacob of Serugh. In the sixth century this was also to be found in the hymns of Romanos.[75] Some of the most lyrical of the Greek hymns date from the period in the eighth century when it was feared that the iconoclast emperors would attack not only religious images but actual devotion to the Virgin, and it seems to have been in this context also that the hymns about the Virgin later absorbed into the eastern liturgy began to be composed.

Surveying the various kinds of evidence about a developing cult of the Virgin in Late Antiquity, one is struck by what seems to be a co-existence of several distinct strands. The period continued to be dominated by fierce debates about Christology. Ephesus marked only a stage; it was followed in 451 by Chalcedon, a Council whose results were widely disputed in the east, producing a division which Justinian's fifth Ecumenical Council in 553 failed to heal. The debates over images in the following centuries were a further stage in this Christological argument. Not surprisingly then, the status of the Virgin often seems to have been implicated in this debate about the human and divine natures of Christ. This was of course even more the case as icons of the Virgin herself increased in number. Images of the Virgin and Child, in their turn, especially those from this earlier period, are not usually to be

---

[74] See Mary Cunningham, 'The Mother of God in early Byzantine homilies', *Sobornost*, 10 (1988), 53–67; Robert Caro, *La homiletica Mariana griega en el siglo V*, Marian Library Studies, 3 (Dayton, OH, 1971). This evidence is also discussed in Tsironis, *The Lament of the Virgin Mary*; see also eadem, 'The Mother of God in the Iconoclastic controversy', in Vassilaki, 27–39. For Jacob of Serugh (fifth–sixth centuries) see P. Bedjan, ed., *S Martyrii, qui et Sahdona quae supersunt omnia* (Paris and Leipzig, 1902).

[75] Pauline Allen traces Mariological development in the fifth and sixth centuries, with an emphasis on the homilies of Severus of Antioch and the hymns of Romanos, in 'Severus of Antioch and the homily: the end of the beginning?', in Pauline Allen and Elizabeth Jeffreys, eds, *The Sixth Century. End or Beginning?*, Byzantina Australiensia, 10 (Brisbane, 1996), 163–75.

read by us as spontaneous artistic creations: they should be seen rather as themselves expressions of and guides to Christological truths. It is natural, then, that some of the most striking writings about her were composed by defenders of images – Germanos of Constantinople, for instance, and indeed John of Damascus – and that they should be deeply theological in nature. Nevertheless, different strands of religious feeling often develop simultaneously, and just as stories of the Virgin's infancy had circulated since the second century, so it was particularly in the period after the Council of Chalcedon that the apocryphal narratives of her 'glorious end' began to take shape and to be repeated.[76]

* * *

Modern writers on the subject of the cult of the Virgin in this period slip easily into the language of 'popular religion', a term not usually intended to convey approval and one which stems from an inadequate understanding of the functioning of religion in society. In the same way the 'rise of icons' has traditionally been seen as a sign of popular piety creeping up from below.[77] This sharp distinction between 'popular' and 'official', or perhaps elite, religion, does justice neither to the evidence nor to the complexities of religious history. I believe on the contrary that religious development on such a scale can only come about when a variety of factors operate in relation to each other to make change possible. As the evidence from the past two millennia shows so amply, the figure of Mary has been and still is capacious enough to permit of an almost infinite number of different ever-changing and developing approaches.

A book which I read a long time ago when I first became interested in this subject, Marina Warner's *Alone of all her Sex* (1978), brought home to me this extraordinary capaciousness of the model of the Virgin or Mother of God – how possible it is and has been for her to be all things to people at different times and places. Perhaps it is a mistake to be looking for the explanations, the whys and wherefores, in any case, certainly for any single explanation. But I would still insist on the importance and centrality of the twin themes, the Christological and

---

[76] The phrase is from Daley, *On the Dormition of Mary*, 7, and cf. 12 on the date. At 6, Daley says that after Chalcedon, 'the figure of Mary emerged like a comet in Christian devotion and liturgical celebration throughout the world'. For comments on the liturgical and theological preoccupations in the texts which Daley translates cf. 28, 30.

[77] E. Kitzinger, 'The cult of images in the age before iconoclasm', *Dumbarton Oaks Papers*, 8 (1954), 134–50.

the ascetic, or perhaps better the virginal, which came together in the late fourth century and for the first time brought the Virgin to the very centre of attention. Nevertheless, if Christology provided the impetus emotion was not far behind. In the sixth century Romanos's poetry represented Mary as a very human mother, addressing her Son on the cross and lamenting over his body.[78] Emotion entered even in relation to the formal apse mosaics. Patriarch Germanos in the early eighth century expresses this in the language of personal religious experience: the apse of a church, he says, is symbolic of the cave in Bethlehem where the Virgin gave birth to Christ, so that we too are drawn into it and can share in the intercession which the Mother of God offers to all people.[79]

Keble College, Oxford

---

[78] For this see Tsironis, *The Lament of the Virgin Mary*, ch. 2.

[79] *Ecclesiastical History*, 3, cited by Robin Cormack, 'The Mother of God in apse mosaics', in Vassilaki, 95; idem, 'The Mother of God in the mosaics of Hagia Sophia in Constantinople', ibid., 111.

FROM 'GOD-BEARER' TO 'MOTHER OF GOD' IN THE LATER FATHERS

by D.F. WRIGHT

THE interest of this paper lies in the distinction between θεοτόκος ('*Theotokos*'), 'God-bearer',[1] and words or phrases which are more precisely translated as 'mother of God', especially μήτηρ θεοῦ ('*mētēr theou*') and θεομήτωρ ('*theomētōr*') in Greek and *mater Dei* in Latin. It concentrates on the usage of Greek and Latin Christian writers between the later fourth century and the eighth century. For those who believe that 'mother of God' is the only proper rendering in English of θεοτόκος,[2] it must seem a non-issue. Indeed, insofar as they have most of the tradition on their side, this enquiry may appear redundant, impertinent, or sectarian. To leave the matter there, however, would be to leave important questions unasked. Historical study is not best served by the indiscriminate translation of θεοτόκος as 'mother of God', or at least by a translation that fails clearly to distinguish between θεοτόκος and direct equivalents of 'mother of God'.

The first question is why it was this particular Greek word, θεοτόκος, which gained a key position in the fifth-century conciliar definitions. The answer lies in its pre-history in eastern Christianity for more than a century before the Council of Ephesus in AD 431.[3] This answer, however, merely pushes the question back also: why did μήτηρ θεοῦ or θεομήτωρ not enter Christian usage in those early fourth-century decades when θεοτόκος is first incontrovertibly attested – if, that is, the meaning of the latter is best conveyed in English by 'mother of God'? Had not Elizabeth hailed Mary as 'the mother of my Lord' as early as Luke 1.43? Yet it was θεοτόκος that a

---

[1] I use the commonest translation of θεοτόκος, while recognizing that the meaning of the Greek extends from conception to giving birth. Some of the evidence in this paper was presented in a more popular format in ' "Mother of God"?', in D.F. Wright, ed., *Chosen by God. Mary in Evangelical Perspective* (1989), 120–40.

[2] Eric L. Mascall, 'The Mother of God', in Alberic Stacpoole, ed., *Mary's Place in Christian Dialogue* (Slough, 1982), 91–2; T.M. Parker, 'Devotion to the Mother of God', in E.L. Mascall, ed., *The Mother of God* (Westminster, 1949), 68.

[3] On pre-431 use of θεοτόκος, see briefly, with literature, Michael O'Carroll, *Theotokos*, 2nd edn (Wilmington, DE, 1983), 342–3; more fully, Marek Starowieyski, 'Le Titre θεοτόκος avant le concile d'Ephèse', *Studia Patristica*, 19 (1989), 236–42.

full half-century before the Ephesian Council had already attained an informal canonical status, as the comments of the Emperor Julian and of Gregory of Nazianzus illustrate in different ways.[4]

It has generally been assumed that θεοτόκος had in its favour the lack of any history of use outside of Christianity.[5] This assumption no longer seems secure;[6] but it remains true that the word was almost completely free of the undesirable pagan associations of the explicit vocabulary of 'mother of god/gods'. Yet it is important not to overestimate the advantage of the unsullied ancestry of θεοτόκος over that of, for example, μήτηρ θεοῦ. If most early occurrences of θεοτόκος point to Egypt as its provenance, its origins in a Coptic (or even Greek?) designation of the goddess Isis cannot be ruled out.[7] Certainly, its meaning was by no means beyond misconstrual, as Antiochene and Nestorian objections made clear. Cyril of Alexandria's third letter to Nestorius, canonized by the Council of Ephesus, found it necessary to declare that 'We say of her that she is θεοτόκος, not as though the nature of the Word had its beginning of being from the flesh', followed by the first verses of John's Gospel.[8] The same disclaimer required regular repetition, so that John of Damascus in *The Orthodox Faith* in the eighth century needed to clarify that 'We say that God was born of her, not because the divinity drew the principle of its existence from her.'[9] So even if 'mother of God' might have trailed clouds of confusing or contaminating implications, θεοτόκος itself was not simplicity itself.

The question, then, why θεοτόκος and not a precise Greek equivalent of 'mother of God' found early favour may elude a satisfactory answer, especially if one obvious answer is debarred almost a priori:

---

[4] Julian, cited by Cyril of Alexandria, *Contra Julianum*, 8 (PG 76, col. 901), 'You [Christians] never stop calling Mary θεοτόκος'; Gregory of Nazianzus, *Epistle* 101 (PG 37, col. 1177), 'Whoever fails to accept holy Mary as θεοτόκος is bereft of the Godhead'.

[5] A fourth-century neologism, according to Heiner Grote, 'Maria/Marienfrömmigkeit II. Kirchengeschichtlich', in G. Krause *et al.*, eds, *Theologische Realenzyklopädie* (Berlin, 1977–), 22:121.

[6] A second-century inscription from Sidyma (on the coast of Asia Minor directly opposite Rhodes) almost certainly reads της θεοτόκου γης (only 'εο' are unclear): E. Kalinka, ed., *Tituli Lyciae*, Tituli Asiae Minoris, 2 (Vienna, 1920), 63, recorded in E.A. Barber, ed., *Greek-English Lexicon. A Supplement* (Oxford, 1968), 70, but noted only by Starowieyski, 'Le Titre', 240, to my knowledge.

[7] Starowieyski, 'Le Titre', 240; Theodore Klauser, 'Gottesgebärerin (θεοτόκος)', in T. Klauser *et al.*, eds, *Reallexikon für Antike und Christentum* (Stuttgart, 1950–), 11:1095–9.

[8] Conveniently in J. Stevenson, *Creeds, Councils and Controversies*, rev. W.H.C. Frend (1989), 306.

[9] *Orthodox Faith*, 3.12 (PG 94, col. 1028).

namely, that the tradition of the Church, later canonized in the fifth century, had recruited a word that specifically did not affirm Mary to be 'mother' of God. The question itself is sharpened not only if the currency of θεοτόκος can be reliably demonstrated some decades before its first undisputed uses in the early fourth century, say, in Origen in the first half of the third,[10] but more particularly by a recognition of the slowness with which, even after Ephesus and Chalcedon, Greek writers who repeatedly used θεοτόκος took to 'mother of God' language. The issue has attracted little scholarly attention. John Pearson, later Bishop of Chester from 1673 to 1686, made some remarkably insightful comments in 1659 in his *Exposition of the Creed*: 'those ancient Greeks which call'd the Virgin θεοτόκος, did not call her μητέρα τοῦ Θεοῦ'.[11] This assessment remains largely valid, although an exhaustive investigation has yet to be carried out. It would have to contend with the traditional imprecision of translation of works extant only in Syriac, Coptic, and other languages, and with numerous writings carrying pseudonymous ascriptions and of uncertain date.

Only once, it seems, and then slightly tentatively, did the arch-champion of θεοτόκος, Cyril of Alexandria, state that the one who gave birth in the flesh to God who appeared in the flesh for our sake 'might be called "mother of God", μήτηρ δ'ἄν λέγοιτο Θεοῦ'.[12] The verbal sense makes the phrase synonymous with θεοτόκος. Perhaps the first Greek Father to use μήτηρ θεοῦ and θεομήτωρ routinely was John of Damascus (d. *c.*750), especially in his homilies on Mary's Nativity and Dormition.[13] Once, in a bold gloss on the words of Jesus in Mark 10.18 (compare John 17.3), John called Mary 'the mother of the only good God'. He loved to pile up honorifics for Mary, 'the queen, the

[10] Starowieyski, 'Le Titre', 236–7, accepts the testimony of Socrates Scholasticus, *Historia ecclesiastica*, 7.32 (*PG* 67, col. 812) to an extended discussion by Origen in his Romans commentary, of which the original is lost.

[11] *An Exposition of the Creed* (1659), 362; 3rd edn 1669 (the last by Pearson), ed. R. Sinker (Cambridge, 1882), 340 n. 1.

[12] *Homilia paschalis* 17.3 (*PG* 77, col. 777); S. Alvarez Campos, ed., *Corpus Marianum Patristicum*, 7 vols in 8 (Burgos, 1970–85) [hereafter *CMP*], 4/i:226, no. 3282, and less precisely *Homilia paschalis* 17.2 (*CMP* 4/i:225, no. 3281). Texts from Cyril fill 250 pages in *CMP*. An occurrence of θεομήτωρ found earlier in *Epistola* 45.2 (in *PG* 77, col. 229) is absent from editions since *ACO*, 1/vi:151. *CMP*, 4/i:312, no. 3405, has the correct Greek text, but the parallel Latin version has not lost *Deique matre*.

[13] See references in G.W.H. Lampe, *Patristic Greek Lexicon* (Oxford, 1961), 629 (θεομήτωρ), 868 (μήτηρ); S. Jean Damascène, *Homélies sur la Nativité et la Dormition*, ed. P. Voulet, *Sources Chrétiennes*, 80 (Paris, 1961), 58, 60, 62, 68, 74, 108, 122, 124, 130, 134, 136, 144, 146, 150, 154, 158, 160, 162, 174, 178, 180, 184, 188, 192, 194. Several pages contain more than one occurrence.

sovereign lady, the mistress, the mother of God, the true θεοτόκος'.[14] It may be significant, however, that in *The Orthodox Faith* θεοτόκος is used almost invariably, with only two instances of θεομήτωρ and none of μήτηρ θεοῦ.[15] Before John of Damascus, Sophronius of Jerusalem (d. 638) employed θεομήτωρ at least ten times and μήτηρ θεοῦ four or five times.[16] By the seventh century these expressions and others of similar force are appearing with greater frequency.

Earlier, however, in the Greek Fathers of the later fifth and the sixth centuries, one can trace only an emerging trickle of occurrences, whose infrequency suggests deliberate reserve. The indexes to Schwartz's *Acta Conciliorum Oecumenicorum* furnish only one reference, to a report to the Emperor Justinian from Syrian bishops in AD 536.[17] The church historian Sozomen in the early fifth century used τὴν θεοῦ μητέρα once of Mary, the anti-Nestorian Theodotus of Ancyra (d. *c.* 445) came very close in naming her as 'the divine mother' and ἡ θεία μητροπαρθένος ('he theia metroparthenos', 'the divine virgin-mother'), while in the sixth century Romanos 'the Melodist' (d. *c.*560) wrote 'μήτηρ θεοῦ' three times and Leontius of Jerusalem (fl. *c.*540) used θεομήτωρ once.[18]

No claim is being made here that such a listing is comprehensive. This paper cannot track down every occurrence of the words and phrases in question. In any case, identification of use would naturally lead on to a more analytical study of genre, context, rhetorical and theological intention, and so on. Nevertheless, despite present limitations and uncertainties, the case seems clear that μήτηρ θεοῦ as a designation of Mary was slow to take hold in the eastern Church and never threatened to oust θεοτόκος from its central place. A letter of Isidore of Pelusium (d. *c.*450) may throw some light on this reticence. He seeks to explain the difference between the pagan cult of 'mother of gods' and the Christian belief in the 'mother of God'. The absence of male seed and of lust distinguishes the one whom Christians call 'the mother

[14] Ibid., 84, 116.

[15] *Orthodox Faith*, 3.12, 4.14: PG 94, cols 1032, 1161; ed. B. Kotter, *Die Schriften des Johannes von Damaskos*, 2, Patristische Texte und Studien, 12 (Berlin and New York, 1973), 136, 202.

[16] *CMP*, 4/ii: 306 no. 4538, 314 no. 4546, 328 no. 4559, 330 no. 4560, 335 no. 4565, 342 no. 4582, 344 no. 4586, 346 no. 4590, 348 no. 4595, 349 no. 4597, 354 no. 4607–8, 360–1 no. 4620.

[17] *ACO*, 3:31, 4/ii:311–12.

[18] *CMP*, 4/i:493, no. 3682; 134 no. 3119, 131 no. 3117; 4/ii:120, no. 4101, 167 nos 4245, 4247, 98 no. 4059.

of God incarnate'. Isidore twice qualifies as 'incarnate' the 'God' of whom Mary was μήτηρ.[19]

The earliest Christian appearance of the Greek θεοῦ μήτηρ is found surprisingly enough in the Emperor Constantine's *Oratio ad sanctos*, as I have shown elsewhere.[20] The authenticity of this speech has been generally accepted in more recent discussion, but on neither date nor place of delivery is there yet consensus.[21] The text records that for his incarnation 'the Son . . . devised a novel [νόθν, nothēn] form of birth for himself . . . θεοῦ μήτηρ κόρη ['a maiden (was/became) mother of God']'. One or two editors have rejected or bracketed the phrase on the grounds of its supposed anachronism, but without support from the manuscripts.[22] There is no good reason to excise it from a Greek text which by general judgement has been poorly translated from a lost Latin original. Whatever was Constantine's Latin phrase, the Greek version of his address was ahead of the pack in the detail which is our concern. Only very few isolated occurrences of μήτηρ θεοῦ predicated of Mary have been identified in the century prior to the Council of 431. A catena on Matthew's Gospel preserves an exegetical fragment explaining why the Gospels omit the genealogy of Mary, to whom it befell to become μητέρα τοῦ θεοῦ. This is assigned by Joseph Reuss to Theodore of Heraclea, who died *c.*351–5.[23] Although an ascription to so early a writer may seem questionable – this would be the first appearance of the phrase in original Greek – the possible alternative of Theodore of Mopsuestia (each Theodore is named by one manuscript) is in this case no less problematic, for the very same reason that raises a question about a mid-fourth-century expositor.[24] The only other

---

[19] *Epistle* 1.54: *PG* 78, cols 216–17; *CMP*, 4/i:436–7, no. 3589.

[20] 'Constantine and the "Mother of God": *Oratio ad sanctorum coetum* 11: 9', *Studia Patristica*, 24 (1993), 355–9.

[21] Robin Lane Fox, *Pagans and Christians* (1986), 627–62, 777–81; Mark Edwards, 'The Constantinian circle and the *Oration to the Saints*', in Mark Edwards, Martin Goodman, and Simon Price, eds, *Apologetics in the Roman Empire* (Oxford, 1999), 251–75; H.A. Drake, *Constantine and the Bishops* (Baltimore and London, 2000), 292–305, 516–17. Earlier literature in Siegmar Döpp and Wilhelm Geerlings, eds, *Dictionary of Early Christian Literature*, trans. Matthew O'Connell (New York, 2000), 141–2.

[22] Bracketed by I.A. Heikel, ed., in *Eusebius Werke*, I, Griechischen Christlichen Schriftsteller, 7 (Leipzig, 1902), 168 (*CMP*, 2:52, no. 524). A new edition in Griechischen Christlichen Schriftsteller is awaited from Friedhelm Winkelmann.

[23] *CMP*, 2:119, no. 684; ed. J. Reuss, *Matthaus-Kommentare aus der Griechischen Kirche*, Texte und Untersuchungen, 61 (Berlin, 1957), 55. Döpp and Geerlings, *Dictionary*, 561–2.

[24] Cf. Reuss, *Matthaus-Kommentare*, xxvi–xxix; M. Geerard, *Clavis Patrum Graecorum*, 5 vols and Suppl. (Turnhout, 1983–98), 2:284–5 no. 3562, 349 no. 3840.

pre-Ephesian usage is found in a poem by Gregory of Nazianzus, linking the recent flourishing of 'the virginal life' with the manifestation of 'θεοῦ ... μήτηρ παρθένος', 'the virgin mother of God'.[25]

A rather different picture emerges from the writers of the Latin west, although here too, if Constantine's own wording had been *mater Dei*, 'mother of God', he would still have been some decades ahead of his time. The erudite John Pearson in the mid-seventeenth century explained that the Latins translated θεοτόκος as *Dei genitrix*, literally 'generator of God', as well as *Deipara*, 'God-bearer', and with 'the Greeks translating *Dei genitrix* θεοῦ μήτηρ, they both at last call'd her plainly the Mother of God'.[26] This account is again highly perceptive, except that it leaves out *mater Dei* altogether.

What is beyond doubt is that Christian Latin fastened on no one uniform rendering of θεοτόκος, although *Dei genitrix/genetrix* seems the commonest equivalent. This much is evident from the *Acta Conciliorum Oecumenicorum* when parallel texts are available. But *mater Dei* came into mainstream use earlier than its Greek counterpart. Ambrose of Milan (d. 397) claimed that parturition without intercourse was no less possible *in Dei matre* than in vultures. What is more noble, he asked on another occasion, than *Dei matre*? And in his *Exposition of Luke* in a succinct phrase he declares that *Mater Domini Verbo feta, Deo plena est*, 'the mother of the Lord, pregnant with the Word, is full of God'.[27] As an influential channel of Greek thought to the Latin Church, Ambrose's vocabulary may imply his awareness of θεοτόκος. At the same time Latin writers' more frequent citation of 'mother of the Lord' than seems true of the Greek Fathers may have eased their adoption of *mater Dei*.

The translation of θεοτόκος into both *mater Dei* and *Dei genitrix* is seen openly in John Cassian's *On the Incarnation of the Lord*, written on the eve of the Council of Ephesus. It is throughout anti-Nestorian, and readily resolves Nestorius's confrontation of θεοτόκος with his preferred Χριστοτόκος ('Christotokos', 'Christ-bearer') into the difference between 'mother of God' and 'mother of Christ'. Cassian uses *mater Dei* six times and *genitrix Dei* twice.[28]

[25] *Carmina moralia* 8:22–4 (*PG* 37, col. 650; *CMP*, 2:258, no. 917).

[26] As n.11 above.

[27] *Hexaemeron*, 5:65 (*PL* 14, cols 233/248); *De virginibus*, 2:7 (*PL* 16, cols 209/220); *Expositio in Lucam*, 2:25 (*PL* 15, cols 1561/1644); *CMP*, 3:78, no. 1718, 141 no. 1988, 93 no. 1779.

[28] *De incarnatione*, 2.2, 5, 6; 3.12; 5.1; 7.25, 29 (*PL* 50, cols 32, 36–7, 43, 46, 68, 98, 254, 266).

Nestorius's own writings have survived largely in Latin or Syriac. The Latin fragments show some evidence of *mater Dei* alongside *Dei genetrix*.[29] On occasions the shape of the argument, in which Nestorius opposes 'mother of Christ' or 'mother of Emmanuel' to 'mother of God' or 'mother of God the Word', strongly suggests his use of μήτηρ θεοῦ in condemnation. More importantly for our purposes it also illustrates as in Cassian the early entry of *mater Dei* into wide currency in the Latin of the western Church, at a time when the Greeks seem quite purposefully to have refrained from μήτηρ θεοῦ. A heterodox usage that has passed unnoticed may be mentioned also. The so-called Monarchian Prologue to John's Gospel states that 'God, going to the cross, entrusted his mother to [John], so that a virgin might look after a virgin'. This could, of course, be straight patripassian Monarchianism, but these Prologues are of Priscillianist provenance, which places them around the end of the fourth century.[30]

Pearson's hypothesis of the transmission by translation of 'mother of God' from Latin into Greek receives some confirmation not only from the broad priority of the Latin usage over the Greek but also from observation of parallel texts in *Acta Conciliorum Oecumenicorum*. More particular support is advanced by Pearson from two lost letters of Ephraim, Patriarch of Antioch 526–44, cited by Photius in the ninth century. According to the latter, Ephraim claimed that 'mother of God' was first uttered when Elizabeth in Luke 1.43 greeted 'the mother of my Lord'. Subsequently Pope Leo I was the first, according to Ephraim, to give expression to the title in a letter to the Emperor Leo: 'Let Nestorius be anathematized for believing that the blessed and θεοτόκος Mary is μητέρα not τοῦ θεοῦ but of the human only.' Pearson points out that this Greek translates not *Dei . . . matrem* but *Dei . . . genetricem*. (Not untypically, Henry's bilingual Greek-French edition of Photius obscures the issue by translating both phrases as 'mère de Dieu'.)[31] It is especially noteworthy that an Antiochene bishop in the sixth century should credit a Roman colleague of the mid-fifth century with being the first to give clear testimony to Mary as 'mother of God'.

[29] See F. Loofs, *Nestoriana. Die Fragmenta des Nestorius* (Halle, 1905), 167–8, 245–7, 252; *CMP*, 4/i:25–6, no. 2959, 23–4 nos 2956–8, 28 no. 2966. Loofs, *Nestoriana*, 212 (*CMP* 4/i:10 no. 2931) is spurious: Geerard, *Clavis*, 3:126, no. 5761.

[30] Ed. John Chapman, *Notes on the Early History of the Vulgate Gospels* (Oxford, 1908), 219. Cf. Henry Chadwick, *Priscillian of Avila* (Oxford, 1976), 102–9.

[31] Pearson, *Exposition*, 362–3 (ed. Sinker, 340 n.1); Photius, *Bibliotheca* codex 228, ed. R. Henry, 8 vols (Paris, 1959–77), 4:117, 121; Leo, *Epistola* 165.2 (*PL* 54, cols 1157–8).

Not only did he recognize its difference from θεοτόκος but, so it seems, he knew no obvious candidate among Greek churchmen who merited the accolade.

This linguistic investigation touches the outskirts of some of the major shifts that took place in the developing Mariological tradition. In his Aquinas Lecture in Glasgow in 1999, Eamon Duffy talks of the east's θεοτόκος being 'softened' in western usage to *mater Dei*, but he also commends the Greek Church's continuing focus on θεοτόκος by contrast with the Latin west's preoccupation with Mary's virginity and attendant issues such as her parents' conception of her.[32]

It is fruitless to speculate what might have happened if Marian reflection had continued to be governed by vocabulary of the fairly precise semantic force of θεοτόκος, with its concentration on her conceiving and giving birth to the God-man. What can be said with confidence is that 'mother of God' language facilitated, in a manner that θεοτόκος itself did not, the elaboration of notions of the Son's dependence on and subjection to his mother, not only during the early years of his earthly life but throughout it and also beyond it, into his continuing ministry at the Father's right hand through the Spirit in the Church, and even to the Day of Judgement itself. These notions came to their most grotesque expression in both the Latin west and the Greek east in portrayals of the exalted Christ as needing the breast-milk or suasion of his mother before he could be induced to show mercy.[33] It is hard to conceive of a more flagrant, even blasphemous, misrepresentation of the core New Testament witness to Christ. Yet there is a paradox at work here, for an essential ingredient in the Son's maternal subservience is the experience of the breast-dependent child. Thus although the 'motherhood' of God incarnate has been stretched to encompass the whole of eternity in the frame of the mother-son relationship, it has retained often an echo of θεοτόκος. It is as though, almost despite the tradition, God-bearing is truly the defining character of being mother of God, or, to put it another way, Christ never ceases to be a baby. This de-historicizing of the human biography of the Son is ironical, given that the very earliest emergence of 'born of a virgin' as a

---

[32] *Madonnas that Maim* (Glasgow, 1999), 4–5. 'The Church after Vatican II has ... been curiously coy about the material fact of Mary's motherhood: Mary's womb, like her milk, has become invisible' (23).

[33] See Sarah Jane Boss, *Empress and Handmaid. On Nature and Gender in the Cult of the Virgin Mary* (London and New York, 2000), 37–8, 49–50, with pl. 3–4 (after p. 126). For the east, see the paper by Jane Baun elsewhere in this volume.

quasi-credal statement is found in Ignatius of Antioch in an anti-Docetic context.[34]

The title 'mother of God' also allowed, or fostered, those various tendencies in the proliferating tradition which, to one degree or another, assimilated the being of Mary to the divinity of the Son. Thus of the Akathistos hymn of the sixth or seventh century George Tavard comments that 'At work in such a hymn is nothing less than a reflection of actions and attributes of God on the vision of the *Theotokos*.'[35] Similarly Vasiliki Limberis says it 'represents the Theotokos as a divine entity like the mother of the gods'.[36] These tendencies are observed even in one of the most fundamental phrases used in Mariological discussion, 'the divine maternity of Mary'. One would normally construe it of the mother's being divine rather than of her offspring's being divine (or, less problematically, of her act of giving birth being divine). This is how the parallel phrase 'the divine paternity' functions.[37] It is not easy to think of a comparable expression intended to be exegeted as Mary's 'divine maternity' normally is.

It is simplistic, however, to suppose that a linguistic transition such as this paper deals with is alone responsible for large-scale developments in Marian theology and cult. These are almost bound to be multi-factorial. It must also be pointed out that signal promoters of the glories of Mary such as the Akathistos hymn, Andrew of Crete, and earlier Proclus of Constantinople, did not use 'mother of God' terminology. Nevertheless, given the vast industry of Marian studies, it remains remarkable that the emergence of 'mother of God' designations of Mary, patently retarded in the Greek tradition (but now, it seems, more dominant there than θεοτόκος), has so far received minimal attention. If word-use matters – a proposition incontrovertible for historians – the neglect calls for rectification.

University of Edinburgh

---

[34] Ignatius, *Smyrnaeans*, 1.1.

[35] George H. Tavard, *The Thousand Faces of the Virgin Mary* (Collegeville, MN, 1996), 78.

[36] Limberis, 140.

[37] For example, in Tavard, *The Thousand Faces*, 76. Another question to be pursued is when 'the Mother' without further qualification entered Christian use. It seems to be established in John of Damascus.

MARIAN PIETY AND THE NESTORIAN CONTROVERSY

by RICHARD M. PRICE

CONVENTIONAL wisdom on the Nestorian controversy has long held that the dispute was over Christ rather than Mary, that the attribution of the title *Theotokos* (or God-bearer) to the Virgin became a battlefield not because the status of Mary was a lively issue but because of its implications for the doctrine of the Incarnation. Associated developments in Marian piety have been seen as a consequence of the approval of the title at the ecumenical Council of Ephesus (431) rather than its cause. The confidence with which this has been repeated reflects, one may suspect, both a prejudice that Christology was a more worthy subject for debate than Mariology and a presumption that theological debate among bishops must be more important than developments in popular piety where lay women played a leading role. We may therefore be grateful to a series of recent writers who have called the conventional wisdom into question and argued that the main cause of the controversy, as it developed in Constantinople, was a development in Marian devotion during the preceding quarter century.

The scholar who has the distinction of having first marshalled the evidence is Kenneth G. Holum. In his book *Theodosian Empresses: Women and Imperial Dominion in Late Antiquity* (Berkeley, CA, 1982), he argued that Theodosius II's virgin sister, the Augusta Pulcheria, linked her own authority to the status of the Virgin and skilfully promoted both. As soon as Nestorius arrived in Constantinople as the new Patriarch (at Easter 428), he attempted to put Pulcheria in her place and to combat what he saw as an 'excessive worship and near-deification of Mary' (p. 154). Pulcheria swung both her brother and the people of Constantinople against their Patriarch, and it was Mary herself to whom they attributed Nestorius' discomfiture at the Council of Ephesus (p. 173).

Holum's thesis was adopted as proven fact by Vasiliki Limberis in her book *Divine Heiress: The Virgin Mary and the creation of Christian Constantinople* (1994). She treated Nestorius' defeat as the key episode that 'brought the cult of the *Theotokos* to the foreground of Constantinopolitan civic religion' (144–5). Let us note in passing a certain indifference to chronology, since the decisive period in the city's adoption of Mary as its supreme protector (replacing the Tyche of the city) began with the attribution to her patronage of the defeat of the Avars in the early seventh century.

The thesis of Holum and Limberis was subjected to a careful analysis by Kate Cooper in an article published in 1998,[1] which pointed to the lateness of much of the evidence and showed how the Pulcheria legend grew in the telling. Nevertheless, Cooper's conclusion was that there is just enough contemporary evidence to support the thesis that Marian piety in Constantinople was the major cause of Nestorius' downfall, and that 'a thorough re-reading of the half-century leading up to the Council of Ephesus may ultimately reveal that Mariology developed from a grounding in both tradition and lay piety, and that Christology was adjusted to accommodate it' (p. 42).

Does the history of the Nestorian controversy need to be rewritten?

* * *

For all these writers a key episode was a dramatic confrontation between Pulcheria and Nestorius at his first Easter celebration in Constantinople, as narrated in the *Letter to Cosmas*. The text is preserved in a nineteenth-century Nestorian manuscript, and was supposedly written by a number of Nestorius' supporters soon after his fall. The story deserves to be quoted *in extenso*:

> At the great feast of Easter the Emperor used to receive communion in the Holy of Holies. Pulcheria wanted to do the same: she won over Bishop Sisinnius [of Constantinople, d. 427], and began to receive communion in the Holy of Holies together with the Emperor. Nestorius did not allow this. On one occasion when she was making her way as usual to the Holy of Holies, he saw her and asked what this meant. Peter the archdeacon explained the matter to him. Nestorius ran, met her at the entrance of the Holy of Holies, stopped her, and would not let her enter. The Empress took offence and said to him, 'Let me enter according to my custom.' But he said, 'This place is reserved for priests.' She said to him, 'Why? Have I not given birth to God?' He replied, 'You have given

---

[1] 'Contesting the Nativity: wives, virgins, and Pulcheria's *imitatio Mariae*', *Scottish Journal of Religious Studies*, 19 (1998), 31–43. A more recent treatment, that reached me too late for discussion in this paper, is John A. McGuckin, 'The paradox of the Virgin-*Theotokos*: evangelism and imperial politics in the fifth-century Byzantine world', *Maria*, 2 (2001), 8–25. He does not address the critical questions raised here.

birth to Satan!', and chased her from the entrance to the Holy of Holies. She left in a rage, and went and reported the incident to the Emperor [her brother Theodosius II]. 'On your life, my sister,' he replied, 'and by the crown that is on your head, I will not rest till I have taken vengeance on him.' From that day forth Nestorius enjoyed no credit with the Emperor.[2]

This is such a good story that one wishes it were true. But there are a number of problems about it, which doubtless explain why Church historians have generally ignored it. The *Letter to Cosmas* is standardly dated to *c.*436, since a *terminus post quem* of 435 is provided by the letter's reference to Nestorius' Egyptian exile;[3] but all we can say with confidence is that the main part of the letter has a dramatic date sometime between 435 and Nestorius' death in *c.*450. It is disturbing that the supposed co-authors of the letter include Count Candidianus, a supporter of Nestorius who was appointed by Theodosius II to chair the Council of Ephesus of 431: the appointment is clear evidence that Theodosius was well-disposed towards Nestorius as late as 431, in which case the claim in the letter that he turned against him as early as 428 cannot be true, and Candidianus will have known this better than anyone. Nestorius, himself, when he wrote the *Book of Heraclides*, claimed that, at the height of the controversy, he enjoyed the Emperor's support against Cyril.[4]

There is also reason to question Pulcheria's hostility to Nestorius before the Council of Ephesus. In a sermon preached in December 430, immediately after receiving hostile letters from both Cyril of Alexandria and Celestine of Rome, Nestorius expressed his continuing confidence because 'the emperor is pious and the Augustae love God'.[5] In other words, he still enjoyed the support of the imperial family, including Pulcheria. There also survive in Latin translation two letters from agents of Cyril discussing bribes to be offered to various persons

---

[2] F. Nau, 'Documents pour servir à l'histoire de l'église nestorienne', *Patrologia Orientalis*, 13 (Paris, 1919), 279.

[3] Holum, 153 n. 35. Nau ('Documents', 273) dated the main section of the letter (containing the Pulcheria episodes) to 'peu après 435'.

[4] Nestorius, ed. F. Nau, *Le Livre d'Héraclide de Damas* (Paris, 1910), 89. The often repeated argument that the summoning of the council of 431 to Ephesus is proof that the emperor intended it to condemn Nestorius, since Ephesus was a centre of Marian devotion, must be rejected in the light of the more direct evidence for Theodosius II's intentions at the time he convened the council. In fact the evidence for Marian devotion at Ephesus before the council is slight; the only solid fact is the dedication of its cathedral to the Virgin.

[5] *ACO*, 1.5, 40, ll. 13–14.

at court in 432 or 433 in order to secure their active hostility to Nestorius;[6] these letters reveal that Cyril's particular concern was to win over Pulcheria. In one of the letters his *syncellus* Epiphanius laments Pulcheria's lack of zeal for the anti-Nestorian cause, despite the numerous *benedictiones* (meaning bribes) which she had received. This evidence tells against the claim in the *Letter to Cosmas* that Pulcheria was a bitter enemy of Nestorius' even before the Council of Ephesus. The reason why most scholars have supposed the contrary is Nestorius' statement in the *Book of Heraclides* that Pulcheria opposed him 'because I refused to compare to the bride of Christ a woman corrupted by men'.[7] In view of the more immediately contemporary evidence just discussed this statement must surely be read as the elderly Nestorius a decade or more later playing his part in the development of the Pulcheria legend, in which Pulcheria's opposition to Nestorius mirrors that of her predecessor Eudoxia's hostility to John Chrysostom, while both echo Herodias' responsibility for the death of John the Baptist. Nestorius had no inclination to forgive Pulcheria for stabbing him in the back after the Council of Ephesus; but the weight of the evidence continues to be that she had supported him up to that date.

There are other suspicious elements in the letter. Apart from narrating the confrontation over communion, it also tells the story that Nestorius had a portrait of Pulcheria in the cathedral defaced: this is wholly incredible, since defacing the image of an empress would have constituted a treasonable act, as in the affair of the statues at Antioch in 387; moreover, the story is manifestly a blown-up version of a story found elsewhere, less impossible though probably equally fictitious, to the effect that Pulcheria asked Nestorius to have her image placed above the altar and was refused.[8]

In all, the *Letter to Cosmas* is a product of Nestorian propaganda after the event that cannot be treated as reliable evidence for tensions in the church and court of Constantinople in the period before the Council of Ephesus.

---

[6] J.D. Mansi, *Sacrorum conciliorum amplissima collectio*, 53 vols in 58 (Paris, 1759–1827), 5:987–9 (Epiphanius to Maximian of Constantinople); Nau, *Le Livre*, 367–9 (which lists various bribes, including fifty pounds of gold to one of Pulcheria's *cubiculariae* 'ut Augustam rogando persuadeat').

[7] Ibid., 89.

[8] The Syrian historian Barhadbeshabba (late sixth century) tells a conflation of both stories: F. Nau, 'Documents pour servir à l'histoire de l'église nestorienne: La seconde partie de l'histoire de Barhadbešabba 'Arbaïa et Controverse de Théodore de Mopsueste avec les Macédoniens': *Patrologia Orientalis*, 9 (Paris, 1913), 565–6.

* * *

What other evidence is there for a wave of Marian piety in court circles in this period? Holum, Limberis, and Cooper all describe Bishop Atticus of Constantinople (406–25) as promoting a court devotion to the Virgin Mary and encouraging the noble ladies of Constantinople, and particularly the female members of the imperial house, to identify themselves with the Virgin. The evidence is as follows. Gennadius of Marseilles refers to a lost work of Atticus, *On Faith and Virginity*, 'addressed to the daughters of Arcadius, in which Atticus attacked in advance the teaching of Nestorius'. Holum, in his discussion of the work,[9] surmises that it presented Mary as the model for the three imperial sisters to imitate. However, Gennadius could simply mean that the book commended virginity as an ideal for all the friends of God; referred incidentally to Mary as the model of virgins and *Theotokos* (whence its anti-Nestorian complexion in the eyes of later readers); and was dedicated to the imperial sisters as an act of courtesy. Holum also quotes a Christmas sermon by Atticus, preserved in Syriac, that is largely dedicated to Mary.[10] But the recent identification of a homily preserved in Church Slavonic as the authentic text of the sermon shows that one of the passages quoted by Holum is not by Atticus at all.[11] It is true that the other passage he quotes is authentic and develops a striking Marian theme:

> And you, women, who gave birth in Christ [*in the Syriac version*: have been renewed in Christ] and have cast off every stain of sin and have participated in the blessing received by holy Mary, receive in the womb of faith the one who is today born from the Virgin; for holy Mary, having first purified by faith the temple of her womb, then received into this temple the King of the ages.

Here Atticus urges his female hearers to imitate the faith of Mary. But it would be an over-interpretation to read this passage as an exhortation to cultivate a specifically Marian piety, involving a vivid and abiding sense of identification with the Virgin; it is in fact the only section in the authentic version of the homily that develops a Marian theme.

---

[9] Holum, 138–9.

[10] Ibid., 139–41.

[11] The Slavonic text, with translation and discussion, is in Francis J. Thomson, 'The Slavonic translation of the hitherto untraced Greek *Homilia in nativitatem domini nostri Jesu Christi* by Atticus of Constantinople', *Analecta Bollandiana*, 118 (2000), 5–36.

If one wants to find Constantinopolitan homilies that give a more prominent place to the Virgin, one must move forward to the homilies of Proclus, a leading presbyter in Constantinople in the 420s and bishop of the city in the post-Nestorian period.[12] The most famous of all his homilies was one he preached for a feast of the Virgin Mary in the very presence of Nestorius (Homily 1). The homily has some memorable things to say about Mary and about the way in which women can take a special pride in her. The fact remains, however, that the homily, like all Proclus' homilies, is predominantly not Marian but Christological. The problem of interpretation is raised in a similar way in another homily (Homily 4):

> Let women rush forward, because a woman . . . is giving birth to the fruit of life. Let virgins rush together, because a virgin gave birth . . . Let mothers rush forward . . . Let daughters rush together . . . Let fathers . . . Let children . . . Let shepherds . . . Let kings . . . Let consuls . . . Let common folk . . .

It is manifest that the women and virgins come first since, through Mary, their contact with the Word incarnate is the most intimate. But the thought is not explicitly developed. These homilies do not enable one to say that Proclus was concerned to promote a specifically Marian piety in Constantinople.[13]

The evidence from the sermons of Proclus is most fully exploited by Vasiliki Limberis, but her treatment of the text exhibits a remarkable indifference to exegetical niceties. A quotation from Homily 1 in praise of the Virgin Mary is compared to the striking panegyric of Pulcheria in Homily 12, with the comment, 'These praises to the Virgin differ very little in form or content from his panegyric to Pulcheria.'[14] Certainly, the literary style is similar; but there is not a single point of close similarity in content. What is said of Pulcheria is quite distinctive, and does not read in the least like the praises of Mary by the same author; Proclus might have chosen to liken Pulcheria to Mary, but he did not do so.

---

[12] Proclus, *Homilies on the Life of Christ*, tr. with an introduction and notes by J.H. Barkhuizen (Brisbane, 2001).

[13] Nicholas P. Constas, 'Weaving the body of God: Proclus of Constantinople, the Theotokos, and the loom of the flesh', *Journal of Early Christian Studies*, 3 (1995), 169–94, brings out the significance and innovatory character of Proclus' Mariology, but its dominance in his thought remains questionable.

[14] Limberis, 87.

Holum tries to strengthen the evidence for Pulcheria's public commitment to Marian piety by adducing her foundation of a number of churches in the capital dedicated to the Virgin.[15] But Cyril Mango has pointed out that the evidence for Pulcheria's involvement in the building of the great Marian churches of Blachernai, Hodegoi, and Chalkoprateia is post-iconoclastic and inconsistent.[16] Holum also refers to a story in the sixth-century anti-Chalcedonian historian John Rufus about Nestorius blaspheming the Virgin and being struck down by an act of God in a church dedicated to Mary in the Daphne complex of the imperial palace.[17] This he takes as evidence for imperial promotion of her cult even before the Council of Ephesus; but the story is a later fiction, and cannot be used as evidence for actual church dedications a century earlier.

* * *

This scepticism about Marian devotion in Constantinople in the time of Nestorius may seem exaggerated: is not the offence caused by Nestorius' attacks on the *Theotokos* itself evidence of a well-developed Marian piety in the capital? But we must again ask whether Mariology or Christology was the main issue. Writing to Celestine of Rome, Nestorius saw as the root of the trouble the promotion by some of his clergy of an exaggerated doctrine of the union of the divine and human in Christ that undermined belief in divine impassibility.[18] The historian Socrates, writing in Constantinople only a decade after the event, says that Nestorius' criticisms of the *Theotokos* caused offence by seeming to imply that her Son was a mere man.[19] This reinforces the impression left by the homilies of Proclus that even in Constantinople Mariology was subordinate to Christology.

The evidence relating to the Nestorian controversy of 428–31 may be reinforced if we allow ourselves to look ahead two decades to the Council of Chalcedon. Pulcheria's great hour came when, at the death of her brother in 450, she effectively took control of the religious policy

[15] Holum, 142–3.

[16] *Studies on Constantinople* (Aldershot, 1993), p. 4 of the Addenda to 'The development of Constantinople as an urban centre'.

[17] F. Nau, 'Jean Rufus, éveque de Maïouma, "Plérophories. temoignages et révélations contre la Concile de Chalcédoine", version syriaque et traduction française', *Patrologia Orientalis*, 8 (Paris, 1912), 11–12.

[18] *ACO*, 1.2, 12–14.

[19] Socrates, *Historia ecclesiastica*, 7.32: G.C. Hansen ed., *Socrates: Kirchengeschichte*, Die griechischen christlichen Schriftsteller der ersten Jahrhunderte, n.f. 1 (Berlin, 1995).

of the empire. Hers was the unseen but guiding hand at the Council of Chalcedon, which through the imperial officials who chaired the council dictated its agenda and secured the approval of a new definition which accorded with the religious policy of the government. How important was the *Theotokos* title at Chalcedon?

At the beginning of the fifth session the doctrinal committee produced a draft definition of the faith; the Acts do not include it, but it is clear from the reaction of the bishops that it was a solidly Cyrillian document (asserting famously that Christ is not *in* two natures but *from* two natures) and as such unwelcome to the Antiochenes and the Roman delegates. The relevant page of the Acts runs as follows:

> Asclepiades, deacon of Constantinople, read out the definition, which it has been decided not to include in these Acts . . . Anatolius of Constantinople said: 'Did everyone yesterday approve the definition of faith?' The bishops said: 'Everyone approved the definition . . . Anathema to whoever believes otherwise . . . Exclude all falsity from the definition. Write that the blessed Mary is *Theotokos* and insert it in the definition.' . . . The bishops exclaimed: 'The blessed Mary is *Theotokos* . . . The Virgin Mary is *Theotokos* . . . "Mary the *Theotokos*" must be added to the definition.'[20]

These episcopal exclamations reveal that the draft definition did not call Mary *Theotokos*.[21] This is very unexpected, since the draft was drawn up by a committee chaired by Archbishop Anatolius of Constantinople, who, like virtually all the bishops at the council, constantly appealed to the authority of Cyril of Alexandria and of the Council of Ephesus of 431, at which Nestorius had been condemned and the *Theotokos* title approved. The omission was open to serious misinterpretation and was immediately rectified. It can only have been accidental, but it remains deeply revealing of what was perceived as essential and inessential in the debate. It adds to the evidence in favour of the traditional view that the status of Mary as *Theotokos* was *not* the prime issue in the Nestorian controversy.

Heythrop College, University of London

---

[20] *ACO* 2.1.1, 123.
[21] Some scholars find this incredible, and strained attempts have been made to give a different interpretation to the page of the *Acts* quoted here. But the omission can be accounted for by reference to the sources used in the final section of the Definition. See G.D. Martzelos, *Genesê kai pêges tou orou tês Khalkêdonas* (Thessalonica, 1986), 94–8.

EMPRESS AND *THEOTOKOS*: GENDER AND PATRONAGE IN THE CHRISTOLOGICAL CONTROVERSY

by KATE COOPER

SCHOLARS have long suspected that the Byzantine cult of the Virgin Mary owed its early success to the efforts of the early Byzantine empresses. Among them, it is Aelia Pulcheria, *Augusta* from 414 to 453 and herself a professed virgin until her politically-charged marriage in 451, who is best known for having asserted Mary's right to be known as *Theotokos* – the one who gave birth to God. Many sources suggest that the Nestorian controversy debated at the Council of Ephesus in 431 arose from an altercation between Nestorius, Bishop of Constantinople from 428 to 431, and Pulcheria. On this view, the debate over Christ's human and divine natures turned on whether Mary had given birth to God the Son, or only to Jesus the man. It was with this in mind that in 1982 Kenneth Holum suggested that by refusing to support the cult of the Virgin as *Theotokos*, Nestorius had in effect challenged the imperial family's religious authority in early fifth-century Constantinople.[1]

Holum's *Theodosian Empresses* made possible a new kind of work on gender, patronage, and imperial piety. His thesis on Pulcheria's contribution to the early cult of the Virgin, however, has recently been challenged.[2] This paper brings to witness the fifth-century historian Socrates of Constantinople, acknowledged by many as the most reliable historian among Pulcheria's contemporaries, in support of a revised version of Holum's thesis. Before turning to Socrates and his handling of the fall of Nestorius, however, we must review very briefly the issues surrounding imperial authority and Marian piety in early fifth-century Constantinople.

Holum saw Pulcheria as the *impresario* of a powerful current of popular Marian devotion. The Empress used this devotion, he argued, as a source of 'sacral *basileia*',[3] a form of royal charisma indispensable to

---

[1] Holum.

[2] See n.11 below, and the contributions of Averil Cameron and Richard Price in this volume.

[3] Holum, 174.

the imperial family for mobilizing their subjects' co-operation. This notion of *basileia* drew on the Pauline ideal of unity in Christ, which was then in use variously to describe the relationship between a bishop and his city, an emperor and his people, or indeed within the imperial family. In her aspect as *Theotokos*, Holum argued, the Mother of God was particularly suited to this role. In support of this contextual interpretation, he called attention to evidence from material culture traditionally ignored by historians of theology. A strikingly clear example is the inscription on a casket for the shroud of the Virgin placed by Leo I, successor to Pulcheria's husband Marcian, and his Empress Verina in the chapel which they built as an annex to the Church of the Blachernai, a Constantinopolitan church recorded by Byzantine sources as founded by Pulcheria and dedicated by her to the Virgin. The inscription, which could hardly have been more appropriate to Holum's argument, reads: 'By showing reverence here to the *Theotokos*, they secured their *basileia*.'[4]

In 1994, Vasiliki Limberis took Holum's line of reasoning one step further.[5] Her study of the Virgin's cult situated the problem of *basileia* against the wider backdrop of pagan and Christian civic and religious culture in fourth- and fifth-century Constantinople. Limberis stressed the inter-dependence of imperial and civic religion, and, like Holum, accorded a key patronage role to the female members of the imperial family. For Limberis, the allegiance between virgin Empress and Virgin Mother was the fruition of a long inheritance of divine and human female power in the cities of Asia Minor, stretching back through the cults of Tyche, Isis, Artemis, and Cybele.[6] That the House of Theodosius drew on this inheritance with good sense and enthusiasm, Limberis argued, was a sign to contemporary eyes that their brand of Christian rulership was firmly rooted in the traditions of the imperial city.

Both writers gave special attention to what seems often to have been a tense relationship between the imperial family and the Bishop of

---

[4] Ibid., 227, citing A. Wenger, 'Notes inédites sur les empereurs Théodose I, Arcadius, Théodose II, Léon I', *Revue des études byzantines*, 10 (1952), 54–9.

[5] Limberis, with a discussion at 121–42 of the Virgin as protectress of the city, based largely on the Akathist hymn, to complement the earlier studies of N.H. Baynes, 'The supernatural defenders of Constantinople', *Analecta Bollandiana*, 67 (1949), 171–2, and Averil Cameron, 'The Theotokos in sixth-century Constantinople', *JThS*, 29 (1978), 79–108.

[6] Limberis' thesis is accepted by Philippe Borgeaud, *La Mère des dieux: de Cybèle à la Vierge Marie* (Paris, 1996), 182.

Constantinople. Divergence over Marian cult emerges in both studies as a factor in a larger opposition. An imperial, civic Theodosian Christianity, which valued the religious leadership provided by male and female lay members of the imperial family, stood in opposition to a clerically-orientated vision of Christian liturgy and polity, which sought to limit the power and symbolic function of members of the royal family, and to dissociate the Church from the religious and political aims of the Emperor.

Both Holum and Limberis brought a dazzling range of material together into evocative, kaleidoscopic pictures, but due to the notorious limitations of the sources, the pictures were necessarily provisional. Important in Holum's view, for example, is the fact that the Council at which the natures of Christ were debated was held at Ephesus, a city whose ancient cult of the virgin goddess Artemis had given way to the cult of the Virgin *Theotokos,* and that the Council was held in the great basilica dedicated to Mary.[7] If the venue for the Council was already dedicated to the Virgin in 431, Holum suggested, this would indicate that the Emperor saw special importance in the Marian implications of the Christological controversy, and that assertion of the Virgin as *Theotokos* was an intended outcome of the Council. This picture has subsequently come to seem less than perfectly convincing, because both the dedication of the basilica at Ephesus to Mary and the role of Pulcheria as foundress of other Marian basilicas depend entirely on late sources.[8] The possibility has to be considered that the picture of Pulcheria as Marian patroness is an anachronistic projection of the Marian interests of later empresses. There is no evidence to prove that the late sources are mistaken, but their witness is unconfirmed.

The problem of late or suspect evidence is as vexing for textual sources as it is for material culture. I have shown elsewhere that the interest in Pulcheria shown by a number of sources, both earlier and later, owes much to literary and rhetorical forces that can distort the evidence if they are not taken into account.[9] A *tableau vivant* was handed

[7] Holum, 164.

[8] Cyril Mango, 'Constantinople as Theotokoupolis', in Vassilaki, 17–25, suggests at 19, drawing on his earlier 'The origins of the Blachernae shrine at Constantinople' (*Acta XIII Congressus Internationalis Archaeologiae Christianae,* 2 (Vatican City and Split, 1998), 61–76, at 65–6), that in the absence of early evidence for Pulcheria as patroness of the Marian basilicas, 'the somewhat disreputable Verina, rather than the virginal Pulcheria, emerges as the chief promoter of Marian devotion in the fifth century'.

[9] Kate Cooper, 'Contesting the Nativity: wives, virgins, and Pulcheria's *imitatio Mariae*', *Scottish Journal of Religious Studies,* 19 (1998), 31–43.

on and elaborated from writer to writer, deploying the altercation between Nestorius and Pulcheria as the dramatic engine for the story of the bishop's fall – and thus, by extension, of the Nestorian Controversy. Its literary pattern is arguably based on accounts of the earlier face-off between John Chrysostom, Nestorius' predecessor as Bishop of Constantinople, and the Empress Aelia Eudoxia, Pulcheria's mother.[10]

But to say that work on the early cult of the *Theotokos* needs to be adequately source-critical by no means implies that the sources can tell us nothing. The persistent emphasis of the narrative sources on Pulcheria must be accounted for, and I will suggest below that there may be a way to identify the historical grain on which the rhetorical pearl was formed. My earlier study showed that the bizarre description of Pulcheria's Marian piety in one early source, the pro-Nestorian *Letter to Cosmas*, can be accounted for if it is read against the wider fifth-century evidence for women's pious imitation of Mary. Such contextual reading can derive valuable information even from a distorted and tendentious account of the Empress's character and actions. At the same time, close analysis of the sermons of Proclus, presbyter of Constantinople in the 420s and early 430s and bishop of the city from 434 to 446, supports a picture of Pulcheria as Marian *impresario*.[11] This article, by contrast, calls for a re-reading of another valuable but under-studied source, the *Ecclesiastical History* of Socrates of Constantinople, written between 439 and 450.[12] Socrates, it will be argued, gives evidence for a link between Marian piety and imperial *basileia* which is all the more valuable for the fact that Pulcheria herself is never mentioned.

Socrates is a particularly important witness to the early Nestorian controversy for several reasons. Not only was he a contemporary of both Nestorius and Pulcheria, but he also wrote self-consciously within the tradition of ancient critical historiography. This is evident in his

---

[10] On the sources for Chrysostom and Eudoxia, see Kate Cooper, *The Virgin and the Bride: Idealized Womanhood in Late Antiquity* (Cambridge, MA, 1996), 17–19, and literature cited there.

[11] Nicholas Constas, 'Weaving the body of God: Proclus of Constantinople, the Theotokos, and the loom of the flesh', *Journal of Early Christian Studies*, 3 (1995), 169–94, to be followed by a book-length study currently in progess.

[12] On the date of Socrates, see Hartmut Leppin, *Von Constantin dem Großen zu Theodosius II: Das Christliche Kaisertum bei den Kirchenhistorikern Socrates, Sozomenus und Theodoret* (Göttingen, 1996), 274–9 (opting for a date between 444 and 446; Theresa Urbainczyk, *Socrates of Constantinople: Historian of Church and State* (Ann Arbor, MI, 1997), 34, arguing for a date early in the 440s; Martin Wallraff, *Der Kirchenhistoriker Socrates: Untersuchungen zu Geschichtsdarstellung, Methode und Person* (Göttingen, 1997), 210–12, arguing for a date before 443.

copious verbatim citation of the documents to which he gained access, and in his revision, on obtaining new evidence, of Books I and II of the *Ecclesiastical History*. If Socrates does have an identifiable bias, it is a tendency to suspect bishops and churchmen of being overly interested in self-promotion. Henry Chadwick put this memorably, saying that for Socrates theology was merely a fig-leaf for politics.[13] But the historian's anticlericalism, if it is that, may simply represent a conservative Theodosian view. Socrates seems to have seen the Emperor as guarantor of the unity of the Church, responsible for and responsive to the best interest of the whole despite – or, perhaps, because of – his lay status, while the clerics who peopled the Church's hierarchy fought for lesser diverging interests. This kind of reasoning reflected the contemporary view that the Emperor could best serve the temporal interest of his empire by cultivating God's favour.[14]

Where Pulcheria is concerned, Socrates offers a reasonably balanced treatment, indulging neither in the semi-hysterical criticism of the Nestorian sources, nor in the fawning of his later contemporary Sozomen. Leppin has argued that Socrates intensely disliked the Empress, suggesting that the fact that her name never appears in the text – though she is alluded to at least once – constituted a diplomatic way of not praising her.[15] Similarly, Urbainczyk suggests that Socrates may have failed to exhibit the enthusiasm for Pulcheria shown by his contemporary Sozomen because he was writing during Pulcheria's period of semi-exile in the 440s;[16] but this picture may alter if a more

---

[13] On Socrates' tendency to attribute schism within the Church to the conflicting power strategies of individual bishops, see Leppin, *Von Constantin,* 227–43.

[14] See, for example, *Letter* 19 of Celestine I to Theodosius II: 'Major vobis fidei causa debet esse, quam regni; ampliusque pro pace ecclesiarum clementia vestra debet esse sollicita, quam pro omnium securitate terrarum' (*PL* 50, cols 511–12), discussed in Stewart Irwin Oost, *Galla Placidia Augusta: a Biographical Essay* (Chicago, 1968), 250; Leppin, *Von Constantin,* esp. 206–24 on 'Kaiserliches Handeln und göttliches Wirken', and also Joachim Szidat, 'Friede in Kirche und Staat: zum politischen Ideal des Kirchenhistorikers Sokrates', in Balbina Bäbler and Heinz-Günther Nesselrath, eds, *Die Welt des Sokrates von Konstantinopel: Studien zu Politik, Religion und Kultur in späten 4. und frühen 5. Jh. n. Chr. zu Ehren von Christoph Schäublin* (Munich and Leipzig, 2001), 1–14. For a relevant discussion of the religious significance of the person of the emperor, see François Heim, *Virtus: Idéologie politique et croyances religieuses au IVe siècle* (Berlin, 1991), 187–218.

[15] Leppin, *Von Constantin,* 240.

[16] Urbainczyk, *Socrates,* 34, assuming a later date for Sozomen, after Pulcheria's re-emergence into the limelight on the death of Theodosius in 450. Alan Cameron, 'The empress and the poet: paganism and politics at the court of Theodosius II', *Yale Classical Studies,* 27 (1982), 217–89, suggests that Pulcheria's withdrawal from court from roughly 439 was the product not of rivalry with Eudokia – indeed, Cameron paints Eudokia and

43

precise date and context for either writer is reached. Socrates himself was not a member of the imperial circle,[17] so his treatment of his cast of characters may not reflect discernible political motivations.

For immediate purposes the most important point about Socrates is that he gives clear evidence that the fall of Nestorius was caused by his attitude to the *Theotokos* while studiously avoiding the temptation to lay the fall of the bishop at Pulcheria's door. This is important because there are good methodological reasons for questioning any source that places the controversy in the shadow of the Eudoxia-Chrysostom dispute. We will see below that while Socrates places considerable emphasis on Nestorius' refusal to use the term *Theotokos*, using it as the frame story for his narrative of the Council of Ephesus, he does so in a way which seems designed to safeguard the dignity of the imperial family.

This is his account of the initial episode of the controversy between Nestorius and Pulcheria:

> Nestorius had an associate whom he had brought from Antioch, a presbyter named Anastastius; for this man he had high esteem, and consulted him in the management of affairs. Anastasius, preaching one day in church, said, 'Let no one call Mary *Theotocos*, for Mary was but a human being, and it is impossible that God should be born of a human being.' This caused a great sensation, and troubled both the clergy and the laity, as they had been heretofore taught to acknowledge Christ as God, and by no means to separate his humanity from his divinity.[18]

Clarifying that Nestorius was not in fact a proponent of Docetism as some people believed, Socrates suggests that his error arose from ignorance of Church history. The term *Theotokos*, he reminds the reader, had been established in ecclesiastical usage by Eusebius and Origen.[19]

Pulcheria as collaborators rather than rivals – but rather of Pulcheria's status as a victim, like Eudokia, of the machinations of the eunuch Chrysaphius in the period from 439 until 450.

[17] Wallraff, *Sokrates*, 220–1.

[18] Socrates, *Historia ecclesiastica*, VII.32.1–3, in Günther Christian Hansen, ed., *Socrates: Kirchengeschichte*, Griechischen christlichen Schriftsteller der ersten Jahrhunderte, n.f. 1 (Berlin, 1995), 80. Neither Holum nor Limberis lays particular emphasis on Socrates' testimony in this respect; both refer to portions of Socrates VII.32 – Holum at p. 154 nn.37–8, and Limberis at p. 54 n.50 – but in support of different points. Here and below I use the translation by A.C. Zenos, 'The Ecclesiastical History of Socrates Scholasticus', in Philip Schaff and Henry Wace, eds, *A Select Library of Nicene and Post-Nicene Fathers of the Christian Church, second series*, 2 (Oxford and New York, 1891), 170.

[19] See Jaroslav Pelikan, *Mary through the Centuries: Her Place in the History of Culture* (New Haven, CT, 1996) on the history of the term.

Similarly, Socrates' account of the end of the Council returns to the *Theotokos* epithet, underlining its centrality to the dispute:

> When affairs reached this confused condition, Nestorius saw that the contention which had been raised was thus tending to the destruction of communion; in bitter regret he called Mary *Theotokos*, and cried out: 'Let Mary be called *Theotokos*, if you will, and let all disputing cease.' But although he made this recantation, no notice was taken of it; for his deposition was not revoked, and he was banished to the Oasis, where he still remains.[20]

According to this version of events, Nestorius still believed that he could bring an end to the dispute by showing adequate reverence to the Virgin.

We should pay close attention to the passage where Socrates illustrates the history of the term *Theotokos* alluded to in the opening passage. To accuse a Bishop of Constantinople of not knowing his Eusebius was no mean slight, but the accusation is in fact a cover for an even more serious charge. 'Ignorance of Church history' turns out to be a euphemism for an affront to the dignity of the imperial family. By offering a direct citation from Eusebius' *Life of Constantine*, Socrates links the term *Theotokos* directly to patronage by the women of the imperial family, so that a Byzantine reader could not have missed what the historian clearly viewed as Nestorius' slight to the women of the House of Theodosius.

The passage which he imports from Eusebius' text reads as follows:

> And in fact Emmanuel submitted to be born for our sake, and the place of his nativity in the flesh is by the Hebrews called Bethlehem. Wherefore the devout Empress Helena adorned the place where the *Theotokos* gave birth with the most splendid monuments, decorating that cave with the richest ornaments.[21]

Helena's patronage of the Church of the Nativity at Bethlehem would have been important from a Theodosian point of view not just because she was the mother of the first Christian Emperor. More specifically she was the mother of a son who styled himself the earthly representative of the One whose birth was remembered at Bethlehem. That Helena could claim special privilege as both protégée and earthly patroness of

---

[20] Socrates, *Historia ecclesiastica*, VII.34.10–11 (ed. Hansen, 383; tr. Zenos, 172).
[21] Eusebius, *Life of Constantine*, 3, in Socrates, *Historia ecclesiastica*, VII.32.15–16 (ed. Hansen, 381; tr. Zenos, 171).

the *Theotokos* is offered as self-evident. For Socrates, her gesture enhancing commemoration of Mary's act of birth amounts to an assertion of her own spiritual authority as mother of Christ's earthly counterpart.

It is no accident that it was Helena's memory that Nestorius stood accused of slighting. In 1997 Leslie Brubaker argued that from the fourth to sixth centuries *Augustae* and other women of the imperial family self-consciously structured their own considerable patronage activity in imitation of the benefactions of the first Christian *Augusta*.[22] Examples of this activity appear in Ravenna, where Galla Placidia established a church of the Holy Cross in 424/5 on her return from Constantinople,[23] and Rome, where the same Empress with her children Honoria and Valentinian III embellished Helena's Church of the Holy Cross in the Sessorian Palace some time before 438.[24] The pilgrimage of Eudokia, Pulcheria's sister-in-law and rival, to Jerusalem soon after the marriage in 437 of her only surviving child, Licinia Eudoxia, to Valentinian III can be read as an imitation of Helena's earlier journey.[25]

This context for the question of Pulcheria's Marian patronage, which Brubaker has called an early Byzantine 'matronage' tradition, was not well understood in the early eighties when Holum wrote. But in the interim, the groundwork for beginning to draw patterns from the evidence for women's patronage activity in Constantinople has become firmer, through the publication of Martin Harrison's study of Anicia Juliana's Church of St Polyeuktos in 1989 and by a ground-breaking article by Elizabeth Clark in 1990, in addition to Limberis' above-mentioned study.[26] Brubaker's article demonstrates

---

[22] Leslie Brubaker, 'Memories of Helena: patterns of imperial female matronage in the fourth and fifth centuries', in Liz James, ed., *Women, Men and Eunuchs: Gender in Byzantium* (1997), 52–75.

[23] Oost, *Galla Placidia Augusta*, 275–7, with sources at 276 n.88.

[24] Ibid., 270–1, with sources at 271 n.77.

[25] And was so by Socrates, *Historia ecclesiastica*, VII.47, where she is explicitly called a new Helena. Holum (183–5) discusses the circumstances of Eudokia's departure in early 438 at the urging of Melania the Younger according to the latter's biographer.

[26] Martin Harrison, *A Temple for Byzantium: the Discovery and Excavation of Anicia Juliana's Palace-Church in Istanbul* (1989); Elizabeth A. Clark, 'Patrons not priests: gender and power in late ancient Christianity', *Gender and History*, 2 (1990), 253–73 (see also Mary Taliaferro Boatwright, 'Plancia Magna of Perge: women's roles and status in Roman Asia Minor', in Sarah Booth Pomeroy, ed., *Women's History and Ancient History* (Chapel Hill, NC, 1991), 249–72). In addition, see now Liz James, *Empresses and Power in Early Byzantium* (London and New York, 2001).

that the patronesses of the Constantinopolitan church not only exercised great scope, but did so in a way that was highly strategic and self-conscious, crafting and enhancing their status as specifically female representatives of a well-chosen and sometimes fictional lineage by imitation of the commissions of chosen female forebears. Though Pulcheria and the other Theodosian women could not claim blood relationship to Helena, they had every reason to model their own activity on that of their illustrious predecessor. Pulcheria's aunt Galla Placidia and her sister-in-law Eudokia established very different strategies for laying claim to the memory of Helena. That Pulcheria's activity on behalf of the *Theotokos* should be read in this light is supported by the acclamations addressed to Pulcheria by the bishops gathered at Chalcedon in 451: 'Pulcheria the new Helena! You have shown the faith of Helena! You have shown the zeal of Helena!'[27]

It is important that Socrates invokes Helena and Eusebius simultaneously. By calling attention to Eusebius' status as author of the *Life of Constantine*, Socrates reminds his readers of his own privileged lineage as a historian of imperial Christianity. Nestorius, by contrast, is cast very much as an outsider – to Constantinople and to tradition itself. The role given to the memory of Helena in Socrates' account of Nestorius' downfall has a precise rhetorical function. Unlike the version of the face-off with Nestorius offered by Pulcheria's more strident critics, here the concern of the Theodosian women for their imperial dignity is treated with oblique respect, by offering the legitimate grounds on which it must have been based. Socrates is by no means emphasising Pulcheria's involvement for sensationalistic rhetorical reasons. Indeed, the passage refers to no living empress as heir to Helena's memory, which may be a way of showing tact in handling a potentially serious affront. Rather, the role of empress is stressed in order to project a comparatively serious message about the lay, civic, imperial tradition of the Constantinian and Theodosian Church, against which – intentionally or inadvertently – Nestorius had aligned himself.

If Socrates' discretion in refusing to name the Empress or Empresses thus slighted remains a stumbling-block, there are nonetheless reasons to connect this passage to the sources which cite a conflict between

---

[27] *ACO*, 2/ii/I:155; I have followed Holum's translation (216), though he uses the passage in support of a different point.

Nestorius and Pulcheria. Unlike her married aunt and sister-in-law, both of whom had legitimate children, Pulcheria as a professed virgin could not emulate Helena in drawing the parallel between imperial and divine maternity. It was the paradox of Mary's fecund virginity which Pulcheria wished to stress, and in so doing she underlined the Virgin's miraculous power.

In the century that separated Helena and Pulcheria the special relationship of virgins to the Virgin had become a staple of the ideology of virginity. David Hunter has shown that in the Latin West a half-generation earlier, Helvidius had argued that how Mary was interpreted theologically placed limits on who could use her power. Helvidius wanted to stress Mary's post-Incarnation life as a mother and married woman, arguing that she could be claimed as a model by all women and not only by virgins.[28] He saw too complete an identification of the Virgin with the Church's human virgins in the assertion, put forward by Ambrose and supported ferociously by Jerome, that her virginity persisted *in partu* and *post partum*. Even Origen, the great theorist of virginity, had stressed that Mary's virginity, though perpetual, miraculously included a full and proper opening of the womb in parturition, thus safeguarding the theology of virginity against the claim that it would lead to a Manichaean rejection of the body.[29] The late fourth-century writer Jovinian asked related questions about the politics of identification. His meditation on the relationship between virgins and the married included a rather pointed critique of the famous letter from Jerome to Eustochium outlining the merits of virginity. For Jovinian, the identification of the professed virgin (as against the Church herself) as the bride of the Song of Songs could not be taken for granted, despite Jerome's assurances to the virginal Eustochium. That we know of Jovinian and Helvidius only through Jerome's refutation of their views[30] is evidence of the eventual victory of the virginity party in the West.

The debate in the East did not follow an identical pattern and has yet to receive the sustained inquiry that Hunter has offered for the West,

[28]   David Hunter, 'Helividius, Jovinian, and the Virginity of Mary in late fourth-century Rome', *Journal of Early Christian Studies*, 1 (1993), 47–71, and Giancarlo Rocca, *L'Adversus Helvidium di San Girolamo nel contesto della letteratura ascetico-mariana del secolo IV* (Berlin, 1998), 24.

[29]   *Homily in Luke*, 14.8; cited in Hunter, 'Helvidius, Jovinian, and the Virginity of Mary', 69.

[30]   In his *Contra Helvidium* and *Adversus Jovinianum*.

but the link between virgins and the Virgin undoubtedly received strong theological support.[31] In light of these dynamics and the evidence, discussed elsewhere,[32] that both Greek and Latin-speaking women in the late fourth and early fifth centuries were interested in *imitatio*, whether of Mary or of other holy women such as the martyrs, we can infer that Pulcheria saw the link between her claim on the memory of Helena and her role as a special patron of the cult of Mary. She is also likely to have believed – correctly, it seems – that how the Virgin was defined theologically would influence the extent and social meaning of her spiritual power.

In this respect, the Council of Ephesus seems to have amounted to a compromise. The claims of virgins on the Virgin had to be reconciled with an assertion of Christ's flesh. All parties to the debate seem to have agreed ultimately that Jesus' body had to be a properly enfleshed body to resist the dangers of Manichaeism and Docetism.

The compromise was developed further twenty years later at Chalcedon, where the *Theotokos* epithet is explicitly mentioned with regard to the full enfleshment of Jesus:

> born from the Virgin Mary, the *Theotokos*, as touching the manhood . . . to be acknowledged in two natures, without confusion, without change, without division, without separation; the distinction of natures being in no way abolished because of the union.[33]

In his account of the later Council, Holum again stressed factors suggesting Pulcheria's influence, such as its location in the basilica of the virgin Euphemia, its above-mentioned acclamations for Pulcheria, and Pulcheria's negotiations with Pope Leo I beforehand.[34] The evidence for this argument, too, may bear revisiting – but that the Empress played a central role in brokering East-West relations through her correspondence with Pope Leo is not in doubt.

[31] See Susanna Elm, *'Virgins of God': the Making of Asceticism in Late Antiquity* (Oxford, 1994), 336–7, on Mary as an exemplar for virgins in Athanasius of Alexandria's *Letter to Virgins*.

[32] Cooper, 'Contesting the Nativity', 35–41.

[33] *The Chalcedonian Definition*, 4. I cite here the English version from J. Stevenson, *Creeds, Councils, and Controversies: Documents Illustrating the History of the Church AD 337–461*, new edn rev. W.H.C. Frend (1989), 353.

[34] P. Goubert, 'La Role de Sainte Pulcherie et de l'eunuque Chrysaphius', in Alois Grillmeier and Hermann Bacht, eds, *Das Konzil von Chalkedon*, I (Würzburg, 1951), 303–21. Holum summarizes: 'During the year of Chalcedon she directed preparations from her palace, and the council unfolded according to her plan' (216).

Given the limitations of the historical evidence, it is unlikely that Pulcheria's actions or intentions will ever be securely understood. But more remains to be done in charting the dynamics of religious patronage by women of the imperial family in the first half of the fifth century, and the effect that their patronage had on theological developments. This would, for example, allow us to revisit the collaboration between Pulcheria and Leo in the period leading up to Chalcedon as the fruit of Leo's relationship with Pulcheria's 'Western' aunt Galla Placidia and with Pulcheria's niece, Eudokia's daughter Licinia Eudoxia, who moved West from Constantinople in 437 on her marriage to Valentinian III, Placidia's son. The evidence for Placidia's role has long been acknowledged,[35] but we should perhaps give weight to the enhancement of dynastic unity as a motive for the theological allegiance. Likewise, we can imagine that Pulcheria's good relations with Placidia and Valentinian were one of the assets which allowed her, at her brother's death in 450, to choose a husband and install him as Emperor of the East.

It is with East-West relations that this contribution reaches its conclusion. We have seen that comparing the Eastern and Western developments can be useful where the evidence for either side is insufficient. But it is worth stressing that the Christological controversies emerged following the division of a previously united Empire into Eastern and Western halves on the death of Theodosius I in 395. It was Theodosius the Great's daughter Galla Placidia in the West and his grandson Theodosius II, son of Placidia's half-brother Arcadius, who attempted to restore the unity of the Empire and consolidate the future of the dynasty by marrying their children, Valentinian III and Licinia Eudoxia, on 29 October 437.[36] It is well known that the gambit failed, and that after Valentinian's murder in 455 – only two years after Pulcheria's death – his family were taken hostage by Gaiseric, King of the Vandals, and the dynasty came to disaster.[37] The two territories

---

[35] Galla Placidia's letters to Theodosius II and to Pulcheria on behalf of Leo are in *ACO*, 2/i/I:5–6, letters 2–3, and 49–50, letter 14. In *ACO*, 2/iv:29, letter 28 (60), Leo thanks Pulcheria for her letter to him (which is not preserved). The letters are discussed by Oost, *Galla Placidia Augusta*, 289–90.

[36] Holum, 129 (on the imperial cousins' betrothal in 424, drawing on Marcellinus Comes *a.* 424), 183 (the sources for the marriage).

[37] On the fate of the mother and daughters, see Carmelo Capizzi, S.J., 'Anicia Juliana (462 ca–530 ca): ricerche sulla sua famiglia e la sua vita', *Rivista di studi Bizantini e neoellenici*, n.s. 5 (1968), 191–226.

would not again be reunited until Justinian's reconquest, and then only temporarily.

In this context, the Theodosian Empresses' attempt to enhance what Holum called their sacral *basileia*, and particularly their attempt to do so by invoking the memory of Constantine and Helena, takes on far-reaching political significance. As Empress Regent and mother of a legitimate emperor, Galla Placidia seems in this matter to have been a traditionalist very much to the taste of Socrates. Pulcheria, in her seeming unwillingness to be displaced in the popular imagination by her brother's legitimate consort Eudokia, put forward a more idiosyncratic vision of imperial Christianity, but in her own way she too drew attention to the miraculous connection between fertility and divine power. That the two *Augustae* collaborated in the period from Valentinian's marriage in 437 through to Placidia's death in November 450 shows that their visions were not patently incompatible. Whatever their differences may have been, the dynasty's future was at stake.

In the end neither piety nor propaganda could compensate where fertility failed. That the sources for Marian piety in Theodosian Christianity are limited is a direct consequence of the dynasty's abrupt end, which is to say of Valentinian's failure to produce a male heir. It remains an open question whether with better planning and luck either of his daughters could have commandeered the succession in 455 as their great-aunt Pulcheria had done in 450 on the death of Theodosius II. Such a gambit might well have included a role for the cult of the Virgin *Theotokos*, but in the event it was for the women of other dynasties to inherit and develop what Pulcheria seems to have begun.

University of Manchester

THE MEETING OF THE OLD AND THE NEW: THE TYPOLOGY OF MARY THE THEOTOKOS IN BYZANTINE HOMILIES AND HYMNS

by MARY B. CUNNINGHAM

THIS article presents a preliminary report on a research project which will examine the homiletic and hymnographic treatment of the Virgin Mary in eighth-century Byzantium. The texts requiring detailed study are numerous and not without their problems.[1] Some of the surviving hymns[2] and homilies remain unedited, while the authorship of many texts, including those which have been edited, is still disputed. The first stage of the project will therefore be concerned with identifying all eighth-century Marian homilies and hymns; only after that will it be possible to study the historical, theological, and spiritual content of this material.[3]

It must be stressed at the outset that any conclusions at this stage of the research project are tentative; so far there are more questions to be posed than answers given. This paper will focus on one important and striking aspect of the eighth-century Byzantine liturgical texts written in honour of the Theotokos: namely, their use of typology to express her connection with the events and prophecies of the Old Testament. It will examine the homilies of three eighth-century preachers, Andrew of Crete, Germanos of Constantinople, and John of Damascus.[4]

---

[1] For a full list of Greek homilies dedicated to the Virgin Mary, see F. Halkin, ed., *Bibliotheca hagiographica graeca*, 3 (Brussels, 1957), App. III, 123–74.

[2] The hymnography written in honour of the Theotokos represents a large body of material which is closely related to the homiletic corpus. For reasons of space, hymns will not be examined in detail in this paper, but they will feature in the larger research project being undertaken.

[3] No comprehensive study of eighth-century Byzantine homilies and hymns on the Theotokos yet exists. For fifth-century background on the homiletic tradition and a good model of the treatment needed by later Byzantine Marian homilies, see R. Caro, *La homiletica Mariana Griega en el siglo V*, 1–3, Marian Library Studies, 3–5 (Dayton, OH, 1971–3). For background on the development of homilies concerned with the Dormition of the Virgin, see M. Jugie, *La Mort et l'assomption de la sainte Vierge*, Studi e Testi, 114 (Vatican City, 1944); A. Wenger, *L'Assomption de la très sainte Vierge dans la tradition byzantine du VIe au Xe siècles*, Études et Documents, Archives de l'Orient Chrétien (Paris, 1955).

[4] These homilies are all listed in M. Geerard, *Clavis patrum graecorum*, 3 (Turnhout, 1979) [hereafter *CPG*], 505–10, 519–21, 532, 537, 539–45, 553; idem, *Clavis patrum graecorum: Supplementum* (Turnhout, 1998) [hereafter *CPG:Suppl.*], 461, 464–5, 467, 469–72.

The reasons for the proliferation of homilies dedicated to the Mother of God in the eighth century are varied and still under discussion. It is certainly likely, as N. Tsironis suggests, that this development was related to the outbreak of Iconoclasm,[5] but it also must reflect (more obviously) the growth in importance of the cult of the Theotokos in the formative period which preceded Iconoclasm, beginning in the late sixth century.[6] In any case, it is clear that the eighth and ninth centuries represented a crucial phase in the history of the veneration of the Virgin Mary, as Mother of God, in the Byzantine Orthodox Church.[7]

For immediate purposes, it is necessary to define typology, a method of biblical exegesis which developed at a very early date in the Christian Church and which has to do with the history of human salvation beginning with the creation of the world in Genesis.[8] Typology seeks to make symbolic connections between persons, objects, and events in the Old and New Testaments. Thus, an event such as God's creation of Adam out of untilled earth in the Old Testament foreshadows the incarnation of Christ from the Virgin Mary in the New. This method of biblical interpretation has usually been viewed as historical, since in contrast to allegorical exegesis it does not deny the importance of an historical framework for the events, persons, or objects which are symbolically connected.[9] Indeed, this historical framework is significant since it represents the working out through time of God's plan for the salvation of humankind.

As Frances Young points out in her penetrating discussion of the subject, however, the division between typological and allegorical exegesis is not always clear-cut. The concept of typology is in fact a

[5] Niki J. Tsironis, 'The Lament of the Virgin Mary from Romanos the Melode to George of Nicomedia. An aspect of the development of the Marian cult' (University of London, Ph.D. thesis, 1998), 122–6, 179–80.

[6] For background on the growth of the cult of the Virgin from the late sixth century onward, see Averil Cameron, 'The Theotokos in sixth-century Constantinople: a city finds its symbol', *JThS*, 29 (1978), 79–108; eadem, 'The Virgin's robe: an episode in the history of early seventh-century Constantinople', *Byzantion*, 49 (1979), 42–56.

[7] Scholars disagree on the question whether iconoclast emperors supported or opposed the cult of the Theotokos. For a survey of the problem, see Tsironis, 'The Lament', 124–6. She questions K. Parry's view that the iconoclasts venerated the Theotokos. See K. Parry, *Depicting the Word. Byzantine Iconophile Thought of the Eighth and Ninth Centuries* (Leiden, 1996), 191–2.

[8] J.N.D. Kelly, *Early Christian Doctrines*, 5th edn (1977), 69–75.

[9] On the different types of biblical exegesis, which were variously defined as threefold or fourfold in the course of the patristic and medieval periods, see Henri de Lubac, *Medieval Exegesis, 1: The Four Senses of Scripture*, trans. Mark Sebanc (Edinburgh, 1998).

modern one; ancient exegetes do not appear to have distinguished between typology and allegory, and the two methods of interpretation frequently overlap. Whereas, for example, images such as Jacob's ladder or Noah's ark continue to be linked with their historical contexts, they also attain a more eternal, or timeless, significance when used as types, or foreshadowings, of the incarnation of Christ through the Virgin Mary. As Young, following Sebastian Brock, expresses it, 'superimposition shifts the "type" into a different frame . . . called "sacred" or liturgical time, suggesting a universal or eternal truth played out in time, time and again.'[10]

Typology is thus rooted in the exegetical tradition of the early Church.[11] The strong Jewish background of early Christians in the first century, and the Church's rejection of Gnosticism and all its teachings in the second, both played an important role in the acceptance – one might even say, *appropriation* – of the Old Testament as Christian scripture. If the Old Testament is, as orthodox Christians since then have believed, a witness to God's plan of salvation for his chosen people – salvation which would culminate in the incarnation and resurrection of Christ – then everything which takes place in its historical and prophetic books must be significant from a Christian point of view. Just as Christ, according to theologians from Justin Martyr and Irenaeus of Lyons onwards, is foreshadowed in many people and events in the Old Testament, so, logically and inevitably, is the figure who was responsible for bringing him as a baby into this world; the Theotokos, or *Meter Theou*, Mother of God, as she came to be called somewhat later in the Byzantine period.[12]

Although exploration of the typology surrounding the Virgin Mary began early, being especially visible in the writings of the second-century writer Irenaeus,[13] it only came into its full flowering in the fourth and fifth centuries. Sebastian Brock, Robert Murray, and others have edited, translated, and discussed the rich Syriac tradition of Marian typology;[14] it requires no further elaboration here, although it is

[10] Frances Young, *Biblical Exegesis and the Formation of Christian Culture* (Cambridge, 1997), 154.

[11] A classic study of the early Christian use of typology may be found in J. Daniélou, *Sacramentum futuri: Études sur les origines de la typologie biblique* (Paris, 1950).

[12] I. Kalavrezou, 'Images of the mother: when the Virgin Mary became *Meter Theou*', *Dumbarton Oaks Papers*, 46 (1991), 97–105.

[13] See R.M. Grant, *Irenaeus of Lyons* (1997); D. Minns, *Irenaeus* (1994); J. Behr, *The Way to Nicaea* (Crestwood, NY, 2001), 111–33.

[14] Sebastian Brock, *Bride of Light: Hymns on Mary from the Syriac Churches*, Moran 'Eth'o, 6

worth noting the significance of Syriac poetic influence on Byzantine liturgical texts in later centuries.[15] Another, possibly even more important, influence on the development of typology surrounding the Virgin Mary was the Christological controversy initiated by the patriarchs of Constantinople and Alexandria, Nestorius and Cyril, among others, in the early fifth century. It is clear that a cult of the Virgin already flourished by this time, but it lacked theological justification in Christological terms.[16] Nestorius' distrust of the term 'Theotokos' for Mary seems to have been based on the idea that the true humanity of Christ is compromised if we speak of the Virgin 'bearing God'. As Proclus, one of Nestorius' main opponents in Constantinople, argued in return, however, God's salvation of humanity is impossible if any aspect of our existence, including birth, was not experienced by Christ. Proclus sums this up in the words: 'Had the Word not dwelt in a womb, the flesh would never have sat on the throne.'[17]

The recognition of Mary's title as Theotokos, or 'God-Bearer', at the Council of Ephesus in 431 represented a response to Christological dispute over the two natures of Christ. Once it was accepted that Christ was fully divine and fully human from the moment of his conception, Mary could, and should, be called the 'one who bore God'.[18] One of the effects of this Council was to grant official sanction for the first time to veneration of the Mother of God within the Church. It is from this period onward that we see a proliferation of hymns and homilies written in the Virgin's honour, as well as the establishment of feasts dedicated to various important events in her life.[19]

(Kottayam, 1994); Robert Murray, *Symbols of Church and Kingdom* (Cambridge, 1975), 144–50; idem, 'Mary, the Second Eve in the early Syriac Fathers', *Eastern Churches Review*, 3 (1971), 372–84.

[15] See Averil Cameron, *Christianity and the Rhetoric of Empire. The Development of Christian Discourse*, Sather Classical Lectures, 55 (Berkeley, Los Angeles, and Oxford, 1991), 161–2, 203.

[16] For general background, see Frances Young, *From Nicaea to Chalcedon. A Guide to the Literature and its Background* (1983); J. McGuckin, *St Cyril of Alexandria. The Christological Controversy. Its History, Theology and Texts* (Leiden, 1994). A more personal and political approach to the council is adopted in Kate Cooper, 'Contesting the Nativity: wives, virgins, and Pulcheria's *imitatio Mariae*', *Scottish Journal of Religious Studies*, 19 (1998), 31–43.

[17] N. Constas, *Proclus of Constantinople and the Cult of the Virgin in Late Antiquity* (Leiden, 2003), 139.66–7.

[18] J. Pelikan, *The Christian Tradition. A History of the Development of Doctrine, 1: The Emergence of the Catholic Tradition* (Chicago and London, 1971), 261.

[19] On the development of Marian feasts in the Eastern Church, see M. Jugie, 'Homélies

In his second homily on the Nativity, Proclus asks his ideological adversaries, the Jews, to 'give heed to the writings of the prophets and see the entire mystery of the Incarnation theologized; behold the entire miracle of the virgin birth hidden in the shadows'.[20] The use of the phrase 'hidden in the shadows' here is interesting: it suggests that the prophecies and types which foretell the role of the Theotokos in the incarnation of Christ are not necessarily easy to spot. This is a matter of close study and exegesis of the Bible, in which it is necessary to build on the work of the Evangelists and earlier Christian Fathers.

Proclus appears to be the first preacher to develop this typology, exploiting fully in his homilies a series of Old Testament images symbolizing the Theotokos.[21] The poetic foundations laid by Proclus and a few other fifth-century preachers inspired a rich tradition of homilies and hymns which continued to be produced in Byzantium in subsequent centuries. The Akathistos Hymn, whose dating and author-ship is still disputed, represented another decisive influence on the content and style of later homilies and hymns.[22]

At this point we may turn to the homilies in honour of various feasts of the Theotokos delivered by various preachers in the course of the eighth century. To begin with Andrew of Crete, who delivered his sermons either in Constantinople or in Crete before his death in 740, we find trilogies of homilies on the Virgin's Nativity and Dormition, a single homily on the Annunciation, a homily on the Akathistos, and a fourth homily on her Nativity whose attribution is less certain.[23] At

mariales byzantines: textes grecs édités et traduits en latin, II', *Patrologia Orientalis*, 19 (Paris, 1926), 289–438; idem, 'La première fête mariale en Orient et en Occident, l'avent primitif', *Échos d'Orient*, 22 (1923), 129–52.

[20] PG 65, cols 698–700; Constas, *Proclus of Constantinople*, 172.

[21] See the fascinating study by N. Constas, 'Weaving the body of God: Proclus of Con-stantinople, the Theotokos, and the loom of the flesh', *Journal of Early Christian Studies*, 3 (1995), 177.

[22] *Triodion Katanyktikon* (Athens, 1983), 321–8. Translated into English in various schol-arly and liturgical sources, for example, V. Limberis, *Divine Heiress. The Virgin Mary and the Creation of Christian Constantinople* (London and New York, 1994), 149–58; Mother Mary and Kallistos Ware, trans, *The Lenten Triodion* (London and Boston, 1978), 422–36. A number of studies have attempted to determine the date at which the Akathistos hymn was composed. Most recently, Leena Mari Peltomaa has argued for the period between the third and fourth Ecumenical Councils (431 and 451) in *The Image of the Virgin Mary in the Akathistos Hymn* (Leiden, 2001), *passim*. Scholars previously have ascribed it either to an anonymous author in the sixth or early seventh centuries, or to the famous sixth-century hymnographer, Romanos the Melodist. See, for example, E. Wellesz, 'The "Akathistos": a study in Byzantine hymnography', *Dumbarton Oaks Papers*, 9–10 (1956), 141–74.

[23] *CPG*, nos 8170–4, 8181–3, 8197.

least two homilies on the Presentation of the Virgin into the temple remain to be edited and securely attributed to Andrew.[24] During about the same period, Germanos, patriarch of Constantinople (715–30), wrote at least nine sermons intended for various feasts of the Theotokos, including her Annunciation, Presentation in the Temple, Dormition, and various miscellaneous subjects connected with her cult.[25] John of Damascus, a monk and priest at the Monastery of St Sabas in Palestine, composed a trilogy of homilies on the Dormition, as well as one on the Nativity of the Virgin.[26]

Several aspects of this eighth-century homiletic corpus merit attention in the context of this paper. First, these works are without exception characterized by a strong element of emotion. In these highly rhetorical orations, which must have been delivered in succession during all-night vigils, the various preachers employ exclamation, repetition, rhythm, and allusive imagery to express lyrical praises to the Mother of God.[27] Secondly, the Christological reference of the imagery applied to the Theotokos is always explicit. Even though they may seem at times to resemble hymns of praise more than paraenetic orations, the eighth-century Marian homilies retain a didactic, as well as a devotional purpose.[28] Finally, and most importantly for our purposes, these sermons are filled with typology; this allusive symbolism helps to convey the message of incarnational theology more effectively than would any amount of more discursive theological reasoning.

Andrew of Crete's first homily on the Nativity of the Virgin Mary represents a good example of the function of typological exegesis in eighth-century preaching. In the first sentence of this oration, Andrew establishes the significance of Mary's birth in the context of the old and new dispensations. This feast, he states, represents the meeting-place between old and new, between the eras of law and grace, shadows and

---

[24]   *CPG*, nos 8201–2. For further background on Andrew of Crete's life and works, see S. Vailhé, 'Saint André de Crète', *Échos d'Orient*, 5 (1902), 378–87; M.-F. Auzépy, 'La Carrière d'André de Crète', *Byzantinische Zeitschrift*, 88 (1995), 1–12.

[25]   *CPG*, nos 8007–15. On Germanos' homiletic style, see J. List, *Studien zur Homiletik Germanos I von Konstantinopel und seiner Zeit* (Athens, 1939).

[26]   *CPG*, nos 8060–3. For the most recent study of the life and writings of John of Damascus, see Andrew Louth, *St John Damascene. Tradition and Originality in Byzantine Theology* (Oxford, 2002).

[27]   See Tsironis, 'The Lament', 179–80.

[28]   See M.B. Cunningham, 'Andrew of Crete: a high-style preacher of the eighth century', in M.B. Cunningham and Pauline Allen, eds, *Preacher and Audience. Studies in Early Christian and Byzantine Homiletics* (Leiden, 1998), 278–86.

light, the beginning and the completion of God's dispensation for humankind. Andrew continues in this Pauline vein until he arrives at the role of the Theotokos in enabling the old world to be transformed into the new: as Mother of God she mediates between 'the height of divinity and the humility of flesh'.[29] Whereas a woman (Eve) brought about the beginning of sin, another woman (Mary) now initiates salvation. She who was condemned in former times is now revealed as God's chosen one. Andrew then goes on in the next paragraph to describe the reaction of the cosmos to the birth of the Virgin:

> Let the whole of creation sing and dance ...
> Let there be one new day of heavenly and earthly feasting!
> Let the whole company of earthly and heavenly [beings] keep the festival ...[30]

Typological and metaphorical allusions to the Virgin Mary are supported in this homily by an exposition of her lineage, which, Andrew argues, may be traced from David, the singer of Psalms.

One of the most extensive usages of typology occurs in the fourth homily on the Nativity of the Theotokos which has been attributed variously to Andrew of Crete, John of Damascus, Germanos, and others.[31] Here, in a manner reminiscent of the Akathistos Hymn, we find long lists of metaphors describing the Virgin Mary. The short, rhythmic manner in which the images are listed, one after another, suggests that the supply of epithets for the Theotokos is inexhaustible. Without quoting the full list, Mary is described as:

> maiden, prophetess, bridal chamber, house of God, holy temple, second tabernacle, holy table, sanctuary, mercy-seat, golden censer, tablets of the testimony, priestly staff, sceptre of the empire, ... rock, earth, paradise, land, untilled field, spring ...[32]

Andrew goes on to cite specific types representing the Theotokos, along with the Old Testament passages in which they are mentioned. The burning bush, the root of Jesse, the mountain from which a rock was cut without hands, the tabernacle, the closed gate, the bed of Solomon, the fleece of Gideon, and many other images feature here.[33]

---

[29] *PG* 97, col. 808: Ἡ μὲν μεσιτεύει θεότητος ὕψει καὶ σαρκὸς ταπεινότητι ...'.
[30] Ibid., col. 809.
[31] See the remarks by the editor, F. Combefis, Ibid., col. 861 n.26.
[32] Ibid., col. 868.
[33] Ibid., cols 869–73.

Andrew is of course building on a long-standing tradition of typological references to the Virgin which had begun to be developed in the early fifth century.

The impression that a rich stock of types and epithets for the Theotokos was understood and appreciated by preachers and their audiences in the eighth century is reinforced when we look at the homilies of Andrew of Crete's contemporaries, Germanos and John of Damascus. In Germanos' homily on the Annunciation, a list of typological epithets follows the traditional greetings, or *chairetismoi*, to the Virgin. This serves to link this event, or feast-day, as in the case of Mary's Nativity, to the old dispensation in which it was foretold and anticipated.[34] John of Damascus' homily on the Nativity of the Mother of God, which perhaps represents the most lyrical and exhuberant of all the sermons to survive from this period, draws extensively on the well-known Old Testament types, but interweaves them in a quite innovative and startling manner.[35] It is worth quoting a longer passage from this homily in order to illustrate John's poetic use of typology. He writes:

> Leap with joy, mountains,[36] reasonable natures, which also stretch up towards the summit of spiritual contemplation. For the mountain of the Lord, the most visible one, is born, who surpasses and transcends every hill and every mountain,[37] that is to say, the height of angels and men; from her, without <human> hand, Christ, the corner-stone,[38] has been pleased to be cut out,[39] the one substance, who unites things that have been separated, divinity and humanity, angels and men, and <joins together> the gentiles and the corporeal Israel into one spiritual Israel. The mountain of God is a rich mountain, a swelling (or 'curdled') mountain, a rich mountain, the mountain which God has delighted to dwell in![40]

It is possible that the emphasis on Old Testament prefigurations of the Theotokos in eighth-century homiletics has some connection with

---

[34] *PG* 98, col. 321.
[35] Published in P. Voulet, ed. and trans., *S. Jean Damascène. Homélies sur la Nativité et la Dormition*, Sources Chrétiennes, 80 (Paris, 1961), 46–79.
[36] Cf. Ps 113:4 (LXX).
[37] Cf. Isa. 40.4.
[38] Eph. 2.20.
[39] Cf. Dan. 2.34, 45.
[40] Cf. Ps 67.15–18 (LXX); Voulet, *S. Jean Damascène*, 60–2.

hymnographic developments in this period. It is thought that the kanon, a long hymn with an elaborate structure based on the nine canticles of the Old and New Testaments which was sung in the monastic office of Orthros (Mattins), first developed in the late seventh or early eighth century.[41] Although composed in honour of important events in the lives of Christ or his mother, or to commemorate individual saints, the kanon evokes typologically in each of its odes important events in Old Testament history. This emphasizes the meeting of the old and new dispensations through the incarnation of Christ. In the final, ninth ode, the kanon reaches its climax with the Magnificat, Mary's song of praise after accepting her role as the Mother of God.[42]

Typology is thus used in both homilies and hymns, especially kanons, to express God's continuous and undeviating plan for the salvation of humankind. This began from the moment when he first created Adam through to the decisive moment at the Annunciation when Mary became Theotokos. God's dispensation would only reach completion with the restoration of the heavenly Kingdom at the final Day of Judgement.

From all this material it is possible to draw several conclusions concerning the use of typology in eighth-century Marian homiletics. First, it seems possible, on the basis of the juxtaposition of typology with the preachers' own lyrical praise of the Virgin, that certain ideas are intended to be linked together. For example, Old Testament imagery seems consistently to be associated with poetic representations of the created world. Both Andrew of Crete's and John Damascene's homilies continually stress in language reminiscent of the Psalms the involvement of the whole of creation in celebrating the new dispensation – this is graphically illustrated by images of mountains leaping for joy, the heavens rejoicing, the earth exulting, and the sea being moved. Not only is all creation involved in this mystery, however, but Mary herself is frequently identified with the material world. She is herself a mountain, untilled earth, unkneaded bread, a threshing-floor, and so on. As John of Damascus puts it, 'The spiritual ladder, the Virgin, has been set up on earth, for she takes her origin from the earth, but her head is lifted up to heaven.'[43]

---

[41] See E. Wellesz, *A History of Byzantine Music and Hymnography* (Oxford, 1961), 198.

[42] Ibid., 206–16.

[43] Voulet, *S. Jean Damascène*, 52.

Secondly, it is perhaps worthwhile to view some of these issues within a broader historical context. Niki Tsironis has suggested most convincingly a connection between eighth-century veneration of the Theotokos, especially as this is expressed in contemporary homilies and hymns, and the iconophile defence of images.[44] She argues that in developing a response to the challenge of Iconoclasm, iconophile writers such as John of Damascus, Andrew of Crete, and Germanos of Constantinople focused on the Mother of God as a symbol of orthodoxy and of incarnational theology. The Virgin Mary, as the sole source of Christ's human nature, was perceived as having played an essential role in the incarnation. In addition, and in response to iconoclasts' inability to believe in the sanctification of material creation, iconophiles emphasised Mary's connection with the physical world. It is for this reason that by the end of the controversy, when the holy icons were restored to the Church after the Triumph of Orthodoxy in 843, the Theotokos herself increasingly became a symbol of the iconophile orthodoxy and, by extension, the affirmation of God's material creation.[45]

It is unfortunate that we will never know what the iconoclasts actually believed concerning these various but related issues. It is obvious that they disapproved of icons and their cult as superstitious idolatry, but their position regarding the Theotokos, saints, and relics is much less clear. It is likely that whereas the holiness of Mary's person, and the appropriateness of the epithet 'Theotokos' remained unquestioned, some iconoclasts were uneasy with her role as intercessor and mediator between the human and divine spheres.[46] The proliferation of homilies and hymns honouring the relatively recently established feast-days of the Theotokos in the early eighth century, and the fact that most of these are written by the defenders of images, certainly seems significant and deserves further investigation. What remains unclear, however, is whether such expressions of devotion were delivered in the face of active opposition to the Marian cult. The typological treatment of the Theotokos in these liturgical sources expresses metaphorically the

---

[44] N. Tsironis, 'The Mother of God in the iconoclastic controversy', in Vassilaki, 27–39.

[45] An eloquent witness to the Virgin's importance after the restoration of orthodoxy is the homily delivered by the Patriarch Photios in March 867 at the inauguration of her mosaic image in the apse of St Sophia. See C. Mango, *The Homilies of Photius Patriarch of Constantinople* (Cambridge, MA, 1958), esp. 293–5.

[46] See the thought-provoking ideas on this subject by G. Dagron, 'L'Ombre d'un doute: L'hagiographie en question, VIe–XIe siècle', *Dumbarton Oaks Papers*, 46 (1992), 65–6.

transfiguration of creation by the incarnation of Christ. Whatever the iconoclasts may have believed about matter and about the relationship of the old dispensation with the new, iconophile writers seem successfully to have linked their views with those of dualist and Marcionite gnostics of the second century. This was done by adopting a strongly affirmative stance towards typology, and by analogy, the sanctification of matter and of all humanity through the incarnation of Christ. Thus the Virgin Mary, or Theotokos, came to symbolize in Byzantine liturgical texts the meeting-place between the divine and the created worlds.

University of Birmingham

DISCUSSING MARY'S HUMANITY
IN MEDIEVAL BYZANTIUM

by JANE BAUN

NINETEENTH-CENTURY Protestant missionaries toiling in the vineyard in Ottoman Armenia found the native women receptive to many of their ideas – until the subject of Mary came up. An American missionary recorded the following encounter in 1877:[1]

> There was another very religious woman, I once met with in one of the villages on Harpoot plain. She said, 'Lady, I love you, and think you are a real Christian, but one thing you say I cannot receive. You say the Virgin Mary is not our intercessor. What should we women do, if we could not call upon the Virgin when in trouble, or suffering? She was a woman, and knows how to pity women like us'. This is what they all say.

Another Armenian woman spoke similarly: 'What should we do without the Virgin? She was a woman like us, and knows how to pity us when we sorrow'.

But was Mary 'a woman like us'? The answer of the Church, traditionally, has been 'No'. Mary transcended normal female humanity in remaining a virgin after giving birth, and the curse of Eve did not apply to her. Both her conceiving and her birth-giving were painless and unstained by sin. The idea that Christ's birth was both virginal and painless surfaces very early, in New Testament apocrypha such as the *Protoevangelion of James* and the *Odes of Solomon*.[2]

Alongside these early apocrypha, however, and all the high-level theological talk of *virginitas in partu*, can be found other texts, and lay pious practices, that insist with a stubborn certainty that the Mother of God was in every sense a woman 'like us', and *homoiopathes*, subject to the same human emotions, frailties, and pains as ordinary people, albeit without sin. For example, a Coptic magical text preserved in a tenth-

[1] S.A. Wheeler, *Daughters of Armenia* (New York, [1877]), 25–6; quotation following, 19.
[2] Michael O'Carroll, *Theotokos: a Theological Encylopedia of the Blessed Virgin Mary* (Wilmington, DE, 1983), 357–62.

century manuscript not only affirms that Mary did indeed suffer labour pains, but even turns them into names to conjure with. Among the many incantations the spell puts into the mouth of the Archangel Michael is the following:[3]

> I adjure you today by the first labor pain that [Mary] had with your only-begotten Son on the day when she gave birth to him, the name of which is Choroei; the second labor pain is Abko, the third labor pain is Hanautos.

Rather than betraying human weakness, Mary's pains are claimed as sources of power. A millennium apart, the author of the Coptic spell and the Armenian women express a similar conviction that Mary's full humanity is a source of strong help for those in need. Because she has been through what we have been through, they seem to say, she knows how to help us, and she will help us. The sure hope of her intercession is founded on her humanity.[4] This conviction runs like a steel thread throughout Eastern Orthodox Marian piety, medieval and modern. With it is often associated a second conviction: that Mary, human like us, is part of the family, and works tirelessly on behalf of her kinsfolk. Humanity, family, intercession: these Marian themes have a long history as an inter-related cluster. The first half of this paper samples a few moments in that broad continuum, exploring how the modern may possibly be used to illuminate earlier ages. Against this background of continuity, of course, distinct periods emerge. Each age has its own questions about humanity, family, and intercession in Mary's care for Christians. Accordingly, the second half of the paper will consider how Christians in a particular place and time, Byzantium between the ninth and eleventh centuries, connected the three themes.

* * *

Orthodox popular piety has long taken as its starting point that Mary is a member of the extended family, and appreciates the same small courtesies one would offer one's kin. In a practice with deep pagan roots, folk custom in parts of southern Russia observed the second day of

3 *Ancient Christian Magic: Coptic Texts of Ritual Power*, ed. Marvin Meyer, Richard Smith, and Neal Kelsey (San Francisco, 1994), 335.
4 Mary's full humanity also ensures our hope of resurrection. Eastern Orthodoxy insists on the *Dormition* (*Koimesis*, 'falling asleep') of Mary, as opposed to the Assumption, because the notion that Mary did not die a real human death, but was simply assumed bodily into heaven, compromises her as a perfect model of redeemed humanity.

Christmas by bringing fish, meat, and vegetable pies (*pirogi*) to the village church.[5] The modern Orthodox priest and his wife who noted this custom explained that the women in bygone days did this,

> much as they did for their neighbors who had just borne a child. As they did take the perogs to the home of the earthly mothers, they took the perogs to the church which they felt was the home of the Virgin Mother. This was a very old custom and it was discouraged late in the sixteenth century by Metropolitan Michael of Kiev.

The social logic of the Russian women is impeccable. Mary, after all, has just had a baby. The obvious thing to do is to stop by the house with a casserole. Might such folk practice provide a potential context for the mention of women offering loaves to the Virgin, preserved in the fourth-century *Panarion* of Epiphanios? In a passage which has long tantalized scholars of the early Church, Epiphanios, a bishop in Cyprus in the fourth century, excoriates the practice among some women 'in Thrace and Arabia' of baking small loaves and offering them to the Virgin on a certain day.[6] He does not say what the day was, but might it have been the day after the Nativity feast? Epiphanios insists on understanding the women as an organized sect, intent on usurping the male sacerdotal role, and their pious practice as a sham Eucharist. The whole history and tendency of Marian lay piety, however, suggests that the women were simply paying familial homage to Mary by baking bread for her on a special day.

Family rally round especially at times of birth . . . and death. Part of the traditional Greek Orthodox devotion to the feast of the Dormition derives from the deeply-held conviction that one should turn out for the funerals of kin and neighbours. People who rarely fast or go to church during the rest of the year will often keep some version of the Dormition fast, and will return to the family or the village to give the *Panagia* ('All-Holy One') a proper send-off.

Going home to attend the funeral of the Panagia is, in the eyes of the Church, the acceptable face of Marian lay piety. Offering small loaves and fish pies to Mary as part of one's family, however, is suspect. Clearly, the human family model for incorporating Mary into one's devotional life is problematic. The family model for understanding

---

[5] 'The second day of Christmas', in *The Orthodox Herald*, ed. W. Basil Stroyen and Nina Bohush Stroyen (Hunlock Creek, PA), 41 (1992), 43, 46.

[6] *The Panarion of Epiphanius of Salamis*, trans. Frank Williams (Leiden, 1994), 620–9.

Mary's intercession also functions within a theological danger zone. Beliefs and practices associated with treating Mary as part of the family, as 'a woman like us', can easily go out of bounds, and cross over into the 'paracanonical'. Such boundaries require continual renegotiation between the faithful and their religious guides.

* * *

We will now examine where these boundaries lay in the Middle Byzantine period. Mary's intercession is one of the big theological topics that bursts out after Iconoclasm. Images of Mary interceding for the living and the dead begin to saturate the visual arts in the tenth and eleventh centuries, and the theme appears frequently in literature and liturgy as well.[7] The intercession of Mary was of course not a new topic. Mary was credited, famously, with helping to save Constantinople from enemy siege in the seventh century, and the growth of her cult in the Empire was intimately bound up with her intercessory powers.[8] Yet each generation has its own particular needs regarding Mary's intercession. The special Middle Byzantine flavour was to work out the family relations between God the Father, God the Son, and God's Mother. In particular, authors, theologians, and artists of the period begin to ponder how the most traumatic event in the life of the divine family, the Crucifixion, affected its relationships. The theme is treated by canonical authors, writing in high-level Greek, such as George of Nikomedia (later ninth century) and John Geometres (later tenth century). It is also treated, very differently, by anonymous *para-canonical* authors of the period, those who crafted popular visions of heaven and hell such as the *Apocalypse of the Theotokos* and the *Apocalypse of Anastasia*. In what follows the paracanonical view is contrasted with the canonical. Middle Byzantine authors were beginning to describe and understand things divine in newly human – and sometimes in all too human – ways.

The intersection of the Crucifixion and Mary's intercession also surfaces in the material culture of the Middle Byzantine period, on double-sided crosses which feature Christ and Mary. Beginning in the tenth century, both large, public, processional crosses and small, personal, pectoral crosses begin to appear on which Christ is shown crucified on the front, while Mary stands with arms raised in inter-

---

[7] See my forthcoming monograph, *Tales from Another Byzantium: Celestial Journey and Local Community in the Medieval Greek Apocrypha* (Cambridge, 2005).

[8] Limberis; also the paper by Averil Cameron in this volume.

cessory prayer on the back.[9] How were these objects understood? As will be seen at the end of the paper, the texts suggest that two very different interpretations of the message of such crosses were available to the Middle Byzantine believer.

First, for the paracanonical side, we shall examine the *Apocalypse of the Theotokos*, a visionary journey to heaven and hell, adapted by an anonymous author from the Late Antique *Apocalypse of Paul*, probably sometime around the ninth century.[10] Wildly popular, the tale of the Mother of God's descent to see the sinners being punished in the Other World survives in hundreds of manuscripts and many languages, dating from the eleventh century to the nineteenth.

The problem with the *Apocalypse* is not so much that Mary is too human, but that *all* its characters are too thoroughly human. Doubtless unintentionally, its author presents a thoroughly dysfunctional divine family. God is a distant, impatient, unapproachable Father; Christ, his equally impatient, stubborn son, constantly rehearsing old grudges. Mary appears as the hapless mother trying to make some progress with these two intractable men. The dramatic climax of her journey through the punishments is a tense scene of mass intercession for sinners. Mary argues valiantly with her obdurate son, and will not take no for an answer. Again, doubtless unintentionally, but with fascinating implications, their dialogue recalls the Gospel parable of the Unjust Judge (Luke 18.1–8): because Mary keeps on pestering Christ, he finally relents, and gives her what she asks for.

The exchange between mother and son differs in each manuscript version; in most, Christ and Mary argue back and forth, with Christ raising objections, and Mary discounting them; Christ insisting on justice, Mary on mercy. What follows is the dialogue from one of the earliest surviving versions of the apocalypse, that of an eleventh-century manuscript in the Bodleian Library.[11] Mary opens, 'Have mercy, Master, on the Christian sinners, for I have seen them being punished and I cannot bear their lamentation'. Her next idea is shocking: she offers herself up, crying: 'May I go forth, and may I myself be punished with the Christian sinners!' The editor of this particular version liked this line so much that he (or she) actually used it twice.

---

[9] Vassilaki, esp. 199–204, 229, 298–9, 308–12.
[10] Baun, *Tales*, includes a complete study of the *Apocalypse*.
[11] Bodley, MS Misc. Greek 77. Except where indicated otherwise, the dialogue following is translated from the edition of M.R. James, *Apocrypha Anecdota* (Cambridge, 1893), 124–6.

God the Father apparently takes Mary's offer as rhetorical, because there is no explicit reply to it, in any of the versions. In the Bodleian version, Christ replies, 'How can I have mercy on them, since they themselves did not have mercy?' Another version substitutes, 'since they make me very angry!'[12] Two other versions continue, 'I see the nails in my hands'.[13] Who are 'they'? Mary's reply makes the answer, hitherto potentially ambiguous, chillingly specific: 'I do not pray, Master, for the unbelieving Jews, but for the Christians I invoke your compassion'. The Christians are not off the hook, however. Christ responds, with inexorable biblical logic, 'How can I have mercy on them, since they did not have mercy on their own brothers?' Undaunted, Mary tries again: 'Master, have mercy on the sinners! Behold the punishments, for every creature on earth calls upon my name: and when the soul comes forth out of the body, it cries out, saying, "Holy Lady Theotokos!"' Finally moved, for his mother's sake, Christ softens somewhat: 'Listen, Panagia Theotokos, if anyone names and calls upon your name, I will not forsake him, either in heaven or on earth.'

But Mary is not yet satisfied. She marshals all the heavenly hosts to cry 'Kyrie eleison', and calls in the heavy brigade – Moses, John, and Paul – to argue for mercy. Implacable, Christ vows that each sinner will be judged, precisely according to Moses's law, John's gospel, and Paul's epistles. Indomitable, Mary tries again: 'Have mercy, Master, on the Christians, because they kept your law and heeded your gospel, and they were simple folk.' Christ rejoins,

> Listen, Panagia: if anyone did evil to them and they did not repay them evil, you say rightly that they attended to both my law and my gospel, but if they did not do them evil and they repaid them evil, how may I say that these are holy people? Now it has been paid back to them according to their evil deeds.

Mary finally wears Christ down, to the point that he agrees to give the sinners a respite from punishment for the fifty days of Easter. He declares explicitly that he did not want to do this, but has given in to his mother's incessant prayers and weeping.

Throughout, Mary is identified, not only as Christ's mother, but also

---

12 BAV, MS Barberinianus Graecus 284, fol. 38r.
13 BN, MS Supp. Graec. 136, fol. 177; Bodley, MS Rawlinson G.4, fol. 122v.

as our mother – our grandmother, in fact. The first time that she offers herself up for sinners, she cries, 'May I myself be punished with the Christians, for they are the children of my Son'.[14] She storms into the heavens as a fierce matriarch, intent on protecting her grandchildren from the terrible treatment meted out in the Other World. Mary's extreme activism on behalf of sinners, shaming a reluctant God into showing mercy, is a new attitude for the 'Tour of Hell' genre.[15] Her Late Antique predecessors in the genre, such as Baruch, Enoch, Peter, and Paul (her journey's immediate model), are not set by their apocryphal authors in opposition to the heavenly establishment. A second innovation in the medieval apocalypse is its explicit link between the Crucifixion and Mary's intercession, an interest that helps anchor the text in its times.

We saw earlier how, in the *Apocalypse*, Christ is still angry about the Crucifixion – 'How can I have mercy on them? I see the nails in my hands' – and still demanding satisfaction for it. The Crucifixion, in the mind of the apocryphal author, rather than removing guilt for sins, seems to have increased it. The speech by Christ which ends the vision strings together a list of *improperia*, making explicit reference to the Passion ('I asked for water, and you gave me vinegar mixed with gall').[16] For this, and for its continued sinfulness and ingratitude, the speech concludes, mankind justly deserves condemnation, averted only because of the prayers and tears of 'my mother Mary'. Only through Mary can mankind be delivered from this terrible burden. The *Apocalypse* opposes Mary to an angry Christ, badgering him to show mercy in spite of mankind's great sins, including the Crucifixion.

Why should Mary do this? Because she is a mother, our mother as well as Christ's, and because she is a human person like us. The Christ of the Theotokos *Apocalypse*, although conceived by the apocryphal author in an all-too-human way, has become totally divine, and has forgotten what it is to be human. He has forgotten, in the words of the Armenian women with whom we opened this paper, 'how to pity us'. The family model of understanding the divine, however, dictates that Christ will never forget, or disappoint, his mother, and it is on this assurance that the intercession scene of the *Apocalypse* rests.

---

[14] James, *Apocrypha*, 124.
[15] Jane Baun, 'Middle Byzantine "Tours of Hell": outsider theodicy?', in D. Smythe, ed., *Strangers to Themselves* (Aldershot, 2000), 50–5.
[16] James, *Apocrypha*, 126.

There is another way, however, to link the Crucifixion and Mary's intercession, and this can be seen in the work of two other authors, John Geometres and George of Nikomedia, writing around the same period as the *Apocalypse*, but from a very different perspective. For both, the Crucifixion, far from generating tension between Mary and Christ, actually brought them closer together. Mary's voluntary, active suffering in union with Christ on the Cross forged the closest possible bond of empathy and mutual love between them, such that Christ and Mary now work in perfect harmony in all things. George's homilies on Mary at the Cross have been studied in recent articles, so this paper will concentrate on John's work.[17]

A sometime imperial official, John Geometres was highly-placed at the court of Nikephoros II Phokas (r. 963–9). While the *Apocalypse of the Theotokos* represents Marian devotion gone too far, John's major work, his *Life of Mary*, is the paramount example of the acceptable face of Marian devotion in the Middle Byzantine centuries. A series of extended theological, mystical, and poetical meditations on major events in Mary's life, the work deserves to be better known.[18] (Because of its great length, and the impenetrable elegance of its high-style medieval Greek, it remains largely unpublished.) In each discourse, John probes the deeper spiritual significance of a particular episode, spinning complex webs of theology and rhetoric around the simple event. Nothing could be further from the medieval *Apocalypse*, with its disjointed, repetitious narrative and its plain, unvarnished Greek.

Despite their extreme intellectual and stylistic divergence, however, the *Life of Mary* and the medieval *Apocalypse* belong to the same basic thought world, one in which Mary is acclaimed as the mediatrix between God and man, and clung to as the most powerful intercessor for sinners, both living and deceased. If anything, John makes an even stronger statement of Mary's role in the economy of salvation, with the remarkable assertion that while Christ died one time for us on the Cross, he has allowed that his Mother should die each hour, for each person, in her willingness to offer herself for the safety of her children.[19] Here is the Orthodox counterpart to Mary's shocking

---

[17] See esp. Maria Vassilaki and Niki Tsironis, 'Representations of the Virgin and their association with the Passion of Christ', in Vassilaki, 457–60.

[18] The *Life* has not been fully edited; see O'Carroll, *Theotokos*, 203–4. Quotations here are translated from the Greek text in A. Wenger, *L'Assomption de la très sainte Vierge* (Paris, 1955).

[19] Ibid., 407.

challenge to God in her *Apocalypse*, noted earlier: 'May I myself be punished with the Christians, for they are the children of my Son.'

There are many points of contact between the Mariology of the *Apocalypse* and that of the *Life*, and the paracanonical and canonical authors write with equal love and fervour for Mary – but from radically divergent perspectives. John, entirely and optimistically Orthodox, is careful at all times to stress two things that the *Apocalypse* has lost faith in: the tight, loving bond between mother and son, and the great mercy of Christ himself as the first Mediator.[20] In the Theotokos *Apocalypse*, Christ no longer functions as mediator between God and man, or as intercessor with the Father. The *Apocalypse* radiates the desperation of those who have lost all hope in any central authority, including God, whose only hope is the compassion of Mary. It projects this sense of alienation onto its Other World, setting Mary and Christ at odds with each other.[21] For both John and the *Apocalypse*, Mary as mother gives herself continually for her children, but for John, she does so *in union* with the sacrifice of Jesus, as part of the unbreakable bond forged by both her maternity and her suffering with Christ in his Passion. They are united in all actions, attitudes, and will: two distinct persons, but as close as a body and its shadow, as indeed the two natures of Christ himself.[22]

* * *

For John Geometres, Christ on the Cross and Mary engaged in intercessory prayer are two sides of the same coin – or indeed, of the same Cross. The Middle Byzantine discussion about the relationship of the Crucifixion and Mary's intercession was given literal expression in the production of double-sided pectoral crosses, many of them reliquaries. A truly popular form, such crosses were manufactured for every budget, from mass-produced cheap bronze models, recovered from graves all over the Empire, to the most deluxe silver niello and gold enamel examples.[23] How did Middle Byzantine believers understand these crosses? And how did they wear them, with which side out? The design of the hinges suggests that Christ's side was the front; his Mother's, the back, but if one were to wear Mary facing out, would that

---

[20] Ibid., 405–7.

[21] See further Baun, 'Middle Byzantine "Tours of Hell" '.

[22] J. Galot, 'La plus ancienne affirmation de la corédemption mariale', *Recherches de science religieuse*, 45 (1957), 192.

[23] See n.9 above.

be considered disrespectful to Christ? The double-sided crosses are thus ambiguous of use. They are even more ambiguous of meaning. The *Apocalypse of the Theotokos* and the work of John Geometres suggest that quite different views of the significance of the pairing of Christ and Mary were possible, and circulating at the time.

The pairing illustrates nicely the new interest in Mary's participation in the Crucifixion that theologians such as John Geometres and George of Nikomedia were beginning to explore. Those who moved in erudite circles may have had such thoughts upon donning their pectoral crosses in the morning, but a more immediate, functional, personal link between the two figures on one's cross is suggested by the Theotokos *Apocalypse*: Christ died for me, yet I continue to sin, and so am worthy of hell; Mother of God, please ask your Son to forgive me yet again. Just this kind of thought process is evident in the closing dialogue from the Theotokos *Apocalypse* examined above.

The paracanonical and canonical texts both witness to a discussion in the Middle Byzantine period regarding the implications of the Crucifixion, the family relationships between Christ, his Mother, and humanity, and the meaning and efficacy of Mary's intercession. The two types of text link these themes in diametrically opposed ways. The paracanonical answer to why Christ was on one side of the pectoral cross, and Mary on the other, was that the burden of human sinfulness symbolized in the Crucifixion necessitated Mary's intercession. In this, we can see popular confusion regarding the Atonement, and also the conviction that Mary, being human and a mother, understands our human frailties with more compassion. The canonical understanding of the connection between the Crucifixion and Mary's intercession was that Mary and Christ had become through their shared Passion two sides of the same coin, intensely close in mutual love, in identity of wills and action, and in compassion for sinners.

Two ways of looking at the same cross. The canonical way to wear a Middle Byzantine pectoral cross was presumably with Christ, the Saviour, facing out. One should consider well, however, where this would place the Mother of God, hands raised in prayer: next to the believer's heart.

Greyfriars Hall, Oxford, and King's College London

THE COUCH OF SOLOMON, A MONK, A BYZANTINE LADY, AND THE SONG OF SONGS*

by KALLIRROE LINARDOU

IN the early twelfth century, the Byzantine monk James of the monastery of *Kokkinobaphou* composed six sermons on the early life of the Virgin Mary.[1] Two copies of these sermons, known collectively as the *Kokkinobaphos* manuscripts, have survived: BN, MS gr. 1208 and BAV, MS gr. 1162.[2] Based on a combination of internal and external evidence, scholars have dated the manuscripts to the second quarter of the twelfth century, and furthermore suggested that their production and decoration was undertaken during the lifespan of James.[3] Both copies bear an extensive and almost identical narrative and typological cycle of illumination, which has been securely connected to the imperial environment of the Byzantine court of the twelfth century and was linked, more tentatively, with the *Sevastokratorissa* Eirene, a prominent patroness of the court, widow of the *Sevastokrator* Andronikos, the second son of the Emperor John II Komnenos (1118–43).[4] The miniatures illustrating the text of James are renowned for their artistic quality and their iconographical peculiarities.

* The completion of this paper would have been far more difficult if Prof. E. Jeffreys and Dr I. Hutter had not provided me with their transcriptions of both unedited sermons of James of *Kokkinobaphou*. I would like to express my sincere gratitude to both. I am also grateful for the advice of my supervisor, Dr Leslie Brubaker.

¹ *PG* 127, cols 544–700, incomplete and with numerous mistakes. On the dating of the text and the manuscripts see J.C. Anderson, 'The illustrated sermons of James the monk: their dates, order, and place in the history of Byzantine art', *Viator*, 22 (1991), 69–120, esp. 85; I. Hutter and P. Canart, *Das Marienhomiliar des Mönchs Jakobos von Kokkinobaphos* (Vatican City, 1991), 11–17.

² BN, MS gr. 1208: H. Omont, *Miniatures des homélies sur la Vierge du moine Jacques (Ms. Grec 1208 de Paris)*, Bulletin de la société française de reproductions de manuscrits à peintures, 11 (Paris, 1927); BAV, MS gr. 1162: C. Stornajolo, *Miniature delle omilie di Giacomo monaco (cod. Vatic. gr. 1162) e dell' evangeliario Greco urbinate (cod. Vatic. Urbin. Gr. 2)*, Codices e Vaticanis selecti phototypice expressi iussu Pii p.p. X consilio et opera procuratorium Bibliotheca Vaticanae, series minor, 1 (Rome, 1910).

³ See Hutter, *Marienhomiliar*, 14; Anderson, 'Sermons', 85.

⁴ F. Chalandon, *Les Comnène: études sur l'empire byzantin au XIe et au XIIe siècle*, vol. 2: *Jean II Comnène et Manuel I Comnène* (Paris, 1912), 2:212–13; K. Varzos, Ἡ γενεαλογία τῶν Κομνηνῶν, 2 vols (Thessalonica, 1984), 1:357–79. Anderson has pointed out the connection of the manuscripts with the court environment, and more tentatively the association with Eirene; 'Sermons', 101. On the association of the manuscripts with Eirene see also R.S.

Every sermon in both manuscripts opens with a full-page prefiguration miniature illustrating events recounted in the Old Testament.[5]
These episodes were interpreted allegorically through Christian
exegesis as prefigurations of the Mother of God.[6] The Christological
cycle of typological imagery was introduced in Christian art as early as
the sixth century. Its Mariological counterpart was, however, developed
later, adapting itself to the motifs of the homiletic tradition and
hymnography on Mary.[7]

The prefiguration miniature introducing James's fourth sermon
shows the Couch of Solomon (fig. 1).[8] The subject matter of the sermon
is the betrothal of Mary to Joseph and her departure from the Temple
when she became twelve years old.[9] James reserved a preferential and
exceptional treatment for this specific typological image: he not only
provided this miniature with a long exegetical explanation, significantly
missing from the five remaining prefiguration miniatures, but also
instructed the reader/viewer to search for the interpretation of the
image in this text.[10] The original caption above the miniature reads:

Nelson, 'Theoktistos and associates in twelfth-century Constantinople: an illustrated New
Testament of A.D. 1133', *The J. Paul Getty Museum Journal*, 15 (1987), 53–78, esp. 75–6; I.
Spatharakis, 'An illuminated Greek grammar manuscript in Jerusalem', *Jahrbuch der
österreichischen Byzantinistik*, 35 (1985), 231–43, esp. 242–3. On Eirene, see E. Jeffreys, 'The
Sevastokratorissa Eirene as literary patroness: the monk Iakovos', *XVI. Internationaler
Byzantinistenkongress: Akten, 2/3* (Vienna, 1983), 63–71; E. Jeffreys and M. Jeffreys, 'Who was
Eirene the Sevastokratorissa?', *Byzantion*, 64 (1994), 40–68.

[5] BN, MS gr. 1208, fols 29v, 73v, 109v, 149v, 162r, 181v; Omont, *Miniatures*, pls IV, X,
XIV, XVIII, XXI, XXIII. BAV, MS gr. 1162, fols 22v, 54v, 82v, 110v, 119v, 133v; Stornajolo,
Miniature, 7, 21, 32, 46, 52, 58.

[6] D. Mouriki, 'Αἱ Βιβλικαὶ Προεικονίσεις τῆς Παναγίας εἰς τὸν Τροῦλλον τῆς
Περιβλέπτου τοῦ Μυστρᾶ', *Ἀρχαιολογικὸν Δελτίον*, 25 (1970), 217–51.

[7] S. Der Nersessian, 'Program and iconography of the frescoes of the Parecclesion', in
P.A. Underwood, ed., *The Kariye Djami, 4: Studies in the Art of the Kariye Djami and its Intellectual
Background* (Princeton, NJ, 1975), 311–13. For the homiletic tradition on the Virgin and her
prefigurations see below nn.17–20. For prefigurations of Mary in hymnography see P. Maas
and C.A. Trypanis, eds, *Sancti Romani Melodi Cantica- Cantica Genuina* (Oxford, 1963),
289–93; S. Eustratiades, *Ἡ Θεοτόκος ἐν τῇ ὑμνογραφίᾳ* (Paris, 1930), 36.

[8] BN, MS gr. 1208, fol. 109v; BAV, MS gr. 1162, fol. 82v; Omont, *Miniatures*, pl. XIV;
Stornajolo, *Miniature*, 32; Hutter, *Marienhomiliar*, 48–50.

[9] The fourth sermon and the second half of the sixth are missing in Migne. I was able to
study the text of both missing sermons from the personal transcriptions of Prof. E. Jeffreys
and Dr I. Hutter.

[10] The exegetical text exists in both manuscripts but is not included in the Migne
edition. It is situated between the end of the third sermon and the prefiguration miniature
introducing the fourth sermon, and covers approximately three folios: BN, MS gr. 1208, fols
107v–109r, with miniature on fol. 109v; BAV, MS gr. 1162, fols 80v–81v, with miniature on
fol. 82v. Fol. 80v of the exegetical text is reproduced in Stornajolo, *Miniature*, 22, 92, where
the editor recognizes and analyses the script as characteristic of twelfth-century minuscule.

'The Couch of Solomon, which is surrounded in a circle by the sixty valiant ones. – Seek for the interpretation on the back of the folio'.[11] Palaeographical and codicological examination of both the text and the caption testify that they were part of the original design of the manuscripts and not later insertions.

In other words, in the original design of his sermons, James included an exegetical text to complement an image. This indicates that our monk was indeed alive during the production of the manuscripts and assigned an active role.[12] This also raises the question, to what extent did the author participate in the design of the illustration? Was he himself the commissioner? Or was he simply trying to comply with the demands and needs of a potential patron who needed his spiritual instruction? We know that in Byzantium deluxe manuscripts were normally produced for particular patrons on commission. Even had the sermons themselves been composed as oral exercises to be delivered to a congregation, the two *Kokkinobaphos* manuscripts can only have been made by the order of an individual patron, who James, the author, felt needed spiritual guidance in interpreting highly sophisticated allegorical scenes. But why did not James provide an exegetical text for each of the five remaining prefiguration miniatures in the manuscripts? Their existence is hardly justified or even interpreted by the inadequate hints in the text of the accompanying sermons. Thus, what was the thought or the need that dictated the exceptional treatment of the Couch of Solomon miniature by the author?

In order to answer this question we must examine both the exegetical text and the image more closely. The first scholar to drag this rare combination of word and image interaction from obscurity was S. Der Nersessian.[13] She concentrated on the iconographical development of the theme as a prefiguration of the Virgin, its interpretation, and its proliferation during the Palaiologan era. The text did not provide the iconographical explanation of the image that she anticipated and so she dismissed it, saying that it was not an original composition of James but a compilation of phrases and words from a fourth-century sermon

---

[11] 'Ἡ κλίνη τοῦ Σολομῶντος, ᾗ κύκλῳ δορυφοροῦσιν ἑξήκοντα δυνατοί. Ζήτει τὴν ἑρμηνείαν ὄπισθεν τοῦ φύλλου.'

[12] I. Hutter, 'Die Homilien des Mönchs Jakobus und ihre Illustrationen' (University of Vienna, Ph.D. thesis, 1970), 240–1.

[13] S. Der Nersessian, 'Le lit de Salomon', in her *Études byzantines et arméniennes* (Louvain, 1973), 49–54.

of Gregory of Nyssa (335–95) on the Song of Songs.[14] James's text is indeed a summary paraphrase of the last part of Gregory's sermon, which analyses Song of Songs 3.7–8: 'Behold Solomon's couch; sixty mighty men of the mighty ones of Israel are round about it. They all hold a sword, being experts in war: every man has his sword upon his thigh because of fear by night.'[15]

Nevertheless, Der Nersessian noted that James made a slight alteration in his text in order to make it appropriate for a commission dedicated to the Virgin. While Gregory provided a spiritual and mystical exegesis of the Song, which was interpreted as a symbol of the union of the human soul with God, James introduced his text with the sentence: 'The Couch prefigured primarily the all-holy Mother of God, and then the soul of each one [of the mortals] to be saved.'[16] So, although James had copied one of the Cappadocian Fathers, he did not follow Gregory's mystical interpretation, making it unmistakably clear from the first sentence of his exegesis that the Couch of Solomon was to be seen and interpreted as a prefiguration of Mary.

The motif of the Couch of Solomon as a prefiguration of the Mother of God was not unknown in Byzantine homilies dedicated to her. Especially after iconoclasm (c.730–843) the Couch/Mary came to be understood as the symbol of the union of the divine *Logos* with human nature through the concept of Incarnation. She became the nuptial bed on which to accomplish the mystical alliance. We find this interpretation as early as the eighth century in the fourth homily on the Nativity of the Virgin by Andrew, metropolitan of Crete (660–740), and in a homily on the Presentation of Mary by Tarasios, Patriarch of Constantinople (784–806).[17] It was not only the Couch of Solomon that inspired Mariological connections, but also other parts of the Song of Songs. Obvious references to the Book may be found in the writings of John Damascene (675–749) and Germanos I, Patriarch of Constanti-

[14] Ibid., 50–1. For Gregory's sixth sermon on the Song of Songs see H. Langerbeck, ed., *Gregorii Nysseni in Canticum Canticorum* (Leiden, 1960), 171–9, esp. 189–99.

[15] A. Rahlfs, ed., *Septuaginta*, 2 vols, 3rd edn (Stuttgart, 1949), 2:263–4. For an introduction and modern commentary on the Song of Songs, see M.H. Pope, *Song of Songs. A New Translation with Introduction and Commentary*, The Anchor Bible, 7C (New York, 1977), 112–32, 434; R.E. Murphy (ed. S. Dean McBride, jr), *The Song of Songs. A Commentary on the Book of Canticles or The Song of Songs* (Minneapolis, MN, 1990), 11–28, 148–52.

[16] ''Η μὲν κλίνη πρῶτον μὲν, εἰκόνιζε τ(ὴν) ὑπεραγίαν Θ(εοτό)κον ἔπειτα δὲ, ἑνὸς ἑκάστου ψυχὴν τῶν σωζομένων.'

[17] For Andrew of Crete see A. Kazhdan (in collaboration with L.E. Sherry and C. Angelidi), *A History of Byzantine Literature (650–850)* (Athens, 1999), 37–54; 'In Nativitatem B. Mariae IV', *PG* 97, cols 868–73, col. 869.

nople (715–30).[18] However, as far as Byzantine commentaries and homilies on the Song of Songs are concerned, no example brings forward an interpretation of the Bride of the Song as the Virgin until the fourteenth century.[19] Even Michael Psellos (1018–78), who composed a superficial commentary in political verse on the Song, based his paraphrase on the work of Gregory of Nyssa, with only an occasional introduction of new material.[20] Yet, although James was copying the same Cappadocian Father as Psellos, he chose to adopt a rather different interpretation, closer to the clichés of the homiletic tradition on the Virgin.

Let us now turn to the miniature (fig. 1). In the middle of the picture we see Christ lying on an embroidered couch surrounded by sixty arch-angels. They all carry lances except two on the far left who hold swords, and an archangel in the middle who holds a disk. One might expect to see the Virgin reclining on the couch since she is the one to be prefig-ured. However, according to James the Virgin was the Couch, and Solomon was to be understood as Christ himself, the antitype of Solomon, the Peaceful King. As James says in his exegesis: 'Therefore, it is obvious that another Solomon is signified through him, he himself a descendant of David, according to the flesh, whose name is Eirene [peace], the true King of Israel.'[21] James – who here deviates from Gregory of Nyssa – interprets the iconography of the image perfectly.

As if he wished to avoid any misunderstandings of the meaning of the picture and to stress the allegorical interpretation of the motif, James introduced the same Marian symbolism of the Couch of Solomon in two other pictorial representations, where Mary herself replaces the Couch. The first accompanies the third sermon, on the

[18] For John Damascene see Kazhdan, *Literature*, 75–94; 'Homilia II in Nativitatem B. V. Mariae', *PG* 96, cols 692–96. For Patriarch Germanos see Kazhdan, *Literature*, 55–74; 'In Presentationem SS. Deiparae I', *PG* 98, cols 292–3.

[19] Matthaeus Cantacuzenos, 'In Canticum Canticorum Solomonis. Expositio religiosissimi regis', *PG* 152, cols 997–1084.

[20] Michael Psellos, 'Alia expositio in Canticum Canticorum a Psello versitibus civilibus explicatum', *PG* 122, cols 540–685.

[21] 'Οὐκοῦν εὔδηλον ὅτι ἄλλος Σολομῶν διὰ τούτου σημαίνεται· ὁ καὶ αὐτὸς ἐκ τοῦ σπέρματος Δα(υ)ὶδ τὸ κατὰ σάρκα γενόμ(ενος) ᾧ ὄνομα Εἰρήνη· ὁ ἀληθινὸς τοῦ Ἰσραὴλ βασιλεὺς·' The name 'Eirene' (peace) has probably a metonymic sense and it is used because Solomon was renowned as the peaceful King in contrast to David. Nevertheless it is also possible that this insertion alludes to Eirene the *Sevastokratorissa*, on whom see below. Allu-sions to the name of Eirene have been reported by E. and M. Jeffreys in the letters James composed and which were addressed to the *Sevastokratorissa*. BN, MS gr. 3039, fols 17r, 25v, 150v, 157v, 158r.

Fig. 1   BN, MS gr. 1208, fol. 109v: The Couch of Solomon
(photo: Bibliothèque nationale de France, Paris)

Fig. 2   BN, MS gr. 1208, fol. 86r: The procession of Mary to the Temple
(photo: Bibliothèque nationale de France, Paris)

Fig. 3   BN, MS gr. 1208, fol. 123r: Mary in the Temple, protected by the sixty
mighty ones (photo: Bibliothèque nationale de France, Paris)

Presentation of Mary in the Temple (fig. 2), and the second illustrates the fourth sermon (fig. 3).[22] In the first miniature, Mary is the central figure of the procession to the Temple, and sixty armed representatives of the archangelic orders surround her. The text just above the miniature reads: 'Accept the glorious throne, the royal vessel inside which the Word in flesh was carried and dwelled. Embrace the Couch of Solomon, which is surrounded in a circle by the sixty valiant ones.'[23] In the second miniature Mary sits inside the temple, holding on her knees an open inscribed book, which alludes to the lower part of the composition and explains it.[24] She is protected in the same way by the sixty valiant ones.[25] In the lower part of the miniature the angels propel the demons over which they triumphed, into the darkness of Hell. The same connotations exist in James's exegetical text: 'And they cause fear and surprise to the dark thoughts of the moonless, darkest night, which pierce and wound with arrows the heart of the righteous.'[26] And later, 'Through these [weapons] fear and surprise is caused to the dark enemies, for whom the night and the darkness of desire becomes the right time to plot against souls.'[27]

Earlier pictorial allegorical representations of the Virgin were extensively used in the illustration of ninth-century Psalters with marginal decoration.[28] She is primarily prefigured as the Holy Mountain and the

---

[22] The first scholar to notice this was Der Nersessian, 'Le lit', 51; BN, MS gr. 1208, fols 86r, 123r; Omont, *Miniatures*, pl. XI, XV; BAV, MS gr. 1162, fols 64r, 92r; Stornajolo, *Miniature*, 26, 37; Hutter, *Marienhomiliar*, 44–5, 52–3.

[23] *PG* 127, col. 612: 'Δέξαι . . . τὸν θρόνον ἔνδοξον τὸν τὸ βασιλικὸν ὄχημα, ἐν ᾧ ὁ Λόγος ὀχούμενος, μετὰ σαρκὸς ἐπεδήμνε· περίλαβε τὴν Σολομώνειον κλίνην ᾗ κύκλῳ δορυφοροῦσιν οἱ ἑξήκοντα δυνατοί'. The caption of the miniature reads: 'Couch is surrounded by sixty which must be perceived as the soul': 'Κλίνην ὑπὸ ἑξήκοντα κυκλουμένην, τ(ὴν) ψυχ(ὴν) νοητέον'.

[24] 'Τοῦ ἐχθροῦ [ἐξέλιπον αἱ ῥομφαῖαι εἰς τέλος]' (Ps 9.6), see Hutter, *Marienhomiliar*, 52–3.

[25] The caption reads: 'On the way that the Holy Virgin remained unharmed by the arrows of the villainous one, thanks to an invisible force': 'ὅπως ἀοράτῳ δυνάμει συνετηρεῖτο ἡ ἁγία παρθένος ἀβλαβὴς τῶν τοῦ πονηροῦ βελῶν'.

[26] '. . . θάμβον καὶ ἔκπληξιν ἐμποιοῦσι τ(οῖς σκοτεινοῖς λογισμοῖς τοῖς ἐν νυξί τε καὶ σκοτομήνῃ τοῖς εὐθέαι τῇ καρδίᾳ λογχῶσί τε καὶ τοξεύουσ(ιν)'.

[27] '. . . δι'ὧν γίνεται θάμβος καὶ ἔκπληξις τοῖς σκοτεινοῖς ἐχθροῖς ὧν καιρὸς εἰς τὴν κατὰ τῶν ψυχῶν ἐπιβουλὴν ἡ νὺξ γίνεται καὶ τὸ σκότ(ος) τῶν παθῶν'.

[28] A. Grabar, *L'Iconoclasm byzantin. Dossier archéologique* (Paris, 1957), figs 147–8, 151; K. Corrigan, *Visual Polemics in the Ninth-Century Byzantine Psalters* (Cambridge, 1992), 37–40, 76–7 and figs 50, 99, 102; S. Dufrenne and S. Der Nersessian, *L'Illustration des psautiers grecs du moyen âge*, 2 vols, Bibliothèque des cahiers archéologiques, 1, 5 (Paris, 1966–70), 1:32 and pl. 18, 28 and pl. 12, 34–5 and pl. 26, 61 and pl. 54; 2:37 pl. 46 and fig. 136, 38 pl. 51 and fig. 149, 44 pl. 69 and fig. 191.

Fig. 4   BN, MS gr. 1208, fol. 1v: The prefatory miniature, with John Chrysostom, Gregory of Nyssa, and James the monk (photo: Bibliothèque nationale de France, Paris)

Holy City and quite frequently as the Fleece of Gideon. Prefigurations of Mary are also to be found in an eleventh-century illustrated Greek *Physiologos*.[29] The repertoire of allegorical representations of the Virgin in this manuscript is rich: Mary is prefigured as the Ark, the Tabernacle, the Table, the seven-stemmed Lamp, the Blooming Rod of Aaron, the Burning Bush, and the Pot of Manna. However, no representation of Mary as the Couch of Solomon has yet been found earlier than those in the *Kokkinobaphos* manuscripts. Der Nersessian pointed out that these miniatures provide the earliest surviving examples of the theme, which was to be developed and fully exploited during the thirteenth and fourteenth centuries.[30]

Although our monk had merely used a cliché from the homiletic tradition to address the Virgin, it is clear that when he came to the difficult task of pictorial representation, he realized that the Couch of Solomon, if not unknown, was at least a pictorial oddity.[31] James must have been conscious of the fact that the image was uncommon, if not unknown, in Byzantine iconography, and he treated it cautiously and exceptionally by providing it with an exegetical text and additional visual allusions. James must also have been responding to attitudes towards the Song of Songs, which was considered a very difficult and highly allegorized piece of work by all its commentators in East and West from the time of Origen (middle of the third century).[32] The only people who were authorized to study the Song were the spiritually mature, the perfect souls, so that its mysticism might not be misinterpreted as an expression of carnal desires. This sense of caution in the treatment of the Song exists already in the work of Gregory of Nyssa, and James was undoubtedly aware of it.[33]

The work of E. and M. Jeffreys and J.C. Anderson has shown that the author of our sermons also wrote forty-three letters and a treatise on

[29] J. Strzygowski, *Der Bilderkreis des Griechischen Physiologus des Kosmas Indikopleustes und Oktateuch nach Handschriften der Bibliothek zu Smyrna* (Leipzig, 1899), 56–7, pls XXV–XXIX; M. Bernabò, *Il Fisiologo di Smirne. Le miniature del perduto Codice B.8 della Biblioteca della Scuola Evangelica di Smirne* (Florence, 1998), pl. 76–81, 85–6.

[30] Der Nersessian, 'Le lit', 53.

[31] Ibid., 54.

[32] For the 'manipulation' of monastic reading in the twelfth century and a specific reference to the Song see J. Waring, 'Monastic reading in the eleventh and twelfth centuries: divine ascent or Byzantine fall?', in M. Mullett and A. Kirby, eds, *Work and Worship at the Theotokos Evergetis 1050–1200* (Belfast, 1997), 400–19, esp. 412–13.

[33] E. Jeffreys, 'The Song of Songs and twelfth century Byzantium', *Prudentia*, 23 (1991), 42.

the Holy Ghost.[34] The addressee of the letters was the *Sevastokratorissa* Eirene, the lady of the Byzantine court with whom our manuscripts have also been cautiously connected.[35]

Scholars have pointed out that James used Gregory's sermons on the Song of Songs extensively throughout his letters. He did not only address his patron with phrases and words from the Song but also offered her spiritual and contemplative advice inspired by Gregory. In other words, James was trying to introduce her to a mystical interpretation of the union of the soul with God by copying Gregory's stages of spiritual progress and development.[36]

The significance of the Song and the acknowledgement by James of the authority of Gregory as its commentator are signalled in the prefatory miniature of the sermons in the Paris copy (fig. 4).[37] Here James is introduced to Gregory by another Early Father, John Chrysostom. Gregory is presented seated on the right in front of an opened inscribed book that quotes the second verse of the Song: 'Let him kiss me with the kisses of his mouth' (Song of Songs 1.2).[38]

James's works all seem to demonstrate a profound interest in the Song of Songs and its several interpretations. His letters are addressed to Eirene, and the manuscripts of his sermons are probably associated with the same person. Should we connect this interest in the Song with James or with Eirene? It seems rather unlikely that an ordinary monk of an insignificant monastic establishment would impose his literary preferences on a lady of the court with a great reputation for patronage in twelfth-century Byzantium.[39] Moreover, Eirene seems to have composed a sermon on the symbolism of the Song of Songs, which she sent to James.[40] Can we believe that the Song was Eirene's obsession,

[34] Elizabeth and Michael Jeffreys have prepared an *editio princeps* of the 43 letters of James contained in BN, MS gr. 3039, to appear in a forthcoming volume of *Corpus Christianorum. Series graeca*; Anderson, 'Sermons', 85–95.

[35] J.C. Anderson, 'Anna Komnene, learned women, and the book in Byzantine art', in T. Gouma-Peterson, ed., *Anna Komnene and her Times* (2000), 125–48, esp. 142.

[36] Jeffreys, 'Song of Songs', 47–50; C. Laga, 'Entering the library of Jakobus Monachus. The exemplar of Jacobus quotations from the commentary on the Song of Songs by Gregory of Nyssa', in K. Demoen and J. Vereecken, eds, *La Spiritualité de l'univers byzantin dans le verbe et l'image*, Series Instrumenta Patristica, 30 (Turnhout, 1997), 151–61.

[37] BN, MS gr. 1208, fol. 1v; Omont, *Miniatures*, pl. I; Anderson, *Sermons*, 71–2.

[38] 'Φιλησάτω με ἀπὸ φιλη[μάτων στόματος αὐτοῦ]'.

[39] She has been associated with works by Ioannes Tzetzes, Konstantinos Manasses, Theodore Prodromos, Manganeios Prodromos and an anonymous encomiast; see Jeffreys, 'Who was Eirene?', 40–1 nn.3–10.

[40] BN, MS gr. 3039, Letter 10, fols 33r–40r, esp. 36r–36v. See the forthcoming edition of the letters by E. and M. Jeffreys.

and that James was simply trying to comply with the tastes of his patron? If that was the case, he also made sure that the aristocratic lady would enter this 'garden of delights' spiritually mature and protected from traps of interpretation. As a good spiritual advisor, James smoothed the path towards a world that Eirene cherished.

But despite what this rare pictorial example may signal for the author, his patron, and their relationship, the *Kokkinobaphos* miniature undoubtedly constitutes the earliest surviving representation of the Virgin as the Couch of Solomon. By the twelfth century Mary was linked with the Song of Songs pictorially as the vehicle of the mysterious incarnation to accomplish and fulfil the divine plan of salvation. According to James's interpretation, it was only through her that all pure and perfect souls could be saved and hopefully become a couch for the King of the Song. A new 'Era of Marianic/Messianic' interpretation had already begun and Mary was to be understood as 'The Woman Who is the All'.[41]

University of Birmingham

[41] Hutter, *Marienhomiliar*, 50. For parallel developments in the West see E.A. Matter, *The Voice of My Beloved. The Song of Songs in Western Medieval Christianity* (Philadelphia, PA, 1990), 151–70; A.W. Astell, *The Song of Songs in the Middle Ages* (1990), 42–72.

THE IDEA OF THE ASSUMPTION OF MARY
IN THE WEST, 800–1200

by HENRY MAYR-HARTING
(Presidential Address)

IF one were studying the whole cult of Mary in the early and high Middle Ages, there might seem little justification for regarding the period 800 to 1200 in the West as having any coherence of its own. It is true that the doctrinal issues in late antiquity were largely Christological. But not only so. As Peter Brown has said of Ambrose, he knew, in defending the perpetual virginity of Mary, that he was not only elevating the mother of the Lord; he was also showing an intense concern not to allow the boundaries of his own time between the sacred and the secular to become mixed up, not to allow the *integrity* of virginal chastity in actual celibates to be exposed to taint from the outside.[1] *Mutatis mutandis* these remained concerns of our period; the inviolate Virgin was one of the keynotes of its Marian language. I have a particular question in mind, however, which stated in a sentence is this: Why were the ninth, tenth, and eleventh centuries, in the West, satisfied with a spiritual assumption of Mary into heaven, while in the twelfth century people wanted to develop the idea of a bodily assumption? And here there is much point in taking the period 800 to 1200. For the celebrated letter, *Cogitis me*, composed probably in the 840s, in effect authoritatively ruled out any but a spiritual assumption, whereas after the visions of Elizabeth of Schönau in the 1150s and the commentary on the *Song of Songs* by the Yorkshireman, William of Newburgh, the idea of the bodily assumption became widely (though not yet universally) acceptable in the West. My period, therefore, is bounded by *Cogitis me* in the 840s and William of Newburgh's commentary in the 1190s.

The lengthy letter *Cogitis me* had a large circulation in the early Middle Ages. Attributed to Jerome for reasons not hard to guess at, Dom Lambot made a strong case in 1934, which has been generally accepted, that it was composed by Pascasius Radbertus of Corbie.[2] It

---

[1] Peter Brown, *The Body and Society* (1988), 353–6.
[2] C. Lambot, 'L'homélie du Pseudo-Jérôme sur l'Assomption et l'Évangile de la Nativité de Marie d'après une lettre inédit d'Hincmar', *Revue Bénédictine*, 46 (1934), 265–82; sup-

was used copiously for Carolingian liturgical antiphons and lections;[3] the hey-day of its considerable circulation appears to be the tenth century, but it was still going strong in the early twelfth.[4] *Cogitis me* is known as the text which forbade belief in the bodily assumption, just as *Humanae vitae* is known as the text which forbade contraception; but there is much more to each than that. *Cogitis me* is a brilliant piece of hyperbolic rhetoric. It begins with its warning not to accept the eastern *Transitus* legends, with their double assumption, first of Mary's soul and then of her body re-united to her soul, which were known in the West from the sixth century, which evidently exercised a magnetic pull on western imaginations, and which (in the opinion of Pascasius) tempted people to 'accept doubtful things as certainties'. How or when Mary's body could have risen was not known. Nothing, indeed was impossible to God; but better to commit everything to Him, than try to define for ourselves 'what cannot be known without danger' ('quod sine periculo nescitur').[5] But all this quickly transpires as only a kind of *captatio benevolentiae*, which paves the way for a prolonged outburst of baroque language, expressing Mary's heavenly praise and the glory of her *spiritual* assumption, her unique combination of *fecunditas* and *integritas*, her virginal motherhood, her sufferings of soul greater than those of the martyrs who suffered in the flesh, her seeming to be the subject of the *Song of Songs*, 'come, my love, my dove', (and, as Pascasius adds on his own account) 'my immaculate one'.[6]

It is a paradox that Pascasius Radbertus, who above all among Western theologians established the argument of Christ's corporeal presence in the Eucharist, should also be the selfsame one who most held back, for three centuries in the West, belief in Mary's corporeal rising to heaven. But we have to remember that corporeality, its goodness or badness, was not particularly an issue in the ninth century, as it had been in the fourth and would again become in the twelfth. Peter Brown was long since quiescent, and Caroline Walker Bynum had not

---

ported by H. Barré, 'La Lettre du Pseudo-Jérôme sur l'Assomption: est-elle antérieure à Paschase Radbert?', ibid., 68 (1958), 203–25.

[3] *William of Newburgh's Explanatio sacri epithalamii in matrem sponsi: a Commentary on the Canticle of Canticles*, ed. John C. Gorman, in Spicilegium Friburgense 6 (Fribourg, 1966), 39–40, with refs to earlier literature.

[4] *Paschasii Radberti De partu virginis*, ed. E. Ann Matter, and *De assumptione sanctae Mariae virginis* [i.e. Pseudo-Jerome, *Cogitis me*], ed. A. Ripberger, CChr.CM, 56C (Turnhout, 1985) [hereafter CChr.CM 56C], discussion of the MSS used for the edition at 99–105.

[5] Ibid., 114–15.

[6] Ibid., e.g., 116–17, 151, 134–5.

yet been stirred into life! Pascasius wrote, rather, under the shadow of the Iconoclastic Controversy and the continuing and intense Carolingian discussion about the role of images in worship. The Byzantine Iconoclastic Council of 754 had maintained that the only true image of Christ was the bread and wine of the Eucharist. Similarly Theodulph of Orleans in the *Libri Carolini* said that Christ constituted the commemoration of his Passion not through mundane works of art but in the consecration of his Body and Blood.[7] Pascasius himself presented the truth, *veritas*, as the Body and Blood of Christ, and the *figura* (or image) as what the priest enacted externally at the altar by way of the memory of the Sacred Passion.[8] When we understand this context of Pascasius's eucharistic thought, we see that his stress on corporeality here need not at all carry with it any idea of Mary's corporeal assumption.

One may ask, therefore: What was the point of making much of Mary's purely spiritual assumption, which hardly differentiated her from the martyrs, whatever Pascasius might say about their respective sufferings? The answer, already present in Ambrosius Autpertus,[9] comes through loud and clear in *Cogitis me*; though Pascasius was rhetorician enough to build up the tone before he let his major argument out into the open. Because Mary had the fullness of grace, because an angel was sent to her (virginity always having to do with angels), because while to be an angel was felicity to be a virgin required virtue, Mary deserved to be exalted above the choirs of angels in heaven, to be as the Mother of God escorted by angels to the throne prepared for her before all time, to be in fact a queen or ruler of angels.[10] Hence she became a paradigm, indeed under God a source, of earthly rule.

Now there will certainly be some to say that while the technicalities of the heavenly constitution might be all very interesting for those who like that sort of thing, they surely cannot have had much to do with

---

[7] Cyril Mango, *The Art of the Byzantine Empire 312–1453* (Englewood Cliffs, NJ, 1972), 166 (for 754); *Libri Carolini*, ed. Ann Freeman, *Mon. Germ. Hist. Concilia* ii, *supplementum* i (Hanover, 1998), ii.27 (290–6, esp. 290 ll.17–25, 292 ll.20–5, 293 l.1519).

[8] *Pascasius Radbertus, De corpore et sanguine domini*, ed. B. Paulus, CChr.CM, 16 (Turnhout, 1969), 28.

[9] H. Barré, 'La croyance à l'Assomption corporelle en Occident de 750 à 1150 environ', *Études Mariales*, 7 (1950), 67–70; and Henry Mayr-Harting, *Ottonian Book Illumination: an Historical Study*, 2 vols (1991), 1:139 and 224 n.52.

[10] CChr.CM 56C, 121 ll.228–9, 121 ll.219–20 ('et bene angelus ad virginem mittitur, quia semper est angelis cognata virginitas'), 121 ll.222–3, 125 ll.302–4, 130 ll.403–4, 127 l.344 ('super choros angelorum exaltata'), 129 ll.384–6 ('ad cuius profecto exsequias, quantum fas est credere, famulabantur angeli').

realities on earth. That would be a very mistaken view of the ninth and tenth centuries. When *Cogitis me* was written, Hilduin of St Denis, whom Pascasius must have known, had already made an attempt, albeit botched, to translate Pseudo-Dionysius's *Heavenly Hierarchy* from Greek into Latin, and around 860 Eriugena succeeded in the same task.[11] The Carolingians – and the Ottonians, for Pseudo-Dionysius was demonstrably well known under the Ottonians and Salians also – were interested in this work, of course, because they were interested in hierarchy.[12] And here we have to remember something which the study of saints' cults has made very evident, that the sharp boundary line between the natural and the supernatural which came to be drawn later was, like that between *regnum* and *sacerdotium*, a practically unthought of demarcation in the ninth and tenth centuries.

The significance of inserting Mary into a place immediately under God but above the angels in the heavenly hierarchy, however, went beyond a mere generalized interest in the relations between heaven and earth or in hierarchy. The idea of Pseudo-Dionysius was that the light of divine illumination passed first of all into the minds of the highest angels – the Seraphim, Cherubim, and Thrones, who were nearest to the Throne of God by reason of their contemplative power[13] – and thence through the other orders of angels into the minds of men, and then on in a kind of cascade of light to illuminate material things, first the most translucent gems, down to the most opaque matter, where it was still (albeit minimally) present. This gave a real earthly meaning, in that highly angel-conscious society, to phrases like '*domina mundi*' in the Uta Codex of *c.*1020,[14] or '*dominatrix inclita celi*' and '*lucida stella maris*' at

---

[11] David Luscombe, 'The reception of the writings of Denis the pseudo-Areopagite into England', in Diana Greenway, et al., eds, *Tradition and Change: Essays in Honour of Marjorie Chibnall* (Cambridge, 1985), 116–21.

[12] E.g. A. Boeckler, 'Das Erhardbild im Utacodex', in Dorothy Miner, ed., *Studies for Belle da Costa Greene* (Princeton, NJ, 1954), 219–30; Henry Mayr-Harting, *Perceptions of Angels in History* (Oxford, 1998), 15, 25 n.61.

[13] Cf. Trevor Johnson, on Mary, 'filled with grace and gifts above the highest seraphim', citing Maria de Jesus de Agreda, *The Mystical City of God*: below, p. 262.

[14] Munich, Bayerische Staatsbibliothek, Clm. 13601 (Uta Codex), fol. 2r; Adam S. Cohen, *The Uta Codex: Art, Philosophy and Reform in Eleventh-Century Germany* (University Park, PA, 2000), 47. The phrase is perhaps not as rare as Cohen maintains. To give some easily to hand eleventh-century examples, Thietmar of Merseburg uses it around the same time: *Thietmar of Merseburg, Chronicon*, ed. R. Holtzmann (Berlin, 1955), 173 l.11. *Domina gentium*, which amounts to much the same thing, is used by Maurilius of Rouen (*PL* 158, col. 947C), and *regina mundi* by Peter Damian (*Sancti Petri Damiani Sermones*, ed. J. Lucchesi, CChr.CM, 57 (Turnholt, 1983), 281 l.245).

the beginning of Hrotsvita of Ganderheim's poem, *Maria* (and Hrotsvita was a cousin of Otto I).[15] 'Stella maris', says Walafrid Strabo (the hymn *Ave maris stella* was already well known in his time): 'star of the sea for us who sail on the sea of this world'. Christ is the light of this star, he adds.[16] Given the continuum, therefore, between heavenly hierarchy and divine illumination of humanity, which was part of the Carolingian and Ottonian mind-set, Mary's rule over angels had a very clear significance for human rule.

The greatest known devotee of Mary in the tenth century was the Emperor Otto III. It cannot be argued that devotion to Mary otherwise reached the pitch between 800 and 1050 that it would subsequently attain, though it was by no means at such a low as the most reproachful writers, like Ohly and Sabbe, have implied.[17] It is always hard to prove a negative; it is particularly hard when one is ignorant of most of the positive evidence.[18] However, Otto III was undoubtedly exceptional. That does not mean that he is not worth considering. One may be both exceptional and characteristic. The fact that Marian devotees like Otto III did not grow on every tree does not mean that the forms of his devotion were not characteristic for his age.

Otto's devotion, which was particularly directed towards Mary's assumption, was probably derived from his mother, the Byzantine Theophanu. After her marriage to Otto II in Rome on Easter Sunday 972, there is documentary evidence which virtually proves that the imperial party, the Emperors Otto I and Otto II, and the Empress, as Theophanu was now styled, while making their way back north, celebrated the feast of the Assumption, its patronal feast, at the great monastery of Reichenau on Lake Constance.[19]

Otto III associated his rule with Mary's rule of the world, particularly during the last three years of his short life, 998 to 1001, when he actually set up an imperial court on the Aventine Hill in Rome. There is little doubt that in these years he thought of Mary not only as his

---

[15] *Hrotsvit Opera omnia*, ed. Walter Berschin (Munich and Leipzig, 2001), 4 ll.13–14.

[16] Homily on the beginning of St Matthew's Gospel, *PL* 114, col. 859B, cited by Hilda Graef, *Mary: A History of Doctrine and Devotion*, 2 vols (1963), 1:175; and for the likely eighth-century date of the *Ave maris stella*, ibid., 174.

[17] Friedrich Ohly, *Hohenlied-Studien* (Wiesbaden, 1958), 69–92, and 92 n.1; E. Sabbe, 'Le Culte Mariale et la genèse de la sculpture mediévale', *Revue belge d'archéologie et d'histoire de l'art*, 20 (1950), 101–25.

[18] E.g. of *Cogitis me*, largely of Otto III, or Hrotsvita of Gandersheim, or the Uta Codex, of Reichenau culture, etc.

[19] Mayr-Harting, *Ottonian Book Illumination*, 1:141, 225 n.61.

protector but also, like the Theotokos in Constantinople, as that of the city of Rome.

Two poems show how Otto III associated his rule as Roman Emperor with Mary's. One was composed for the procession in Rome of 15 August 1000, in which an image of Christ in Majesty was carried. Here Rome addresses Mary as if, so remarked Schneider, she were a pagan city goddess. 'Holy Mary, who hast scaled the heights of heaven', it begins, 'be kind to your people'; and it ends, 'be not slow to spare your Otto III who offers you what he has with a devout heart; let every man rejoice that Otto reigns, let every man rejoice in his rule'.[20] The second poem is attached to a text of *Cogitis me* in a manuscript at Bamberg written at Cluny about 1000.[21] Both Otto III and his successor Henry II, the latter not without devotion to Mary, had a close connection with Abbot Odilo of Cluny. This poem begins, 'behold there shines forth the day on which the holy mother of God ascended to the highest heaven, a virgin as parent, a virgin still, a virgin for ever.' It refers to Mary as 'helper of your own Henry, ever your pupil', and as *'domina per saecula'* ('ruler for ever'). The word 'Henry' has been written over an erasure; probably the text originally read 'Otto'.[22]

During these years (*pace* Kuder) the Gospel Book of Otto III now in Munich was made by Reichenau artists. It was bound in sheets of gold encrusted with gems, and into its front was set a fine tenth-century Byzantine ivory depicting the Dormition of the Virgin, with Christ by her bedside handing her soul up to two angels to be assumed into heaven.[23] Otto's favourite subject could obviously not be illustrated in a gospel book, so with 'Greek cunning' (he liked to think of himself in this way) he had it placed on the outside! The ivory could have come by way of Reichenau, which had many Greek connections in the tenth

[20] *Die Lateinischen Dichter des Deutschen Mittelalters, Die Ottonenzeit*, ed. Karl Strecker and Gabriel Silagi, MGH, Poetae Latini Medii Aevi, 5, 3 parts (Leipzig, Berlin, and Munich, 1937–79; pts 1–2 reprinted in 1 vol., Munich, 1978), 465–8.

[21] Ibid., 468–9, cf. Hartmut Hoffmann, *Bamberger Handschriften des 10. und des 11. Jahrhunderts*, MGH Schriften, 39 (Hanover, 1995), 160–1 (MS Patr. 88).

[22] That there is an erasure is clear. The name of Otto cannot be read underneath it, and therefore caution is necessary, but that is the likeliest explanation; see note in Strecker and Silagi, *Lateinischer Dichter*, 468.

[23] Munich, Bayerische Staatsbibliothek, Clm 4453; *Das Evangeliar Ottos III: CLM 4453 der Bayerischen Staatsbibliothek München*, ed. F. Dressler, F. Mütherich, and H. Beumann, 2 vols (Frankfurt, 1977–8), 1, esp. 23–4. Ulrich Kuder, 'Die Ottonen in der ottonischen Buchmalerei: Identifikation und Ikonographie', in Gerd Althoff and Ernst Schubert, eds, *Herrschaftsrepräsentation im ottonischen Sachsen* (Sigmaringen, 1998), 193–4, would date this book to the reign of Henry II (1002–24); but his brief arguments lack all conviction.

Fig. 1   The Dormition of Mary: tenth-century Byzantine ivory set into the front cover of the Gospel Book of Otto III (998–1001). Munich, Bayerische Staatsbibliothek, Clm. 4453. (Reproduced by permission of the Bayerische Staatsbibliothek, Munich)

Fig. 2   The Dormition, Spiritual Assumption, and Coronation of Mary by the Hand of God. Prüm Antiphonary, late tenth century. BN, MS Lat. 9448, fol. 60v. (Reproduced by permission of the Bibliothèque Nationale de France)

Figs 3 (left) and 4 (right) The Dormition and Spiritual Assumption of Mary. Book of Collects, Reichenau, c.1010–30. Hildesheim, Dombibliothek, MS 688, fos 76v, 77r. (Reproduced by permission of the Dombibliothek, Hildesheim)

94

century, or it could have been left to Otto by Theophanu. Reichenau, the one monastery north of the Alps with which Otto had really close and entirely friendly relations, had a near monopoly in Dormition and Assumption iconography according to the surviving evidence. One important exception is in an antiphonary from Prüm, an abbey with which Otto was on amicable terms, which shows Mary's soul being carried to heaven by angels, whence the Hand of God appears to place a crown on her head.[24] Reichenau developed the basically Byzantine iconography of the subject to combine the affecting scenes around Mary's bed with her apotheosis in heaven. The earliest of these representations can with virtual certainty be dated to 1001 and be said to have been made for Otto III.[25] The early eleventh-century book of collects at Hildesheim, perhaps made for Otto's mentor Bishop Bernward of Hildesheim, divides the subject between two pages; the first, the Dormition, with Jesus and Mary seeming to look at each other poignantly, while of the apostles around the bed, Peter and John are in tears; the second, the spiritual assumption, with Mary, *orans*, as the *imago clipeata*, with the Hand of God reaching down to her, out of a cosmos and against a victory cross, as if constituting her a ruler of angels.[26] This idea of the ruler of angels is also found in a book of Regensburg influence, commissioned by Bernward himself. In two delightful dedication pages facing each other, Bernward hands over his gospel book to Mary by placing it on an altar before her; and then she is shown, stiff and hieratic, with the Pantocrator on her lap, as if in a church, if not *as* the Church, in an unusual iconography being crowned by angels.[27]

There is a paradox at this time in the whole Reichenau Marian culture. All the time they were producing these images, they had sitting in their library a Latin translation of the *Transitus* legend, which was explicit as to the bodily assumption of Mary, and a manuscript of excellent Latin translations of Greek homilies by Andrew of Crete, Cosmas Vestitor, and others, which held the same doctrine.[28] Cosmas stressed a point that would be made much of in the twelfth-century western

[24] Mayr-Harting, *Ottonian Book Illumination*, 1:147, fig. 86; BN, MS lat. 9448, fol. 60v; *Ottonis III diplomata*, MGH Diplomatum regum et imperatorum Germaniae, 2/ii (Hanover, 1893), no. 262.

[25] Mayr-Harting, *Ottonian Book Illumination*, 1:151–2 and Colour Plate XXII.

[26] Ibid., 1:150 and Colour Plates XIV–XVII.

[27] Ibid., 1:95–105 and figs 49–50.

[28] Karlsruhe, Badische Landesbibliothek, MSS Aug. CXXIX, LXXX. See A. Wenger, *L'Assomption de la T.S. Vierge dans la tradition Byzantine du VIe au Xe siècle: études et documents* (Paris, 1955), 17–95, 209–69.

Figs 5 and 6 Bishop Bernward of Hildesheim presents his Gospel Book, by placing it on the altar, to Mary, with Christ seated on her lap in hieratic posture, as she is crowned by angels. Gospel Book, c.1015. Hildesheim, Domschatz, MS 18, fos 16v, 17r. (Reproduced by permission of the Diözesanmuseum, Hildesheim)

96

discussions, that as Mary and Jesus were of one flesh, Mary should therefore share the corporeal incorruptibility and resurrection of her Son.[29] Yet in Reichenau art there was never a question of anything but a spiritual assumption being represented, with Mary's soul a child naked or mummified. One has to remember here, I think, that much of this Byzantine material had a legitimate devotional use (in *Cogitis me* terms), which was probably quite as important to the prayerful and highly-strung religiosity of the youthful Otto III as the apotheosis aspect was. In it the idea was developed, in the death-bed scene, of a loving relationship between Mary and her Son, as well as between the apostles and Mary, with which the reader, listener, or meditator could identify, and in which they could participate.[30] Personal religion of this sort was by no means an invention of the Twelfth Century Renaissance.

The early medieval West also knew an iconography of Mary's heavenly glorification without representation of the dormition. We see it in a rather provincial Augsburg manuscript of *c.*1030 where, at the bottom of the mandorla, in an eleventh-century hand, are the words *Maria stella maris*, 'Mary star of the sea'. The model for this could have come from Rome itself, for by around 800 the church of Sta Maria Maggiore seems to have had two altar frontals, one depicting the *transitus*, the other the *adsumptio Mariae*.[31]

One might be tempted from all the foregoing on Otto III to draw the conclusion which Marina Warner draws in her ever brilliant and challenging book, *Alone of All Her Sex*, in the chapter 'Maria Regina': 'the cult of Mary as queen served for centuries to uphold the status quo to the advantage of the highest echelons of power'.[32] I do not disagree with this but I think there is more to be said. The Assumption of Mary must have meant a great deal personally to Otto. He lost his potent but amiable mother, Theophanu, as a boy of eleven. When he succeeded to the kingship in 983, aged three, she, alongside Archbishop Willigis of Mainz, had fought like a tiger for his rights in the intense succession dispute of 983–85. Unlike his second cousin, Henry II, who succeeded him, he did not know what it was to struggle for his own succession. Thietmar of Merseburg, for all his anti-Byzantine prejudices, says of her:

---

[29] Ibid., esp. 319, para. 4; cf. 160.

[30] Mayr-Harting, *Ottonian Book Illumination*, 1:142–3.

[31] O. Sinding, *Mariae Tod und Himmelfahrt* (Christiania, 1903), 33–4, citing the *Liber pontificalis*.

[32] Marina Warner, *Alone of All Her Sex* (1974), 104.

Fig. 7 The Spiritual Assumption of Mary. Augsburg Sacramentary, *c.*1030.
BL, MS Harley 2908, fol. 123v. (Reproduced by permission of the British
Library)

Despite being of the weak sex, she was a woman of gentleness and
trustworthiness, and what is rare in Greece, led an honourable way
of life, and she preserved the kingdom of her son with masculine
alertness [*custodia virili*], nurturing the devout and scaring the
proud.[33]

Theophanu would not have objected to being called masculine, for a
diploma of hers issued in Ravenna on 1 April 990, styled her 'Theophanius

---

[33] Thietmar of Merseburg, *Chronicon*, 4.10 (ed. Holtzmann, 142).

gratia divina imperator augustus'![34] To Otto, Theophanu and Mary must have looked much like each other, two great rulers both spiritually assumed into heaven, both his protectoresses. He could not have remained unaffected by the Dormition scenes, with their reflection on the relations between a son and his dying mother.

Caroline Walker Bynum has written of how men retreat to what she calls 'the womanliness and weakness of liminality' in order to re-emerge, girded with consolation, to play the more effective role as leaders of men. St Francis compares himself to a mother and takes on the sufferings of Christ in the stigmata, she says, adding, 'from the liminality of weakness, nudity and womanliness comes the leader and model who changes the religious life of the thirteenth century'. Men (popes, emperors, bishops, and so forth) had recourse to actual women, such as Hildegard of Bingen or St Catherine of Siena, as 'a means of escape from, and reintegration into, status and power'.[35] Otto III, with all his tears and vigils, may not have been everyone's notion of an ideal ruler, though he had some notable successes in the field of battle; but surely these penetrating words tell us something also of Otto III, in the liminality of his prayer, the sinking of his own rule into Mary's heavenly rule, and his re-emergence to be no small force as a leader of men. Otto III gave a boost to the holiness of the empire as an institution, his devotion to Mary playing a major role in this. And holiness is not a quality of institutions that can be produced to order, for 'the advantage of the highest echelons of power'.

One might have supposed that the tidal wave of devotion to Mary, which swept the West between 1050 and 1150 – and however one thinks scholars have underplayed the phenomenon in the previous centuries, it is undeniable that there was this surge – would be a direct cause leading to belief in the bodily assumption. But it was not at all direct. One might have thought that the world of the Gregorian Reform, Gregory VII himself, Peter Damian, Anselm, the promoters of

---

[34] The Byzantine precedents for this do not make it less striking in its context; see F.-R. Erkens, 'Die Frau als Herrscherin in ottonish-frühsalischer Zeit', and Johannes Laudage, 'Das Problem der Vormundschaft über Otto III', both in Anton von Euw and Peter Schreiner, eds, *Kaiserin Theophanu*, 2 (Cologne, 1991), 256–57, 268–71. See also Karl Leyser, 'Theophanu divina gratia imperatrix augusta: western and eastern emperorship in the later tenth century', in his *Communications and Power in Medieval Europe: The Carolingian and Ottonian Centuries*, ed. Timothy Reuter (1994), 143–64.

[35] Caroline Walker Bynum, 'Women's stories, women's symbols: a critique of Victor Turner's theory of liminality', in her *Fragmentation and Redemption: Essays on Gender and the Human Body in Medieval Religion* (New York, 1991), esp. 34–7.

the Immaculate Conception, Bernard, the Cistercians, to name but some of the most famous, would quickly bring about this development of doctrine. But it was not so. In fact rule, and Mary as a model of rule, continued to be a major theme of Marian devotion for most of that hundred years, which remained by and large satisfied (if that is the right word) with a spiritual assumption. The prayer to the Virgin of Archbishop Maurilius of Rouen, Anselm's counsellor, struck in a sense a new note around 1050–60 by hyperbolizing the wretchedness of the sinful supplicant and the craving for the 'tendency to chastity'.[36] To chastity I come in a moment; clerical chastity was to become a keynote theme of the Gregorian Reform. Of the wretchedness of the supplicant, I will say here only that this idea was a pregnant one. For in the enormous economic explosion of 1050 to 1150, the new materialistic opportunities, the competitiveness, the social upheavals and dislocations that accompanied this, Mary came to be seen as the refuge of the left-behind and marginalized, and even of the immoral, the refuge of those who did not always deserve help, the mother of men as well as of God. In literature, that was a driving force in the genre of Marian Miracles.[37] What one particularly notices about Maurilius's prayer, however, is that Mary is addressed in the language of rulership, the Lady of Peoples (*domina gentium*), the Queen of Angels (*regina angelorum*), and – here a phrase applied from the *Song of Songs* (4.15) – the Fountain of Gardens (*fons hortorum*).[38] Such terminology is reflected in the early twelfth century, in a manuscript of Jumièges provenance containing the text of *Cogitis me*. The text is headed by a fine representation of Mary, infused with the Holy Spirit, in a mandorla supported by her subjects, as queen of angels. Maurilius's letter in art, one might call it.

The Gregorian Reform, however much it may have been a party to unleashing the new surge of Marian devotion, actually had the effect of reinforcing Mary's spiritual assumption and reaffirming her image as a paradigmatic ruler, rather than leading on to the idea of her bodily assumption. Rupert of Deutz, whose whole lengthy commentary on the *Song of Songs*, composed in the mid-1120s, had the originality, even as against that of Ambrose, of being a meditation on the Virgin Mary, makes this point for us. If the Bride of the *Song of Songs* had been mainly interpreted as the Church during the so-called Dark Ages, the idea of

---

[36] *PL* 158, cols 946–7.
[37] R.W. Southern, *The Making of the Middle Ages* (1953), 246–54.
[38] *PL* 158, col. 947C.

Fig. 8   The Assumption of Mary, before the text of *Cogitis me*, early twelfth century. Rouen, Bibliothèque municipale, MS Y109, fol. 4r. (Reproduced by permission of Collections de la Bibliothèque municipale de Rouen. Photographie: Didier Tragin et Catherine Laucien)

relating her to Mary, herself a type of the Church, was by no means lost on them, least of all in *Cogitis me*.[39] But in the totality of the Marian approach to the *Song*, Rupert was original.[40] We must not hijack Rupert to our own purposes. His central interest in this work was the role of Mary in salvation. Within that, however, this writer, who had been firmly aligned with the party of the Gregorian reformed papacy at Liège in the days of Urban II,[41] expanded the concept of Mary's spiritual rule to signify rule, in the world, by the reformed church.

First of all, says Rupert, she (that is, Mary, Church, Bride) wielded only a spiritual sword, her Beloved having taken from her the material sword. In the Old Testament the material sword may have been necessary, but now the only necessary things were the testimonies of the Scriptures.[42] Gregory VII might have thought this a trifle optimistic, but he certainly thought that the pope could not wield the material sword himself.[43] And he emphatically thought that the Church of Rome was the ultimate authority in the teaching of the Scriptures. This has been clearly shown by Fichtenau in his study of the production of Giant Bibles in eleventh-century Italy, and by Ian Robinson in his study of Donizo of Sutri on Genesis.[44] Hence it is very interesting that Rupert, commenting on the phrase *fons hortorum*, which we have related above to his use of the language of rulership, says of Mary that she is the fountain of gardens, that is the mother of churches (a phrase constantly used of Rome by the reformed papacy); and that she is the well of living waters, *puteus aquarum viventium*, that is the repository (*secretarium*) of all the holy Scriptures.[45] The idea of this

---

[39] In *Cogitis me*, e.g. CChr.CM 56C, 149–52. See also Mayr-Harting, *Ottonian Book Illumination*, 2:42 (where the lack of Mariological significance is exaggerated), and Cohen, *Uta Codex*, 47–8.

[40] See Rachel Fulton, 'Mimetic devotion, Marian exegesis and the historical sense of the Song of Songs', *Viator*, 27 (1996), 85–116. This important paper, to which Susan Boynton drew my attention, raises wide issues. My purposes in the study of these commentaries have been more limited.

[41] John H. van Engen, *Rupert of Deutz* (Berkeley, CA, 1983), 26–42.

[42] *Ruperti Tuitiensis Commentaria in Canticum canticorum*, ed. H. Haacke, CChr.CM, 26 (Turnholt, 1974) [hereafter CChr.CM 26], 65 ll.193–6, 163–4.

[43] R.W. and A.J. Carlyle, *A History of Medieval Political Theory in the West*, 6 vols (Edinburgh and London, 1903–36), 4:291. Rupert closely anticipates Gerhoh of Reichersberg, who though no outright papalist, was even less of an imperialist, ibid., 4:356–7.

[44] H. Fichtenau, 'Riesenbibeln in Österreich und Mathilde von Tuszien', in his *Beiträge zur Mediävistik*, i (Stuttgart, 1975), 163–86; I.S. Robinson, 'The metrical Commentary on Genesis of Donizo of Canossa', *Recherches de théologie ancienne et médiévale*, 41 (1974), 5–37.

[45] CChr.CM 26, 89 ll.164–7; cf. ibid., 24 l.495, where in the same connection (S. of S. 1.6) Mary is called 'magistra magistrorum, id est apostolorum'. This, rather than a general

last exegesis is that the Gospel, because of Christ, had its origins in Mary.[46]

Rupert also saw in Mary an embodiment of all the virtues aimed at by the reformed church – freedom from avarice, humility, *justitia*, the right balance of the contemplative and active lives.[47] The last was one of the many points where teaching and liturgy interact on each other in our period, since a common gospel reading for the feast of the Assumption was that on another Mary, and Martha, the types of the contemplative and active lives. Not least Mary – the Virgin – consummately embodied the virtue of chastity, that reforming rock on which was founded clerical celibacy and thereby the whole distinctness of the *sacerdotium* from the world. Commenting on the phrase, 'your navel is like a rounded bowl which never lacks wine' (*Song of Songs*, 7.2), for instance, Rupert says of Mary, 'perfect in you is the virtue of chastity; you are free from every appetite of carnal desire'. Because of her virtues, Mary is not only the mother of churches, but also a perfect *mirror* to all churches.[48] In all this Rupert does not refer to any assumption of Mary, but a purely spiritual one is understood throughout, and that is all, within the persisting concept of rulership, that is needed.

It would not be unreasonable to suppose that the development of the doctrine of the Immaculate Conception, propagated in the West above all by a group of English Benedictine abbots in the 1120s, prepared the ground for the development of the doctrine of Mary's bodily assumption. After all it was not only that the Son of God shared her flesh, but also that she was neither conceived in concupiscence, nor in principle was able to feel concupiscence, which made it right that her flesh should not see corruption. But in the first place, the incorruptibility of Mary's body was generally believed, regardless of belief or non-belief in the Immaculate Conception or bodily Assumption. Secondly, there are good grounds for saying that the main drive behind the development of the Immaculate Conception was not theological – its theological

---

connection to the Immaculate Conception, a feast propagated by Abbot Geoffrey of St Albans but a doctrine denied by Rupert, is the likeliest explanation for the novel Pentecost iconography and the exceptional prominence (for the time) given to Mary in the St Albans' Psalter *c*.1130, rather than a source such as Odilo of Cluny's sermon on the Assumption, as Otto Pächt would argue, in Otto Pächt et al., *The St Alban's Psalter* (1960), 67–70. For Rupert represents Mary as a *teacher* of the Apostles. True, Rupert's circulation was in the Empire (van Engen, *Rupert*, 291), but imperial artistic influence figures large in the Psalter.

[46] van Engen, *Rupert*, 296.
[47] Ibid., 296–7.
[48] CChr.CM 26, 147 ll.534–5; and on the mirror to churches, ibid., 106 ll.39–47.

discussion, *pace* those who admire Eadmer, was jejune – but liturgical. It was the desire to bring in a new feast and a new devotion to Mary by the black monks,[49] whose religion, though sincere and devout, was at that time highly ritualized. Thirdly, and most of all, this argument does not work in terms of twelfth-century religious alignments. The Cistercians, who in England at least were the great propagators of the idea of a bodily assumption, were apparently to a man opposed to the Immaculate Conception.[50]

What made all the difference, more than is sometimes thought, to the acceptance of the bodily assumption, if not yet universal belief in it, were the visions of the Rhineland mystic Elizabeth of Schönau. Elizabeth, a younger contemporary of Hildegard of Bingen, experienced her visions of the bodily assumption between 1156 and 1159 when she was in her late twenties. Her brother Ekbert said that she normally spoke in German, but after her ecstasies she sometimes spoke in Latin, *non sine evidenti miraculo*. In other words, since she was not much of a Latinist, her brother was needed to write up her experiences in Latin if they were to be taken seriously in the Church. Also, there was the fear that if her visions were not to be taken as mere figments of a woman's imagination (*muliebria figmenta*), and Elizabeth herself as an inventor of novelties (*inventrix novitatum*) – an index of how little ground the bodily assumption had made up to then – they would have to be published under male authorship.[51] Hence the *Visio de resurrectione beate virginis Marie*. It is a work of but a few pages – ideal if one wanted to be read! Elizabeth says that, advised by one of her elders, she asked Our Lady, the *domina celorum*, straight out, whether she was assumed into heaven only in the spirit or also in the flesh.[52] She was not vouchsafed an answer for another year when, as she says,

[49] This is made very clear in the celebrated letter of Osbert of Clare, Prior of Westminster to Anselm of St Saba, Abbot of Bury St Edmund (1129): *The Letters of Osbert of Clare*, ed. E.W. Williamson (Oxford, 1929), no. 7 (65–8). Against the challenge of Roger of Salisbury and Bernard of St Davids on the day itself, the monks carried the celebration of the festival through (ibid., 65).

[50] *Sermones inediti Aelredi abbatis Rievallensis*, ed. C.H. Talbot, Series Scriptorum S. Ordinis Cisterciensis, 1 (Rome, 1952), 20, on the Cistercians and the Immaculate Conception, which was very much a black-monk agendum. For the Cistercians and the Assumption see below and n.55 below. Also for Ailred himself, see *Sermones*, 136 ll.21–2: 'Fecit [i.e. Christ] et sibi hodie thronum beatissime virginis corpus et animam.'

[51] *Die Visionen und Briefe der hl Elisabeth, sowie die Schriften der Aebte Ekbert und Emecho von Schönau*, ed. F.W.E. Roth (Brünn, 1886), 53–5. See Anne L. Clark, *Elisabeth of Schönau: a Twelfth-Century Visionary* (Philadelphia, PA, 1992), 14–16, 28–9, 40–1, 107–11.

[52] Roth, *Die Visionen*, 53: 'utrum solo spiritu assumpta sis in celum an etiam carne'.

I saw in a very remote place a sepulchre engulfed in a great light, and in it, apparently, the form of a woman, and a large multitude of angels stood about it. After a little while she was raised up from the tomb, and, together with that multitude standing by, she was lifted up on high.[53]

Elizabeth asked an angel, another of her heavenly interlocutors, 'my Lord, what does this great vision that I saw mean?' He said, 'this vision has shown you how Our Lady was taken up into heaven in flesh as well as in spirit'. The York Psalter, of the 1170s, now in Glasgow, illustrates this vision to perfection. It must be the first representation in Christian art of the bodily assumption of Mary.[54]

The *De resurrectione* spread like wildfire, which shows that it struck a chord. Rarely is it lacking from the numerous manuscripts of Elizabeth's complete works, and it usually stands out in them as a separate item.[55] Elizabeth died in 1164, and only after Ekbert became abbot of Schönau in 1165 did he 'publish' her visions. Yet by the 1170s they were in circulation in England, as the York Psalter shows. A Cistercian monk, Roger, sent a copy of them in that decade to the Cistercian Baldwin, Abbot of Ford in Devon, who would later become Archbishop of Canterbury. A manuscript from the northern province (Oxford, St John's College, MS 149), dating from the later twelfth century, is another early evidence. This might have been connected with the Cistercian, Roger, Abbot of Byland in Yorkshire, who was present at the death-bed of Ailred of Rievaulx, and was abbot 1142 to 1196. It was for Roger that the Augustinian canon and Yorkshireman, William of Newburgh, wrote his commentary on the *Song of Songs* in the 1190s.[56] This commentary interpreted the whole work in the light of Mary, and was apparently innocent of Rupert of Deutz, whose circulation had been largely in the Empire. It is very different from Rupert,

---

[53] Ibid.: 'Vidi in loco valde remoto sepulchrum quoddam multo lumine circumfusum, et quasi speciem mulieris in eo, et circumstabat multitudo magna angelorum.'

[54] T.S.R. Boase, *The York Psalter* (1962), pl.6 in colour.

[55] Kurt Köster, 'Elisabeth von Schönau: Werk und Wirkung im Spiegel der mittelalterlichen Handschriftlichen Überlieferung', *Archiv für mittelrheinische Kirchengeschichte*, 3 (1951), 243–315, esp. 251–76. Also this vision had a considerable circulation as the only one of Elizabeth's works in a manuscript, with eight not later than c.1200 (ibid., 285–93). From the first fifty years or so, the manuscripts show a considerable Cistercian circulation: see ibid., nos 12, 13, 16a, 17, 18, 24, 27, 32, 72, 73, 82, 83a, 93.

[56] Boase, *York Psalter*, 10–11; Gorman, *William of Newburgh's Explanatio*, 21–4.

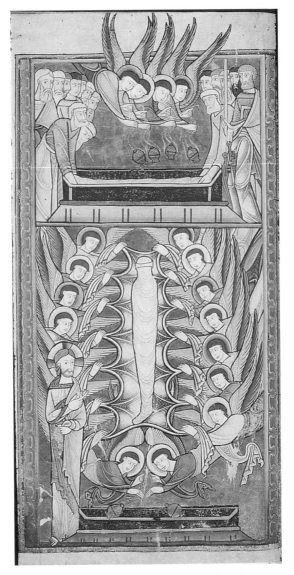

Fig. 9 The Bodily Assumption of Mary. York Psalter, c.1170.
Glasgow University Library, MS Hunter 229, fol. 19v.
(Reproduced by permission of Glasgow University Library,
Department of Special Collections)

and William gives as his principal source his own prayer.[57] Interestingly, William is never explicit about the bodily assumption; but he obviously has a bodily assumption in mind throughout, particularly where he speaks of Mary's incorruptibility of flesh and of her resurrection together. He imagines Jesus saying to his mother – and this kind of use of the imagination is a marked feature of Cistercian prayer – 'I have first been taken up to the Father; come now, pious mother, to the Father and join me at the feast; formerly I came to you to be incarnate of you; now come to me to be glorified by me.'[58] Incidentally, William denies the Immaculate Conception. Being conceived by the concupiscence of her parents, he says, Mary could not have been exempted from original sin at conception. Christ sanctified his future mother shortly *after* her conception, and she was perfected at the Incarnation, though she was necessarily exempted from concupiscence *ab initio*.[59] So much, with this hair-splitting, for the *purely* theological issues felt to be at stake in the twelfth-century debate on the Immaculate Conception.

Whatever one thinks of the idea of Mary's bodily assumption, it is undoubted that this idea gained currency in the Western Church, as the result of taking the religious experiences of a woman, Elizabeth of Schönau, seriously. That was not necessarily *because* she was a woman, for the less paramount the external importance of the male priestly mediator, and the greater the stress on the interiority of religion, the less relevant the status or gender of the person having religious experience. Hence a barrier was broken down, or partly broken down, *against* taking the religious experiences of women seriously. And if one considers the reliance of Abbot Geoffrey of St Albans on the prayer and spirituality of Christina of Markyate,[60] or the fame that accrued to Hildegard of Bingen from her visions recorded in the *Scivias*,[61] or the remarkable registering of emotion on the face of one of the sisters of Lazarus as she witnesses the raising of her brother from the dead on one of the Chichester Reliefs,[62] all in the few decades before Elizabeth of Schönau's visions, or the way Ailred of Rievaulx wrote about prayer for

---

[57] Ibid., 364, cf. 23, 56–7. One may note that he and Rupert differ in their whole concept of the Assumption.

[58] Ibid., 133–4, cf. 85–6, 110, 337 ll.10–13.

[59] Ibid., 25–6, with refs to the text.

[60] *The Life of Christina of Markyate*, ed. C.H. Talbot (Oxford, 1959), 134–44.

[61] Sabina Flanagan, *Hildegard of Bingen: a Visionary Life* (1989), 159, 172.

[62] For a fine general discussion of these reliefs, see F. Saxl, *English Sculptures of the Twelfth Century* (1954), 32–8.

his sister in the decade after,[63] one sees some of the many evidences that these visions occurred in a culture that was taking the religious experience of women seriously in a new way and to a new degree.

What we must ask, as historians, about Elizabeth of Schönau is not why she received the answers about the corporeal assumption which she did, but why she put the question (when she put it) in the first place.

First of all, it was a matter by the 1150s much mooted, but of real doubt. Honorius Augustodunensis is said by Hilda Graef, in her altogether very useful work on Mary, to have taught her bodily assumption in his *Sigillum* of *c*.1100.[64] But in fact he is very clipped and cautious on the subject. Referring to the words in the *Song of Songs* about Solomon's bed, which he interprets as the body of the blessed Virgin, he says that 'they *seem* (*videntur*) to be the words of the Church on the assumption of the body of Mary'.[65] That is virtually all. In any case he went back on this approach some thirty years later in his commentary on the *Song*, and he then interpreted it as a dialogue of Christ with his Church.[66] Graef is equally optimistic about the Pseudo-Augustine letter of perhaps the early twelfth century, saying that it gradually ousted the influence of Pseudo-Jerome (that is, *Cogitis me*).[67] But this letter put its arguments from first principles rather than from authority. They are what one might call arguments from fittingness, rather like Eadmer's on the Immaculate Conception.[68] What people wanted in that age was authority, with the conflicts of authority ironed out, as one can see from Abelard or Gratian. And what greater authority could one have than the authenticated words of the Virgin herself?

Then there was St Bernard. Bernard notoriously sat on the fence over this issue in his sermons on the Assumption. 'She who first received the Lord when he entered into the castle of this world, now is received by him when she enters the heavenly city. But with how much

---

[63] *De institutione inclusarum*, in *Aelredi Rievallensis Opera omnia*, ed. A. Hoste and C.H. Talbot, CChr.CM 1 (Turnhout, 1971), 635–82. In this work Ailred encourages his sister to imagine, in her meditation, what it was like to be one of the people, one of the women especially, around Jesus.

[64] Graef, *Mary*, 1:228. Valerie Flint, 'The commentaries of Honorius Augustodunensis on the Song of Songs', in her *Ideas in the Medieval West: Texts and their Contexts* (1988), at XI, 203, is wisely more cautious.

[65] *PL* 172, col. 505A.

[66] Flint, 'Commentaries', 197.

[67] Graef, *Mary*, 1:222.

[68] *PL* 40, esp. cols 1143–4, cf. Graef, *Mary*, 1:222–4. For Eadmer, R.W. Southern, *St Anselm and His Biographer* (Cambridge, 1963), 290–6.

honour, do you think? With how much glory?' Ah ha!, one supposes. The great man, the dominating influence in the second quarter of the twelfth century, the outspoken prophet, is going to say what he thinks about the corporeal assumption. His answer has all the skill of many a Vatican monsignor. With how much glory is the Virgin received in heaven? It is an *inestimable* glory! There is no place in heaven more worthy![69] One would not wonder if one significance of the date when Elizabeth's visions of Mary started, 1156, was that St Bernard, who had made such a fuss to the canons of Lyon about the Immaculate Conception, and who opined that a novelty (*novitas*) could never please Mary,[70] had been safely in his grave for just three years.

There is a more important point, and one so obvious that I wonder whether I have overlooked its being made somewhere. The Rhineland was infested in the mid-twelfth century with Cathar heretics, whose main tenet was that all spirit was good and all flesh, all created matter, was evil. And their principal adversary was none other than Ekbert of Schönau, Elizabeth's brother who wrote down her visions about the bodily assumption. Ekbert began his *Sermons against the Cathars* only in 1163, but his experience of them in the Rhineland went back into the 1140s.[71] This is how he described their beliefs in his first sermon:

> They teach that there were two creators, one good and one evil: God and the prince of darkness. They created the universe. The souls of men and all the other living animals and the quality which gives life to trees, plants and seeds, owed their beginning to God, and were created from his good nature. Everything of flesh which lives on the earth, whether man or animal, originates from the prince of darkness, the devil, and is founded in his evil nature.[72]

Can one imagine a more robust challenge to this kind of belief than Mary, glorified in soul *and body* by her assumption? Of course this was not the only answer to the Cathars. Both Ekbert and Elizabeth held that the Catharist views obtained such wide credence because of the materialism and pastoral neglect of so many clergy.[73] The standard needed to

---

[69] *Sancti Bernardi Opera V, Sermones*, ii, ed. J. Leclercq and H. Rochais (Rome, 1968), 230 ll.6–15.

[70] Epistola 174: *PL* 185, cols 332–6, esp. 336B.

[71] R.I. Moore, *The Origins of European Dissent* (1977), 175–6; Malcolm Lambert, *The Cathars* (Oxford, 1998), 19–23.

[72] *PL* 195, col. 17B–C. Translation of R.I. Moore, *The Birth of Popular Heresy* (1975), 93.

[73] Clark, *Elisabeth of Schönau*, e.g. 23–5 (Hildegard of Bingen in here also), 63–7.

be raised in this respect. But one can hardly doubt that the idea of Mary's bodily assumption was *an* answer to the Cathars.

It would be cheap, however, to end there. I have said that in the ninth century, despite arguments about the Eucharist, corporeality was not particularly an issue. By the mid-twelfth century it very much was. Caroline Walker Bynum, writing of the later Middle Ages, has wisely commented that in late medieval spirituality,

> a concern to give the proper significance to flesh was not so much a concern that characterized orthodox as opposed to heterodox, as it was a concern that bound all religious reactions of the period together (however much they might differ over what the proper significance was) . . . *All* the religiosity of the period was animated in deep ways by the need to take account of (rather than merely to deny) matter, body, and sensual response.[74]

In the mid-twelfth century we have already arrived at this point. Think of the whole phenomenon of Romanesque sculpture in its second phase, its concern for the tactile and the three-dimensional in the shaping of the human body, compared with the zoomorphism, geometricality, and two-dimensionalism of the first phase. What could take greater account of the 'sensual response' than Gislebertus's Eve of the 1130s at Autun? Think of the efforts of the early Gothic sculptors of the 1140s to express the inner soul in the outer body, as brought out by Katzenellenbogen.[75] Think of the early Cistercians' stress on the material as well as moral improvement of mankind, as evidenced in the superbly engineered mill race at Fountains and sewers at Rievaulx. Think of the great concern shown in several distinctions of Peter Lombard's *Sentences*, composed probably in the very years that Elizabeth was experiencing her visions of the Assumption, for the way that body and soul are integral to each other.[76] When one thinks of all these things, *there* is the culture in which the idea of Mary's bodily assumption into heaven began to be established.

Obviously the idea of Mary as Queen of Angels was not soft-

---

[74] Caroline Walker Bynum, *Holy Feast and Holy Fast: The Religious Significance of Food to Medieval Women* (Berkeley and Los Angeles, 1987), 253.

[75] Adolf Katzenellenbogen, *The Sculptural Programs of Chartres Cathedral* (Norton, NY, 1959), 43–4.

[76] *Magistri Petri Lombardi Sententiae*, 2 vols (Grottaferrata, 1971), esp. 1.8.5 (1:99, cf. 265); 2.1.6 (1:334–6); 2,19.1–3 (1:422–4); 2.31.4 (1:506–8); 4.44 (on the Resurrection of the Dead).1, 2, 3, 5, 7 (all 2:516–21).

pedalled in the middle decades of the twelfth century; this was indeed the very period when the iconography of the coronation by Christ in heaven caught on in the west. But the development of the other idea, added to it, of the bodily assumption, was part of a new era in the history of Christian humanism.

Christ Church Oxford

EARLY MEDIEVAL LATIN POETRY OF MARY

by WALTER BERSCHIN

IN the tenth century Gandersheim was a small, proudly independent principality ruled by women. All who belonged to Gandersheim (except for the servants) were of noble birth, taking vows as canonesses – that is, free to leave the abbey, if they wanted.[1] Hrotsvit, born around 935, was one of these canonesses. She was well aware of her talent for writing Latin[2] and – as she confessed later in a rhyming prose-preface – 'was not to lie sluggish in the heart's dark cavern and be destroyed by the rust of negligence, but rather struck by the hammer of unfailing diligence, was to echo some small ringing note of divine praise.'[3] 'In complete secrecy' she began to write poems based on writings she had found in the library of Gandersheim.

Her first work was the life of Mary, covering the period from her birth until the flight to Egypt with her son Jesus and her bridegroom Joseph. Mary's parents Joachim and Anna had remained childless for twenty years. A comment about this by the scribe of the temple so offended Joachim that he disappeared for some time. After five months Anna having finished her prayer 'raised her eyes and beheld in the branches of a laurel some birds carolling in sweet melodies and covering their young with downy wings'

(122) His ita finitis sublatis cernit ocellis
     in ramis lauri resonantes murmure dulci
     Pullos plumigeris volucres circumdare pennis.

Passionately Anna continues to pray and solemnly promises: if she were to have a child, it would be offered to God in the temple. Joachim returns. Waiting at the Golden Gate Anna 'beheld him with astonished eyes' and 'across those flowery fields she sped to meet him and she threw herself into his cherished embrace':

---

[1] Cf. H. Goetting, *Das reichsunmittelbare Kanonissenstift Gandersheim*, Germania Sacra, ns 7 (Berlin and New York, 1973).
[2] There is a new Teubner-edition of her works: *Hrotsvit: Opera omnia*, ed. Walter Berschin (Munich and Leipzig, 2001).
[3] Hrotsvit, Liber I: Legendae, praef. (ed. Berschin, 2). The English translations of the *Maria* below are cited from Gonsalva Wiegand, *The Non-dramatic Works of Hrosvitha* (St Louis, MO, 1936), 14–65.

(253)   Scilicet attonitis quem cum conspexit ocellis,
      Caro florigerum percurrerat obvia campum
      Ipsius et collo sese suspendit amando . . .

In the later Middle Ages this scene became a favourite subject for paintings.

Exactly nine months later the longed-for child is born and a mighty voice from heaven names her Maria, that is 'sea star', because she will shine forever in the Crown of Christ.

(276)   'Stella maris' lingua quod consonat ergo latina;
      Hoc nomen merito sortitur sancta puella,
      Est quia praeclarum sidus, quod fulget in evum
      Regis <in> aeterni claro diademate Christi.

(In the English translation of Gonsalva Wiegand: 'Stella maris, as our Latin tongue has it! Fittingly was this name conferred upon that holy child, because she is the brightest star shining for aye in the beautiful diadem of the eternal Christ.')

When Mary is two years old, she is presented to the Temple; she hurries up the fifteen steps without looking back to her parents. This scene is well known to art-historians as well. Now the little Mary begins living a saintly life in the temple with other girls, praying the psalter and working with purple threads and wool. Later her special task is to weave the purple curtain of the Temple of Jerusalem – the same curtain which according to Matthew and Luke 'was rent in twain from the top to the bottom' in the hour of the death of Mary's son. She is spinning the purple wool when the Angel enters her room and announces that she is to become the Mother of Christ:

(518)   Post haec secreta residebat in aede quieta
      Purpureos digitis filos operans benedictis.
      Angelus et summus Gabrihel conspectibus eius
      Astitit astrigera celorum lapsus ab aula.

(Hrotsvit has here made use of the dactylic metrical foot to give an idea of the manner of spinning. Besides the thread – *filos* – everything moves quickly.)

While Mary was in the Temple, the High Priests had engaged her to be married to an old man named Joseph. 'And it came to pass in those days, that there went out a decree from Caesar Augustus, that all the world should be taxed.' Joseph travels with his pregnant fiancee to

Bethlehem, the *patria* of his stock. Near Bethlehem, 'with the eyes of her mind', the young wife sees two crowds of people on the path, one laughing and the other weeping. Mary tells Joseph about her vision, but he angrily answers: 'Keep upright on your mount and do not talk a lot of nonsense, please!'

> (549) Aspexit non corporeis, sed mentis ocellis
> Comminus alma duos virguncula stare popellos,
> Unum ridentem necnon alium lacrimantem.
> Quod Ioseph vetulo narrans audivit ab illo:
> 'Contine subiecto tantum te rite iumento
> Et noli, posco, narrare superflua verba!'

The child is born in an underground cave at midnight. Two midwives are in attendance, Zelemi and Salome. Zelemi immediately is convinced that this birth is an extraordinary one; Salome tries to examine whether the mother of the child might still be a virgin or not. When she touches Mary, her right arm is paralyzed, but by grazing the swaddling clothes of the child, Salome is healed and believes.

The stories of the shepherds abiding in the field and visiting the babe lying in a manger, and of the wise men from the East, who came to worship the Saviour, are mentioned by Hrotsvit in a few words only; for these tales were well known from St Luke and St Matthew. She concentrates upon what is found about Mary in other writings; for example, what happened during the flight to Egypt.[4]

Once Mary stopped to rest beside a hollow in the desert. While she was sitting there with her child, many dragons came out. But the little boy stood up in his mother's lap and the dragons adored him; he walked on and they followed him. The parents began to fear this child, but he said: 'Why do you see my childlike limbs and not the eternal power of my mind? I seem to be a little child, but I am also an almighty man and so it is quite suitable that all the wild animals become tame before me.'

> (725) 'Quamvis humanis sim parvus homuntio membris,
> Vir tamen omnipotens summo sum numine pollens,

---

[4] Hrotsvit's principal source was the so-called *Protevangelium Iacobi* (or Pseudo-Matthaeus): *Liber de ortu beatae Mariae et infantia salvatoris*, ed. C. Tischendorf, *Evangelia apocrypha*, 2nd edn (Leipzig, 1876), 51–111. For other editions see M. Geerard, *Clavis apocryphorum Novi Testamenti* (Turnhout, 1992), no. 51.

> Condecet atque feras silve mansuescere cunctas
> Me coram rabie dimissa rite priore.'

Indeed, the artists of the middle ages often showed Christ in the lap of his mother with the limbs of a two-year-old child, but with the strong facial expression of an adult.

Lions and leopards join the dragons and show the way through the desert – which Hrotsvit seems to imagine like the tremendous woods then covering a great part of Germany. As the beasts guide them, they feed on grass along with the flock of Joseph; the wolf and the lamb feed together, the lions do not attack the oxen, because the peace of God has descended upon the earth.

And again Mary, exhausted by the tiresome flight through the desert, needs a rest. Sitting under a palm she looks up at the leaves of the tree, sees the coconuts and says: 'If I could have one . . .' Again she is sharply criticized by Joseph, the *senior vetulus iustus* (v. 760); what is really needed, he says, is not a coconut, but water! Mary is consoled immediately by her little boy, who with words alluding to the hymn on the Cross by Venantius Fortunatus,[5] orders the palm to bend down so that his mother 'may pluck from' the tree 'as much fruit as she wishes':

> (775) 'Arbor, flecte tuos summo de vertice ramos,
> Ut, quantum libeat, de te mater mea carpat.'

The palm obeys, and is rewarded by the divine child. An angel descends and takes the tree with him to plant in the new Paradise. Where the palm had been rooted, a spring gives water to Joseph, his servants, the cattle, and the beasts which accompany the Holy Family along the way through the desert.

Arriving in Egypt, Mary and her child enter a temple full of idols. In the presence of the true Son of God all the false images of gods fall down. The priests of the temple hope that the head of the town will punish the strangers severely. But one man, Afrodisius, is the first outside Palestine to adore Jesus, and Hrotsvit joins in the praise of God, who has shown himself to mankind in a paradoxical way: he who is able to enclose the whole world in the palm of his hand does not despise to be wrapped in swaddling clothes of little worth:

> (873) Quique vales proprio mundum concludere palmo,
> Panniculis stringi non raris haut respuisti.

---

[5] Venantius Fortunatus, *Pange, lingua, gloriosi proelium certaminis* (carm.II 2) str.9: *Flecte ramos, arbor alta . . .*

* * *

Salve, regina misericordiae,
vita, dulcedo et spes nostra, salve!
Ad te clamamus exsules filii Evae,
ad te suspiramus gementes et flentes
in hac lacrimarum valle.
Eia ergo, advocata nostra,
Illos tuos misericordes oculos ad nos converte
et Iesum, benedictum fructum ventris tui,
nobis post hoc exsilium ostende.
O clemens, o pia,
o dulcis Maria.

The *Salve regina*[6] is a poem, but not a metrical or regularly rhythmical one. The form is that of emphatic speaking which was and is known through the psalter and the so called *cantica* like *Benedictus* and *Magnificat*. Their irregular form of poetry, very uncommon in the Roman world, had already found its way into Latin Christianity in the third or fourth century with the *Gloria in excelsis deo* or the so called *Canticum Ambrosianum (Te deum laudamus, te dominum confitemur . . .)*. It was an Englishman who discovered and described the rules on which this archaic or oriental form of poetry is organized: Robert Lowth from Winchester, later Bishop of London, was the first to speak of the *Parallelismus membrorum* in his book *De sacra poesi hebraeorum* (Oxford 1753), which five years later appeared in a German version.[7] Since that time the rhetoric of Biblical poetry and its successors has been no problem for philologists: everything is said twice with slight variations. So we read in Psalm 2.4:

> Qui habitat in caelis inridebit eos
> et dominus subsannabit eos

> (He that sitteth in the heavens shall laugh:
> the Lord shall have them in derision.)

Qui habitat in caelis is the *dominus*, and *inridere* and *subsannare* are almost the same, so that indeed the two halves of the verse form a parallel.

---

[6] The text given here represents the older form of the poem; later it was slightly extended: *mater misericordiae* and *dulcis virgo Maria*.

[7] R. Lowth, *De sacra poesi Hebraeorum* (Oxford, 1753; repr. London, 1995). German translation by J.D. Michaelis, *Roberti Lowth A.M., collegii novi socii et poeticae publici praelectoris, De sacra poesi Hebraeorum praelectiones* (Göttingen, 1758).

The *Te deum* imitates this repetitious style (*Wiederholungsstil*): *Te deum laudamus / te dominum confitemur*. *Deus* and *Dominus* mean the same; one of the three senses of *confiteri* is 'to praise'. Repetition is also one of the secrets of the *Salve regina*, but it occurs in a more sophisticated way at the beginning and the end. The salutation formula *Salve* stands at the beginning and at the end of the first sentence:

> *Salve*, regina . . ., *salve*
>
> (Hail Queen of mercy, our life, our sweetness and our hope. Hail to thee.)

The two most heavily stressed parts of the Latin sentence are the first and the last words. In the *Salve regina* these two points are marked by biblical parallelism. The rest of the clause is formed by a series of four invocations, following each other like the pearls of a necklace: *regina misericordiae - vita - dulcedo - spes nostra*.

The second sentence describes the situation of the speakers or singers:

> Ad te clamamus . . .
> Ad te suspiramus . . . in hac lacrimarum valle
>
> (To thee we do cry, poor banished children of Eve. To thee we send our sighs, mourning and weeping in the valley of tears.)

As we can see, this part of the song also fits quite neatly into the concept of the *Parallelismus membrorum*.

The third sentence begins with an exclamation and an unusual (fifth) invocation –

> Eia ergo, advocata nostra
>
> (Oh thou, our Advocate)

– and continues with a request

> Illos tuos misericordes oculos ad nos converte et . . . ostende
>
> (Turn thine eyes of mercy towards us. And after this our exile show unto us the blessed fruit of thy womb, Jesus.)

So the poem seems to be a prayer with its typical triple step:[8]

---

[8]   Cf. J.A. Jungmann, *Missarum sollemnia*, 1, 3rd edn (Vienna, 1952), 480.

invocatio
↓
praedicatio
↓
petitio

It ends with three other invocations: *O clemens, o pia, o dulcis* (O clement, O loving, O sweet), so that we are – as it were – climbing up a ladder of eight invocations and the ninth and final rung is the name Maria.

In other words, t3he Salutation goes through the whole poem; no fewer than eight times the Queen of Heaven is addressed, from *regina misericordiae* to *dulcis*, and finally these emphatic invocations lead to the name *Maria*.

In around 1500 this famous prayer was ascribed to Hermannus Contractus – Hermann the Cripple – of Reichenau.[9] Much earlier a note by Jacobus de Voragine states that a Spanish bishop, Petrus of Compostela (*c*.986–1000), was the author of the *Salve regina*.[10] Another writer of the thirteenth century, however, Alberich of Trois-Fontaines, says that the *Salve regina* was composed by a French bishop, Ademar of Le Puy-en-Velay (1087–1100).[11] The *Vita quarta* of Bernard of Clairvaux, written between 1180 and 1182, knows that St Bernard heard the prayer from the mouth of an angel and sent the text to Pope Eugenius III in order to notify it to the whole of Christendom.[12] All these attributions, including that to Hermannus Contractus, seem to be fabulous. Manuscript evidence of the *Salve regina* goes back to the eleventh century.[13]

* * *

Alma redemptoris mater, quae pervia caeli
porta manes et stella maris, succurre cadenti,
surgere qui curat, populo, tu, quae genuisti

---

[9] Johannes Trithemius (d.1516), *Chronica insignis monasterii Hirsaugiensis ad a.1047*, in *Johannis Trithemii opera historica*, ed. M. Freher, 2 vols (Frankfurt, 1601), 2:50–1.

[10] Jacobus de Voragine (d.1299), *Legenda aurea*, c. 177 (181), 'De sancto Pelagio papa': ed. G.P. Maggioni, 2 vols, Millennio medievale, 6 (Florence, 1998), 2:1272; ed. T. Graesse, 3rd edn (Breslau, 1890), 836.

[11] Alberich of Trois-Fontaines (d. after 1252), *Chronica ad a.1130*: P. Scheffer-Boichorst, 'Albrici monachi Triumfontium Chronicon', *MGH Scriptores*, 23 (Hanover, 1874), 828.

[12] Johannes Eremita, *Vita (IV) S.Bernardi*, II.7 (*PL* 185, col. 544). For this Life in the context of the other biographies of St Bernard, W. Berschin, *Biographie und Epochenstil im lateinischen Mittelalter*, 4/ii (Stuttgart, 2001), 326.

[13] H. Oesch, *Berno und Hermann von Reichenau als Musiktheoretiker* (Berne, 1961), 149–50.

natura mirante tuum sanctum genitorem,
virgo prius ac posterius, Gabrielis ab ore
sumens illud Ave, peccatorum miserere.

Like the *Salve regina* the *Alma redemptoris mater* is attributed by the later medieval tradition to Hermannus.[14] The ascription has a higher degree of probability, if we consider the sophisticated form of the poem.[15] Like the *Salve regina*, the *Alma redemptoris mater* is a prayer. It begins with the *invocatio* 'Gracious mother of the Redeemer', which is followed by the *praedicatio* of Mary

'quae . . . porta manes et stella maris'

('who dost remain the open gate to heaven and the star of the sea.')

The third part of the Christian prayer is the *petitio*, which follows immediately:

succurre . . . populo

('Help a falling people who seek to rise.')

What is very special about this poem or Marian Antiphon is that these three steps are repeated in a slightly larger expanded form:

2nd *invocatio*: *tu* ('thou')
2nd *praedicatio*, first half: *quae genuisti . . . tuum sanctum genitorem* ('who while Nature stood amazed, gavest birth to Him who made thee')
   second half: *virgo . . . sumens illud 'Ave'* ('Virgin before and after [his human birth], Thou who didst receive the greetings of Gabriel')
2nd *petitio*: *peccatorum miserere* ('have mercy on sinners')

In the 1950s and 1960s, when there was still a lot of Latin to be heard in the churches, the *Alma redemptoris* was often read like a prose prayer. But the Antiphon consists of six perfect hexameters. The poet shows his finesse, for example, in not putting the break exactly in the middle of the poem, but in the third line, so that he had a little more space for the second series of three steps. The verse form reveals another stylistic

---

[14]   Here our first instance is the *Legenda aurea*, c.177 (181); see n.10.
[15]   Cf. W. Berschin, *Eremus und Insula. St.Gallen and die Reichenau im Mittelalter – Modell einer lateinischen Literaturlandschaft* (Wiesbaden, 1987), 17–18.

feature of the poem, that is the enjambment. One sentence runs from line 1 to 2 and another from line 5 to the end with little or no pause: 'quae pervia caeli porta manes ... Gabrielis ab ore sumens illud Ave ...'.

Some other peculiarities could be mentioned. The essence of our interpretation is that, on the formal level, by doubling the prayer the poet expressed the emphasis of his devotion to Mary. Repetition no longer meant saying the same thing in the same or slightly different words; this old form of religious speaking now was refined by the rules of Latin poetry and the result was a new mixture of the oriental and classical western traditions. Another innovation – on the level of content – seems to be the fact that at the end of the poem Mary is addressed not only as an intercessor, but directly as the Mother of the Saviour; she shall 'have mercy on sinners'.

* * *

(1) Ave, preclara
maris stella,
in lucem gentium,
Maria divinitus orta.

(2a) Euge, dei porta,
que non aperta
veritatis lumen
ipsum solem iusticie
indutum carne
ducis in orbem.

(2b) Virgo decus mundi,
regina celi,
preelecta ut sol,
pulchra lunaris ut fulgor,
agnosce omnes
te diligentes.

(3a) Te lignum vite
virgam alme stirpis Iesse
nascituram priores
desideraverant
patres et prophete.

(3b) Te plenam fide
sancto rorante pneumate
parituram divini
floris amigdalum
signavit Gabriel.

(4a) Tu agnum, regem,
terre dominatorem
Moabitici
de petra deserti
ad montem filie
Syon transduxisti.

(4b) Tuque furentem
Leviathan,   serpentem
tortuosumque
et vectem, collidens
dampnoso crimine
mundum exemisti.

. . .

(6a) Fac fontem dulcem,
quem in deserto
petra premonstravit,

(6b) Fac igni sancto
patrisque verbo,
quod rubus ut flammam

degustare   tu portasti,
cum sincera fide   virgo mater facta,
renesque constringi   pecuali pelle
lotos in mari,   discincto pede
anguem eneum   mundis labiis
in cruce speculari.   cordeque propinquare.

(7a)   Audi nos,   (7b)   Salva nos,
       nam te filius   Iesu, pro quibus
       nihil negans honorat.   virgo mater te orat.

(8a)   Da fontem boni visere,   (8b)   quo hausto sapientie
       da pure mentis oculos   saporem vite valeat
       in te defigere,   mens intelligere,

(9)   christianismi fidem
     operibus redimire
     beatoque fine
     ex huius incolatu seculi,
     auctor, ad te transire.

Ave, praeclara maris stella, formally a sequence, is also ascribed to Hermannus Contractus and according to recent investigations rightly so.[16] Hermannus Contractus was a pioneer in mathematics, astronomy, historiography, and musical theory. For Matthew Paris (d.1259) of St Alban's he was one of the great philosophers. He drew him between 1240 and 1250. Matthew's manuscript, Oxford Ashmole 304, shows Hermannus together with Euclid.[17] Hermannus holds in his right hand the Astrolabium, the astronomic instrument whose construction he had described in a very successful booklet, *De mensura astrolabii*.[18] Matthew Paris did not know anything about Hermann's handicap. It is, however, certain that Hermann was a cripple. According to the biography which one of his students wrote, Hermann 'suffered even as a child from paralysis down both sides. His limbs were so stiff that he could not

[16] B. Klein-Ilbeck, *Antidotum vitae. Die Sequenzen Hermanns des Lahmen* (Dissertation, University of Heidelberg, 1992; microfiche 1998). The Latin text of the sequence is from this dissertation. Previous edn: C. Blume and G.M. Dreves, *Hymnographi latini: lateinische Hymnendichter des Mittelalters*, Analecta Hymnica, 48, 50 (Leipzig, 1905–7), 2:313–15.
[17] F. Saxl and H. Meier, *Verzeichnis astrologischer und mythologischer illustrierter Handschriften des lateinischen Mittelalters*, 3 (1953), 287–8, and pl. 55 (ill. 141). For the date of the drawing see R. Vaughan, *Matthew Paris* (Cambridge, 1958), 230.
[18] Edited in J. Drecker, 'Hermannus Contractus: Über das Astrolab', *Isis*, 16 (1931), 200–19. Many manuscripts are cited by Oesch, *Berno und Hermann*, 162–4. Somewhat speculative is A. Borst, *Astrolab und Klosterreform an der Jahrtausendwende* (Heidelberg, 1989).

Plate 1   Between 1240 and 1250 Matthew Paris of St Alban's wrote a
collection of fortune-telling tracts and illustrated it with a number of
drawings. The first of them shows *Euclid* and *Hermann*. Hermann of
Reichenau holds in his right hand the *Astrolabium,* whose construction
he had described in a successful booklet: Bodley, MS Ashm. 304, fol. 2v.
(Reproduced by permission of the Bodleian Library, University of Oxford)

move away from the place where he had been seated . . . In his chair, however, he was a good teacher, although he spoke slowly and could be understood only with great difficulty.' This according to his disciple Berthold of Reichenau.[19]

There is another and hagiographically better story in an English manuscript from St Augustine's in Canterbury from the early twelfth century.[20] An angel came to Hermann and provided the following choice for the course of his further life: health without special wisdom, or a great step forward in the sciences at the price of the weakness of his body. Herman chose science and wisdom and therefore he was struck by paralysis.

As a poet Hermann wrote only five sequences. *Ave praeclara maris stella* seems to have been his contribution to the principal religious holiday of Reichenau,[21] which was (and is) the Assumption of the Virgin Mary on 15 August.

What is a sequence? It is a new kind of sacred chant invented and developed on the basis of existent Alleluia-melodies in the ninth century.[22] The Alleluia sung between the Epistle and the Gospel of the mass was replaced by a chant, which gave to each note of the Alleluia one syllable of the poem. Since the Alleluia was sung by two choirs, that of the abbot's side and that of the prior's side – and the melody the first choir sang was repeated by the second – the sequence consists of couplets with the same number of syllables and sung to the same melody. Excepted are the introductory and final stanzas. Instead of the monosyllable – 'a' – of the word 'Alleluia', the melody now bore a text fitting to the holidays; and additionally the text had a mnemotechnical function: now it was easier for the monks to keep in mind the difficult and long melodies of that Alleluia between Epistle and Gospel.

Considering a well-edited sequence you see at first glance the paral-

[19] 'Bertholdi annales, a. 1054–1080', *MGH Scriptores*, 5 (Hanover, 1844), 267.

[20] 'corporis salutem sine magna sapientia vel maximam scientiam cum corporis inbecillitate': Bodley, MS Digby 174 , fol. 210v, printed by Borst, *Astrolab*, 91. Another legend of this type was edited from Cambridge, Corpus Christi College, MS 111 (twelfth century), by J. Handschin, 'Hermannus Contractus-Legenden – nur Legenden?', *Zeitschrift für deutsches Altertum*, 72 (1935), 1–8.

[21] 'Reichenau . . . has a virtual monopoly of the Dormition and Assumption of the Virgin in the surviving manuscript art of the Ottonians': H. Mayr-Harting, *Ottonian Book Illumination. An Historical Study*, 2 vols, 2nd edn (1999), 1:145.

[22] The best introduction to the form of the sequence is the preface which Notker Balbulus of St Gall (d.912) wrote to his *Liber hymnorum*, ed. W. von den Steinen, *Notker der Dichter und seine geistige Welt*, 2 vols (Berne, 1948), 2:8–10.

Plate 2 *Ave preclara maris stella,* one of the five sequences by Herman the Cripple was well known in medieval England. The manuscript, BL, MS Royal 2.B.IV (fol. 178v–179r) belongs according to R.M. Thomson (*Manuscripts from St Albans Abbey, 1066–1235* (Woodbridge, 1982), 1:29) to the books of high quality which survive from the abbacy of Ralph Gubiun of St Alban's (1146–51). (Reproduced by permission of the British Library)

lelism of the couplets. They do not only have exactly the same number of syllables, but sometimes also the same words at the beginning of the strophes, *Te-Te, Tu-Tu,* and so on. Often the last words of the strophes echo those of the preceding one by a rhyme: *transduxisti – exemisti, honorat – orat, defigere – intelligere.* Also, the first word of the whole sequence and the last one should be noticed. AVE is said and sung at the beginning. It was a very common idea during the Middle Ages that this AVE was not a casual salutation of Mary; for read backwards the word is EVA; 'Ave' means that the new Eve, namely Mary, would repair the failure of the mother of mankind, would not follow the suggestion of the serpent, but would be she who 'shall bruise' 'the head' of the serpent (Genesis 3.15). The last words are those of the petitio directed to Jesus – *Da . . ., auctor, ad te transire.*

It is impossible to mention here the images which follow each other stanza by stanza and sometimes even line by line. An almost 'baroque flamboyance of language and imagery'[23] goes through the text, with a lot of citations which for Hermann could be very brief, since his audience – the monks – knew the Bible and the Fathers. In the couplets beginning with *Fac*, for example, the spring in the desert coming out of the rock is followed by the 'loins girded' (Exodus 12.11), the waters of the Red Sea (*lotos in mari*) and the 'Serpent of brass upon the pole' (Numbers 21.9).

The answering choir evokes the flame of fire out of the 'midst of a bush' (Exodus 3.2), which is interpreted as the Word of the Father; whilst the bush itself is Mary, who has given birth to the flame. She will help us to pull off our shoes and to draw nigh hither to the fire with pure lips and a pure heart.

Music became Poetry through the Carolingian invention of the sequence; now Poetry becomes Theology in the High Middle Ages. One could try to go further and show how in the well-known sequence *Stabat mater* at the end of the thirteenth century theology was transformed into compassion. Latin medieval poetry of Mary is fascinating because it expresses most clearly and often emphatically what men longed for in their epoch.

Ruprecht-Karls-Universität, Heidelberg

---

23 P. Dronke, *The Medieval Lyric*, 2nd edn (London, 1978), 44–5.

KING HENRY III AND THE BLESSED VIRGIN MARY*

by NICHOLAS VINCENT

UCH has been written of the Marian devotions of King Louis IX of France. Louis, so we are told, would mortify his flesh on the vigils of the four principal feasts of the Virgin.[1] Regular pilgrimages were made by the King to the great Marian shrines of France, most notably those of Chartres and Rocamadour.[2] Day by day, in his own chapel, the King listened to matins, tierce and compline sung with the appropriate offices of Our Lady, and on Tuesdays and Saturdays the Mass itself was dedicated to the Virgin.[3] When the King took communion, which he did on six principal feast-days each year, two of these feasts, the Assumption and the Purification, were those of the Virgin.[4] Rather than listen to ribald or secular songs, Louis preferred the singing of the *Ave Maria stella*.[5] Amongst Louis' contemporaries, a similar devotion to Mary inspired King Alfonso X of Castile, composer of the elaborate *Cantigas de Santa Maria*. For both Louis and Alfonso, these devotions are assumed to have had political as well as spiritual overtones.[6] Jacques Le Goff, for example, has commented upon the three great objects of Louis IX's piety – the Virgin Mary as chief intercessor between the French nation and Christ, St Denis as saintly patron of French nationhood, and Christ himself, represented in the Passion relics of the Sainte-Chapelle – as a potent triumvirate, intended to foster the spiritual and dynastic ambitions of Capetian

---

* I am indebted to Paul Binski for valuable discussion and for several bibliographical references. To my former tutor, Henry Mayr-Harting, I owe whatever merits this article may possess.

[1] Geoffroy de Beaulieu, 'Vita et sancta conversatio piae memoriae Ludovici', in *Recueil des Historiens des Gaules et de la France*, ed. M. Bouquet *et al.*, 24 vols (Paris, 1738–1904), 20:10–11.

[2] J. Le Goff, *Saint Louis* (Paris, 1996), 538–40.

[3] *Vie de Saint Louis par Guillaume de Saint-Pathus confesseur de la reine Marguerite*, ed. H.-F. Delaborde (Paris, 1899), 33–5.

[4] Ibid., 39.

[5] Ibid., 19.

[6] For an introduction to the secondary literature on Alfonso's great collection, emphasising the political dimension in which Alfonso appears as intercessor with Mary on behalf of the people of Spain, see J. Le Goff, 'Le Roi, la Vierge, et les images: le manuscrit des "Cantigas de Santa Maria" d'Alphonse X de Castille', in P. de Clerck and E. Palazzo, eds, *Rituels: Mélanges offerts à Pierre-Marie Gy, O.P.* (Paris, 1990), 385–92.

France.[7] Amongst the symbols of Capetian kingship, the fleur de lys and perhaps the colour blue were both appropriated from the attributes of the Virgin Mary. Chroniclers, from Suger onwards, report the special protection afforded by the Virgin to the Capetians and their realm.[8] To this extent, the cult of Mary is recognized to have provided yet further expression to the Capetian pretensions to sacral as well as political authority.

By contrast, historians of the Norman and Plantagenet kings have shown almost complete indifference to the relationship between English kingship and the cult of the Virgin. Just as historians have assumed that, from the twelfth century onwards, royal sacrality began and ended south of Calais, so, with very few exceptions, the Marian devotions of the Norman and Plantagenet kings have been written out of English political history.[9] Not until the late fourteenth century, and then only as the result of the fortuitous survival of just one work of art, the Wilton Diptych, has the Virgin Mary been permitted to intrude upon our otherwise thoroughly desacralized notions of English kingship.[10] In what follows, I hope to demonstrate that Mary occupied a more prominent place in the thinking of England's twelfth- and thirteenth-century kings than has previously been admitted. In particular, I intend to show that King Henry III (1216–72) expressed a life-long devotion to the Virgin, and that Henry's piety, like that of Louis IX, was rich in both personal and political resonances. The documents to be cited – principally, the enrolled administrative evidences of English royal government – are of a very different nature to the biographical and hagiographical evidence used by Le Goff and others in their studies of the kings of France. For Henry III, we have a great wealth of administrative records but no hagiography and little, even in

---

[7] Le Goff, *Saint Louis*, 540.

[8] C. Beaune, *The Birth of an Ideology. Myths and Symbols of Nation in Late-Medieval France* (Berkeley, CA, 1991), 204–11, and for evidence of even more ancient devotions by the kings of France, see D. Iogna-Prat, 'Le culte de la Vierge sous le règne de Charles le Chauve', in *Marie: Le Culte de la Vierge dans la société médiévale*, ed. D. Iogna-Prat, E. Palazzo and D. Russo (Paris, 1996), 65–98.

[9] For the general background to Anglo-French approaches to 'sacrality', see N. Vincent, *The Holy Blood: King Henry III and the Westminster Blood Relic* (Cambridge, 2001), esp. 188–96; idem, 'The pilgrimages of the Angevin Kings of England 1154–1272', in C. Morris and P. Roberts, eds, *Pilgrimage, the English Experience from Becket to Bunyan*, (Cambridge, 2002), 12–45, esp. 30–45.

[10] For brief remarks on the Marian devotions of Richard II, see S. Mitchell, 'Richard II, kingship and the cult of saints', in D. Gordon, L. Monnas, and C. Elam, eds, *The Regal Image of Richard II and the Wilton Diptych* (1997), 123–4.

Matthew Paris, that can be considered as deliberate biographical reporting. For Louis IX, by contrast, we have a wealth of biography but little save charters by way of administrative record. Even Louis' charters are not as yet properly surveyed. Nonetheless, this great contrast between the evidences for France and England should not be allowed to obscure the great similarity, in intention if not in outcome, between Capetian and Plantagenet approaches to the holy and in particular to the cult of the Blessed Virgin Mary.

That Mary should have loomed large in English royal spirituality is hardly surprising. From a very early date, England stood at the forefront of Marian devotion.[11] In the immediate aftermath of the Norman Conquest, it was in England that writers such as Dominic of Evesham, Anselm of Bury, or William of Malmesbury assembled some of the earliest and most influential collections of the miracles of the Virgin.[12] Specifically, it was in England that the feast of the Immaculate Conception was most vigorously championed, at the royal foundations of Ramsey, Bury, St Albans, Gloucester, Westminster, and Reading.[13] Here, at the very start of our enquiry, we meet evidence of a royal interest in the cult of the Virgin. King Henry I, himself the subject of at least one later Marian miracle story (albeit as the victim rather than the beneficiary of Mary's intercession), is said to have prayed to the Virgin before his victory over Louis VI at the battle of Brémule in 1119.[14] A

---

[11] For the general background and for an introduction to the secondary literature for English Marian devotions both before and after 1066, see the important studies by M. Clayton, *The Cult of the Virgin Mary in Anglo-Saxon England* (Cambridge, 1990), and N. Morgan, 'Texts and images of Marian devotion in thirteenth-century England', in W.M. Ormrod, ed., *England in the Thirteenth Century*, Harlaxton Medieval Studies, 1 (Stamford, CA, 1991), 69–103.

[12] R.W. Southern, 'The English origins of the "Miracles of the Virgin"', *Mediaeval and Renaissance Studies*, 4 (1958), 176–216.

[13] The classic article here remains that by Edmund Bishop, 'On the origins of the Feast of the Conception of the Blessed Virgin Mary', in his *Liturgica Historica* (Oxford, 1918), 238–59. For an introduction to the more recent secondary literature, see C.H. Talbot, 'Nicholas of St Albans and Saint Bernard', *Revue Bénédictine*, 64 (1954), 83–117; R.M. Dessì and M. Lamy, 'Saint Bernard et les controverses mariales au Moyen-Age', in P. Arabeyre et al., eds, *Vies et légendes de Saint Bernard de Clairvaux*, Cîteaux: Commentarii Cistercienses Textes et Documents, 5 (Cîteaux, 1993), 230–60. For Gloucester, see *The Original Acta of St Peter's Abbey, Gloucester, c.1122 to 1263*, ed. R.B. Patterson, Gloucestershire Record Series, 11 (1998), xxv.

[14] *Liber monasterii de Hyda*, ed. E. Edwards, RS (1866), 317, and for a miracle story involving Henry I, preserved in the vast fifteenth-century collection now at Cambridge, Sidney Sussex College, see M.R. James, *A Descriptive Catalogue of the Manuscripts in the Library of Sidney Sussex College, Cambridge* (Cambridge, 1895), 101 no.98, from Sidney Sussex College, MS 94, fol. 190v, where the Virgin is said to have rescued a nun threatened with rape by the King.

decade later, it is King Henry who is said to have insisted upon the observance of the feast of the Conception at his own foundation, Reading abbey, supplied with an appropriate Marian dedication and richly endowed with Marian relics, including portions of the Virgin's hair and garments.[15] Amongst Henry's successors, his grandson Henry II, the first Plantagenet king of England, demonstrated unmistakable devotion to the cult of Our Lady.

We might begin here with the King's itinerary. No doubt, by the 1150s, we should read no special significance into the timing of royal councils held at Candlemas (2 February, the feast of the Purification) or the Assumption (15 August). It was only natural that the King should hold great councils on the greater feasts of the saints. Nonetheless, was it mere coincidence that it should have been on 7 December 1154, the eve of the Virgin's Conception – that most English and most controversial of Marian feasts – that Henry first crossed the Channel, arriving in England on the feast-day itself, to be crowned King at Westminster a few days later?[16] Likewise, was it mere coincidence that led him to return to Normandy, presumably for his first post-coronation crown-wearing at the ducal capital in Rouen, on 2 February 1156, the feast of the Purification?[17] In 1158, Henry once again crossed to Normandy, sailing on 14 August, the vigil of the feast of the Assumption. A few weeks later, on the feast of the Virgin's Nativity (8 September), at Argentan, he summoned his expedition against Brittany.[18] The feast of the Assumption, it might be noted, was widely advertised in an Anglo-Norman poem by Master Wace, canon of

[15] For the claim that it was *prece regis Henrici* that abbot Hugh celebrated the feast at Reading, and for evidence of the introduction of the associated feast of St Anne, the mother of Mary, at Worcester Cathedral Priory, see *The Letters of Osbert of Clare Prior of Westminster*, ed. E.W. Williamson (Oxford, 1929), 11–15, 65–8 no. 7, esp. 67 ll. 19–21. For the Reading relics of Mary, recorded early in the thirteenth century, see BL, MS Egerton 3031 (Reading cartulary), fol. 6v: 'Reliquie de domina nostra sancta Maria: capillus sancte Marie ut putatur; de terra ubi nata fuit beata virgo Maria; de vestimento eius in quattuor locis; de lecto eius in duobus locis; de zona eius; de sepulcro eius in viii. locis.'

[16] Pending the appearance of the revised itinerary of Henry II by Dr Judith Everard, see R.W. Eyton, *Court, Household and Itinerary of King Henry II* (1878), 1, based upon Robert de Torigni, 'Chronica', in *Chronicles of the Reigns of Stephen, Henry II and Richard I*, ed. R. Howlett, 4 vols, RS (1885–9), 4:181–2, dated 7 Ides Dec.

[17] Eyton, *Court, Household and Itinerary*, 15–16, based upon Torigni, 'Chronica', in Howlett, *Chronicles*, 4:186. The King sailed in late Jan., in time to be in Rouen by 2 Feb.

[18] Eyton, *Court, Household and Itinerary*, 40–1, based upon Torigni and upon the Bec continuation of Torigni in *Chronicles*, ed. Howlett, 4:196, 318.

Bayeux and author of the *Roman de Rou*, this latter dedicated to and apparently commissioned by King Henry II.[19]

Around the feast of the Assumption, 15 August 1170, Henry fell ill in Normandy. Seeking a cure for both his personal and his political misfortunes, he made pilgrimage to the shrine of the Virgin Mary at Rocamadour – a pilgrimage whose significance has been thoroughly explored by Emma Mason.[20] Less well known is the timing of events a few years later, when Henry faced the gravest crisis of his reign, confronted by the rebellion of three of his four sons acting in alliance with the kings of Scotland and France. The Norman chronicler, Robert de Torigni, tells us that the raising of the French siege of Rouen on 14 August 1174, the vigil of Mary's Assumption, was widely interpreted as a portent of divine deliverance.[21] Thereafter, with the rebellion's collapse, it was on 8 September 1174, the feast of the Virgin's Nativity, that Henry met with Louis VII of France to discuss peace at Gisors, and on 8 December 1174, the feast of the Conception, that Henry negotiated his peace with the captured rebel, William I of Scotland, at Valognes. Two months later, at Le Mans, it was the feast of the Purification (2 February 1175) that was chosen to initiate the settlement with the King's sons, Richard and Geoffrey.[22] The Virgin, just as much as St Thomas of Canterbury, appears to have had a part to play in the great rebellion of 1174.

Besides his visit to Rocamadour, Henry issued charters for the Marian pilgrimage churches of Chartres and St-Pierre-sur-Dives.[23] In

---

[19] For a critical edition, see A. Pantel, *Das Altfranzösische Gedicht über die Himmelfahrt Mariä von Wace und dessen Überarbeitungen* (Greifswald, 1909).

[20] E. Mason, ' "Rocamadour in Quercy above all other churches": the healing of Henry II', *SCH*, 19 (1982), 39–54.

[21] Torigni, 'Chronica', in *Chronicles*, ed. Howlett, 4:265.

[22] Eyton, *Court, Household and Itinerary*, 184–8, based upon Torigni, 'Chronica', in *Chronicles*, ed. Howlett, 4:265; *Radulfi de Diceto decani Lundoniensis Opera historica*, ed. W. Stubbs, 2 vols, RS (1876), 1:396, 398; *Chronica Magistri Rogeri de Hovedene*, ed. W. Stubbs, 4 vols, RS (1868–71), 2:71.

[23] For Chartres, see *Recueil des Actes de Henri II roi d'Angleterre et duc de Normandie concernant les provinces françaises et les affaires de France*, ed. L. Delisle and E. Berger, 3 vols (Paris, 1916–27), 1:228–9 no.123, 2:142–3 no.563. For Henry and St-Pierre-sur-Dive, whose miracles worked by the Virgin after 1145 are set out in a report published by L. Delisle, 'Lettre de l'abbé Haimon sur la construction de l'église de Saint-Pierre-sur-Dive en 1145', *Bibliothèque de l'École des Chartes* [hereafter *BÉC*], 21 (1860), 113–39, see *Rotuli chartarum*, ed. T.D. Hardy (1835), 35. Amongst other Norman churches patronized by Henry, note the miracles of the Virgin reported earlier in the twelfth century at Coutances cathedral: E.-A. Pigeon, *Histoire de la cathédrale de Coutances* (Coutances, 1876), 367–83, including at 378–9 reference to a hair-relic of the Virgin.

June 1187, the impending confrontation between Henry and Philip of France was brought to a sudden halt by events at Déols in the suburbs of Châteauroux, where a mercenary in the service of Richard, Henry's son, struck off the arm of an image of the Virgin and Child, giving rise to a miraculous flow of blood. The miraculous blood and the subsequent wonders, in which the statue of Our Lady is said to moved and to have bared her breast, were interpreted on all sides as divine portents. Henry is said to have viewed the relics of the miracle. Richard, the future King of England, is said to have offered to defend the miracle's authenticity by trial of arms. Even John, the youngest and arguably the least pious of Henry's sons, was sufficiently impressed to make off with the stone arm, removed from Déols by stealth to add to John's private relic collection.[24]

Under both Richard and John, the Kings' itineraries supply little evidence of deliberate timing according to the feasts of Mary.[25] Nonetheless, both Kings maintained an interest in the Virgin's cult. Richard is said to have taken a personal interest in the Marian miracles of Chartres, receiving the canons on their fundraising tour after the disastrous fire of 1194 and personally carrying the reliquary which they brought with them, on his own shoulders.[26] Under John, and even at the height of the papal interdict, the fragmentary accounts of royal alms-giving supply clear evidence of a continuing awareness, if not necessarily a continuing observance, of the five feasts of the Virgin, including, most significantly, the feast of the Conception.[27] John's one

---

[24] J. Hubert, 'Le Miracle de Déols et la trève conclue en 1187 entre les rois de France et d'Angleterre', *BÉC*, 96 (1935), 285–300, esp. 298–300, with further details of the interest taken in the miracle by Henry II and his sons Richard and Geoffrey the chancellor in the brief excerpts from John Agnellus' once extensive collection of miracle stories, in P. Labbe, *Novae bibliothecae manuscriptorum librorum*, 2 vols (Paris, 1657), 1:319–22. The thief of the arm relic, described by Agnellus merely as *quidam vir illustris*, is identified as John by the Capetian chronicler Rigord: *Oeuvres de Rigord et de Guillaume le Breton*, ed. H.F.Delaborde, 2 vols (Paris, 1882–5), 1:79–80, whence Vincent of Beauvais, *Bibliotheca mundi seu speculi maioris*, 4 vols (Douai, 1624), 4:1199–1200.

[25] Under Richard, note perhaps the King's sailing from Genoa on 14 August 1190, his moving into winter quarters at Ramleh on 8 December 1191, and his judgement over Limoges on 25 March 1196: *The Itinerary of King Richard I*, ed. L. Landon, Pipe Roll Society, n.s. 13 (1935), 39, 58, 111.

[26] A. Thomas, 'Les Miracles de Notre-Dame de Chartres. Texte Latin inédit', *BÉC*, 42 (1881), 531.

[27] The 'Missae Roll 11 John' (1209–10), employs a calendar that includes the feasts of the Assumption, the Nativity, the Conception, the Annunciation and the Purification: *Rotuli de Liberate ac de Misis et Praestitis*, ed. T.D. Hardy (1844), 127, 130, 141, 148, 158. The 'Missae Roll 14 John' (1212–13), notes all feasts save that of the Conception, but nonetheless includes a payment of the King's gambling debts on 2 February 1213, suggesting a less than assiduous

religious foundation, at Beaulieu, was a Cistercian abbey and therefore necessarily dedicated to the Virgin Mary. Rather intriguingly, however, in 1206 an unnamed clerk is said to have carried letters into England addressed to King John from the Virgin Mary.[28] Much later, we find the most violent of all the many condemnations of King John, the so-called *Invectivum contra regem Iohannem*, composed in the 1250s or '60s, couched in the form of a letter addressed from Christ to the Virgin Mary; whilst at the Council of Oxford in 1222, the bishops are said to have sentenced to perpetual imprisonment a woman who had assumed the identity of Mary, acting in league with a man who had mutilated himself so as to assume the wounds of the crucified Christ.[29] The false Mary of 1222 was almost certainly deranged, claiming the power to celebrate mass with a chalice and a paten which she had fashioned from wax.[30] Nonetheless, these events should remind us that the cult of the Virgin could take on distinctly subversive features, in the case of the *Invectivum* and probably the letters of 1206 serving not so much to protect the King as to focus criticism upon royal misdeeds. In the *Invectivum*, for example, the Virgin not only seeks intercession for the people of England, but calls upon all the citizens of heaven and upon Christ, her son, to join her in saving mankind from the misgovernment of Church and state.[31] Rulers who ignored the retributive powers of the Virgin did so at their peril: a lesson that was brought home most forcefully in 1251 when the shepherds and poor people of northern France were inspired to millenarian lawlessness by letters supposedly sent from Mary, calling upon them to rise up and make pilgrimage to the Holy Land, promising them a victory that would be denied to the proud and

religious observance: *Documents Illustrative of English History in the Thirteenth and Fourteenth Centuries*, ed. H. Cole (1844), 238, 240, 251, 257, esp. 251.

[28] *Annales monastici*, ed. H.R. Luard, 5 vols, RS (1864–9), 1:58, 4:393–4.

[29] For the 'Invectivum', BL, MS Cotton Vespasian E iii, fols 171r–178v, see N. Vincent, 'Master Simon Langton, King John and the Court of France' (forthcoming). For the events of 1222, see *Councils and Synods with Other Documents Relating to the English Church II: 1205–1313*, ed. F.M. Powicke and C.R. Cheney, 2 vols (Oxford, 1964), 1:105–6.

[30] *Memoriale fratris Walteri de Coventria*, ed. W. Stubbs, 2 vols, RS (1872–3), 2:251–2.

[31] BL, MS Cotton Vespasian E iii, fol. 174v (164v, 171v): 'Cumque mater et virgo Maria pietate plena cum omni celesti curia perspiceret populos Anglie, Scotie, Hybernie in libro malorum operum cleri et prelatorum exemplari obcecatos infernalibus ministrare et obedire, ait omnibus sanctis et celi civibus universis: Venite dilecti mei mecum, et dominum Ihesum Cristum, quem genui, quem uberibus meis lactavi, quem infantulum more matris diligenter nutrivi, humiliter deprecemur ut in multitudine miserationum suarum omnium nationum et populorum et cleri totius mundi misereatur, ne infernis insatiabilis genus humanum morte et passione preciosa redemptum absorbeat, deglutiat in tenebris palpapilibus, in tormentis eternis, in penis millenis sine fine puniat'.

mighty of France and by inference to the crusading King Louis. For several weeks, the Capetian realm, from Paris to Bourges, was riven by civil disorder.[32] To what extent King Louis' subsequent devotion to the Virgin reflects a desire to stave off a recurrence of the affair of the 'pastoureaux' is a question which students of the King's religion have not seen fit to address. Even so, historians are in no doubt that the religiosity of Louis IX increased beyond measure on his return from the disastrous crusade of the 1250s: a disaster which he blamed in no small part upon his earlier failure to bring the laws and government of France into line with the laws and government ordained by God.[33]

At much the same time that Louis' government was attempting to suppress the disorders of the 'pastoureaux', the King of England, Henry III, passed the feast of the Annunciation, 25 March 1251, on pilgrimage to the shrine of Our Lady at Walsingham, his stay there made all the more memorable by a gift which he made of two silver candlesticks and an elaborate chasuble of red samite, purchased at a cost of more than £13.[34] The principal Marian shrine in England, Walsingham had been founded in the previous century supposedly as the result of a command from the Virgin to build a copy in England of the Holy House of Nazareth – the place where Mary had first received the announcement of Christ's conception from the archangel Gabriel. Henry's Walsingham pilgrimage of 1251 was but one of at least eleven pilgrimages he made to the shrine, and was the second such journey, the first having been made in March 1242, timed specifically to coincide with the feast of the Annunciation, the feast most intimately associated with Walsingham.[35] Henry III was indeed probably the first King to have visited the shrine at Walsingham, his earliest approach being made in April 1226.[36] He returned in August 1229, July 1232, June 1238, for the feast of the

[32] Matthew Paris, *Chronica majora*, ed. H.R. Luard, 7 vols, RS (1872–84), 5:246–54; Le Goff, *Saint Louis*, 195–8.

[33] In general, see W.C. Jordan, *Louis IX and the Challenge of the Crusade* (Princeton, NJ, 1979), ch. 6–8.

[34] For Henry's stay at Walsingham in March 1251, see *Close Rolls of the Reign of Henry III preserved in the Public Record Office*, 14 vols (1902–38) [hereafter CCR], *1247–51*, 425; *Calendar of the Patent Rolls preserved in the Public Record Office: Henry III*, 6 vols (1901–13) [hereafter CPR], *1247–58*, 91; *Calendar of the Liberate Rolls preserved in the Public Record Office: Henry III*, 6 vols (1916–64) [hereafter CLR], *1245–51*, 343. For the gifts, see CCR *1247–51*, 423; CLR *1245–51*, 343–4, 354.

[35] In general, for the shrine and for a summary of Henry's visits, see J.C. Dickinson, *The Shrine of Our Lady of Walsingham* (Cambridge, 1956), esp. 4–11, 17–19.

[36] For the visit in April 1226, see *Rotuli litterarum clausarum*, ed. T.D. Hardy, 2 vols (1833–44), 2:105.

Annunciation in March 1242 and March 1251, shortly before the feast of the Annunciation in March 1235, March 1245, March 1248 and March 1256, and again during his final tour of the shrines of East Anglia in September 1272, a few weeks before his own death.[37] As J.C. Dickinson has pointed out, the first of these pilgrimages appears to have had no particular Marian overtones, since in granting the canons of Walsingham an annual fair during his visit in April 1226, the King specified that the fair was to be held on the vigil and feast day of the Holy Cross, rather than on any of the feasts of Our Lady.[38] Thereafter, however, there are clear signs that it was the cult of the Virgin Mary that drew the King to Walsingham: in June 1239, for example when he ordered a wax taper to be burned before the Virgin's altar;[39] in December 1240 when he ordered 2,000 tapers to be burned there and at Bury St Edmunds for the feast of the Virgin's Conception;[40] in August 1241 and August 1242 when he ordered more than 3000 tapers to be burned for the feast of the Assumption;[41] on 25 March (the feast of the Annunciation) 1251, when he transferred the priory's fair to the feast day of the Virgin's Nativity each year in return for a wax candle to be burned in perpetuity before the great altar of Mary;[42] and in January 1246 when he ordered 20 marks to be spent on a golden crown to place upon the head of the image of Our Lady at Walsingham.[43] Some at least of these visits and gifts had political overtones. The pilgrimage of 1242, for example, and the elaborate ceremonial that surrounded it, came shortly before the King's proposed military expedition to Poitou. It was at Walsingham on 24 March 1242, the vigil of the feast of the Annunciation, that Henry first issued his summons to the knight service of England to attend him in arms in France.[44]

---

[37] For the King's visits, see *CCR 1227–31*, 199; *CCR 1231–4*, 82; *CCR 1234–7*, 59; *CCR 1237–42*, 58, 407–8; *CCR 1242–7*, 295; *CCR 1254–6*, 286; *CCR 1268–72*, 527; *CPR 1225–32*, 487–8, 520; *CPR 1247–58*, 10, 466; *CPR 1266–72*, 679; *Calendar of the Charter Rolls preserved in the Public Record Office*, 6 vols (1903–27) [hereafter *CChR*], *1226–57*, 165, 354; *CChR 1257–1300*, 184, 319; *CLR 1245–51*, 171; *CLR 1251–60*, 276, and for 1251 see above.

[38] Dickinson, *Shrine of Our Lady*, 17–18, citing *Rotuli litterarum clausarum*, 2:105.

[39] *CLR 1226–40*, 398; London, Public Record Office [hereafter PRO], E372/83 m.13.

[40] *CLR 1240–5*, 9.

[41] *CLR 1240–5*, 66, 143; *The Great Roll of the Pipe for the Twenty-Sixth Year of the Reign of King Henry the Third*, ed. H.L. Cannon, Yale Historical Publications: Manuscripts and Edited Texts, 5 (New Haven, CT, 1918), 190.

[42] *CChR 1226–57*, 354, and cf. 377.

[43] *CLR 1245–51*, 18.

[44] *CCR 1237–42*, 435, and note the 25 lbs of wax that the King awarded on the vigil of the Annunciation for making tapers: *CLR 1240–5*, 114.

Walsingham was merely the greatest of the Marian shrines of England to which the King rendered devotion. At Caversham, just across the river Thames from Reading, he is to be found as early as April 1235 presenting the chapel of St Mary with an expensive silk cloth.[45] In October 1238, he commanded timber to make a boat to transport pilgrims to the chapel, and thereafter regular gifts of timber for the chapel roof.[46] Tapers were burned there at the King's command in June 1239, and in August 1241 both at St Mary's Caversham and at St Mary's in the Strand at London, for the feast of the Virgin's Nativity.[47] In February 1246, Henry granted the chaplain of Caversham a richly embroidered chasuble in which to celebrate for the preservation of the King's spiritual health,[48] and in March 1254 offered a brooch there on behalf of his daughter Katherine, born a few months earlier but destined to die in infancy, perhaps from some congenital handicap.[49] Although there is no record of a royal visit to Caversham at any of the Virgin's feasts, it is worth remarking that the King was at Reading – less than two miles away and itself, as we have seen, a centre of Marian devotions – for the feast of the Annunciation in March 1228, the Conception in December 1234 and December 1241, the Assumption in August 1237, and the Purification in February 1246.[50]

Images of the Crucifixion with the Virgin and St John the Evangelist, of the Virgin with the three Magi, of the Virgin and Child, or of Mary alone, abound among the artistic commissions of Henry III recorded in the Close and Liberate Rolls.[51] Petitioners approaching the

---

[45] PRO, C47/3/4/1. For the Caversham shrine, served by the canons of Notley abbey, including a much later record of its relics, most notably the statue of the Virgin, see *Three Chapters of Letters relating to the Suppression of the Monasteries*, ed. T. Wright, Camden Series, 38 (1843), 221–7 nos 108–110; *CCR 1237–42*, 111.

[46] *CCR 1237–42*, 108, 111, 164, 375; *CLR 1245–51*, 31; *CLR 1251–60*, 260; *CCR 1256–9*, 397; *CCR 1259–61*, 121.

[47] *CLR 1226–40*, 398; *CLR 1240–5*, 66.

[48] *CCR 1242–7*, 393; *CLR 1245–51*, 36.

[49] PRO, C47/3/43 m.6, and for Katherine, born 25 Nov. 1253, died 3 May 1257, see M. Howell, 'The children of King Henry III and Eleanor of Provence', in P.R. Coss and S.D. Lloyd, eds, *Thirteenth Century England IV* (Woodbridge, 1992), 57, 63–4.

[50] See the typescript 'Itinerary of Henry III', on open access in the Map Room of the PRO.

[51] For crosses with Mary and John, see *CLR 1226–40*, 221, 260, 414, 452–3; *CLR 1240–5*, 216, 218; *CLR 1245–51*, 45, 83, 157, 239, 292, 294–5; *CLR 1251–60*, 57, 511. For images of Mary with her tabernacle, of the Annunciation, of Mary with the Magi, and of the Virgin and child, see e.g. *CLR 1226–40*, 51, 350; *CLR 1240–5*, 14; *CLR 1245–51*, 158, 182, 296, 363, 372; *CCR 1247–51*, 380–1. Many of these paintings and statues, it should be noted, were intended for the Queen's chapels as well as those of the King.

court, seeking to buy the King's favour with gifts, were clearly aware of Henry's devotion to the Virgin. In 1235, for example, the King was presented with a jewelled ebony image of Mary by the prioress of Amesbury, and a few weeks later, by the Hospitallers, with a small silver image of the Virgin containing oil from the icon of Saidnaiya – an eastern image of Mary believed miraculously to weep oil.[52] Even on the evidence which survives, it appears that Mary was to be seen and touched in each of Henry III's principal chapels and residences. That such images were the object of deep contemplation by the King is suggested by an order of 3 February 1251, the morrow of the Purification which the King had spent at Woodstock, requiring the painted image of Mary by the Queen's seat there to be improved.[53] Amongst the more interesting of these commissions, in April 1237 the King commanded the keeper of the London exchange to have prepared before Easter five portable square panels, showing God's Majesty, the Blessed Virgin, the Crucifixion with Mary and John, God's Majesty crowning the Blessed Virgin, and the Transfiguration of Christ, all five of these panels to be used henceforth in the King's processions.[54] The Marian significance of these images is undeniable, and suggests that the painting of the five portable icons marks an attempt to institute something along the lines of the famous procession held in Rome each year on the vigil of the feast of the Virgin's Assumption, in which the 'unpainted' icon of Christ, stored in the Lateran, was ceremonially processed for a reunion with the Virgin at S. Maria Maggiore.[55] In the immediate term, the processions of Easter 1237 may have been inspired by Henry's recent marriage and the coronation of his Queen, Eleanor of Provence, an earthly model of the crowned Virgin whose marriage could be said, no doubt, to have transfigured King Henry III, Christ's representative on earth.

Turning from art to liturgy, we possess two enrolled lists of royal masses and almsgiving, covering the months from October 1238 to

---

[52] PRO, C47/3/4/1: 'i. ymaginem eburnei de sancta Mar(ia) ex utraque parte io(co)sa ... i. vasculum vitreum cum oleo de Sardenay est in parva ymagine argent(i) beate Marie', and for the oil and icon, see B. Hamilton, 'Our Lady of Saidnaiya: an Orthodox shrine revered by Muslims and Knights Templar at the time of the Crusades', *SCH*, 36 (2000), 207–15.

[53] *CLR* 1 245–51, 332.

[54] *CLR* 1 226–40, 261.

[55] See H. Belting, *Likeness and Presence: a History of the Image before the Era of Art* (Chicago, IL, 1994), 323–9, 498–502, a reference that I owe to Paul Binski. The ceremony is described in detail with numerous illustrations by H.L. Kessler and J. Zacharias, *Rome 1300: on the Path of the Pilgrim* (New Haven, CT, and London, 2000), esp. 62–3.

May 1239, and from January to August 1265, both of which demonstrate keen observance of the Virgin's feast days, including in 1238 the
feast of the Conception.[56] The feast of the Conception, it should be
noted, appears in the liturgical calendar prepared for the King's Exchequer, composed in the 1250s or early 1260s, many years before the
Conception was decreed as a general feast of the Church throughout
England.[57] In addition, the almoners' rolls reveal that the Lady Mass
formed a regular feature of the King's devotions, just as it did for Louis
IX. In the six months to May 1239, the King attended the Lady Mass on
at least six occasions besides his celebration of the feasts of the Conception and the Purification, on the latter occasion with two masses.
Intriguingly, however, the dates of these masses follow no particular
pattern, being held on Wednesday 27 April 1239, Thursday 16 and 23
December 1238, Friday 26 November 1238 and 11 March, and
Saturday 19 March 1239.[58] In general, as was the practice at the court of
Louis IX, we would expect Saturday to have been the favoured day for
the Lady Mass, since it was on Easter Saturday that, alone of Christ's
followers, the Virgin had kept faith with her son: a theme which,
according to report, had been expounded to Louis IX in person.[59] In
due course, Saturday was indeed instituted as the regular occasion for
Henry III's Lady Mass. The change was already in place by 1265, when
the King attended the Mass of the Virgin on twelve Saturdays and the
two great feasts of the Purification and the Annunciation, on this latter
occasion making oblations at the relic of the Virgin's girdle in Westminster abbey.[60] Probably, Saturday was instituted as Mary's day shortly

[56] PRO, C47/3/44 mm.1–2 (Oblations 28 Oct. 1238–7 May 1239); E101/349/30 (Oblations 2 Jan.–6 Aug. 1265).
[57] For the Exchequer calendar, see PRO, E36/266 (Black Book of the Exchequer), fols 2v,
3r, 5v, 6r, 7v, specifying the five principal feasts of Our Lady, together with the octave of the
Virgin's Nativity, 15 Sept., noted as the feast of relics in Salisbury cathedral, itself a centre of
Marian devotion. The date of the feast of relics at Salisbury had been altered at least twice,
before 1161 from an unknown date to 17 Sept., and thereafter to 15 Sept., the octave of the
Nativity: A. Saltman, *Theobald Archbishop of Canterbury* (1956), 467–8 no. 243. It is worth
noting that the Exchequer calendar forms part of a gathering of gospel readings and religious
images, with strong Marian overtones, including drawings (fols 10r, 17v) of the Virgin and
Child and the Crucifixion with Mary and John. For a description, see N. Morgan, *Early
Gothic Manuscripts 1190–1250*, 2 vols (1982–8), 1:130 no. 83 and illustrations 276–8.
[58] PRO, C47/3/44, mm.1–2. In 1239 the feast of the Annunciation coincided with Good
Friday, whose solemnities took precedence.
[59] Le Goff, *Saint Louis*, 372, and for the specific association of miracles of the Virgin with
Saturdays, see Suger, 'Liber de rebus', *PL* 186, cols 1223–4, and the miracle of Déols, said to
have taken place on Saturday 30 May 1187: Hubert, 'Le Miracle de Déols', 298.
[60] PRO, E101/349/30.

after 1239, since in February 1244 the King commanded that fifteen tapers be burned continually in the royal chapel at Oxford on Saturday each week, during the celebration of the Mass of Our Lady.[61]

Elsewhere, we find the Lady Mass being celebrated in the King's chapel at the Tower of London at least as early as 1240.[62] A permanent lamp was endowed to burn before the altar of St Mary in the royal chapel of Salisbury castle in 1247, and in 1250 the King commanded that a chapel be built in the Virgin's honour at Degannwy.[63] Even on pilgrimage to the shrine of St Thomas in Canterbury cathedral in February 1239, Henry rendered devotion and left offerings at the altar of St Mary in the crypt.[64]

Close by, in Dover castle, at least as early as May 1242, he had endowed a chaplain to celebrate Our Lady's Mass.[65] Thirteenth-century Dover would seem to have been conspicuous for its Marian devotions, sponsored both in the castle and in the hospital of St Mary founded by Henry's justiciar, Hubert de Burgh.[66] As the gateway to England, it was perhaps appropriate that Dover should honour Mary, the star of the sea. The idea of England itself as Mary's dower appears to have been a later, fourteenth-century development.[67] It is nonetheless worth remarking the similarity between the image of England portrayed in miniature in the orb at the top of the Virgin's standard recently brought to light in King Richard II's Wilton Diptych, and the miniature of an idealized landscape displayed in the globe held by Christ, flanked by the Virgin and by St John the Evangelist, in the Westminster retable, almost certainly commissioned for the high altar of Westminster abbey in the 1270s or '80s, either by Henry III or his son. The Wilton image is overwhelmingly Marian in focus and iconography, whereas the Westminster retable is Christocentric, with its globe symbolizing universal

[61] *CLR 1240–5*, 220.

[62] *CLR 1226–40*, 499.

[63] *CLR 1245–51*, 156, 300.

[64] PRO, C47/3/44, m.1.

[65] *CLR 1240–5*, 129, 146, 173.

[66] For the hospital, which acquired numerous royal charters during the years of de Burgh's ascendancy, see *CChR 1226–57*, 48, 78–9, 91, 98–9, 101, 126, 129–30, 141–2, 191–2, 202, 315, 330.

[67] D. Gordon, 'The Wilton Diptych: an introduction', and N. Morgan, 'The significance of the banner in the Wilton Diptych', in Gordon, Monnas and Elam, eds, *The Regal Image*, 22–6, 185. However, for a Bury motet in honour of St Edmund, rewritten with connotations of Mary as Queen of the English as well as the Angels, *Ave regina celorum, mater regis angelorum*, perhaps in circulation as early as the thirteenth century, see Mitchell, 'Richard, kingship and the cult of saints', ibid., 118, 124.

rather than specifically English natural abundance.[68] Nonetheless, the very presence of the Virgin on the high altar of Westminster with Christ, and the abbey's patron saints, Peter and (almost certainly) Edward, confirms the ubiquitous nature of the cult of Mary in Plantagenet court art.

With the exception of the almoner's rolls of 1238–9 and 1265, our knowledge of the King's daily liturgy is severely limited. However, from other household accounts, we can establish the quantity of wax that was used each day in the King's chapel for most of the year 1259–60. The consumption of wax surged as we might expect on the feasts of the Purification (Candlemas), the Annunciation, and the Assumption. Intriguingly, however, there seems to have been no particular celebration that year of the feast of the Conception, 8 December 1259, which the King spent at Paris as a guest of Louis IX.[69] Could it be that in 1259 Henry III omitted the celebration of the Conception out of respect for his French host, just as the Conception is signally absent from the list of Mary's feasts observed by King Louis? Elsewhere, however, the shared Marian enthusiasm of the two Kings is most obviously displayed in 1254, when it was at Chartres, the greatest Marian pilgrimage centre in France, that Louis IX came to greet King Henry and to escort him north to Paris for the opening stages of the negotiation of an Anglo-French peace.[70] One further point is worth making about the King's liturgical observance. Kantorowicz long ago drew attention to the great frequency, from the 1230s onwards, with which Henry commissioned the singing of the *Laudes*, the acclamations in which Henry was proclaimed higher than the stars, decked with all the pomp and majesty of Solomon.[71] At least to begin with, it is striking how this ritual acclamation of the King was timed to coincide with the feast-days of Mary: the Purification, Assumption, and Nativity of Our

[68] For the Westminster retable, see P. Binski, *Westminster Abbey and the Plantagenets. Kingship and the Representation of Power 1200–1400* (New Haven, CT, 1995), 152–67, esp. 156–7. For the orb of the Wilton Diptych, see Gordon, 'Wilton Diptych', 22–3.

[69] PRO, E101/349/27. Taking a daily average of 10lbs of wax used 'in the chapel and in alms', 36 lbs were expended on the vigil and 153 lbs on the feast of the Purification; 27 lbs on the Annunciation, and 13 lbs on the Assumption. These compare with a mere 7½ lbs on 8 Dec., 75 lbs used on Christmas day, 123 lbs on Easter Saturday and Sunday, 31 lbs on the feast of St Edward in Oct. 1260, and the quite enormous and unexplained expenditure of 237 lbs on the feast of St Peter ad Vincula in Aug. 1260.

[70] Paris, *Chronica majora*, 5:476–7.

[71] E.H. Kantorowicz, *Laudes Regiae: a Study in Liturgical Acclamations and Mediaeval Ruler Worship* (Berkeley, CA, 1946), 171–9, esp. 175–7.

Lady in 1233; and thereafter regularly on the feasts of the Purification, the Nativity, and in 1239 the Annunciation.[72]

These references by no means exhaust the catalogue of the King's Marian devotions. In 1240, for example, we find the King paying for a cup to contain a relic of the Virgin's girdle belonging to the nuns of Goring.[73] What are we to make, moreover, of such suggestive coincidences as that in 1235, when it was on the feast of the Annunciation that the King ordered the fair at Leicester to be transferred away from the feast of the Virgin's Purification, or in 1266, when it was on the feast of the Virgin's Nativity (8 September) that the King renewed what might otherwise be regarded as a routine arrangement, requiring the abbot of St Mary's York to supply a man to the King's armies carrying the abbey's banner of St Mary?[74] For present purposes, however, there remains only one major theme still to be explored before we attempt to draw some conclusions from this survey.

Of all the churches in England, it is Westminster abbey that is most closely associated with the memory of Henry III. From the 1240s onwards Westminster and its patronal shrine of St Edward the Confessor were sumptuously rebuilt, very much at the King's command and expense. It has long been recognized that Henry's earliest association with the abbey came in 1220, when on the eve of his own coronation at Westminster he laid the foundation stone of the abbey's Lady Chapel.[75] A few months later he offered the golden spurs used at his coronation as a gift towards the fabric of the new chapel.[76] These events should not incline us to suppose that it was Henry, still only thirteen years of age in 1220, who had planned the Lady Chapel, or that Henry devoted much attention to building at Westminster at least until the 1230s.[77] The monks of Westminster possessed an interest in the cult of Mary that long predated Henry's accession, being the possessors of relics of the Virgin, including a portion of her girdle supposedly bequeathed by Edward the Confessor, and a wonder-working statue recorded in various of the early English collections of Marian

---

72 *CLR 1226–40*, 197, 231, 255, 406, 441.

73 *CCR 1237–42*, 233.

74 *CCR 1234–7*, 64; *CPR 1258–66*, 636.

75 Paris, *Chronica majora*, 3:59; *Radulphi de Coggeshall Chronicon Anglicanum*, ed. J. Stevenson, RS (1875), 187–8, noting that the foundations were laid on Saturday (the Virgin's day) 16 May 1220. For the coronation on Sunday 17 May 1220, see D. Carpenter, *The Minority of Henry III* (1990), 187–9.

76 *Rotuli litterarum clausarum*, 1:440b.

77 Binski, *Westminster Abbey*, 10–13.

miracles.[78] Twelfth-century Westminster was one of the first post-Conquest churches to adopt the feast of the Virgin's Conception.[79] After 1220, we have no certain evidence of a royal interest in Westminster's cult of Mary until 1235, when the King offered a silk cloth to be placed upon the image of the Virgin in the abbey's Lady Chapel.[80] Thereafter, however, throughout the 1240s and 50s, we have frequent indications that Westminster was fully integrated into the King's Marian observances. In 1240, for example, Henry paid for the glazing of the Lady Chapel; in 1242 he promised an annual subvention of £40 and in December 1243 offered a silver-gilt censer at the feast of the Conception.[81] In June 1256, to accommodate the rebuilding that he had put in train since 1245, Henry ordered that the upper portions of the post-1220 Lady Chapel be demolished and rebuilt, the discarded materials being offered to the new chapel of St Mary in the London college of St Martin-le-Grand.[82] In 1258 he commissioned paintings for the

---

[78] For the cult of St Mary at Westminster in the twelfth century, see E. Mason, *Westminster Abbey and its People, c.1050–c.1216* (Woodbridge, 1996), 262–3; G. Rosser, *Medieval Westminster 1200–1540* (Oxford, 1989) 47–51. For the abbey's Marian relics, including those given by St Edward and St Thomas of Canterbury, see *The History of Westminster Abbey by John Flete*, ed. J.A. Robinson (Cambridge, 1909), 69–70, and below. For miracle stories involving the Virgin and the monks of Westminster, several of them collected in the later compendium at Cambridge, Sidney Sussex College, MS 94, fols 63v–64r, 145r–146r, 211r–212r, whence the calendar by James, *Catalogue of the Manuscripts of Sidney Sussex College*, 86 no.38, 96 no.12, 104 no.42, two of these also to be found in the earlier, thirteenth-century collections in BL, MS Royal 6.B.x, MS Cotton Cleopatra C x, as noted by H.L.D. Ward, *Catalogue of Romances in the Department of Manuscripts in the British Museum II* (1893), 617 no.38, 645 no.6.

[79] The assumption must be that it was to Westminster that Osbert of Clare was referring when he wrote of his institution of the feast *c.*1129: *Letters of Osbert of Clare*, 11–13, 65–8 no.7. The feast is included in the calendar attached to the Westminster Psalter *c.*1200: *Missale ad usum ecclesie Westmonasteriensis*, ed. J.W. Legg, 3 vols, Henry Bradshaw Society, 1, 5, 12 (1891–7), 3:1396; Morgan, *Early Gothic Manuscripts*, 1:49–51 no.2. The Westminster Customary of *c.*1270 lists the feast of the Conception together with the Purification, the Annunciation, and the Nativity of the Virgin, as one of the abbey's twenty-five lesser feasts, including only the Assumption amongst the eight major feasts. However, it should be remembered that these rankings were applied to the abbey as a whole, not to the Lady Chapel which had its own distinct customs including a daily recital of the Lady Mass and special pittances at the feast of the Conception, endowed by the monk Robert of Moulsham: *Customary of the Benedictine Monasteries of St Augustine Canterbury and Saint Peter, Westminster*, ed. E. Maunde Thompson, 2 vols, Henry Bradshaw Society, 23, 28 (1902–4), 2:77–8, 91–3.

[80] PRO, C47/3/4/1.

[81] *CLR 1226–40*, 442; *CPR 1232–47*, 281; *CLR 1240–5*, 206, 212. These awards are assumed to apply to the monastic Lady Chapel rather than to the chapel of St Mary, not established in the royal palace at Westminster until the 1290s, for which see *The History of the King's Works I: The Middle Ages*, ed. R. Allen Brown, H.M. Colvin and A.J. Taylor, 2 vols (1963), 1:521–3.

[82] *CCR 1254–6*, 314; Brown, Colvin, and Taylor, *King's Works*, 1:144.

altar of the Westminster Lady Chapel at a cost of more than £80.[83] Of Henry's specific devotion to the relic of the Virgin's girdle at Westminster we have the evidence not only of the offerings he made before the relic at the feast of the Annunciation in 1265, but of events in 1242 when three monks of Westminster transported the girdle to Gascony to attend Henry's Queen, then pregnant with her second daughter, Beatrice.[84]

In his pilgrimages, in his artistic commissions, in his private liturgical observance, and in his veneration of Marian relics, King Henry III revealed a devotion to the Virgin at least equal to that displayed by the French King Louis IX. What, however, are we to conclude from these devotions? Mary, as Jacques Le Goff reminds us, was acquiring a status by the thirteenth century little short of that of a fourth member of the Trinity.[85] The people of England were as assiduous as those of any other part of Christendom in their *Aves* and *O Intemerata*'s.[86] The four greater feasts of the Virgin were set aside as pious holidays for ordinary English laymen and women, not merely for kings.[87] Churches in thirteenth-century England, as elsewhere, were acquiring Marian statuary and images by the cartload.[88] King Henry's devotions may have been nothing more than the standard that would have been expected of any pious thirteenth-century ruler. But even had this been the case, and had Henry merely been conforming to the spirit of his age, the very fact that we find a Plantagenet ruler so devout in his approaches to the

---

[83] *CLR 1251–60*, 424, 448.

[84] For the offering of a piece of gold made at the feast of the Annunciation 1265 *ad zonam beate Marie*, see PRO, E101/349/30. For the girdle's journey to Gascony dated 1246, presumably by mistake for June 1242, the date of the birth of Beatrice at Bordeaux, see Maunde Thompson, *Customary of Westminster*, 2:73; Howell, 'Children of King Henry III' 57, 62–3. For the duty of carrying the girdle 'wherever it may be sent', imposed upon the sacrist of Westminster, see Maunde Thompson, *Customary of Westminster*, 2:49, and for its later peregrinations to the court of Edward III both in England and France, see Westminster Abbey Muniments 19621, 19623, 19634. For episcopal indulgences directed to visitors to the relic, after 1287, see Westminster Abbey, MS Domesday, fols 398v–9r.

[85] Le Goff, *Saint Louis*, 425, 772.

[86] Morgan, 'Texts and images', 69–103, and for the earliest English diocesan legislation prescribing prayers to Our Lady before 1240, see Powicke and Cheney, *Councils and Synods II*, 1:61 no.5, 213 no.20, 228 no.2, 269 no.8.

[87] C.R. Cheney, 'Rules for the observance of feast-days in medieval England', *Bulletin of the Institute of Historical Research*, 34 (1961) 117–47; B. Harvey, 'Work and "Festa ferianda" in medieval England', *JEH*, 23 (1972),289–308.

[88] For the insistence that every church obtain an image of Our Lady, set out in the diocesan legislation of the see of Exeter in 1287, see Powicke and Cheney, *Councils and Synods II*, 2:1006.

Virgin must raise questions over the extent to which the Capetians, and in particular Louis IX, are to be regarded as exceptionally or specifically honoured amongst Mary's servants. For all that modern historians may insist that the Capetians espoused a sacral and mimetic style of kingship, far removed from the secularized and bureaucratized style attributed to the Plantagenets; once we know where to look, pious exercises and a resort to the incidental trappings of sacral kingship are as easily found in Plantagenet England as anywhere in Capetian France.

For Henry's interest in the cult of the Virgin there could be any number of explanations, not least his continued devotion to a cult that, as we have seen, was by no means unfamiliar to his ancestors, Kings Henry II, Richard, and John. Beyond mere conformity to the norms of his family and age, however, it is worth reminding ourselves that Henry III came to the throne as a mere boy of nine, and that for most of the first twenty years of his reign, until at least 1234, he was not only deprived of a mother and a father but overshadowed by the influence of the great men of his court: William Marshal, Hubert de Burgh, Peter des Roches, and to some extent Stephen Langton. Most or all of these men were themselves keen devotees of Mary. Stephen Langton, former canon of Notre-Dame in Paris, composed hymns in the Virgin's honour and a lengthy commentary on the *Ave Maria stella*.[89] Peter des Roches founded nearly a dozen houses of religion, most of them dedicated to Mary. In 1231 on his return to England from the Holy Land, he bore witness to the authenticity of a crucifix acquired in the valley of Josophat, supposedly the site of the Virgin's Dormition and Assumption.[90] William Marshal, regent during the first three turbulent years of the reign, was lord of the manor of Caversham. His long deathbed agony there was witnessed by the boy-king some years before the chapel at Caversham became the object of Henry's own Marian devotions.[91] Of all four men, however, it was Hubert de Burgh who demonstrated the most fervent devotion to Mary. Hubert's mother was buried

---

[89] R. Sharpe, *A Handlist of the Latin Writers of Great Britain and Ireland before 1540* (Turnhout, 1997), 631–2; *Gereimte Psalterien des Mittelalters*, ed. G.M. Dreves, Analecta Hymnica Medii Aevi, 35 (Leipzig, 1900), 153–71 no.11. In April 1220, it was on Langton's behalf that the second stone of the new cathedral of Salisbury was laid, the cathedral itself having been founded by Langton's former pupil Richard Poer in consequence, so it was much later alleged, of a vision of the Virgin Mary: *The Register of St Osmund*, ed. W.H. Rich Jones, 2 vols, RS (1883–4), 2:civ, 12–13.

[90] N. Vincent, *Peter des Roches: an Alien in English Politics 1205–38* (Cambridge, 1996), 256.

[91] D. Crouch, *William Marshal. Knighthood, War and Chivalry, 1147–1219*, 2nd edn (2002), 214–16, based closely upon the contemporary *Histoire de Guillaume le Maréchal*.

at Walsingham, the principal Marian shrine both of England and of Henry III. It was almost certainly with Hubert at his side that in 1226 Henry began his long connection with the Walsingham shrine.[92] Earlier, following his successful defence of the castle against the French in 1216 and his naval victory off Sandwich in 1217, it was Hubert who had founded the hospital of St Mary at Dover.[93] Disgraced and imprisoned after 1232, Hubert is said to called upon the aid of the Virgin Mary. In the winter of 1233, when he was sprung from captivity at Devizes, he spent several hours awaiting a ship to carry him to safety across the Bristol Channel. Throughout that anxious night he is said to have been comforted by a heavenly voice that repeated to him, 'Fear not, Our Lady will deliver you'.[94]

It may well have been from Hubert de Burgh that Henry acquired his intense devotion to Mary. Did Mary indeed serve as a surrogate mother to Henry, as a more fitting parent than his own absentee mother Isabella of Angoulême, in much the same way that historians have presumed that the King adopted Edward the Confessor as a surrogate father, more appropriate to a man of peace and piety than Henry's real father King John? I have suggested elsewhere that it was the very fact that St Edward, like Henry III, was the son of an absentee mother who abandoned her children in their infancy, that may have made him that much fitter a model of sanctity to the maternally-abandoned Henry III.[95] From the mid 1230s onwards there can be little doubt that it was St Edward rather than St Mary who occupied the principal place in the King's devotions.[96] It was the shrine of St Edward, rather than the

---

[92] For Hubert's awards to Walsingham, referring to the burial there of his mother Alice, see BL, MS Cotton Nero E vii (Walsingham cartulary), fols 91r, 140r.

[93] For Hubert's charters to the hospital, see BL, Campbell Charter II.12; London, Lambeth Palace Library, MS 241 (Dover cartulary), fol. 41r; Register of Archbishop Warham, fol. 134r.

[94] M.L. Colker, 'The "Margam Chronicle" in a Dublin manuscript', *The Haskins Society Journal*, 4 (1993), 135 (mentioning Hubert's possession of a psalter), 137.

[95] N. Vincent, 'Isabella of Angoulême: John's Jezebel', in S.D. Church, ed., *King John: New Interpretations* (Woodbridge, 1999), 215–16. Beyond the perfunctory obit celebrations cited there (213–14) as having been made by Henry for his mother after 1246, note that in 1251 Henry arranged for his mother's obit to be inscribed in the martyrology of Rouen Cathedral, and that as late as 1265 he was celebrating an obit mass for her on the anniversary of her death: *CPR 1247–58*, 89; PRO, E101/349/30, this latter correctly dated 4 June but assigned by the clerk who compiled the roll to *Alyanora mater domini regis*, suggesting that the clerk, if not the King, was ignorant even as to Isabella's name.

[96] For the fact that Henry III spent the feast of St Edward's translation at Westminster in most years of his reign and certainly from the mid 1230s, and that from 1238 he also made it his practice to be in Westminster for the feast of Edward's deposition in Jan., see Vincent,

Westminster Lady Chapel, upon which the King lavished his most extensive gifts. For all the wax tapers that he burned at Walsingham, nothing in his Marian devotions could compare with the single candle weighing 1,000 lbs that he commanded for the shrine of St Edward in 1247.[97] His masses in 1265 may have included a dozen recitals of the mass of Mary, but over the same period he listened to the mass of St Edward recited on more than twenty occasions, at least once a week and not on any particular day but whenever the King felt it appropriate.[98] Nonetheless, if we care to adopt Le Goff's suggestion that to Louis IX the Virgin formed part of a heavenly triumvirate in company with St Denis and Christ himself, protecting and interceding for the king and kingdom of France, it is at least worth considering the possibility that in the mind of King Henry III the Virgin, St Edward, and Jesus Christ formed a holy and specifically English trinity, to be propitiated for the defence and spiritual health of the king and the realm of England. Consider here the King's commission in 1251 of images of St Mary and St Edward for the royal chapel at Clarendon, or most notably the decoration of the monastic choir at Westminster, where before 1242 Abbot Richard Berkyng ordered the hanging of more than forty tapestries, those on the south side depicting the story of Mary and Christ from the Annunciation to Pentecost with the Coronation of the Virgin and scenes of Abbot Berkyng praying to the Virgin and the Virgin interceding with Christ, faced by those on the north recounting legends from the life of St Edward.[99] With the deposit at Westminster after 1247 of the greatest of the King's Christological relics, a portion of the Holy Blood sent from the church of Jerusalem, the abbey could indeed be said to provide the most magnificent setting for the cult not only of Mary and St Edward but of Christ, present in relics, imagery and the daily sacrifice of the Mass.[100]

Louis IX, the devotee of Mary, was destined for sanctity and great

'The pilgrimages of the Angevin kings', and the digest of a lecture by David Carpenter in *The Westminster Abbey Chorister*, 31 (2000), 37–9, drawn to my attention by Paul Binski.

[97]   *CCR 1247–51*, 18.

[98]   PRO, E101/349/30, recording 22 recitals of the Mass of St Edward, besides celebrations and offerings on the feast of his deposition in Jan.. The Masses were celebrated on Monday (8 times), Tuesday and Saturday (once each), Wednesday (twice), Thursday (6 times), and Friday (5 times).

[99]   *CLR 1245–51*, 362; P. Binski, 'Abbot Berkyng's tapestries and Matthew Paris's Life of St Edward the Confessor', *Archaeologia*, 109 (1991), 85–100, and for Abbot Richard's burial in the Lady Chapel, see Maunde Thompson, *Customary of Westminster*, 2:92.

[100]   For the events of 1247, see Vincent, *The Holy Blood*, 1–19.

posthumous fame. Henry III, just as much the Virgin's obedient son, was not. Both Louis IX and Henry III, however, showed lifelong devotion to Mary, to Christ and to their chosen, national patron saint. Whatever distinctions we care to draw in the wider scheme of things between Capetian and Plantagenet kingship, we would be misguided to suppose that in their religious lives there was much to set Henry III and Louis IX apart. Their style was very much the same, and in both cases afforded great prominence to the cult of the Virgin Mary. To this extent, we must look elsewhere, to politics, and to the ways in which royal policy was received and recorded both by contemporary chroniclers and by later historians, if we are to discover any real distinction between the court styles of England and France.

University of East Anglia

THE VIRGIN AND THE DEVIL:
THE ROLE OF THE VIRGIN MARY IN THE THEOPHILUS LEGEND AND ITS SPANISH AND PORTUGUESE VARIANTS

by IONA MCCLEERY

THE story of Theophilus is one of the oldest and most widespread Marian miracles in Christian literature.[1] Theophilus is said to have been a sixth-century priest of Adana in Cilicia, removed from office by a new bishop. Eager to regain his position, Theophilus went to a Jew known for diabolical practices and through him made a written pact with the Devil, sealed with a ring. Theophilus received back his lost status but then began to repent and, through the intercession of the Virgin Mary, finally won the document from the Devil. Three days later he died.[2]

The story of Theophilus is usually considered from a Faustian perspective.[3] It is not heavily studied as a Marian miracle even though two of its most famous versions survive in important Spanish Marian collections: the *Cantigas de Santa Maria* of Alfonso X, King of Castile (1252–84), and the *Milagros de Nuestra Señora* of Gonzalo de Berceo (died before 1264).[4] The Theophilus miracle can also be compared with the legend of a Portuguese saint, Giles of Santarém. Giles was a physician who became a Dominican friar and eventually Prior Provincial of the province of *Hispania*. He died in 1265 in Santarém, a town about forty miles up the river Tagus from Lisbon. A cult grew up around his tomb, but he was not beatified until 1748. Although the earliest version of his

---

[1]   C.H. Ebertshäuser, H. Haag, J.H. Kirchberger, and D. Sölle, *Mary: Art, Culture and Religion Through the Ages*, trans. P. Heinegg (New York, 1997), 74–8.

[2]   *ActaSS*, Feb. I, 486–97; P.M. Palmer and R.P. More, *The Sources of the Faust Tradition from Simon Magus to Lessing* (New York, 1936), 58–77.

[3]   C. Dédéyan, *Le Thème de Faust dans la littérature européenne*, 6 vols (Paris, 1954–67); J.W. Smeed, *Faust in Literature* (1975); A. Dabezies, *Le Mythe de Faust* (Paris, 1972); E.F. DiAmico, 'The diabolical pact in literature: its transmission from legend to literary theme' (University of Michigan, Ph.D. thesis, 1979).

[4]   Alfonso X, *Cantigas de Santa Maria* [hereafter *CSM*], ed. W. Mettman, 2 vols (repr., Madrid, 1986–8), no.3; Gonzalo Berceo, *Milagros de Nuestra Señora* [hereafter *MNS*], ed. A.G. Solalinde (Madrid, 1958), no.24. The most recent study of these works is D.A. Flory, *Marian Representations in the Miracles Tales of Thirteenth-Century Spain and France* (Washington, DC, 2000), although he does not discuss the Theophilus story.

vita dates from the sixteenth century, there is evidence that the cult originated in the thirteenth century.[5]

According to Giles's legend, he was a noble youth of Coimbra in Portugal who went to study medicine at the University of Paris. On the way he was met by the Devil in disguise and persuaded to go instead to Toledo in Castile to study black magic. Giles made a pact with the Devil, signed with his own blood, and studied magic in Toledo for seven years. He then went to Paris and became a famous physician with the help of his demonic powers. After some years, visions of a knight in armour commanding him to change his ways caused him to hurry back to Portugal. He joined the Dominican Order, but seven years passed before he received back the bloody pact he had signed, thanks to the intercession of the Virgin Mary. What is the relationship between the stories of Giles and Theophilus? What was the role of the Virgin in these popular tales of redemption? Did her role change through time? This paper seeks to analyse the transformation of the legends of Theophilus and Giles in Spanish and Portuguese literature. The stories provide an excellent indication of the mutations of such stories over a long period of time and the changing appreciation of the role of the Virgin in Christian history.

There are obvious differences between the stories of Giles and Theophilus. Their legends developed centuries apart in time and grew out of contrasting geographical and social contexts. On the surface a Cilician priest of the sixth century and a Portuguese physician and friar of the thirteenth have little in common. Yet at heart each story concerns an ecclesiastic who made a pact with the Devil. He repented and, with the help of the Virgin Mary, eventually received back the

---

[5] The main *vita* is the *Liber de conversione miranda D. Aegidius Lusitani* by André de Resende (*c.*1500–73): *ActaSS*, May III, 400–36. The edition used here is V. da C. Soares Pereira, 'O Aegidius Scallabitanus de André de Resende: estudo introductório, edição crítica, tradução e notas' (University of the Minho [Braga], Ph.D. thesis, 1995) [hereafter *Aegidius Scallabitanus*]. The main evidence for Giles's medieval cult is as follows: in 1294 Caterina Eanes stipulated in her will that a lamp was to be maintained at the altar of 'blessed brother Giles' in the Dominican house of Santarém: Lisbon, Archivos Nacionais da Torre do Tombo, S. Domingos de Santarém, antiga colecção especial, maço 1, doc. 15; according to a Dominican catalogue of saints, Giles was venerated by the order in the fifteenth century: *Laurentii Pignon Catalogi et Chronica*, ed. G.G. Meersseman, Monumenta Ordinis Fratrum Praedicatorum Historica, 18 (1936), 2–4; an Italian manuscript of herbal remedies dated to 24 May 1463, attributed to 'maestro Gilio diportogallo dellordine di Sancto Domenico', questions whether miracles recorded at his tomb were performed 'per arte divina' or 'per arte magicha', since Giles was said to have been a 'grande negromante': Washington DC, National Library of Medicine, MS 22, fol. 16.

document. This basic similarity could lead to the dismissal of the legend of Giles of Santarém as simply another Theophilus story. Do personal details and place names matter? Theophilus moved from being a priest of Cilicia to one of Sicily by at least the tenth century.[6] Was this a scribal error or a way of westernizing an originally Greek story? Although there are close similarities between the legends, that of Giles of Santarém is clearly a more complex treatment of the story. The new elements were crucial to the expansion of the theme.

The story of a man who made a pact with the Devil in return for knowledge or power is of course famous in European literature. The sixteenth-century play *Dr Faustus* by Christopher Marlowe, and the eighteenth-century poem *Faust* by Johann von Goethe are both very well known.[7] The links between these works and the medieval stories have long been debated and the matter remains unresolved. Instead of focusing on the connecting feature of the Devil pact, we should perhaps look at these stories from the perspective of the Virgin Mary. Mary was a dominant figure in the medieval legend of Theophilus. Her role declined in the sixteenth-century versions of Giles's legend, and she had all but vanished in seventeenth-century dramatizations of the theme. She plays no part in the Faust stories. This erosion of role is striking, and study of it may shed light on the Devil-pact theme.

* * *

What was the role of the Virgin in the medieval legend of Theophilus? Mary, the Devil, and the Jewish necromancer form a symbolic triangle in this legend.

There had long been a conceptual link between Jews and the Devil in Christian art and literature.[8] In the *Milagros de Nuestra Señora* of Berceo, and to a lesser extent in the *Cantigas de Santa Maria* of Alfonso X, Jews were only depicted positively when they converted to Christianity,

---

[6] Hrotswitha of Gandersheim, *Lapsus et conversio Theophili vicedomini: PL* 137, cols 1101–10. Some later versions still set the story in Cilicia, e.g. Fulbert of Chartres, *Sermones ad populum*, sermo IV (*PL* 141, cols 320–1), but in others it remained in Sicily, e.g. Jacobus de Voragine, *Legenda aurea vulgo historia Lombardica dicta ad optimorum librorum fidem*, ed. T. Graesse (Dresden, 1846), 595–6; *The Golden Legend: Readings on the Saints*, trans. W. Granger Ryan, 2 vols (Princeton, NJ, 1993), 2:157.

[7] C. Marlowe, *Doctor Faustus: A- and B-Texts (1604, 1616)*, eds D. Bevington and E. Rasmussen (Manchester, 1993); J.W. von Goethe, *Faust: Part One*, trans. D. Luke (Oxford, 1987).

[8] J. Trachtenberg, *The Devil and the Jews* (New Haven, CT, 1945); R. Bonfil, 'The Devil and the Jews in the Christian consciousness of the Middle Ages', in S. Almog, ed., *Anti-Semitism Through the Ages* (Oxford, 1988), 91–8.

usually as a result of Marian miracles.[9] Jews represented those who rejected the Christian faith, the greatest of whom was of course the Devil. Mary, on the other hand, led people away from the Devil to Christ. Just as she undermined the effects of Eve's temptation by giving birth to Christ, so she had the power to redeem others who succumbed to the Devil's ploys.[10] She mediated between Theophilus and Christ in much the same way as the Jew mediated between Theophilus and the Devil. The Theophilus miracle in fact appears to have been the first time that the title *mediatrix* was applied to the Virgin. The legend therefore holds an important place in Marian doctrine and has been described as 'one of the most powerful influences in the spread of an ever-increasing belief in the never-failing efficacy of Mary's intercession'.[11]

The Theophilus legend emerged in the eighth century when the cult of the Virgin was only beginning to develop in the west. It continued to be used throughout the Middle Ages as the miracle of choice in sermons promoting her intercessory powers and Marian feasts in general. The story was particularly popular in relation to the Feast of the Nativity of the Virgin (8 September). Fulbert of Chartres, for example, used it in the early eleventh century to promote what was then a relatively new feast.[12] More than two hundred years later, Theophilus was included in the section of *The Golden Legend* that dealt with this same feast. Here it is explained that the Church celebrates just three birthdays: those of Christ, John the Baptist, and Mary, which 'mark three spiritual births, for we are reborn in water with John, in penance with Mary, and in glory with Christ'.[13] Birth and penance are significant in the case of Theophilus. He was apparently an irredeemable sinner who made a pact with the Devil and denied Christ and the Virgin Mary. He had broken the Christian contract and formed a new diabolical one. Originally Theophilus' pact was signed with a ring, but by the thirteenth century it had, perhaps inevitably, come to be written in his own blood.[14] The Devil pact had to match the blood sacrifice of

[9] See A. Bagby, 'The Jews in the *Cantigas* of Alfonso X el sabio', *Speculum*, 46 (1971), 670–88, and the contrasting arguments of V. Hatton and A. Mackay, 'Anti-semitism in the *Cantigas de Santa Maria*', *Bulletin of Hispanic Studies*, 60 (1983), 189–99.

[10] Alfonso X's version of the Theophilus legend links the eating of the apple in the Garden of Eden to Mary's power: *CSM*, no.3, ll.9–14.

[11] H. Graef, *Mary: a History of Doctrine and Devotion*, 2 vols in 1 (1985), 1:170–1.

[12] Fulbert of Chartres, *Sermones*, col. 320B.

[13] Graesse, *Legenda aurea*, 594; Ryan, *Golden Legend*, 154.

[14] See S. Waxman, 'Chapters on magic in Spanish literature', *Revue Hispanique*, 38 (1916), 325–463; DiAmico, 'Diabolical pact in literature', 106 n.32.

Christ that was being rejected.[15] In some versions Theophilus also denied the eucharist.[16] The Virgin Mary was closely linked to the eucharist in medieval theology. She gave birth and brought up the body of Christ that could be seen on the altar.[17] Therefore it was through her Divine Motherhood, her power to give birth, that Theophilus was redeemed. In his poem, Berceo refers to Mary as 'Mother' no fewer than twenty-six times and mentions her own birth once. Alfonso X also refers to the 'Mother of God' and repeats the belief in her influence over her son in each chorus. It was through her special relationship with her son that Mary derived her power to intercede for sinners like Theophilus. Motherhood and all its physical ramifications was probably the most important attribute of the Virgin Mary in the art and literature of the Middle Ages.[18]

One of the ways in which Mary's power was articulated was in the language and imagery of the pact itself. The Theophilus miracles of the thirteenth century contain vocabulary which can be described as 'feudal'.[19] Theophilus' relationship with both the Virgin and the Devil is that of vassal. To each he kneels in homage and swears allegiance, he shows dissatisfaction with lordship, and he makes petitions. In miracle collections like the *Milagros de Nuestra Señora* the Virgin helped some desperate people: murderers, thieves, fornicators, prostitutes, and suicides, who had exhausted all other sources of intercession. This explains why it was crucial that the Virgin recovered the pact from the Devil so that she could reassert lordship over her vassal.

Mary's role in the legend of Giles of Santarém also needs to be considered. First of all, it is necessary to point out that Giles not only made a pact signed with blood but was also a necromancer, a practitioner of black magic. As Giles dealt directly with the Devil, the figure of the Jewish intermediary vanished. If the story of Giles is a variant of the Theophilus legend, how did he become a necromancer? What happened was that an older legend, that of Cyprian of Antioch, a tale

15   Dabezies, *Mythe de Faust*, 307–11.

16   For example, in the early thirteenth-century *Les Miracles de Nostre Dame par Gautier de Coinci*, ed. V.F. Koenig, 4 vols (Geneva, 1955–70), 1:50–176.

17   See Graef, *Mary*, 1:205–6.

18   C.W. Atkinson, *The Oldest Vocation: Christian Motherhood in the Middle Ages* (Ithaca NY, 1991), 101–43; S.J. Boss, *Empress and Handmaid: on Nature and Gender in the Cult of the Virgin Mary* (London and New York, 2000), 26–72.

19   For 'feudal' language in *CSM* and *MNS*, see A. Mackay, 'The Virgin's vassals', in D.W. Lomax and D. Mackenzie, eds, *God and Man in Medieval Spain: Essays in Honour of J.R.L. Highfield* (Warminster, 1989), 49–58.

which also lacks a Jewish figure, became absorbed into the Theophilus story. Cyprian was a pagan magician of Antioch asked by a nobleman to seduce a Christian maiden, Justina. Thanks to Justina, Cyprian saw the error of his ways, converted to Christianity, and died as a martyr along with Justina in the third-century Diocletianic persecution.[20]

It is sometimes thought that Giles of Santarém is merely a combination of Cyprian and Theophilus.[21] He brought together the figures of the learned man and the magician, an important development on the path to Faust. This theory is too simplistic. There are other influential elements in Giles's legend. His magical studies, for example, are related to twelfth- and thirteenth-century stories of black magic practised in the caves of Toledo;[22] and a link may be made to the story of Gerbert of Aurillac, later Pope Sylvester II (999–1003), another churchman who reputedly summoned the Devil and made a pact with him.[23] More importantly, there are crucial differences between the legends of Giles and Cyprian. In the medieval Cyprian legend there was no formal pact with the Devil; Cyprian simply summoned a demon to do his bidding. Also significant is the love theme between Cyprian and Justina. Only one of Giles's *vitae* provides anything of this nature.[24] Finally, the Cyprian legend is not a Marian miracle. It arose in the east long before the cult of the Virgin Mary developed.

The influence of the tale of Cyprian may be one reason why the Virgin Mary is less prominent in the legend of Giles of Santarém. In Giles's main *vita* by André de Resende O.P., written between the 1540s and the 1560s, the Virgin was mainly referred to in connection with the pact. She did not appear herself in a vision when the pact was returned; Giles prayed before her altar image.[25] She only featured once in his later visions.[26] An earlier Dominican *vita* by Baltazar de São João, completed in 1537, is more Marian in tone. However, in both the 'feudal' imagery

---

[20] *ActaSS* Sept VII, 180–243; Palmer and More, *Sources of the Faust Tradition*, 41–58.

[21] Waxman, 'Chapters on magic', 385.

[22] J. Ferreiro Alemparte, 'La escuela de nigromancia de Toledo', *Anuario de estudios medievales*, 13 (1983), 205–68.

[23] William of Malmesbury, *Gesta regum Anglorum, The History of the English Kings*, ed. R.A.B. Mynors, R.M. Thomson and M. Winterbottom, 2 vols (Oxford, 1998–9), 1:278–95.

[24] Baltazar de São João, 'A vida do Bem-aventurado Gil de Santarém por Fr. Baltazar de S. João', ed. A.A. Nascimento, *Didaskalia*, 11 (1981), 113–219, 150–4: a noble woman fell in love with Giles. When he spurned her advances she accused him of assaulting her. Only on her deathbed did she confess the truth.

[25] *Aegidius Scallabitanus*, 239–41.

[26] Ibid., 266.

of vassalage is almost entirely gone; its only vestige is the armed knight who wounded Giles with his lance.[27] This is strikingly reminiscent of Berceo's Theophilus whose sudden repentance was described as being wounded with Christ's lance.[28]

Giles turned to the Virgin Mary for help in this legend more because she was the patroness of the Dominican order than because she was the universal last court of appeal for sinners. Miracle tales in which Mary watched over her erring friars were quite common in the Middle Ages.[29] Giles's sanctity appears to have been promoted by the Dominicans of Santarém from the time of his death, and therefore the fact that he still featured in a Marian legend in the sixteenth century is a clear sign of the continuity of his cult. Times were changing, however. Resende wrote his *vita* of Giles of Santarém during the Council of Trent (1545–63) which did so much to alter the cult of the saints in Catholic Europe. Half a century later Giles's legend would be very different.

The year 1637 saw the performance of *El mágico prodigioso*, written by the Spanish playwright, Pedro Calderón de la Barca.[30] This play tells the story of Cyprian of Antioch who wooed Christian Justina on behalf of two young men but then fell in love with her himself. Cyprian swore he would give his soul to have her. The Devil accepted and agreed to teach Cyprian how to win Justina if he signed a pact with his own blood. Both Cyprian and the Devil failed to win Justina because of the strength of her faith. Cyprian turned to the Christian God and was released from the pact. He and Justina then died as martyrs.

In this version of the Cyprian legend the Virgin Mary was absent, as in the medieval versions. However, the story now featured a formal pact with the Devil signed in blood, which eventually led Calderón's Cyprian to become known as 'the Spanish Faust'.[31] Much effort has been put into discovering whether Calderón had heard of the Faust stories circulating in Germany and England at this time;[32] but what is

[27] Ibid., 237; de São João, 'A vida', 142–4.

[28] *MNS*, no.24, v.746.

[29] Examples in Thomas de Cantimpré, *Bonum universale de apibus* (Douai, 1627), and Gerard de Frachet, *Vitae fratrum ordinis praedicatorum*, ed. B.M Reichert (Louvain, 1896).

[30] P. Calderón de la Barca, *El mágico prodigioso*, ed. M. McKendrick and A.A. Parker (Oxford, 1992).

[31] Waxman, 'Chapters on magic', 367.

[32] See introduction to *El mágico prodigioso*, 41–2, 64–5; Dédéyan, *Thème de Faust*, 1:145; H.W. Sullivan, *Calderón in the German Lands and the Low Countries: his Reception and Influence, 1654–1980* (Cambridge, 1980).

clear is that Calderón got the idea of a blood pact from a play published in 1612, *El esclavo del demónio*, by António Mira de Amescua.[33] The Devil's slave was Giles of Santarém. In this version he is a cleric of Coimbra who dissuaded a young man from climbing up a ladder into Lisarda's room. He then succumbed to temptation and climbed up himself. He and Lisarda turned to a life of crime until Giles met Leonor, Lisarda's sister, who had been brought up to be a nun. He swore that he would give his soul to have Leonor, signed a blood pact with the Devil, failed to win Leonor over, and finally repented and joined the Dominican order. What is most striking is that it was not the Virgin Mary who released Giles from his pact but his guardian angel. The Virgin had vanished.

Why did Mira de Amescua choose not to make the Virgin Mary the agent of Giles's salvation? Without venturing too deep into the fields of literature and modern history, it is possible to suggest some reasons for the legend's transformation. The cult of the Virgin Mary was deeply affected by religious reform in the sixteenth and seventeenth centuries. Saints' cults became subject to far greater regulation, and very few Marian apparitions were officially recognized after 1513.[34] Marian doctrine changed in the early modern period as a result of Counter-Reformation ideals. Although still central to religious belief, Mary became more dependent and spiritual, less powerful and physical, than she had been in the Middle Ages. The idea of Mary having power over her vassals became meaningless. Early-modern theology was Christocentric, and Mary had to be made firmly subordinate to Christ.[35] The idea of Divine Motherhood, prominent in the Theophilus miracle, declined in popularity. There are fewer representations of Mary engaged in the physical activities of motherhood in seventeenth-century Spanish art.

As a result of these changes, Devil-pact stories ceased to have much significance in a Marian context. Instead, they became a way of highlighting the key Counter-Reformation themes of martyrdom, conversion, and the sacraments.[36] The relationship between the Eucharist,

---

[33] A. Mira de Amescua, *Teatro*, ed. Á. Valbuena Prat, 2 vols (Madrid, 1960), 1:5–153; English trans. by M.D. McGaha, intr. by J.M. Ruano, *The Devil's Slave (El esclavo del Demonio)* (Ottawa, 1989).

[34] W.A. Christian, jr., *Apparitions in Late Medieval and Renaissance Spain* (Princeton, NJ, 1991), 150–87.

[35] This is particularly clear in the writings of Ignatius Loyola and other Jesuits. See Boss, *Handmaid and Empress*, 51, 57–8; M.A. Mullett, *The Catholic Reformation* (1999), 93.

[36] See introduction to *El mágico prodigioso*, 29–36.

baptism, and the blood pact is far more obvious in the modern plays. Cyprian, an early-church martyr, was of course more suitable for this role than Giles of Santarém. Giles's decision to join the Dominican order at the end of *El esclavo del demónio* does not have the same force as Cyprian's conversion and martyrdom. The Cyprian legend also offers the major figure of Justina. Theatre audiences demanded a love theme, and the fact that one was already present probably explains why Cyprian's story eclipsed Theophilus' in the modern period. Justina played a decisive role in Cyprian's conversion; even in the medieval versions of the tale Justina was closely associated with the dispensing of justice and with the provision of compassionate aid to the poor and afflicted.[37] She was effectively playing the part ascribed to the Virgin Mary in Theophilus' legend. When Mira de Amescua, almost certainly influenced by the Cyprian legend, tried to introduce a similar female role into *El esclavo del demónio*, the split character Lisarda/Leonor, he rendered the Virgin Mary redundant.

This helps to explain the disappearance of Mary from Giles's story. Why was she replaced with a guardian angel? The Theophilus legend and its variants can be interpreted as elements of the medieval and early-modern 'discovery of the individual'.[38] Tracing the legend from Cyprian and Theophilus to Faust tells the story of restless, dissatisfied intellectuals whose salvation depended on free will, and whose deeply personal relationships with the Devil and the Virgin Mary bear witness to increasingly individual beliefs and desires. This individualism intensified when historically documented figures like Giles of Santarém and Johann Faust were drawn into the legend. The Virgin Mary had been a universal saint who offered hope to many, but from the late Middle Ages the idea developed of having individual guardian angels who forged stronger, more personal, bonds between man and God.[39] Mira de Amescua's play is significant in the history of self-knowledge. If the plot of this play had been a little less convoluted, allowing it more dramatic success, it is possible that the story of Giles of Santarém would have been much better known today.[40]

---

[37] Graesse, *Legenda aurea*, 632; Ryan, *The Golden Legend*, 2:192.

[38] C. Morris, *The Discovery of the Individual, 1050–1200* (repr., Toronto, 1995); I. Watt, *Myths of Modern Individualism: Faust, Don Quixote, Don Juan, Robinson Crusoe* (Cambridge, 1997).

[39] R.N. Swanson, *Religion and Devotion in Europe, c.1215–c.1515* (Cambridge, 1995), 170–2.

[40] Giles appears in nineteenth- and early twentieth-century Portuguese literature that is little known outside Portugal. Modern novels and poems portray him in a Faustian and political, rather than a religious light.

This last point leads to the question of audience. Who formed the audience of 'Golden Age' Spanish plays? To what extent did popular religious beliefs influence the role of the Virgin Mary in religious drama? Can Spanish literary works be used to form an idea of Portuguese religious beliefs? Studies of popular religion in late medieval and early modern Spain have focused on Marian apparitions.[41] They do not adequately explain the transformation of the Virgin's role in Iberian versions of the Theophilus legend, and they provide little insight into the Portuguese context of Giles of Santarém's legend. Much more work needs to be done on the cult of the Virgin Mary in the Iberian Peninsula as a whole. The aim of this paper has been simply to show how the role of the Virgin Mary could change during the course of centuries. The legend of Theophilus and his pact with the Devil was one of the best known Marian miracle tales of the Middle Ages, and it is revealing to see how it mutated under the pressure of modern ideals.

University of Edinburgh

---

[41] Especially Christian, *Apparitions*, and idem, *Local Religion in Sixteenth-Century Spain* (Princeton, NJ, 1981).

MARIAN STUDIES AND DEVOTION IN THE BENEDICTINE CATHEDRAL PRIORIES IN LATER MEDIEVAL ENGLAND*

by JOAN GREATREX

O N 15 November 1407, in the monastic infirmary of Christ Church, Canterbury, Thomas Wykyng breathed his last with a prayer for the intercession of the Virgin Mary on his lips.[1] The brethren in attendance, so the memoir continues, were convinced that at the moment of his departure the Blessed Virgin summoned him to herself ('ad se evocavit') because next to his trust in God he had always placed supreme confidence in her.[2] He was remembered as a model monk who had served his turn in many offices including those of cellarer, sacrist, novice master, and warden of Canterbury College, Oxford. To the many young monks who owed their instruction in the celebration of mass to him he strongly recommended that this same prayer be included as part of their personal devotions as they stood at the altar.[3]

In highlighting this particular detail of Thomas's personal life the account might suggest that such fervent devotion to the Virgin was unusual. On the other hand, abundant evidence of the veneration attached to her person exists for the cathedral priories; we have only to recall the Marian feasts, Lady altars and chapels, shrines, images and other works of art, the liturgical rites and devotions in the daily office and mass, and the abundance of sermons and treatises that celebrated her cult. Bede's sermons for the feasts of the Purification and Annunciation and the *Regularis Concordia*'s provision for the Saturday mass *De beata Maria* confirm the establishment of the cult of the Virgin well

---

* I would like to record my gratitude to Nigel Morgan who shared with me his liturgical expertise in commenting on an earlier draft of this paper.

[1] The opening and closing words of the prayer are provided in the death notice in Canterbury Cathedral Library, Lit. Ms. D.12, fol. 18v, revealing it to be one that is found in monastic breviaries today: 'Beatae et gloriosae semper virginis Mariae, quaesumus, Domine, intercessio gloriosa nos protegat et ad vitam perducat aeternam. Per Dominum.'

[2] Ibid. The exact wording is '. . . post deum in ipsa gloriosa virgine fiduciam obtinuit singulariter.'

[3] Ibid.; see also Joan Greatrex, *Biographical Register of the English Cathedral Priories of the Province of Canterbury, c.1066–1540* (Oxford, 1997) [hereafter *BRECP*], 328–9.

before the Norman Conquest.[4] This paper focuses on the Marian presence in the cathedral priory cloisters by drawing attention to some of the forms in which it was expressed and experienced in the individual and corporate life of these monastic communities.[5]

First, then, dedications. Two of the cathedral priories, Coventry and Worcester, were dedicated to the Virgin Mary, and both possessed widely revered images of her. William of Malmesbury's *Gesta Pontificum* describes the circlet of precious beads (*circulum gemmarum*) that the dying Lady Godgifu placed around the neck of the Virgin on the altar of the church of the Benedictine monastery she and her husband had founded in Coventry.[6] Worcester cathedral was a much frequented pilgrimage centre in the later middle ages because of the shrine of Our Lady until the shrine was completely destroyed in 1538 on the orders of Bishop Latimer, whose reforming zeal caused him to denounce the image as 'the devil's instrument'.[7] It is likely, however, that the common seals of both priories, in their depiction of the crowned and enthroned Virgin holding the Child, have preserved likenesses of these venerated statues.[8]

Six Marian feasts are commonly found in surviving liturgical

---

[4] Bede's homilies in *PL* 94 include one on the Annunciation (cols 9–14), one on the Purification (cols 79–83), and also one on the Visitation (cols 15–22); T. Symons, ed., *Regularis Concordia* (1953), 20.

[5] In a recent article Prof. Nigel Morgan has summarized some of the results of his prolonged researches in Marian studies: 'Texts and images of Marian devotion in English twelfth-century monasticism and their influence on the secular church', in B. Thompson, ed., *Monasteries and Society in Medieval Britain*, Harlaxton Medieval Studies, 6 (Stamford, 1999), 117–36. It is furnished with copious footnote references which amount to an indispensable bibliography of the relevant publications.

[6] William explained the purpose of the string of beads: 'ut singularem contactu singulas orationes incipiens numerum non praetermitteret', N. Hamilton, ed., *Willelmi Malmesburiensis Monachi de Gestis Pontificum*, RS, 52 (1870), 311. This might have been a proto-rosary which was used in the repetition of Paternosters for the purpose of keeping count; see H. Thurston, 'Prayer beads', *The Month*, 129 (1917), pt 1:352–7, and also A. Winston-Allen, *Stories of the Rose: the Making of the Rosary in the Middle Ages* (Philadelphia, PA, 1997), 14. Coventry became a cathedral priory in 1102.

[7] J.S. Brewer *et al.*, eds, *Letters and Papers, Foreign and Domestic, of the Reign of Henry VIII*, 23 vols in 38 (London, 1862–1932), 13/i, no. 1177; 13/ii, no. 543. It should be noted that Durham was dedicated to the Virgin and St Cuthbert; see D. Rollason, ed., *Symeon of Durham, Historian of Durham and the North* (Stamford, 1998), pl. 31. I owe this and other helpful information concerning Durham to Alan Piper.

[8] It should be noted that from time to time a new matrix came into use on which the image might differ from its predecessor in certain details; see the late thirteenth- and the sixteenth-century seals of Worcester cathedral priory in R.H. Ellis, comp., *Catalogue of Seals in the Public Record Office: Monastic Seals*, 1 (1986), nos M963a, 963b; a late thirteenth-century Coventry seal is ibid., M249.

kalendars of the cathedral priories; in the order of the calendar year these are the Purification (2 February), the Annunciation (25 March), the Assumption (*Dormitio, Ascensio*) (15 August), the Nativity (8 September), the Presentation (*Oblatio*) in the temple (21 November) and the Conception (8 December). Bath, Durham, Ely, and Norwich celebrated all but the Presentation, while Canterbury, Winchester and Worcester included it as well.[9] All six were in place at Canterbury before 1220, and at Worcester by or before 1263.[10] Since the feasts of the Assumption and Nativity of Our Lady were commonly observed during the octave the cathedral monks would have appreciated the change in routine with extra liturgical celebrations in choir and more agreeable rations in the refectory.[11]

Next, the Lady altars and chapels. In some monastic cathedral churches there was more than one altar dedicated to the Virgin Mary; at Durham, for example, two Lady altars were in close proximity in the aisle of the south transept.[12] At Worcester there is a late twelfth-century reference to the altar of St Mary in the vestry and later references to an altar or chapel of Blessed Mary 'at the Red Door' in which stood an image of Our Lady.[13] These altars probably remained in use

---

[9] The late fourteenth-century kalendar for Dunster, a cell of Bath which almost certainly observed the same feasts as the cathedral priory, has been printed in F. Wormald, ed., *English Benedictine Kalendars after A.D. 1100*, Henry Bradshaw Society [hereafter HBS], 2 vols, 77, 81 (1939–46), 1:145–60; also printed there are an early thirteenth-century Christ Church kalendar (1:63–79); a Durham kalendar, dated as prior to AD 1170 (1:161–79) and a thirteenth-century Ely kalendar (2:8–19). J.B.L. Tolhurst, ed., *The Customary of the Cathedral Priory Church of Norwich*, HBS, 82 (1948) includes a late thirteenth-century kalendar, 1–12. N.J. Morgan reconstructed the Winchester kalendar by collating kalendars of different dates with the result that he has presented it in the form of a fourteenth- or early fifteenth-century text: 'Notes on the post-Conquest calendar, litany and martyrology of the cathedral priory of Winchester with a consideration of Winchester diocese calendars of the pre-Sarum period', in A. Borg and A. Martindale, eds, *The Vanishing Past: Studies of Medieval Art, Liturgy and Metrology presented to Christopher Hohler*, BAR International Series, 3 (Oxford, 1981), 136–46. For the Worcester kalendar see *Antiphonaire monastique, 13 siècle: Codex F1 60 de la Bibliothèque de la cathédrale de Worcester*, Paléographie musicale, 12 (Tournai, 1922), 29–40. No surviving kalendars for Coventry and Rochester have been identified.

[10] The Canterbury kalendar used by Wormald (n.9 above) is in BL, MS Cotton Tiberius B.iii, fols 2r–7v to which this date has been assigned, and for the kalendar in the Worcester antiphoner, Worcester Cathedral MS F.160, see preceding note.

[11] The widespread observance of these two octaves is exemplified by the liturgical kalendars cited with references in n.10 above.

[12] See J.T. Fowler, ed., *Rites of Durham*, Surtees Society, 107 (1903), 30; the Durham altars were those of Our Lady of Houghall and Our Lady of Bolton, both named after the lands from which the income for the officiating priest was derived.

[13] The vestry altar is named in R.R. Darlington, ed., *The Cartulary of Worcester Cathedral Priory*, Pipe Roll Society (1968), item 340; the image and altar/chapel of Blessed Mary 'at the

after the construction of large and imposing chapels dedicated to the Virgin Mary between the late twelfth and early fourteenth centuries which reflected the growing prominence of her cult and changing liturgical priorities.[14] These chapels frequently took the form of an impressive eastern extension to the cathedral, as at Norwich, Winchester and Worcester, but at Ely of a separate structure on the north side of the presbytery. Where there were major shrines behind the high altar, as at Canterbury and Durham, the Lady chapels were sited elsewhere: at Christ Church in the crypt or undercroft, and at Durham in the Galilee beyond the western extremity of the nave.[15]

The chapels were adorned with statuary, wall paintings and stained glass. Much has been destroyed, but enough remains to allow a partial reconstruction of the interiors of these chapels as they would have appeared to the monks and laity frequenting them. The fourteenth-century sculpture sequence in the Lady chapel at Ely included 147 images depicting the life and miracles of the Virgin Mary, a breath-taking array and a riot of colour as they were all brightly and delicately painted.[16] The murals in the Lady chapel at Winchester which portrayed a series of miracles attributed to the Blessed Virgin were commissioned by Prior Thomas Silkstede around 1500.[17] These are probably among the finest examples of the artistic embellishment of the cathedral priory churches, but we must constantly remind ourselves that there was much more of which only traces remain.

Next, the Mary mass and the office of Our Lady. At some time during the twelfth century, the preconquest mass of St Mary assigned to Saturday became a daily celebration. The obligingly informative Gerald of Wales states that the first Benedictine house to adopt the daily *missa de Dominica* was Rochester cathedral priory during the reign of King

Red Door' occur in the sacrist's accounts, Worcester Cathedral Muniments, C.425–C.430; could this have been situated at the eastern end of the nave against the pulpitum?

14   For example, at Ely where there was a Lady altar in the south aisle of the presbytery, see R.B. Pugh, ed., *Victoria History of the County of Cambridge and the Isle of Ely*, 4 (1959), 59. At Winchester, however, Bishop Wykeham's chantry chapel replaced the nave Lady altar; see *BRECP*, 725 *under* Richard de Pek.

15   At Durham there was an altar of our Lady of Pity on the north side of the Galilee and close beside it the chantry chapel of Bishop Thomas Langley (d. 1437) dedicated to the Virgin, Fowler, *Rites of Durham*, 44.

16   M.R. James, *Life and Miracles of the Virgin in the Sculptures of the Lady Chapel at Ely* (1895); P. Lindley, 'The monastic cathedral at Ely *c.*1320–*c.*1350: art and patronage in medieval East Anglia', 3 vols (University of Cambridge, Ph.D. thesis, 1985), 2:189–249.

17   D. Park and P. Welford, 'The medieval polychromy of Winchester cathedral', in John Crook, ed., *Winchester Cathedral Nine Hundred Years, 1093–1993* (Chichester, 1993), 123–38, at 133–4 with further references.

Stephen; it was certainly common practice by 1249 because the General Chapter of the Black Monks of Canterbury province in that year agreed that a prayer for the king and queen was to be said daily at the Lady mass in all monasteries.[18] Archbishop Winchelsey refers to it in 1298 as an established custom at Christ Church, as do Bishop Walpole at Ely in 1300 and Bishop Salmon at Norwich in 1308/9.[19] By the thirteenth century most English monasteries, including the cathedral priories, were honouring the Virgin in two forms of observance: the 'Little Office' and the Saturday commemorative office. The former, which was said in addition to the regular monastic office and followed the same cursus, was in use in some Benedictine monasteries before the Conquest – for example at Canterbury – but only became widespread in the twelfth century; the c.1230 Worcester antiphoner shows that it was in use there not many years later.[20] Where the office was observed it generally followed on directly after the regular office.[21] By the twelfth century there was also a commemorative office of Our Lady which was confined to Saturday when it replaced the regular monastic office.[22] Regulations concerning performance and attendance at matins and the other hours of Our Lady were issued by the General Chapter in 1277, making it clear that those who were customarily absent from lauds and vespers in choir were expected to make a commemoration of her privately.[23] In addition, memorials and suffrages of Our Lady

[18] J. Brewer et al, eds, *Giraldi Cambrensis Opera*, 8 vols, RS, 21 (1861–91), 4:202; W. Pantin, ed., *Documents Illustrating the Activities of the General and Provincial Chapters of the English Black Monks, 1215–1540*, 3 vols, Camden Society, 3rd ser., 45, 47, 54 (1931–7), 1:45.

[19] R. Graham, ed., *Registrum Roberti Winchelsey, Cantuariensis archiepiscopi, 1293–1313*, 2 vols, CYS, 51–2 (1952–6), 2:820; S.J.A. Evans, ed., 'Ely chapter ordinances and visitation records, 1215–1515', in *Camden Miscellany, xvii*, Camden Society, 3rd ser., 64 (1940), 8; E.H. Carter, ed., *Studies in Norwich Cathedral Priory* (Norwich, 1935), 22.

[20] See J.B.L. Tolhurst, *The Monastic Breviary of Hyde Abbey*, 6 vols, HBS, 69–71, 76, 78, 80 (1930–42), 6:120–2. The Canterbury MS, BL, MS Cotton Tiberius A.iii (dated c.1050), is printed *in extenso* in E.S. Dewick, ed., *Facsimiles of Horae de Beata Maria Virgine*, HBS, 21 (1902), fols 107b–112. The Worcester antiphoner, of which the kalendar is slightly later than the main text, is Worcester Cathedral MS F.160; the Ely breviary is CUL, MS Ii.4.20.

[21] Tolhurst, *Hyde Breviary*, 6:205; see also *Antiphonaire monastique*, 93–6 for details of the Worcester observance.

[22] John Harper refers to this office as the Office of Our Lady, and he describes the other, which was said daily, as the 'Little Office', because it was the shorter form: *The Forms and Orders of Western Liturgy from the Tenth to the Eighteenth Century* (Oxford, 1991), 133–4. The portiforium of St Wulstan, associated with Worcester, contains the earliest surviving evidence of the Saturday commemorative office of Our Lady and was in use before 1100, A. Hughes, ed., *The Portiforium of St Wulstan*, 2 vols, HBS, 89–90 (1956–7), 2:60–2; directions for the weekly commemorative office are also found in the late thirteenth-century Norwich customary, occurring *passim* through the text, Tolhurst, *Customary*.

[23] Pantin, *Black Monk Chapters*, 1:68.

appear in many office books, usually in the form of an antiphon, versicle, and collect at the end of lauds and vespers.[24] The 1343 statutes of the Black Monk General Chapter prescribed that an antiphon in honour of the Virgin be sung daily followed by a collect.[25] An examination of surviving monastic breviaries reveals that custom and practice varied among Benedictine houses, and that changes were made by individual chapters as they responded to new liturgical tastes and requirements. Despite the complexities of the Benedictine office, some of which have yet to be solved, with regard to the attention and honour paid to the Virgin there is no doubt that her praises were said and sung by all black monks each day.[26]

Following this brief survey of the artistic splendour and liturgical ceremony which were visible manifestations of the Marian cult, we now turn to the written word as found in some of the texts that nourished the minds and hearts of the monastic community in the cathedral priories. First, we will be concerned with a few examples of the writings composed, collated, copied, and used by named cathedral monks, and with those assigned for use in specified places, for specified purposes; and secondly, with other titles in the cloister which were available for instruction, study, and devotion.

No more than a handful of cathedral monks are known and recognized as authors whose writings bear the marks of originality. Those who were moved to write and preach about the Virgin were for the most part content to extol her virtues by drawing on the available sources as a basis for their own treatises and compilations. There are, however, two notable exceptions, both monks from Christ Church, Canterbury, who made significant contributions to the early twelfth-century theological debate about the conception of Mary: these were Archbishop Anselm and his young companion and disciple Eadmer.[27] Their treatises were found in many monastic libraries, including at least three cathedral priories in addition to Canterbury.[28] The Archbishop

[24] See S. Roper, *Medieval English Benedictine Liturgy: Studies in the Formation, Structure and Content of the Monastic Votive Office, c.950–1540* (New York and London, 1993), 140–5.

[25] Pantin, *Black Monk Chapters*, 2:33, and reissued in 1444, ibid., 2:197.

[26] Roper has dealt with monastic votive observance in *Medieval English Benedictine Liturgy*, which includes a critical study of the Marian office.

[27] See E. Bishop, 'On the origins of the feast of the Conception of the Virgin Mary', *Downside Review*, 5 (1886), 107–19; with papal authorization the Council of London in 1129 approved the celebration of this feast in England, ibid., 112.

[28] E.g., copies of Anselm's *De conceptu virginali et de peccato originali* were to be found at Durham, Norwich, and Rochester, as well as Canterbury: M.R. James, *The Ancient Libraries of*

also wrote *De laude beatae virginis*, and Eadmer followed suit with *De quatuor virtutibus quae fuerunt in beata Maria*.[29] Among the titles attributed to a Norwich monk and cardinal, Adam Easton, there may have been an *Historia de visitatione beate Mariae virginis*; if so, it probably served to explain his choice of texts for this Marian feast and they were widely adopted after its official institution by Pope Boniface IX in 1389.[30]

Easton is also numbered among the Benedictines who composed sermons for the Marian feasts, in his case *Sermones XXXVII super Magnificat* of which only the attribution survives.[31] Thomas Brinton, a fellow monk at Norwich before his provision to the see of Rochester, has left a sermon collection which includes several for the feasts of the Annunciation and Assumption.[32] Proximity to Oxford was no doubt the reason why Worcester monk students at the university were regularly required to return to preach before their brethren on the greater festivals.[33] On three such occasions, in 1411, 1420, and 1437, the records relate to the feast of the Assumption, and one of these student preachers is named as John Lawerne, whose Oxford notebook contains drafts of his lectures on the Annunciation and the Magnificat.[34]

The profusion of miracle stories surrounding the Virgin, with their bafflingly similar titles and even incipits, reminds us that our demand for authorial identification was not shared by medieval monastic writers whose primary interest lay in the contents themselves. All the cathedral priories were well supplied with *Miracula* texts the sources of which, however, are difficult to trace. Richard Southern paved the way by unravelling some of the complexities, tracing their English origins

Canterbury and Dover (Cambridge, 1903), Eastry catalogue, 23 (nos 62, 63, 65, 66) (Canterbury); *Catalogi veteres librorum ecclesiae cathedralis Dunelm.*, Surtees Society, 7 (1840), 22 (Durham); CUL, MS Kk.4.12 (Norwich); BL, MS Royal 5A.x (Rochester). References to the printed texts of both are given in R. Sharpe, *A Handlist of the Latin Writers of Great Britain and Ireland before 1540* (Turnout, 1997), 59–60 (Anselm), 104 (Eadmer).

[29] Details of the printed editions are in Sharpe, *Handlist*, 60, 105; Eadmer may also be the author of *De excellentia virginis Mariae*, although it was attributed to Anselm in the Middle Ages, ibid., 104.

[30] Adam's *Historia* is listed in Sharpe, *Handlist*, 13. The introduction of the feast into England is discussed in R.W. Pfaff, *New Liturgical Feasts in Medieval England* (Oxford, 1970), 43–4.

[31] Sharpe, *Handlist*, 13.

[32] M.A. Devlin, ed., *The Sermons of Thomas Brinton, Bishop of Rochester (1373–1389)*, 2 vols, Camden Society, 3rd ser., 85–6 (1954), 1, nos 38, 52; 2, nos 82, 98.

[33] The details are given in the precentor's accounts: Worcester Cathedral Muniments C.373, 375, 378; see also *BRECP*, under Richard Barndesley, 773, and John Lawerne, 830–1.

[34] Bodley, MS Bodl. 692, fols 133v, 140, 141. Lawerne was at Oxford during the 1430s and 1440s.

and showing that there were three distinct collections circulating in England by about 1140.[35] Before Prior Eastry's death at Canterbury in 1331 there were in the monastery library seven copies with the title *Miracula*, one or more of which were in verse and composed by the Christ Church monk, Nigel Witeker.[36]

Books were stored in a number of locations within the cloister for the convenience of particular users, monk readers in the refectory for example. The mid-thirteenth-century Norwich customary prescribes the mealtime readings for the feasts of the Assumption and Nativity of Mary; in one surviving sermon collection which was assigned to the refectory there were several sermons designated for use on feasts of Our Lady in accordance with these regulations.[37] An inventory of the reading material appropriated for similar use at Durham in the mid-fourteenth century included Jerome's writings on the Virgin.[38] There is also at Durham a short list of books selected for the novices' book cupboard in the cloister which itemizes a sermon attributed to Bernard, *De compassione beatae Mariae*, and a *Miracula beatae Mariae cum aliis*; there may have been more, but details of the contents of other volumes in the list are lacking.[39] Similarly, at Norwich, there is an incomplete *De sancta Maria tractatus quidam* among other items in a miscellaneous collection of instructional and devotional treatises bound in one volume in the mid-fourteenth century; these may well have been assigned to the novices.[40] An inventory of books missing from Christ Church library in 1338 reveals both previous monk owners and current defaulting borrowers whose names were attached to a *Miracula beatae Mariae* in French, and two Marian psalters, which were probably devotional rather than for use in choir and, if so, would have taken the form of Ave psalters containing 150 Ave invocations in place of the psalms.[41] In the mid-thirteenth century a Coventry monk was diligently

---

[35] R. Southern, 'The English origins of the Miracles of the Virgin', *Medieval and Renaissance Studies*, 4 (1958), 201–2.

[36] James, *Ancient Libraries*, 48–49 (nos 275–280), 139 (no 1724). Reference to the printed edition of Witeker's *Miracula* is in Sharpe, *Handlist*, 401; Witeker's career is summarized in *BRECP*, 320–1 (as Wireker).

[37] CUL, MS Ii.2.19; two were by the founder monk-bishop, Herbert of Losinga, fols 221v, 234v. Another Norwich MS, CUL, MS Kk.4.13, consists of a set of public readings (*lectiones*) from the Fathers for three of the Marian feasts, fols 42v, 55r, 152r.

[38] A.J. Piper, 'The libraries of the monks of Durham', in M.B. Parkes and A.G. Watson, eds, *Medieval Scribes, Manuscripts and Libraries: Essays presented to N.R. Ker* (1978), 230–1.

[39] *Catalogi veteres*, 82; the list is dated 1395.

[40] CUL, MS Kk.3.26, fols 132r–135r.

[41] J.B. Sheppard, ed., *Litterae Cantuarienses*, 3 vols, RS, 85 (1887–9), 2:147, 149, 151. This

copying such service books, including *totum officium de sancta Maria per annum ad missam*; he also completed a copy of the *De virginitate perpetua beatae Mariae* attributed to Ildefonsus of Toledo.[42]

Meditative and devotional writing flourished in the Benedictine cathedral cloisters, and produced a variety of miscellaneous collections and compilations which were passed on from one generation of monks to the next. Many of these works include prayers and meditations addressed to the Virgin, as exemplified in the writings of two contemplative Durham monks who, between the 1350s and 1370s, resided at the Durham cell on the small island of Inner Farne. John de Whitrig's meditation is interwoven with quotations from the Bible, the Fathers, and Marian texts and hymns; Richard de Segbrok's personal prayers and devotions include one accompanied by a papal indulgence.[43] Prayers and invocations are also found in volumes that are not entirely devotional in content as, for example, those in an early fourteenth-century Christ Church miscellany once owned by Thomas Stoyl who may have copied them himself. Two of pseudo-Bernard's *plancti* are also in this collection: *De dolore virginis Mariae*, and *De dolore virginis de morte filii sui*.[44]

Many Marian texts occur as short tracts, expositions, meditations, and sermons, interspersed among the contents of these volumes of miscellanea; the items possibly began life as separate quires before being bound together as the reading material appropriated by an individual monk for private use. Adam de Chillenden, prior of Christ Church (d. 1274), may have owned one fitting this description which after his death was placed in the cloister library; it consisted of over twenty items and included two Marian titles: a *Carmen de beata virgine versifice*, and John of Garland's *Stella maris*.[45] A miscellany at Norwich, in the possession of Robert de Rothewell sometime in the fourteenth century and of John Marton two centuries later, listed among its devotional material the four homilies *De laudibus virginis Mariae* by the perennially popular Bernard, the usual incipit being *Super missus Gabriel*

---

description of the Marian psalter was given to me by Nigel Morgan who referred to the example of the thirteenth-century Reading abbey psalter described in his *Early Gothic Manuscripts*, 2 vols, A Survey of Manuscripts Illuminated in the British Isles, 4 (1988), 2, item 106.

[42] See *BRECP*, *under* John de Bruges, 348.

[43] For Whitrig, see H. Farmer, *The Monk of Farne: the Meditations of a Fourteenth Century Monk* (1961), 119–26. The prayers attributed to Segbrok are in BL, MS Arundel 507, fols 34v–39v.

[44] Cambridge, Corpus Christi College, MS 63, fols 3r–7r, 22r, 29v–31r.

[45] James, *Ancient Libraries*, 69–70 (no. 603).

or *Super missus est*.[46] One or more of these homilies and other similar writings attributed to Bernard occur repeatedly in cathedral priory manuscripts; Eastry's catalogue lists at least four, with his name and with one of the above incipits.[47] Also available for monk readers at Norwich were a *Meditatio super antiphona beatae virginis Marie* (probably the *Salve regina*), and a *meditatio* on the *Ave Maria*; at Rochester, a twelfth-century manuscript is noteworthy for its collection of Assumption sermons.[48]

A few uncommon works have also been noted in the cathedral priories, the *Sigillum Mariae*, for example, by Honorius Augustodunensis found only at Worcester which possessed four copies.[49] Other less familiar writings devoted to the Virgin are worthy of mention. By the middle of the fourteenth century, Winchester monks had acquired a *Summa florum ortorum et deliciarum beatae virginis Mariae* addressed to Cistercians, its author and provenance as yet unknown.[50] Finally, three manuscripts furnish us with examples of Marian compositions and compilations which may have their counterparts beyond the cathedral priories, but within this circle appear to be exclusive to Durham. One is the *Libellus de gestis et laudibus beatae Mariae virginis ex dicto sanctorum patrum canonicis extractus*, which reads like a veritable biography of Our Lady in 143 chapters. Another, entitled *Mariale*, is an untidy fourteenth-century collection of poems, prayers, meditations, and hymns, some with musical notation and to some of which indulgences are attached. The third, also a *Mariale*, is presented in the form of an alphabet of the attributes of the Virgin from *abstinencia* to *vulnerata*. Although the known author's name, James of Voragine, does not appear, the monk who possessed it in the later fifteenth century has inserted his.[51]

---

[46] CUL, MS Ii.1.22, fols 196r–206v.

[47] They are, in James, *Ancient Libraries*, 33 (no. 161), 65 (no. 537), 73 (no. 647), 77 (no. 698); another copy from Norwich is in CUL, MS Ii.1.31, fols 9r–20v; one from Worcester is in Worcester Cathedral Library, MS F.71, fols 150v–157r; and one of several from Durham is in Bodley, MS Laud misc. 345, fols 62r–77v.

[48] CUL, MS Ii.1.18, fols 128v–134r,139r–142v (Norwich); Cambridge, Corpus Christi College, MS 332, pp. 90–152, 180–97 (Rochester).

[49] These are Worcester Cathedral Library, MSS F.71, Q.66 (incomplete); CUL, MS Kk.4.6; BL, MS Royal 4C.xi. V.I.J. Flint lists all but MS F.71 and explains the Worcester connections of Honorius in her 'Honorius Augustodunensis', in *Authors of the Middle Ages: Historical and Religious Writers of the Latin West, Volume II, nos 5–6* (Aldershot and Brookfield, VT, 1995) [also published separately], 173 [79], 102–4 [8–10].

[50] This is found in Bodley, MS Bodley 767, along with the handbook for priests known as *Speculum juniorum*.

[51] These are in Bodley, MS Rawlinson C.4, fols 198r–265r; BL, MS Royal 7A.vi; Durham,

It would be unwise to draw conclusions before the broad and complex topic surveyed here has been subjected to further, more extensive, investigation. It will be necessary, for example, to assess the extent to which the monks, who had been initially influential in the spread of the Marian cult in England, were themselves influenced by the changes in Marian devotion within the Church at large during the later middle ages. Moreover, in the narrower context of the cathedral priories' book collections, questions must be raised. For example, why, apart from Bernard, are there not more Cistercian authors, who wrote prolifically and eloquently in praise of the Virgin? Again, why are Marian texts less conspicuous at Worcester than mendicant sermons?[52] Or are these observations, arising from recent research, merely founded upon the accidents of loss and survival of manuscripts?

There is abundant evidence to attest that the Virgin Mary was daily revered, exalted, and invoked by the cathedral monks, and it should be noted that their prayers and praises were always directed to her in her relationship with her Son. The reason why Benedictine piety remained on the whole restrained, marked by 'une certaine sobriété', as Jean Leclercq succinctly described it, was that it was founded upon scriptural and patristic texts.[53] It follows that Marian devotion in the monastic liturgy was expressed in the prayers, hymns, antiphons, and sequences which drew their origin and inspiration from these texts. A similar restraint can be discerned in the instructional and devotional writings and in the visual representations of Our Lady, but as yet no definitive conclusions can be drawn. It is hoped that this preliminary survey of the potential for Marian studies within the cathedral priories will bear fruit through further research.

Robinson College, Cambridge

DCL MS B.IV.40. It was John Manby who purchased this last MS from a fellow monk, who was unidentified.

[52] See J. Greatrex, 'Benedictine sermons: preparation and practice in the English cathedral priory cloisters', in C. Muessig, ed., *Medieval Monastic Preaching* (Leiden and Boston, 1998), 271–2.

[53] See J. Leclercq, 'Dévotion et théologie mariales dans le monachisme bénédictin', *Maria, Études sur la sainte Vierge*, 2 (Paris, 1952), 576–7; also R. Laurentin, *Court traité de théologie mariale*, 4th edn (Paris, 1953), 69–70.

THE MARIAN ANTHEM
IN LATE MEDIEVAL ENGLAND

by DAVID SKINNER

*A*LMA *redemptoris mater* is one of the four ancient antiphons or anthems in honour of the Blessed Virgin Mary. This anthem may recall Chaucer's *Prioress's Tale*, and the image of a choirboy, seven years of age, who, having learnt his *Alma redemptoris*, sang daily the Virgin's praises even beyond death. Primer in hand he learnt his *Alma* by heart, only to be murdered in a Jewish ghetto for singing the anthem that he took such pains to perfect. With the song on his lips his throat was cut; but Mary intervened, placed a precious pearl on his tongue, saying,

> My litel child, nowe wol I fecche thee,
> Whan that the greyn is fro thy tonge ytake.
> Be not agast; I wol the nat forsake.[1]

The *Tale*, with its antisemitic theme, may be shocking to the modern reader, but it aptly illustrates the power of Marian devotion as a fundamental part of the medieval experience.

Primers were not only an educational tool for children, but from the thirteenth to the sixteenth century, were also the ordinary prayer-books used by the laity. The contents of these books vary widely, but they possess certain common elements which are never absent, the central feature being the Little Office of the Blessed Virgin Mary and the prayers that follow.[2] Here, however, the *Alma redemptoris*, as well as *Regina caeli* and *Ave regina caelorum* are rarely found, but first among what is usually a long list of prayers is the last of the four Marian anthems *Salve regina*.

The singing of the *Salve* was among the most popular of Marian

---

[1] L.D. Benson, ed., *The Riverside Chaucer*, 3rd edn (Oxford, 1987), 212, ll. 667–9. As delivered, this paper began with a recording of *Alma redemptoris mater* sung by The Cambridge Singers, directed by John Rutter, on Collegium Records (COL CD 116).

[2] See E. Hoskins, *Horae Beatae Mariae Virginis, or, Sarum and York Primers with Kindred Books and Primers of the Reformed Roman Use* (1901); C.C. Butterworth, *The English Primers (1529–1545): Their Publication and Connection with the English Bible and the Reformation in England* (Philadelphia, PA, 1953).

devotions throughout medieval Europe. In England, the prayer came with additional verses and was particularly revered. It was the custom that, after the closing prayers of Compline, clerks would process to an image of the Virgin Mary, and there sing the *Salve regina*, while certain devout members of the town, with prayer books in hands, might rehearse privately similar prayers to Mary listed in their books. The devotions would not take long to recite, but replace the prayer book with a choir-book of late-medieval polyphony and the day's final proceedings could easily extend from being a few minutes in length to more than twenty.

One might associate evening prayer book devotions with parish churches; the performance of polyphony (composed music), however, seems chiefly to have been the domain of religious houses with an average income of around £200 or more.[3] During the reign of Henry VIII, England fostered some 200 professional liturgical choirs which, collectively, represented a broad spectrum of organization and competence. The great chapels of royal foundation, collegiate institutions of the nobility, the choral foundations of Oxford and Cambridge, monastic Lady chapel choirs, and even the more humble establishments of private households, hospitals, and religious guilds all maintained a musical repertoire of some description.[4] The music was composed by the singing-men themselves, and their compositions could freely circulate from one town to the next. It has been shown that the Eton Choirbook, perhaps the most famous of the three surviving choir-books from early Tudor England, contains music that was composed in institutions throughout England from as far north as Lincoln to the furthest reaches of the south coast.[5]

The professional singing-men in the fifteenth and early sixteenth centuries were a rare breed who possessed skills which took years to

[3] This is apparent from a comprehensive study of collegiate and monastic churches by the present author (unpublished); average annual incomes, as they stood in 1535, may be seen in the *Valor Ecclesiasticus*, ed. J. Caley and J. Hunter, 6 vols (1810–34).

[4] The most comprehensive studies of musical institutions in late medieval England include F.Ll. Harrison, *Music in Medieval Britain* (1958; 4th edn, Buren, 1980), and R. Bowers, *English Church Polyphony*, Variorum Collected Studies Series (Aldershot, 1999), esp. articles IV–VII. See also M. Williamson, 'The Eton Choirbook: its institutional and historical background' (University of Oxford D.Phil. thesis, 1997); D. Skinner, *Nicholas Ludford I: Mass Inclina cor meum and Antiphons*, Early English Church Music, 44 (2004), and idem, *The Arundel Choirbook: London, Lambeth Palace Library, MS 1 – a Facsimile and Introduction*, Roxburgh Club (Arundel, 2004).

[5] M. Williamson, 'The early Tudor court, the provinces and the Eton Choirbook', *Early Music*, 25 (1997), 229–43.

cultivate, many having begun their training as boy choristers; even rarer, it seems, were those who turned to composition. By the 1530s the festal and Lady Mass, Magnificat, and the so-called votive antiphon (or better termed 'devotional anthem') were the main compositional forms in England. Composers often unified their large-scale compositions by using similar musical material to link the four movements of a Mass (English composers did not set the Kyrie in festal Mass settings, as this was sung to troped plainchant) to certain sections of a Magnificat and an Anthem. In England, the greatest exponent of this technique was Robert Fayrfax. Cyclic compositions are, in fact, a helpful way of visualizing how music might have played a part in a large musical establishment. For example, Fayrfax's great O bone Iesu cycle, which consists of a Jesus anthem, a Magnificat and a Mass (complete with its elevation motet) would, in effect, thematically link an entire day of musical devotion. The Mass would be heard first, probably in the late morning; then the Magnificat at Vespers; and, finally, the antiphon after Compline, the final office of the day. Here are represented the main compositional forms in context.[6]

The scope in performance of Marian anthems would depend on the size of the institution concerned and, in those cities, towns, and villages where musical composition was fostered on a grand scale (such as in monastic or collegiate churches, or wealthy parishes and guilds), this simple private devotion was often transformed into one of great ritual and music. The so-called Salve ceremonies of late medieval England were very much an opportunity for the laity to become directly involved in the daily devotions to Mary. These events often involved a procession from the chancel, the private space of the church, to a more public arena, such as in the nave (usually before the rood or choir screen), where at certain stations anthems would be sung to Mary, Jesus, a patron saint, or any such combination.

There is plenty of evidence of lay attendance at these rituals. Henry VI followed long-established convention in providing for the singing of Marian antiphons in the nave (the public space) rather than in the choir of his chapel at Eton. At Fotheringhay College in Northamptonshire, the Salve ceremony was a composite of memorials to several saints which commenced at the founder's tomb in the quire and moved in procession into the nave of the parish church; similar ceremonies took place at Arundel College in Sussex and at Tattershall College in Lincolnshire. Magnus Williamson has shown that the guild of St Mary

---

[6] See R. Bray, Robert Fayrfax: O bone Iesu, Early English Church Music, 43 (2002).

and St John the Baptist, Lichfield, maintained chaplains and clerks to sing *Salve regina* in the guild chapel in the market place, one of the busiest public spaces in the city; while in 1515 at St James's Church, Louth, in Lincolnshire, an 'anthem bell' was hung in the newly completed steeple expressly to publicize the evening *Salve* to the towns-folk.[7] The *Salve* ceremony was, therefore, a *public* event, and its musical elaboration was an artistic expression of collective piety.

So great was the devotion to Mary in pre-Reformation England that many texts were written in her honour and subsequently set to music, and to understand the nature and conception of Marian anthems is to appreciate the nature of lay devotion within the context of a collegiate or monastic set up. It is no accident of history that nearly all the great composers of church music in late medieval England were attached to institutions that served a dual purpose: first, to perform memorials for a founder (in the case of collegiate churches) or to adhere to the rules of an order (for monastic churches), and second (and in both cases) to serve the needs of the parish. This is often an aspect of collegiate and monastic musical life that tends to be forgotten, or least neglected. It is also important to remember that, by the middle of the fifteenth century, most composers may be counted among the laity and not the clergy. Indeed by the turn of the sixteenth century the majority of singing-men were lay persons who lived outside their institutions; many were married, had children, and sampled the pleasures of secular life while, paradoxically, spending their entire working week within a sober, religious setting (not so different from the modern day lay-clerk of a cathedral). It would not be uncommon to find an entire comple-ment of male family members working together within a musical establishment, as either singing-men, choristers, or even priests. At Arundel College in the 1490s one brother was a priest-chaplain, while another was a singing-man whose two sons served as choristers; at Fotheringhay, the Johnson family dominated college personnel in all ranks, from servants, to choral staff, to fellows and office holders throughout the 1530s and 40s.[8] Such family participation was certainly not unusual, and put in this context, the performance of Marian anthems takes on a more communal perspective.

So, to imagine the situation in a large collegiate church at the turn of

---

[7] M. Williamson, '*Pictura et scriptura*: The Eton Choirbook in its iconographical context', *Early Music*, 28 (2000), 359–80.

[8] For Arundel, see Skinner, *The Arundel Choirbook*, 9–10; an article on the musical history of Fotheringhay is forthcoming by the same author.

the sixteenth century, the late medieval singing-man would finish his long day after the office of Compline, when he would gather with his colleagues round their founder's tomb, and there say or sing the *Pater noster, Ave Maria,* and the appointed suffrages. Once this is done he would then process to the nave – the parish side of the church – where college and community would assemble before ending their day. The clerks and choristers, many in the company of their families, would kneel and sing, before an image of the Virgin Mary, an anthem not dissimilar, perhaps, to any *Salve regina* preserved in the Eton Choirbook.

* * *

It has been noted that of the output of many composers it is their devotional works that tend to shine, both technically and musically. This observation is not difficult to justify. The Mass and Magnificat do serve a functional, liturgical purpose, and the texts, of course, are unchanging. This is not to suggest that wonderful settings of Masses and Magnificats do not exist from this period, but the antiphon, with its variable subject matter and often beautifully poetic texts, seems better at times to inspire many composers; and it might also be suggested that the shared devotional aspects of their performance also helps to give certain anthems the emotional and artistic edge.

There were certainly a great number of texts from which a composer (or patron) might choose, although the *Salve regina* accounts for the majority of surviving English Marian anthems from before the turn of the sixteenth century. After this time other Marian texts were more frequently being set, and it is notable that the appearance of a number of new Marian compositions coincides with the publication of corresponding literary texts in contemporary primers. It seems fairly clear that composers acquired many of their strictly non-liturgical texts from these lay sources. Indeed, two texts that commonly appear in prayer books with the *Salve regina* – *Gaude flore virginali* (celebrating the seven spiritual joys of Our Lady, and attributed to St Thomas of Canterbury) and *Gaude virgo mater Christi* (celebrating the five spiritual joys of Our Lady) – were frequently set to music. Relatively newer devotional texts to Mary, such as *Ave Dei patris filia, Ave cuius conceptio, Salve intemerata virgo* (and others) may be found in prayer books of the early sixteenth century, around the same time that settings of these texts appear in musical sources.[9]

---

[9] For a list of surviving Latin compositions from this period, see M. Hofman and J.

Some texts chosen for musical composition were from among the most inventive devotional poetry found in the prayer books of the time. *Ave fuit prima salus* and *Ave rosa sine spinis* are both meditations on the *Ave Maria*, whose text in both of the prayers may be constructed from the first word of each verse.[10] Most enigmatic is, perhaps, *Plaude potentissima, Parens plasmatoris*, by Stephen Prowett (*c*.1495–1560); the work is made up of a seven-verse poetic text in which all 122 words begin with a 'p', an obvious pun on the name of the composer. Only a few of the surviving Marian anthems are found in prayer books to come with indulgences (these are never transferred to the musical source), such as *Ave Maria ancilla trinitatis*, set by at least four composers, which, according to the prayer book rubric, was shown to St Bernard by the messenger of God, saying 'that as golde is moost precious of all other metall, soo excedeth thys prayer [of] all other prayers, and who that deuoutly sayth it shall have a singular rewarde of our blessyd lady and her swete son iesus'.[11] However, the texts of a great number of anthems – some 30 per cent of the surviving total – cannot be found in contemporary prayer books, although it is thought that these texts may have been commissioned alongside the compositions themselves. The subject matter of some anthems is suggestive: *Salve regina pudica mater* by Nicholas Ludford, a composer who spent his entire working life in the royal chapel of St Stephen in Westminster, contains a prayer for Henry VIII and Catherine of Aragon which, with a petition to the Virgin Mary to protect England from its enemies, is thought to have been written during one of Henry's campaigns against the French and the Scots.[12] Another anthem by Ludford, *Domine Iesu Christe*, is thought to have possible associations with the burial of Abbot John Islip in the Jesus chapel at Westminster Abbey in 1532.[13]

One conclusive link between patron, composer and composition in early sixteenth-century England may be found in Robert Fayrfax's setting of *Eterne laudis lilium*, an anthem to the Virgin Mary and St

Morehen, *Latin Music in British Sources c.1485–c.1610*, Early English Church Music, Suppl. Vol. 2 (1987).

[10] *Ave fuit prima salus* was set by at least two composers (John Mason and ?Richard Lovell). *Ave rosa sine spinis* was set by Thomas Tallis (d.1585), and the literary text may be found in printed prayer books from 1510 (see Hoskins, *Horae*, 124; the text is also found in an early fifteenth-century prayer book, Bodley, MS Douce 1, unfoliated).

[11] See Hoskins, *Horae*, 124; the text is also found in several manuscript prayer books from the fifteenth century.

[12] See Skinner, *Nicholas Ludford*, p. xviii.

[13] Ibid., p. xx.

Elizabeth. Fayrfax, a Gentleman of the Chapel Royal under both Henry VII and Henry VIII, was considered by his own contemporaries as the prime musician of the nation, and a number of royal commissions can be tied to his name. Of his surviving works, however, only *Eterne laudis lilium* can be identified as such. On 28 March 1502 Elizabeth of York, admired and well loved queen to Henry VII, paid Fayrfax a substantial sum of 20s for setting an anthem to Our Lady and St Elizabeth. The text was newly composed (possibly by Fayrfax himself), in which the first letter of each line spells out the phrase ELISABETH REGINA ANGLIE:

> E terne laudis lilium, O dulcis Maria, te
> L audat vox angelica. Nutrix Christi pia.
> I ure prolis glorie detur harmonia,
> S alus nostre memorie omni agonia.
> A ve radix, flos virginum, O sanctificata.
> B enedicta in utero materno creata.
> E ras sancta puerpera et inviolata,
> T uo ex Iesu filio virgo peramata.
> H onestis celi precibus virgo veneraris,
>
> R egis excelsi filii visu iocundaris.
> E ius divino lumine tu nusquam privaris.
> G aude sole splendidior virgo singularis.
> I ssachar quoque Nazaphat nex non Ismaria,
> N ati ex Iesse stipite qua venit Maria,
> A tque Maria Cleophe sancto Zacharia,
>
> A qua patre Elizabeth, matre Sophonia
> N atus est Dei gratia Iohannes Baptista.
> G audebat clauso Domino in matrice cista.
> L ine ex hoc genere est evangelista
> I ohannes. Anne filia ex Maria ista
> E st Iesus Dei filius natus in hunc mundum.
>
> Cuius cruoris tumulo mundatur in mundum; conferat nos
> in gaudium, in evum iocundum, qui cum patre et spiritu
> sancto regnat in unum. Amen.

The work begins in general praise of Mary, and then provides a curious (and perhaps unorthodox) lineage of Christ through Mary and the female line, with St Elizabeth, mother of St John the Baptist, as one of the central themes.[14] It stands, of course, in counter-balance to the genealogy at the opening of St Matthew's Gospel, which traces the lineage of Christ through Joseph and the male line.

We often see the image of a patron appearing in the pages of his or her specially commissioned illuminated prayer book, and here in Fayrfax's anthem we have what is perhaps the closest equivalent to visible patronage in music. The second part of the text, as may be seen, reads simply as a genealogical list of names. It is the composer's task, therefore, to bring those words to life, to give them meaning. So, how does Fayrfax respond? For those not familiar with late-medieval English music, it must be said that, unlike their Continental counterparts, English composers before the generation of Fayrfax rarely constructed a truly musical response to the words. In the refined polyphony of the Franco-Flemish school headed by Josquin Desprez, one hears a more humanistic approach to musical composition; here may be heard a distinct balance between imitative vocal lines and more homophonic (or chordal) compositional techniques which, in their own ways, serve to accentuate key elements in a literary text. English composers, in contrast, tended to highlight the vocal sonorities in their music, often writing for two or three voices, with little or no imitation, and bringing the entire texture together in order to underline particular words or phrases.

In *Eterne laudis lilium* Fayrfax *does* respond, and in ways quite foreign to his predecessors in that there is a clear musical reaction to what is being stated in the text. The genealogy of Christ starts with the letter 'I' of 'REGINA', and here in the music the texture is reduced from all five voices (soprano, alto, tenor, baritone, and bass) to soprano and tenor. Two lines later, at 'atque Maria', the baritone and bass take over, before all voices in turn, including the otherwise silent alto, sing the word 'Elizabeth', highlighting the namesake of the patron of this work. The texture becomes full at the 'L' of 'ANGLIE', where reference is made to St John the Evangelist, a favourite saint of Elizabeth of York. But the highlight of the entire work occurs at the first and only mention of Jesus Christ, being the resolution of this devotional text.[15]

---

[14] As given in the *Golden Legend* and the *Protoevangelium*, and referred to in a sermon on Mary by Johannes Eck, mentioned in the *Acta Sanctorum*. See Andrew Carwood's liner note in a recording of this work by The Cardinall's Musick, on the ASV Gaudeamus label (CD GAU 160).

[15] Here was played a recording of a *Eterne laudis lilium* by Robert Fayrfax (d.1521),

Still, while Fayrfax might respond in a particular way to a text that is placed before him, it does not necessarily follow that we in the twenty-first century will have similar reactions to those who would have heard this composition 500 years ago. Yet one wonders whether it might follow that such anthems were perceived as an extension of the doctrinal and iconographic imagery that is still seen in the naves of a number of churches in England. Just as images of saints, of biblical stories, and of man's morality and mortality once served a didactic purpose for the laity (many of whom, of course, were illiterate), so too might musical anthems had been used to add an extra layer of devotional *and* instructive tapestry to the proceedings? Composers who daily saw such images in the wall paintings and stained glass of their respective institutions would certainly have understood their significance in relation to the *Salve* ceremony. Convincing correlations have recently been shown between the wall paintings in the nave at Eton College, and works by Robert Wilkinson (a singing-man at Eton) in the great choirbook of that place.[16] At Arundel and Fotheringhay, and doubtlessly elsewhere, sermons were delivered in the nave by the college clergy in order to explain and clarify the activity which took place in the chancel. Here one can imagine the orator drawing, time and time again, on the multimedia of visual and aural images around him as an aid to illustrate his message.

It must be admitted that is less clear how music might have been employed as a didactic instrument, but the subject matter of some anthems again might provide a few clues. Like the original four Marian antiphons, polyphonic settings of other devotional texts can also be seasonal, and are often written for a particular saint or Marian festival. But those written for specific key events in the temporal calendar of the church (such as Advent/Christmas, Lent/Easter) are rare. One anthem, again by Robert Fayrfax, seems to fall into this latter category. While *Eterne laudis lilium* may be considered an early work, *Maria plena virtute* probably counts among his last surviving compositions; with regard to the presence of musical rhetoric, it is certainly among the most exceptional of the period. Though technically a Marian anthem and one that may well have been heard in a *Salve* ceremony, *Maria plena virtute* is closer to a private musing on the matter of the Passion than a general

performed by The Cardinall's Musick, directed by Andrew Carwood, on the ASV Gaudeamus label (CD GAU 160).

[16] Williamson, '*Pictura et scriptura*'.

prayer to the Virgin. In primers of the period it is common to find meditations on the Seven Last Words on the Cross, where Christ's words are applied to the devotee's own behaviour. To quote but one example found frequently in the prayer books, 'Lord, as you said, "Father, forgive those who crucify me", grant that for love of you I may forgive all those who do me wrong'. A similar interpolation of Christ's words and personal petitions occurs in Fayrfax's anthem, though Christ's words are here loosely paraphrased and not in the correct order; *In manus tuas, Domine, commendo spiritum meum* ('Into your hands, O Lord, I commend my spirit') is omitted altogether. In the Sarum Rite, this respond was sung at Compline only on Passion Sunday which, if Fayrfax's anthem was intended for such an occasion, *may* account for its omission. But it is Mary, in fact, who is last to be quoted in the anthem: 'Son, in the hour of death, forgive the sins of this your servant'.[17]

It is through Mary's sorrow, as expressed in the Stations of the Cross for example, that those in prayer can relate to the pain of the Passion and Crucifixion. In this text and others (such as the *Stabat mater*), she guides the penitent and makes understandable the mystery of redemption through Christ's death; she also focuses human feeling in an accessible way, providing comfort as death draws near. An emotional text often demands an impassioned delivery, so what better means to convey this narrative to the lay person than through the medium of music and words? Indeed, one can imagine this particular anthem being prefaced with an appropriate sermon, in which key biblical references to the story are emphasised.

This preliminary discussion of *Maria plena virtute* has drawn attention to only a few musical features. For fuller analysis the list is considerably longer. Sadly, the work survives only in post-Reformation sources so cannot be illustrated via an illuminated choir-book. However, a guided tour through this most extraordinary of anthems can highlight certain words and phrases which merit particular attention.

The anthem begins, as expected, with an invocation to Mary (sung by three voices), after which a duet moves swiftly to the Passion and the first reference to St Luke's Gospel: 'Father forgive them, for they know not what they do', and Christ's comforting words to the robber condemned with him: 'Today you will be with me among our fathers in paradise' (23:39–43). As the texture becomes full, the focus is

---

[17] See text on following two pages.

ROBERT FAYRFAX
Maria plena virtute

(Bracketed numbers refer to the original order of the
Seven Last Words on the Cross)

FIRST PART
Alto (A), Baritone (Bar), Bass (B) – Soprano (S), Tenor (T)

Maria plena virtute pietatis gratie mater misericordie, tu nos ab hoste protege.	Mary full of goodness, devotion and grace, mother of mercy, protect us from the enemy.
Clementissima Maria vite per merita compassionis tue pro nobis preces effunde et de peccatis meis erue.	Most merciful Mary, by the merits of your life and compassion pour out your prayers for us and do away mine offences.
Sicut tuus filius petiit pro crucifigentibus, Pater dimite ignorantibus, magna pietate pendens in latronibus dixit uni ex hominibus, in paradiso cum patribus mecum eris hodie.	Just as your son prayed for those who were crucified, (1) 'Father forgive them, for they know not what they do', in great trust as he hung there, he spoke to one of the robbers and said, (2) 'today you will be with me among our fathers in paradise'.

FULL	
Mater dolorosa plena lacrimosa videns ruinosa filium in cruce, cum voce raucosa dixit speciosa, mulier clamorosa filium tuum ecce. Vertens ad discipulum, sic fuit mandatum matrem fuisse per spatium, et ipsam consolare: et sicut decebat filium servum paratissimum custodivit preceptum omnino servire.	Mother of sorrows, full of tears, as you watched your son on the cross of destruction, in a voice of broken beauty he said, (3) 'woman of weeping, behold thy son'. Turning to the disciple, it was his command that she be his mother, and that he comfort her: and thus it was fitting that the servant son was most ready to preserve the rule of serving all.

widened as Fayrfax moves to the scene at the foot of the cross when Christ commits the care of his mother to the Beloved Disciple (John 19:25–7); the section ends with the words of St Mark (10:44), concerning the son of Man who comes not to be served but to serve.

From this point, narrative and personal interjection interweave in the music rather like the chorus in a play. Most unusual, for an English composition, is the syllabic word setting in places, which is certainly more reminiscent of Continental techniques than those practised in England. There is much to listen for. Of particular note is the chordal opening, prefacing Christ's words 'sitio salutem genuis' ('I thirst for the salvation of Man' – not simply 'I thirst', as in St John's gospel narrative (19:28)). This is a cue for personal musing in the soprano, tenor, bass

SECOND PART
ATBarB – STB – TBarB – TB – SATBarB

Dixit Iesus dilectionis, sitio salutum genui. Audi orationibus nostris tue misericordie, O Iesu.	Jesus spoke of his love, saying, (5) 'I thirst for the salvation of all people'. O Jesu in your mercy listen to our prayers.
Rex amabilis quid sustulisti pro nobis! Per merita tue passionis peto veniam a te.	O king of love, what have you taken from us! By the merits of your passion I ask pardon.
Iesu, dicens clamasti Deus meus, quid dereliquisti? Per acetum quod gustasti ne derelinquas me, consummatum dixisti.	Jesus, you cried aloud and said, (4) 'my God, why have you forsaken me?'. By the bitter wine you tasted do not abandon me; you cried, (6) 'it is fulfilled'.
O Iesu fili Dei, in hora exitus mei, animam meam suscipe.	O Jesu, son of God, in the hour of my death receive my soul.
Tunc spiritum emisit, et matrem gladius pertransivit. Aqua et sanguis exivit, ex delicato corpore. Post ab Arimathia rogavit et Iesum sepelivit, et Nicodemus venit ferens mixturam myrrhe.	Then he gave up the ghost, and a sword pierced his mother. Blood and water flowed out from his body. Joseph of Arimathea asked for his body and buried Jesus, and Nicodemus came bringing a mixture of myrrh.

FULL

O dolorosa mater Christi, quales penas tu vidisti, corde tenens habuisti fidem totius ecclesie. Ora pro me, regina celi, filium tuum dicens, fili, in hora mortis, servi tui peccatis suis indulge. Amen.	O sorrowing mother of Christ, what torments you beheld and dept in your heart the faith of the whole Church. Pray for me, queen of heaven, and say to your son, 'Son, in the hour of death, forgive the sins of this your servant'. Amen.

trio at 'Rex amabilis' before a movement to Matthew, 'My God, why hast thou forsaken me?' (27:46), and back to John, 'It is fulfilled' (19:30). Here, note Fayrfax's use of dark textures in the lowest voices, especially at 'consummatum'. Another personal petition follows before further drawing on scripture at the mention of the sword piercing Mary's heart from St Luke (2:35), and the mission of Joseph of Arimathea and Nicodemus from St John (19:38–42). The anthem then comes full circle, when all of the voices unite and attention is again focused on Mary. Fayrfax implements the darkest and most sombre chords in setting 'O dolorosa mater Christi' ('O sorrowing mother of Christ'), after which the harmony is brightened at 'fidem totius ecclesie' ('the faith of the whole Church') as if to underline the strength and confidence of the composer's own belief. Finally, there seems to be an inter-jection of dramatic irony with the words 'regina caeli', a Paschaltide reference to the Virgin, at which point the sopranos reach the highest point in their vocal range for the entire work. Throughout his compo-sition, Fayrfax responds to almost every nuance of his text with remark-able melodic and harmonic subtlety, the like of which would not be a regular feature in English church music until William Byrd put pen to paper later in the century.

Fayrfax's anthem, with its concentration on the Gospel narratives is, of course, ideally suited for performance in Holy Week. While being a Gentleman of the Chapel Royal, he spent much of his career attached to St Alban's Abbey, where he and his family lie buried. In monastic churches where polyphony was cultivated, such as at St Alban's, West-minster, Winchester, and elsewhere, the choir largely sang in the Lady Chapel as opposed to the chancel, the latter being the domain of the monks. We do not know how the *Salve* ceremony was performed at St Alban's, but, as elsewhere in England, it was probably celebrated in the parochial nave of the church or in a public space elsewhere in the town. Meanwhile the seasonal antiphons to Mary would be performed by the community in the chancel. *Ave regina caelorum* was directed to be sung from Candlemas to the Wednesday of Holy Week; *Regina caeli*, the next antiphon in rotation, would not be heard until Compline of Holy Saturday. Special observances such as the Little Office of the Blessed Virgin and the performance of Marian anthems were omitted during the *triduum*, as the liturgical timetable for these three days was excep-tionally crowded.

So what of Fayrfax's *Maria plena virtute*? Being a 'Salve' devotion, it could have been performed at any point in Holy Week, if not on Good Friday itself; but it is the appearance of the words 'Regina caeli', high-lighted musically in such an obvious way, that seems to assign its performance during the *triduum*, when no devotions to Mary would have been sung by the monks at St Alban's. In the darkness of Holy Week, is Fayrfax here giving his community, both lay and religious, a glimmer of light?[18]

Magdalen College, Oxford

---

[18] At the original delivery, the lecture concluded with a recording of *Maria plena virtute* by Robert Fayrfax, performed by The Cardinall's Musick, directed by Andrew Carwood, on the ASV Gaudeamus label (CD GAU 145).

CARDINAL CAJETAN AND
FRA AMBROSIUS CATHARINUS
IN THE CONTROVERSY OVER THE
IMMACULATE CONCEPTION OF THE VIRGIN
IN ITALY, 1515–51

by PATRICK PRESTON

THE development of the doctrine of the Immaculate Conception of the Virgin has a long history. This article deals with a small but important segment of this development, by providing some account of what was at stake and of the main stages by which the contest was fought out, principally within the Dominican Order, between 1515 and 1551.

The development here considered is really sandwiched between two Councils, the Fifth Lateran on the one hand, and Trent on the other, at which the thought of settling a very contentious issue was first entertained and then dismissed. The need for a settlement became apparent in the fifteenth century when the increasing popularity of the doctrine exacerbated the longstanding rivalry between the Franciscans, its principal devotees, and the Dominicans, its traditional opponents. Pope Sixtus IV went some way towards satisfying the Immaculists by the constitution *Cum praeexcelsa* of 1476, but the constitution *Grave nimis* of 1483 gave some satisfaction to their opponents, because it explicitly stated that, in the case of this doctrine, the Church had not yet made up its mind. Meanwhile, in an attempt to reduce the tension, mutual accusations of heresy were forbidden. Pope Alexander VI confirmed *Grave nimis* with the bull *Illius qui* in 1502.[1] It might have been convenient to provide a definitive answer at the Fifth Lateran Council (1512–17). Pope Leo X evidently thought so, for he asked for guidance from the great Dominican theologian, Cardinal Cajetan. The outcome was the *Tractatus* of 1515.[2] Nothing came of it. Nevertheless, while the question

---

[1] P. Giacinto Bosco, O.P., 'Intorno a un carteggio inedito di Ambrogio Caterino', *Memorie Domenicane*, 67 (1950), 142.

[2] Tommaso de Vio Gaetano, *Tractatus de conceptione Beatae Mariae Virginis ad Leonem X*, in idem, *Opuscula omnia* (Lyons, 1575), 2, tract. I.137–142. I have used *The Judgement of Thomas de Vio Cajetan against the Immaculate Conception of the Blessed Virgin Mary*, trans. R.C. Jenkins (1858); all quotations are from this version.

remained unsettled, the doctrine continued to grow in popularity and from time to time occasioned scandal, as at Vigevano in 1537[3] and, much more sensationally, at Siena, in the Tuscan Congregation of the Dominicans ten years earlier. At the centre of the Sienese dispute was Ambrosius Catharinus, O.P., best known perhaps as the most formidable Italian anti-Lutheran polemicist of his day, but also tireless in his advocacy of Marian devotion and the doctrine of the Immaculate Conception of the Virgin. This Sienese dispute has been discussed by Giacinto Bosco,[4] showing how in Siena, a city of which Mary was the patron saint, popular devotion to the Virgin, intensified by the strain of a siege and the subsequent triumph over enemies internal and external, eventuated in a vow that committed the whole city to the annual solemn celebration of the Feast of the Immaculate Conception. For theological reasons endorsed and enforced by the Dominican hierarchy, the Observant Dominicans of Santo Spirito refused to honour the vow in spite of intense pressure from the magistrates. They were supported in their refusal by the Prior of San Marco in Florence, the Prior Provincial of the Tuscan Congregation, to whom the Sienese Observants owed allegiance as members of that Congregation. Probably in early 1527, Catharinus was posted to Santo Spirito, where he very rapidly became prior, in which post he had the responsibility of handling the delicate negotiations between Santo Spirito and the city government. In spite of papal permission to celebrate the feast, the Observants, still supported by the Prior of San Marco, refused to submit. In the ensuing discussions, in which Catharinus, as an ardent Immaculist, sided with the city government against his own community and the Prior of San Marco, ill feeling became so intense that the outcome was an allegation of heresy and an appeal to Rome, which Catharinus was adjudged by Cardinal Cajetan to have lost. His position, his whole career in the Order, was compromised. The Dominican hierarchy never forgave him for what was obviously considered as a lack of loyalty – he had after all entered the Dominican Order at San Marco – and possibly a breach of the monastic vow of obedience. He for his part never forgave Cajetan, whom he blamed, no doubt unjustly, for his failure.

It is therefore ironic that in 1531, the year after his humiliation, Santo Spirito was made to toe the line; and it had become the intention

---

[3] F. Chabod, *Storia religiosa dello stato di Milano durante il dominio di Carlo V* (Bologna, 1938), 189.

[4] In Bosco, 'Intorno', 107–153.

of the Dominican Superiors to extend this obligation to celebrate the Immaculate Conception of Mary to the whole Order.[5] No doubt it was this general amelioration of the situation that induced Catharinus to write the first of his three tracts on the Immaculate Conception and to produce this at the Dominican General Chapter in Rome in 1532:[6] he was intent on pressing home his advantage, but he had no success in face of the hostility against him.[7]

Concurrently, he was working on another by-product of the great controversy of 1527–30: his vitriolic *Annotationes in commentaria Caietani*,[8] which it is easy to see as an act of revenge for the humiliation inflicted upon him. Book IV of these *Annotationes*, in which Catharinus attempts to respond to the influential negative view of the doctrine of the Immaculate Conception presented by Cajetan in his *Tractatus* of 1515, has the title *De his quae attinent ad Beatae Virginis dignitatem et puritatem*. But Catharinus was not the only Dominican with animus to discharge against the recently dead Cajetan. The future Master of the Sacred Palace, Bartolomeo Spina, also published a work against him in 1535.[9] While Catharinus was blaming his victim for having done so little to support the Immaculate Conception, Spina was blaming him for having done far too much. According to Spina, the balanced position assumed by Cajetan was superfluous, illogical, dangerous, and insufficient. It was also contrary to Scripture, to the spirit of the Church, and to the traditions of the Dominican order and its most qualified doctors.[10] Also in 1535, Spina published another work with a bearing on the doctrine of the Immaculate Conception,[11] and Catharinus duly made it the object of his attack in his second improved tract on the subject in 1542.[12] In that year he also produced the second edition of the *Annotationes*,[13] and so repeated the anti-Cajetan case of

[5] Ibid., 154–5.

[6] Ambrosius Catharinus *Disputatio pro veritate Immaculatae Conceptionis Beatae Virginis Mariae ad Patres ac Fratres Ordinis Praedicatorum* (Siena, 1532).

[7] Bosco, 'Intorno', 159.

[8] Ambrosius Catharinus, *Annotationes in excerpta quaedam de commentariis Reverendissimi Cardinalis S. Xisti dogmata* (Paris, 1535).

[9] Bartolomeo Spina, *Tractatus contra opusculum Caietani de conceptione Beatae Virginis* (Venice, 1535).

[10] Bosco, 'Intorno', 148.

[11] Bartolomeo Spina, *De universali corruptione generis humani ab Adam seminaliter propagati* (Venice, 1535). See Bosco, 'Intorno', 159.

[12] Ambrosius Catharinus, *Disputationis pro immaculate divae Virginis conceptione libri tres*, in idem, *Opuscula* (Lyons, 1542), pt III, 1–103.

[13] Ambrosius Catharinus, *Annotationes in commentaria Cajetani* (Lyons, 1542).

1535. Thereafter, Spina replaced Cajetan as Catharinus's principal bugbear. Enmity between the two became public at the time when the doctrine of the Immaculate Conception was being discussed at the Council of Trent.

Catharinus was present at this Council in the role of papal theologian. Yet he took no part in the discussion that ensued in 1546 when Cardinal Pedro Pacheco, Bishop of Jaen, proposed the Immaculate Conception as the first item on the agenda should dogma be discussed as well as reform.[14] Catharinus kept quiet, on the principle that the first task of the Council was the rejection of the Reformers' doctrines. Only after this should controversies among Catholics be dealt with.[15] But Spina, now the Master of the Sacred Palace and a member of the Council Commission in Rome, did his best to prevent the dogmatization of the Immaculate Conception. At the expense of Cardinal John of Toledo, and in association with his pupil and current colleague on the Council Commission, Alberto Duimo de Catharo, he published a hostile work of Torquemada's on the Immaculate Conception from the time of the Council of Basle that had hitherto remained in manuscript. However, the published version contained so many changes that it should really be regarded as a new work. To it he added an index of fifty-eight errors concerning the Immaculate Conception and attributed them to Catharinus.[16] In the event, presumably to Catharinus's bitter disappointment, Trent produced no decree on the Immaculate Conception. But, according to some authors,[17] it did virtually decide in its favour, for in the final paragraph of the decree on Original Sin we read,

> This holy council declares, however, that it is not its intention to include in this decree ... the blessed and immaculate Virgin Mary, the mother of God, but that the constitutions of Pope Sixtus IV ... are to be observed under the penalties contained in those constitutions, which it renews.[18]

[14] H. Jedin, *A History of the Council of Trent*, 2 vols (1957–61), 2:139.
[15] Ambrosius Catharinus, *Disputatio pro veritate immaculatae conceptionis Beatissimae Virginis et eius celebranda a cunctis fidelibus festivate*, in his *Enarrationes in quinque priora capita libri Geneseos* (Rome, 1551–2), the tract occupies pp. 1–115 in the 3rd set of pagination in the volume.
[16] Ibid., 3.
[17] For example, M. Mullett, *The Catholic Reformation* (1999), 5.
[18] H.J. Schroeder, *Canons and Decrees of the Council of Trent*, (Rockford, IL, 1979), 23; see also *Decrees of the Ecumenical Councils*, ed. Norman P. Tanner, 2 vols (London and Washington DC, 1990), 2:*667.

Nevertheless, Catharinus replied to Spina and restated his position on the Immaculate Conception at the request of Julius III and the expense of Cardinal Alvarez of Toledo in the *Disputatio* of 1551.[19]

The first and the last contributions to this running debate merit further attention. On the one hand they show the strength of the case for the traditional Dominican opposition to the doctrine of the Immaculate Conception of the Virgin. On the other, they demonstrate not only the importance of the cult as an element in Catholic Reformation piety, but also the importance of the arguments used in the controversy by Catharinus, as indications of the Catholic Reformation emphasis on the power and the authority of the pope and the church.

The first tract, Cajetan's *Tractatus* of 1515, is a brief, methodical, and judicious discussion in five chapters that begins with a set of general principles for determining belief. We understand that there are three ordinary methods of determining the status of a belief, and one extraordinary method, but all depend on revelation.[20] To be accepted as valid, a doctrine must be supported by divine revelation; but divine revelation is made to, and declared by, different human agencies. This permits a distinction to be made between the various methods of determining belief, which are as follows: revelations made to the authors of the canonical books of the Holy Scriptures and to the Apostles in general; revelations made to the Apostolic See; revelations made to the holy doctors of the Church; and revelations made to the recipients of genuine miracles.

The third kind of revelation must be less secure, for Cajetan tells us that we hold doctrines supported by this kind of revelation as probable only,[21] whereas support by the other three revelations will render a doctrine unassailable. A further distinction is to be made, for a revelation may contain a doctrine either implicitly or explicitly: in the former case great care must be taken to ensure the validity of the methods for making the implicit explicit.[22] The thrust of Cajetan's argument is first to show that the status of the doctrine of the Immaculate Conception of the Virgin is probable only (in other words, its strength comes from revelations made to holy doctors), and then to show that, as things stood in 1515, there were two views about Mary that had the support of the doctors, and one was more probable than the other. The question really was, 'Was the Mother of God preserved from sin, or was she cleansed from it?' There are some subtleties to consider here, but to begin with at least all is plain sailing. Mary was not preserved from original sin and all its penalties, for Christ died for all.[23] The text to ponder is II Corinthians 5.14, 'If Christ died for all, then all are dead', that is, dead by the death of sin. However, there is a second sense to be attached to the preservation thesis: that Mary 'was preserved from the stain of original sin and not from the infection of the flesh'. '[S]he had a corrupt nature with the fuel and the guilt of sin, she needed the manifestation of a future remedy through the incarnation and death of Jesus Christ.'[24] This is not contrary to Scripture. Here the preservation thesis modulates into the cleansing thesis, for 'the grace which sanctified her has the character of a grace cleansing, reconciling, redeeming etc.'[25] What is it then that gets cleansed? The answer is that it is the soul. But there is an oddity in such a remark, for Mary's soul *ex hypothesi* was never stained. The point is that the soul would have been stained if grace had not intervened, for the infection of the flesh would inevitably have contaminated it on the junction of the soul with the body. For this reason, Cajetan introduces, explains, and defends an argument that he attributes to Aquinas. It is to the effect that there is a series of terms – preservation is another – that have not only an actual but also a conditional or potential sense, that is they are applicable not only to actual cases, but also to potential cases.[26] 'It is in this sense that the Blessed Virgin is alleged to have been preserved from original sin by those who affirm that she was conceived without original sin.'[27] The upshot of these arguments is that we are left with two Marian claims between which to decide, and both relate to the freedom of her soul from contamination by the body: is this to be described as the consequence of preservation or of cleansing? Chapter IV considers the case for the former position, and Chapter V for the latter.

Here, by the previous argument, we have only probabilities to go on. The cleansing argument, we are told, has received a great deal of support from holy doctors. Cajetan limits the task of assessing the evidence by adducing the names, and selected quotations from the works, of fifteen saints only.[28] The list, though necessary, is also tedious, and need not be rehearsed here. One of the finer points that arises in the course of considering and dismissing attempts to avoid the weight

---

[23] Ibid., 60.
[24] Ibid., 64–5.
[25] Ibid., 65.

[26] Ibid., 65–6.
[27] Ibid., 68.
[28] Ibid., 69.

of this evidence is the notion that there are two conceptions, one before the soul was infused, and one when the soul was infused. Then the evasion is that Mary was immaculately conceived with respect to the second of these conceptions, but not with respect to the first. Cajetan dismissed this evasion with the remark that the fifteen saints always refer to the second 'conception', so that Mary's body was corrupt at the time of the infusion of the soul, 'for original sin cannot be found without a rational soul'.[29] Catharinus later made use of the idea that Cajetan here dismisses.

What then of the argument of the preservationists? Their case receives more varied support. Nine sources are given, but only three are of substance: the support of many doctors; the decision of a council; and the worship of the Church. Cajetan's strategy is to look at all nine and assess their weight, usually unfavourably. Yes, there are many doctors who have supported this view, but most of them are moderns, and in any case, 'in those things which belong to God, we ought rather to think with the ancients than with the moderns'.[30] Yes, the thirty-sixth Session of the Council of Basle did decide for this position, but it was at that time a schismatic body, that is, a synagogue of Satan.[31] And yes, nearly all the Latin Churches celebrate the Feast of the Conception, not of the Sanctification, and the insinuation therefore is 'that the Virgin was not purified from original sin, but conceived without it'. But 'many churches throughout the world celebrate the Sanctification, and not the Conception; and herein the Church suffers everyone to abound in his own sense'.[32] Cajetan's conclusion is therefore that the cleansing hypothesis is more probable, given the evidence considered. His advice to Leo X was, therefore, that if a definition of the question were to be given at the Fifth Lateran Council, it should endorse the cleansing hypothesis, according to the precedent of the Council of Vienne under Clement V, which determined the more probable doctrine.[33]

Catharinus's *Disputatio* of 1551 takes a different tack. His doctrine of the Immaculate Conception of the Virgin is stated early in Part I,[34] and depends on the notion that there are two conceptions, the first at the time of fertilization and the second much later when the rational soul is infused. Sin may only be predicated of a human being with a rational soul. In a nutshell, his doctrine of the Immaculate Conception is that

---

[29] Ibid., 76.
[30] Ibid., 77.
[31] Ibid., 81.

[32] Ibid., 82.
[33] Ibid., 86.
[34] Catharinus, *Disputatio* (1551), 16.

Mary was first conceived in the usual way, but at the moment of the infusion of the rational soul was the recipient of a special divine privilege that rendered her immune from the normal sinful consequences of life in the flesh. Why? Here enters the notion of congruence or decorum: Mary was the future mother and spouse of Christ, and it was therefore fitting for her status to be thus elevated.[35] The rest of Part I is devoted to defending this doctrine from Spina's objections, but of course the notion of congruence allows Catharinus to suggest the rich vein of piety and spirituality latent in the idea of Mary as the Mother, the Bride, and the daughter of Christ – a piety that traditionally draws substance from interpretations of the Song of Solomon. On the title page of this work he cleverly alludes to this piety by a quotation from that source – in fact a learned pun at the expense of Spina's name: 'Sicut lilium inter spinas, sic amica mea inter filias'. In this disputation, Spina and his co-author Duimio are almost always referred to as 'the thorns'. Lest we forget, the work concludes with another quotation from the same source: 'Tota pulchra es Amica mea et macula non est in te'.[36]

In the remarkable Part II, attention turns from doctrine to worship. The obstinacy of the Dominican hierarchy in refusing to accept the Immaculate Conception is no longer an obstinacy in face of what to Catharinus seem overwhelming theological arguments, but an arrogant and presumptuous defiance of a decision made by Peter, God's representative on earth. For Catharinus, their plight is hopeless. On the one hand, they face the overwhelming authority of the Holy See; on the other hand, divine providence is moving against them. Catharinus recalls what Dominicans said to him during the troubles of 1527–30: the Order of Preachers is the greatest and noblest part of the Roman Church,[37] that is, they are the head and the others are the members.[38] They constitute themselves the critics and judges of the whole Church, all the Orders, and all the universities.[39] The truth is that the brothers of the Order are under the Church.[40] In the constitutions of Sixtus IV it was no mere Franciscan who spoke, as Dominicans allege in excuse of their behaviour, but Peter and the whole Church,[41] which cannot err in matters pertaining to the faith.[42] The Church will not suffer an opinion repugnant to divine worship.[43] Bernard of Clairvaux, whose stance on

35 Ibid., 39.
36 Ibid., 115.
37 Ibid., 94.
38 Ibid., 94.
39 Ibid., 113.
40 Ibid., 102.
41 Ibid., 95.
42 Ibid., 96.
43 Ibid., 114–15.

the celebration of the Immaculate Conception was an inspiration for the Dominican case, even confessed as much in his letter to the canons of Lyons. He was then against the Immaculate Conception because the Church was not for it, but now things are different, and he would surely have adjusted his position had he been living in our time.[44]

In all this we detect the hand of God in history.[45] Since Bernard's time there have been 400 years of steady growth in the cult of the Immaculate Conception in spite of massive opposition orchestrated by the Dominicans.[46] Yet no Dominican pope ever attempted to define the doctrine in an adverse sense.[47] Surely the Holy Spirit has controlled the course of events. The Dominicans are subject to a tide that will not ebb.[48]

* * *

Catharinus's *Disputatio* is important for three main reasons. Firstly, it contributed to the acceptance of an influential popular cult immensely important in Reformed Catholicism. Secondly, it introduced an evolutionary view of Christian doctrine as not fixed in the past (as Cajetan seems to suggest) but as advancing in due season in accordance with the prompting of the Holy Spirit. Thirdly, it advocated an unquestioning acceptance of papal authority. Once the pope speaks on behalf of the Church all members, including Dominicans,[49] must toe the line without demur. Here too, it is not difficult to detect the spirit of the Catholic Reformation.

Catharinus's *Disputatio*, then, plainly reflects the way in which the Catholic response to the Lutheran revolt had shifted the debate on the Immaculate Conception of the Virgin to a new level. Cajetan's *Judgement* is, of course, at the old level. Catharinus was still prepared to debate the issue at this level as late as the second edition of the *Annotationes* of 1542, a date often taken to mark the real beginning of the Catholic Reformation. After that date he moved to the new position, from which it was apparent that the real enemy was not Cajetan, but Spina, for Spina and his Dominican supporters, like Luther (though

---

[44] Ibid., 99.
[45] Ibid., 95, 109.
[46] Ibid., 99, 100.
[47] Ibid., 95.
[48] Ibid., 111.
[49] At least one Dominican, Padre Michelozzi, had asserted during the troubles in 1527–30 that the Church could still err in accepting a feast day, and was not infallible in its approval of liturgical festivities and canonization of saints. See Bosco, 'Intorno', 159.

for different reasons), were prepared to challenge the authority and infallibility of the pope. Cajetan had never been guilty of that offence. He had merely offered advice which Catharinus believed to be wrong. Since his loyalty and obedience were unquestionable, he and Catharinus were not at odds over what was now the main issue. Their differences could reasonably be attributed to changed circumstances. To adopt Catharinus's way of speaking, Catharinus was advocating a view of the doctrine of the Immaculate Conception of the Virgin that the operation of the Holy Spirit had made much clearer than it was at the time when Cajetan was writing.

University College, Chichester

MARY AND SIXTEENTH-CENTURY PROTESTANTS

by DIARMAID MacCULLOCH

L ET us contemplate Thomas Cranmer, Primate of All England, sitting on an altar to preside over the trial of Anabaptist heretics. The time is May 1549; the altar, unceremoniously covered over to support the judge, is that of the Lady Chapel in St Paul's Cathedral in London; several of the heretics on trial have denied the Catholic doctrine of the incarnation, and one will later be burned at the stake. In a compelling paradox, an archbishop tramples an altar of Our Lady in the course of defending the incarnation. One witness in the crowd of onlookers was a pious and scholarly Welsh Catholic, Sir Thomas Stradling, who later wrote down his reactions to the occasion. He interpreted it as the uncannily accurate fulfilment of an eleventh-century prophecy to be found in a manuscript in his own library: Cranmer, he pointed out, went on to be punished for his blasphemy first by the 1549 rebellions and then by his fiery death at the stake.[1]

The scandal of Cranmer on the Lady altar tells us a good deal about the ambiguous feelings of the Reformers for Our Lady. On the one hand they saw it as a major work of piety to demolish and demystify the cultic and devotional world of which she was the centrepiece. On the other, they needed her as a bastion to defend the Catholic faith against the more militant forces which the Reformation had unleashed. They wished her to play her part in the biblical narrative which they were proclaiming to the world, and which they felt to be threatened from the two opposed forces of papistry and radicalism. But in the ambiguity of their feelings towards Mary, they were being true to what they found in the biblical text; here was a story of Mary which not only was restricted in scope but also contained elements of both praise and

---

[1] G.C.G. Thomas, 'The Stradling Library at St. Donat's, Glamorgan', *National Library of Wales Journal*, 24 (1986), 402–19, at 408. There are several notices of this incident: [?N. Harpsfield,], *Bishop Cranmer's Recantacyons*, ed. Lord Houghton with introd. by J. Gairdner, Philobiblon Society Miscellanies, 15 (1877–84) 15; *A Chronicle of England . . . by Charles Wriothesley, Windsor Herald*, ed. W.D. Hamilton, 2 vols, Camden Society, 2nd ser., 11, 20 (1875–7), 2:10; *Chronicle of the Grey Friars of London*, ed. J. Gough Nichols, Camden Society, 1st ser., 53 (1852), 58. For the surviving account of the trial of the antinomian radical John Champneis, see Lambeth Palace Library, Reg. Cranmer, fol. 71v; other accounts in the register, notably that of the later martyr Joan Bocher, have been lost.

reserve. The Reformers' task was one of restoration as much as destruction.

* * *

Since so much of the Reformers' relations with Mary was determined by the scriptural text, it is inevitable that the prehistory of their attitudes lies in the mind of Desiderius Erasmus. The young Erasmus, innocent of his later career as a biblical scholar, did what any young humanist cleric with conventional ambitions would have done; he wrote elegant Latin verse in praise of Mary. His *Supplication to the Virgin* has the extravagant note which one expects in late medieval literature: he calls her 'my salvation, my sole and certain refuge'; 'the beautiful moon, sister and mother of the eternal sun'. In his *Paean*, written at much the same time, he styled Mary 'a true Diana', as he also did in the *Supplication*; yet by 1528, in his *Ciceronian*, the mature biblical critic and doyen of humanists was ridiculing those who might seek to portray Jesus as Apollo and his mother as Diana, and his earlier poetry clearly embarrassed him.[2] That note was sounded in a letter to Thomas More even before he gone far in his biblical study, and in the same year, his Christocentric devotional work, the *Enchiridion*, pioneered an observation which became a cliché of Protestant moralizing: 'No devotion is more pleasing to Mary than the imitation of Mary's humility'.[3] In another classic statement, Erasmus pointed out the obvious, but also left a timebomb for the Western Church: 'Christ is the anchor of our salvation, Mary is not'.[4]

When Erasmus turned his scrutiny on the text of the Bible, his work proved a devastating broadside against much of the critical structure created by the doyen of biblical commentary, Jerome, which had been formative in the development of Mariology. If readers of the Bible should note allegory in its text, they should do so with due caution, and direct it aright. Erasmus came to deplore the use of wisdom material from the Song of Songs or the Book of Sirach in relation to Mary; if there was allegory in the figure of the beautiful bride or the pre-

[2] L.-E. Halkin, *Erasmus: a Critical Biography* (Oxford, 1993), 224–5, 229. The *Ciceronian* is tr. in *Collected Works of Erasmus, XXVIII*, ed. A.H.T. Levi (Toronto, 1986): see 381–2. Erasmus's main Marian works are to be found in *Collected Works of Erasmus, LXIX: Spiritualia and Pastoralia*, ed. J.W. O'Malley (Toronto, 1999): cf. 25, 44–5, and for his embarrassment, ibid., 40.

[3] *Collected Works of Erasmus, LXVI: Spiritualia: Enchiridion; De contemptu mundi; De vidua Christiana*, ed. J.W. O'Malley (Toronto, 1988), 71.

[4] Halkin, *Erasmus*, 230.

existent wisdom, this should refer to the Church and its relation with the saviour. Protestant commentaries would ram home this message.[5] An issue over allegory which proved more troublesome to Protestants was the perpetual virginity of Mary: much of the traditional case for this belief was based on a directly allegorical use of Ezekiel 44.2, on the shutting of a gate which only the Lord could enter, bolstered by a Latin reading of Isaiah's prophecy of a young woman conceiving the son Immanuel (Isaiah 7.14). Erasmus could not read these as Jerome had done. In response to shocked complaints about his comments, he set out a precise position: 'We believe in the perpetual virginity of Mary, although it is not expounded in the sacred books.'[6] Other insights of Erasmus proved crucial to the revolution in soteriology which was to come. In his 1519 revision of his New Testament edition, he rewrote the Latin version of the angelic salutation which was quoted devotionally in the Hail Mary; now the Virgin became 'gratiosa' rather than 'gratia plena', and thus became less available as a prop for the theology of merit.[7] He sneered at the misguided piety which led some to use Luke 2.51, the statement that Jesus was subject to his parents, to affirm that Jesus still owed obedience to his mother. This outbreak of common sense might sound trivial, but it was of huge importance, since it was a wedge to split apart the edifice of intercession by Mary to her Son which had become so all-pervasive in Western popular devotion.[8]

After such rethinking of the fundamentals, it was inevitable that the cults of Mary and indeed of all the saints should come into Erasmus's sights. Famously, in his *Colloquies*, he turned his pilgrimage to Walsingham and Canterbury into light comedy for the public.[9] This was part of a vigorous debunking of the physicality and tactility of late medieval popular piety which reflected Erasmus's distaste for lay devotion; for all his loudly proclaimed vision of the labourer reading the Bible at the plough-tail, and his strictures on the clericalism of his age,

---

[5] Ibid., 229. Halkin points out that Erasmus's close friend John Fisher continued in his preaching to make use of the Song of Songs in relation to Mary.

[6] Ibid., 225: cf. *Modus orandi deum: Opera omnia Desiderii Erasmi Roterodami* (Amsterdam, 1969–), 5.1:146–7.

[7] Halkin, *Erasmus*, 209. Cf. *Opus epistolarum Des. Erasmi Roterodami*, ed. P.S. Allen, H.M. Allen, and H.W. Garrod, 12 vols (Oxford 1906–58), 8:421, Ep. 2310, for a preacher's attack on Erasmus for this change.

[8] *Opera Erasmi*, 6.5:490–2.

[9] On the Colloquies, see M. Aston, *England's Iconoclasts I: Laws against Images* (Oxford, 1988), 197–9.

he was profoundly repelled when he observed the everyday reality of Western Christendom's layfolk grasping at the sacred. His nausea would become naturalized in Protestantism, particularly in its Reformed variety.[10] The intellectual genealogy is clear. Erasmus attacked the excesses of the cult of relics, devoting particular wit to the easy target of relics of milk from the Virgin: a particularly heavy-handed (not to say offensive) version of this sarcasm can be found in John Calvin's anti-relic tract of 1544.[11] Erasmus developed the topos of the saints having replaced pagan deities: St Anthony had taken over from Aesculapius and the Virgin Mary had staged a coup d'état against Proserpine. In the *Colloquies* and elsewhere he sneered at sailors in distress who used titles for Mary like 'Star of the Sea, Queen of Heaven, Mistress of the World, Port of Salvation'.[12] All this can be found echoed in a classic and influential demolition of the cult of saints and relics by Heinrich Bullinger, *De origine erroris libri duo*, which via its 1539 edition came to be plagiarized around 1560 in the longest single reference to Mary in all the homilies of the Church of England, a purple passage in the blockbuster-length *Homily against Idolatry*.[13]

Erasmus's revisionism on Mary, together with his irritable sallies of defence against the sniping of conservatives, has to be balanced with his expressions of apparently genuine devotion to the person and work of the Virgin, to be found liberally scattered through his writings throughout his career. Even one of his very last works, a collection of prayers of 1535, is careful to include a notably traditional prayer to the Virgin.[14] As the consequences of his attacks became plain in the first decade of the Reformation, Erasmus had drawn back in alarm and done his best to reaffirm some old certainties. One of the most unexpected of his writings after the Luther explosion is his *Votive Mass of Our Lady of*

[10] Cf. interesting remarks on this in J. Pelikan, *Mary through the Centuries: her Place in the History of Culture* (New Haven and London, 1996), 210–11.

[11] Halkin, *Erasmus*, 106/316: *Collected Works of Erasmus, XXXIX–XL: Colloquies*, ed. C.R. Thompson, 2 vols (Toronto and London, 1997), 2:630–3, 636; *An Admonition showing the Advantages which Christendom might Derive from an Inventory of Relics*, in *Calvin's Theological Tracts and Treatises*, ed. H. Beveridge, 3 vols (Edinburgh, 1844–51), 1:287–341, esp. 316–18.

[12] *Collected Works of Erasmus: Colloquies*, 1:355; *Opera Erasmi* 5.1 (*Modus orandi deum*), 155–6, 172; cf. Halkin, *Erasmus*, 222.

[13] *Certain Sermons or Homilies Appointed to be Read in Churches in the Time of the Late Queen Elizabeth* (1852), 206–8. For discussion, see Aston, *England's Iconoclasts*, 320–5, esp. n.96.

[14] *Precationes aliquot novae* (Basel, 1535): Levi, *Collected Works of Erasmus, LXIX*, 117–52, at 126–7, cited by Halkin, *Erasmus*, 261, 334. Cf. Erasmus's attempts to balance his material in the *Colloquies* and elsewhere in his writings of the 1530s: Aston, *England's Iconoclasts*, 199; Halkin, *Erasmus*, 225.

Loreto, a venture into liturgy unique for him and published in 1523 at the request of a friend who was the parish priest of Porrentruy, not far from Basel. However, what is noticeable in this apparent attempt at reconciliation with the world of holy places is the emphasis on the passion of Christ, together with a complete absence of any positive celebration of the Holy House, something which is quite an achievement in the circumstances. Erasmus included a homily in the mass which managed to dwell on the common late medieval theme of the sufferings of Mary, while at the same time criticizing some of the devotion and iconography which it had attracted:

> She suffered at her son's suffering, but by force of character she restrained the human feelings of her heart, she smothered her sighs, she held back her flowing tears, and while the rest of the disciples fled in fear, she alone stood with John beside her son's cross. Those pictures, which show her fallen down and stricken with fainting, dead with suffering, are damaging. She did not wail, tear her hair, beat her breast, cry out that she was unhappy. She drew more comfort from the redemption of mankind than suffering from the death of her son.[15]

* * *

Here was a possible direction in which reformed Catholicism might travel. Erasmus's biographer Léon-Ernest Halkin has indeed suggested that his revised Mariology made him the predecessor of Muratori and the Catholic Enlightenment.[16] There might have been a future for a Mariology drawing on the Christocentric theology of the Passion in a Catholicism which had not been traumatized by the Reformation. If one considers the *Spirituali* in Italy in the 1530s and 1540s, for instance, there is the example of Vittoria Colonna, lay theologian and patron of Michelangelo. Inspired by Michelangelo's gift to her of a drawing of a *Pieta*, one among his artistic meditations on the Sorrows of the Virgin, Colonna wrote poetry which concentrated on this theme of the bond between mother and son in the Passion, which so illuminated for her the way in which Christ's death transformed death, and the Son's body, caressed by the Virgin, showed forth the divine gifts of the Spirit. Her Mariology could therefore become an organic part of a theology which emphasised the *Spirituale* themes of death, resurrection, and the work of

---

15 Ibid., 226–8: Levi, *Collected Works of Erasmus*, LXIX, 79–108, esp. 98–9.
16 Halkin, *Erasmus*, 331.

the Holy Spirit: themes which strike a chord with the Reformed spirituality of the north. However, it is striking that such Marian themes do not emerge when Colonna corresponded with another outstanding humanist writer, Marguerite of Angoulême. Both women might have been expected to draw on the well of feminine models provided by Mary; the five extant letters between this distinguished devotional pairing bulge with scriptural allusions, yet those relating either directly or allegorically to the Virgin are noticeable by their absence.[17]

Moreover, the fate of *Spirituale* piety was to be driven to the margins of Catholic spirituality, to face systematic suppression or to seek refuge in Protestantism. The *Spirituali* became a might-have-been of Catholic history. A contrast and significant pointer to what would be the actual future is provided by the career of one contemporary of Erasmus who sought to follow in his revisionist or mediating path: the Franciscan friar from Avignon, François Lambert. Around 1520, Lambert published *La Couronne de Notre Seigneur Jésus Christ*, a devotional work modelled on the rosary, but transferring its Marian focus to the person of Christ: it contained thirty-three mysteries of the life of Christ. Yet the work still referred to Our Lady, and sought her intercession as well as those of the angels and saints: it affirmed the Immaculate Conception, and prayed devoutly for the pope.[18] Not long afterwards, in summer 1522, Lambert took it upon himself to travel to Zürich in the middle of the ferment of its Reformation, and he preached in the Fraumünster, on the subject of intercession by Mary and the saints. This was the famous occasion on which Huldrych Zwingli heckled the preacher, bellowing out 'Bruder, da irrest du' – 'That's where you're wrong, Brother'. On the following day Lambert was involved in debate with Zwingli; it was the last time that the friar wore his Franciscan habit, and after that he was launched on his own brief but intensely active life as a champion of Reformation. No more talk of Our Lady's intercession from him.[19]

[17] For the texts of their correspondence, see B. Collett, *A Long and Troubled Pilgrimage: the Correspondence of Marguerite D'Angoulême and Vittoria Colonna 1540–1545*, Studies in Reformed Theology and History, n.s. 6 (2001), 125–43; and for Colonna, the Virgin, and Michelangelo, ibid., 87, 89–92.

[18] B. Cottret, *Calvin: a Biography* (Grand Rapids, MI, and Edinburgh, 2000), 62.

[19] H.A. Oberman, *The Impact of the Reformation* (Edinburgh, 1994), 213, quoting *Die Chronik des Bernhard Wyss, 1519–1530*, ed. G. Finsler, Quellen und Abhandlungen zur schweizerischen Reformationsgeschichte, 1 (Basle, 1901), 16.

* * *

Lambert's apostasy brings us at last to the Reformation itself, and the double legacy of destruction and affirmation which Martin Luther bequeathed to its various outworkings. Erasmus had refocused scripture, subverted pilgrimage and saintly intercession, and emphasised the passion and saving work of Christ. All this was welded into a potent and destructive force by Luther's fiery and single-minded promotion of justification by faith only. It was unlikely that the mediation of the saints would have for long escaped a clash with his message, but the very liveliness of the pilgrimage industry brought an immediacy to the contest. Already in one of his key declarations of war on the old world of devotion in 1520, the *Address to the German Nobility*, Luther drew attention to the most recently- and dramatically-created Marian shrine in Germany. This was the 'Beautiful Mary' of Regensburg, a Frankenstein's monster created (with nice historical irony) by the future radical Balthasar Hubmaier. Hubmaier, then a highly traditionalist preacher at the cathedral, had in winter 1519 incited an anti-Jewish pogrom in Regensburg, after which Our Lady was drafted in to cure a workman badly injured during the demolition of the synagogue. 50,000 pilgrims were reputed to have visited the makeshift shrine chapel within a month of its completion on the Feast of the Assumption 1519. Hubmaier's unappealing combination of antisemitism and Marian fervour (both of which he later regretted) was to have a dire effect on the place of Mary in Protestant Europe: it was the equivalent of Tetzel's indulgence campaign in catalysing a violent reaction in Luther. The year-old Beautiful Mary fired Luther's fury: it formed the climax of his list of offensive shrines that should be 'levelled' ('*vorstoret*') as he launched a bitter diatribe against pilgrimage in the *Address*.[20]

Luther had thus given one particular cue for destructive action to the many people who were beginning to look to him for guidance. There was one further connection which needed to be made to complete the logic of destruction: shrines often centred on a statue, and Marian shrines invariably did. It was Luther's colleague in Wittenberg,

---

[20] *Address to German Nobility*, 75: *D. Martin Luthers Werke* (Weimar, 1883–) [hereafter *WA*], 6:447, 18, and n. For an illustration of a copy of Michael Ostendorfer's 1520 print of the Regensburg pilgrimage, with an added hostile MS comment of 1523 by Albrecht Dürer, S. Michalski, *The Reformation and the Visual Arts: the Protestant Image Question in Western and Eastern Europe* (1993), pl. 3. For the noticeable late medieval association between Marian devotion and anti-Semitism, see M. Rubin, 'Europe remade: purity and danger in late medieval Europe', *Transactions of the Royal Historical Society*, 6th ser., 11 (2001), 101–24, at 118–19.

Andreas Karlstadt, who made the link between shrines and the evil of images generally. In January and February 1522, with Luther away in the Wartburg, crowds destroyed images in some of the churches of Wittenberg, inspired by Karlstadt.[21] Luther promptly stopped this in March, but the following year Zwingli's parallel Reformation in Zürich followed Karlstadt's lead, turning popular vandalism into an orderly and thorough-going cleansing of the churches. Naturally images of Mary, so prominent in the iconography of medieval church interiors, were prime targets in this process: victims of what, by analogy with *hyperdulia*, might be styled *hyperphobia*. Luther had little time for either Karlstadt or Zwingli's Zürich, but he could hardly unsay what he had said about pilgrimage in the *Address to the German Nobility*. In 1522 Wolfgang Russ preached at the Bavarian shrine of Our Lady of Altötting against Marian devotion and miracles: it was the beginning of nearly half a century of eclipse for the shrine until the Counter-Reformation put a special effort into reviving it.[22] Russ's echo of Luther's call for action was repeated all over northern Europe: over the next couple of years, images of Mary which were especial foci of pilgrims' devotion became prime symbols of what needed to be destroyed. In March 1524, enthusiasts for the Reformation in Allstedt were inspired by their preacher Thomas Müntzer to turn on the nearby Marian shrine at Mallerbach; they terrorized its hermit custodian into flight and ended up burning the place down.[23] In the same year far to the north in Riga, a similar group of the godly denounced as a witch the much-venerated statue of the Virgin in the Cathedral, uprooted it and ducked it in the river: since the wooden object floated, they pronounced it guilty and burned it at Kubsberg, the customary place to punish witches.[24]

* * *

This carnivalesque mixture of the spontaneous, the calculated, and the ritualistic, set the pattern for what happened in Reformed Protestant lands over the next century and into the general mayhem of the Thirty Years' War: from England, one could multiply examples of exemplary destruction of Marian images from the time of Thomas Cromwell,

---

[21] Aston, *England's Iconoclasts*, 35–6.

[22] R. Bireley, *The Refashioning of Catholicism, 1450–1700* (1999), 111.

[23] H.-J. Goertz, *Thomas Müntzer: Apocalyptic Mystic and Revolutionary* (Edinburgh, 1993), 114–16.

[24] Michalski, *Reformation and Visual Arts*, 92.

Edward VI, or Elizabeth I. These atrocities spawned a new genre of Roman Catholic Marian devotion, what might be styled cults of battered Marys: images which had been rescued after Protestant vandalism and which were thus seen as especially worthy exemplars of the sufferings of Our Lady. One can cite particular examples from Paris in 1528 (rebattered in 1545 and 1551), pre-Calvinist Geneva in 1532, or Valladolid in 1600: this last battered Mary, victim of the ideologically-fuelled English raid on Cadiz in 1596, was specifically renamed Santa Maria Vulnerata.[25] One has to emphasise, however, that this violent assault on the physical symbols of Mary was a phenomenon of Reformed Protestant Europe, of the heirs of Karlstadt and Zwingli: it died away wherever Protestantism was chivvied into that modified version of Luther's bundle of beliefs which has come to be styled Lutheranism. Luther's horror at the consequences of Karlstadt's actions in Wittenberg drove him furiously to think about the image problem, and led him to the conclusion that there was no problem. Once the more ridiculous or dangerous images had been put aside, the old statues, pictures, and stained glass could be left to bring innocent delight and edification to the faithful.[26] The consequences can pleasurably be seen in Lutheran northern Europe to this day; two examples will suffice. In Lübeck Cathedral, the great Rood group has now survived both the Reformation and Allied air raids, so the attendant Mary and John still guard the crucifix on their fourteenth-century screen. Perhaps most memorable of all Mary's appearances in Lutheran church interiors is Veit Stoss's glorious suspended sculpture of the Annunciation which hangs above the high altar of the parish church of St Lorenz in Nuremberg (admittedly restored in modern times to its original position after some years of discreet withdrawal).

Luther was not simply reacting to what he regarded as the crassness of Karlstadt. He quickly matched his assault on the Marian cult with a positive repositioning of Mary as part of his own announcement of the message of salvation. He first set this out in one of his most eloquent devotional writings, the *Commentary on the Magnificat*, published in

---

[25] On Paris, 1528, and Geneva, 1532, see Cottret, *Calvin*, 49. On the image from Cadiz at St Alban's College Valladolid, see A. Shell, *Catholicism, Controversy and the English Literary Imagination, 1558–1660* (1999), 200–7.

[26] Aston, *England's Iconoclasts*, 39–43. Lutherans nevertheless got no credit from Orthodox Christians for their positive attitude to the visual: the memories of 1520s northern atrocities like Riga remained strong. Michalski, *Reformation and Visual Arts*, 102, 114, 134–5, 148, 154.

September 1521, but begun even before he had left Wittenberg to defy the Holy Roman Emperor at the Diet of Worms.[27] It was no mechanical exercise for Luther to explore Mary's song. He showed how much of traditional devotion to Mary he was prepared to admit, in his para-phrase of the angelic salutation: 'O thou blessed Virgin, Mother of God... Hail to thee! holy art thou, henceforth and for ever ... '. 'Queen of Heaven' was a permissible title 'as much as it is certainly true', without making her a goddess.[28] All this could be preserved because it emphasised a paradox characteristic of Luther's theology: Mary's glory consisted, as she herself sang, in God having lifted her up from lowli-ness. Even before Karlstadt had forced him to face the practical question of images and iconoclasm, Luther was thinking out how devotional art might be redirected suitably to portray Mary, and as he meditated on this, he produced one of the most memorable passages of his work: a sustained contrast of 'the Divine glory joined with her nothingness; the Divine merit with her homage; the Divine greatness with her smallness; the Divine goodness with her lack of merit; the Divine grace with her unworthiness'.[29] Note that God had regarded Mary's lowliness and not her humility, which might be seen as merit: Mary's momentous destiny was not given her because of any merit of her own – a thought in which Luther's core theology coincided with the textual exegesis of Erasmus.[30] This radical repositioning effectively rescued Mary's humanity to emphasise both the reality and the enormous gift of the Incarnation: the huge error of medieval devotion, as was clear in the art which it had produced, was to contrast 'us with the Mother of God instead of her with God'.[31] Luther was then free as his commentary climaxed to

> pray God that He may offer us a right understanding of this *Magni-ficat*, an understanding which does not merely expound and shed light on it but burns and lives in body and soul. May Christ grant us this through the intercession and the intention of His dear Mother Mary. Amen.[32]

[27] Useful treatments in English are P. Newman Brooks, 'A lily ungilded? Martin Luther, the Virgin Mary and the saints', *Journal of Religious History*, 13 (1984), 136–49 and G. Müller, 'Protestant veneration of Mary: Luther's interpretation of the *Magnificat*', in J. Kirk, ed., *Humanism and Reform: the Church in Europe, England and Scotland, 1400–1643. Essays in Honour of James K. Cameron*, SCH.S, 8 (1991), 99–112. The work is to be found in *WA*, 7:538–604.

[28] *WA*, 7:568, 11 and 15–16; 7:573, 32–3.

[29] *WA*, 7:569, 33–570, 3.

[30] Cf. Halkin, *Erasmus*, 105.

[31] *WA*, 7:569, 14–15.

[32] *WA*, 7:601, 8–11.

Luther remained faithful throughout his career as a Reformer to the programme set out in his Magnificat commentary. In 1962 Walter Tappolet produced a remarkable anthology of passages on the subject of Mary from Luther, Zwingli, Bullinger, and Calvin, *Das Marienlob der Reformatoren*. The very thoroughness of Tappolet's achievement reveals the imbalance between Luther and the three Reformed theologians: Luther takes up nearly half the work, and in Tappolet's table of references, Luther scores eight pages, in contrast to the couple of pages encompassing Zwingli, Bullinger, and Calvin.[33] Luther never wrote a specifically Marian hymn (indeed he characteristically modified various medieval pilgrimage hymns in a Christological direction), but his hymnody is scattered with warm references to Mary in the context of the Incarnation. These allusions are unsurprisingly prominent in his Christmas hymns, but they also emerge delicately and beautifully in his sacred love-ballad from the early 1530s, 'Sie ist mir lieb die werte Magd' ('The worthy Maid is dear to me'). In this, Luther keeps three topoi in exquisite tension: his controlling image is of the woman crowned with the twelve stars from Revelation 12, but the woman is traditionally both an image of the Church and an image of Mary; in all three guises she finds her child kept safe from the dragon of sin.[34]

Luther's warmth towards Mary continued to be expressed in his preaching, which remained tied to the liturgical year, because he kept so much more of the kalendar than other churches in the Protestant world. Free to choose which he would retain of the festivals associated with Mary, he kept those which could be seen as centring on Christ rather than Mary: the Annunciation, the Visitation, the Purification. Tappolet points out that Luther preached on these feast-days until the end of his life, while by contrast his last sermon on the Conception of Our Lady was no later than 1520, on her Nativity 1522, and on her Assumption 1523.[35] The subject of the Magnificat remained a favourite with him, to be lovingly and regularly expounded on the feast associ-

[33] W. Tappolet with A. Ebneter, *Das Marienlob der Reformatoren: Martin Luther, Johannes Calvin, Huldrych Zwingli, Heinrich Bullinger* (Tübingen, 1962), 357–65. For further discussion of Luther and Mary, see H. Düfel, *Luthers Stellung zur Marienverehrung* (Gottingen, 1968).

[34] On Luther's hymnology, Tappolet, *Marienlob*, 127–44, and on this poem, 141–4. See also Brooks, 'Lily ungilded', 147, and Pelikan, *Mary*, 13.

[35] Tappolet, *Marienlob*, 156. The editors of the Rheims Testament underlined Luther's rationale when they complained that English Protestants only retained Marian feasts which were really Christocentric, 'so that she by this meanes shal have no festivitie at al': *The New Testament of Jesus Christ* (Rheims, 1582), 191. For Luther's remarks on the feast of the Immaculate Conception in 1516–17, see Rubin, 'Europe remade', 121.

ated with it in scripture, the Visitation, on 2 July. Luther's partiality for the Visitation contrasts with the one non-Lutheran Church of the Reformation to keep the shape of the liturgical year, the Church of England: curiously when Archbishop Cranmer made his own selection of festivals, the Annunciation and Purification still got special liturgical mention, but the Visitation was dropped, even from the ceremonialist provisional rite of 1549. This was despite the pivotal dramatic role which the Magnificat continued to play in the English liturgy of Evensong; moreover, here was an instance in which Cranmer consciously ignored advice from Martin Bucer, who shared Luther's particular affection for the feast, and who advocated retaining it when he gave advice on revising the 1549 rite.[36]

* * *

If the Zürich Reformers were not so vocal as Luther in their praise of Mary, they still echoed the message of his Magnificat commentary, a work which achieved wide popularity, no doubt in large measure thanks to the unusual lack of polemical edge in the work. Like him, they were conscious of accusations from their conservative enemies that they dishonoured the Virgin, and they were eager to make as positive noises as they could. In 1522, the same year that he shouted down Lambert in the Fraumünster, Zwingli preached and published a major sermon 'On the ever pure Virgin Maid Mary the mother of Jesus Christ our Saviour', a careful recounting of the scriptural material on Mary, and a direct response to claims that he had denied Mary's virginity.[37] The Zürich authorities were gradualist in their approach to Marian devotion; the Marian liturgical feasts were not abolished until 1535, and more surprisingly, one would have experienced a liturgical recitation of the scriptural portion of the Hail Mary in the Zürich preaching service right up to 1563, when Bullinger finally did away with it.[38] Bullinger

[36] *Martin Bucer and the Book of Common Prayer*, ed. E.C. Whitaker, Alcuin Club Collections, 55 (1974), 140–1. It is a token of Cranmer's characteristic self-effacement that the Feast of the Visitation was his birthday.

[37] For a modernized and abridged text, Tappolet, *Marienlob*, 221–39. For a similar Marian sermon from Bullinger, preached and published in 1558 because 'contumeliose nos loqui de beate virgine', see ibid., 275–302.

[38] G.W. Locher, *Zwingli's Thought: New Perspectives* (Leiden, 1981), 60; on the Marian festivals, ibid., 89, 91, and K. Biegger, *'De invocatione beatae Mariae Virginis': Paracelsus und die Marienverehrung*, Kosmosophie, 6 (1990), 86. For Zwingli's defence of using the scriptural Hail Mary, see Oberman, *Impact*, 243. Note cautious comments on the liturgical use of the angelic salutation by the prominent Zürich pastor Ludwig Lavater, *De ritibus et institutis*

could be surprisingly old-fashioned when he chose: unlike his mentor Zwingli, he seems to have been prepared to countenance the possibility of the Assumption of Mary, on the reasonable Protestant basis that Enoch and Elijah provided scriptural precedents for such an event. The discussion, admittedly casual enough, occurs in an unpredictable setting: the 1539 version of his well-known book (already cited above) attacking relics and pilgrimages. In a course of a rather tortured dialogue with the writings of Jerome, Bullinger affirms without apparent reservation 'For this reason indeed we believe the sacred body of Mary, the bearer of God, the most pure home and temple of the Holy Spirit, to have been carried by angels up to heaven'.[39]

It is significant that when an edition of Bullinger's *De origine erroris* was published in Geneva in 1549, this remarkable sentence was omitted from the text.[40] With Calvin, a more chilly overall attitude to Mary is perceptible than in either Wittenberg or Zürich. While Luther cheerfully remarked in 1523 that the Hail Mary was no danger to those of firm faith, and while its scriptural text continued to echo around the churches of Zürich, in 1542 Calvin bitterly denounced any use of it as 'execrable blasphemy', together with the titles of honour for Mary which Luther was happy to commend.[41] It is noticeable that the Angelic Salutation is never cited in the *Institutes*: indeed throughout the *Institutes* in its successive versions, the absence of any use of the standard Marian biblical passages, whether direct or allegorical, is very striking. There is only one passing reference even to the Magnificat.[42] Admittedly, when he was forced to face up to the Marian scriptural passages in his biblical commentaries, Calvin could be carried away by his interest in the text, and use his imagination. For instance, in his commentary on Luke 2.48, he chose to defend Mary for telling off the boy Jesus for his truancy in

---

ecclesiae Tigurinae (1559), qu. *Private Prayers put forth by Authority during the Reign of Queen Elizabeth*, ed. W. Keating Clay, PS (Cambridge, 1851), viii.

[39] 'Hac caussa credimus et Deiparae virginis Marie purissimum thalamum et spiritus sancti templum, hoc est, sacrosanctum corpus eius deportatum esse ab angelis in coelum': H. Bullinger, *De origine erroris libri duo* (Zürich, 1539), fol. 69v, and subsequent edns; the sentence does not occur in the much shorter first version, Zürich, 1529. On Zwingli and the Assumption, see Locher, *Zwingli's Thought*, 89–90.

[40] Tappolet, *Marienlob*, 327.

[41] Beveridge, *Calvin's Theological Tracts and Treatises*, 1:118–20; this is Calvin's riposte to 25 Articles put out on 10 March 1542 by the doctors of theology in the University of Paris. On Luther: Tappolet, *Marienlob*, 126.

[42] J. Cadier, 'La Vierge Marie dans la dogmatique réformée au XVIe et au XVIIe siècle', *La Revue réformée*, 9/no. 36 (1958/iv), 46–58, at 46 makes the point that there is no reference to Mary in Marlorat's index to the *Institutes*.

the Temple: 'The weariness of three days was in that complaint', he said sympathetically.[43] Yet such naturalism was not the attitude which the Queen of Heaven might have expected. Calvin's single-minded hatred of anything which could be regarded as an idolatrous obstacle to the worship of God skewed in a negative direction the delicate balance of attitudes to Mary which the Lutheran and Zürich Reformers had managed to sustain, and gradually Calvin's was the influence which coloured the spirituality of non-Lutheran Europe. It was noticeable in England, for example, that the first version of the English Bible to supplant the phrase 'full of grace' in the angelic salutation at Luke 1.28 was the Geneva translation of 1560: there, it became 'thou that art freely beloved', and the Authorized Version did not return to the older phrase in 1611, opting for 'thou that art highly favoured'.[44]

This impact of Calvinism in later Tudor England fused with an older native English strain of negative comment on Mary: this was a mark of Lollard discourse, and it had in turn been distinctively reinforced by the charismatic preaching of Hugh Latimer, diffused into the Elizabethan age through publication. Latimer, as Bishop of Worcester in the 1530s, had taken a savage delight in the nationwide round-up and destruction of cultic images of Mary carried out in 1538, not least the venerated image in his own cathedral.[45] Freed from circumspection after the death of Henry VIII, he took up Erasmus's theme of the negative passages about Mary in Scripture and infused it with a distinctly personal misogyny in his campaign to sweep out the remnants of the once-mighty English cults of Our Lady. The best thing about Mary for Latimer was that she was obedient: that was a positive womanly quality. However, she had not always shown the humility of the Magnificat: she had demanded to speak to her son, 'interrupting his sermon, which was not good manners'. Latimer took great delight in citing John Chrysostom and Augustine to prove his point that 'she was pricked a little with vain-glory; she would have been known to be his mother,

---

[43] W.J. Bouwsma, *Calvin: a Sixteenth Century Portrait* (New York and Oxford, 1988), 123, 267.

[44] Taking their cue from Calvin, the notes to the Geneva Bible are remarkably taciturn on Mary, even in passages where it would be obvious to comment on her, with the notable exception of condemnations of papist misattribution to her of honorific titles at Ezek. 7.18 and 44.17: *The Bible: that is the Holy Scriptures conteined in the Old and New Testament* (1606), sigs HH8v and KK6r.

[45] *Sermons and Remains of Hugh Latimer*, ed. G.E. Corrie, PS (Cambridge, 1845), 393. On Mary and the Lollards, see Aston, *England's Iconoclasts*, 130–9; C. Marsh, *Popular Religion in Sixteenth Century England: Holding their Peace* (Houndmills, 1998), 165.

else she would not have been so hasty to speak with him . . . The school doctors say she was arrogant'. She was even at fault for losing Jesus in the Temple, and she quarrelled with him afterwards 'like a mother' – this phrase might form a clue to Latimer's unconscious feelings. Christ's independent actions on this occasion illustrated for Latimer the limits of earthly obedience: *oportet magis obedire Deo quam hominibus*. All this conveniently served to prove for Latimer, as Chrysostom's remark had already indicated to William Tyndale two decades before, that Mary could not have been conceived immaculately.[46]

* * *

Magisterial reformers, however, were always uncomfortably conscious that they were skating on thin ice when they took to cutting Mary down to size. They shared with their papist opponents a loyalty to the Church as it had emerged by the time of the Council of Chalcedon. But as the devastating response to Luther's call for the levelling of shrines had demonstrated, it was not always possible to predict or control which elements of the early Christian package would now be challenged by more radical spirits. Here the role of Mary was a major area of instability. Some of the reaction was a generalized hostility to what Mary had become in the devotion of the Western Church, and so it was allied to the destruction of shrines and images. All through the Reformation century, one can find offensive talk about Mary which was an extension (albeit injudicious) of some of the more extreme rhetoric of Calvin or Latimer – it was little more than posturing to show what a good Protestant the speaker was. It is unlikely, for instance, that when in 1605 a glover from Buckinghamshire ranted that 'the virgin Marie was the instrument of the divell', he was expressing any sort of coherent radical theology beyond too much beer and anti-Catholicism.[47]

But there was much more to Reformation radicalism than an effort to out-Calvin Calvin. The Reformation had turned back to Scripture, and one obvious issue to rethink was the proposition about Mary most insecurely supported therein: her perpetual virginity. Any reader coming fresh to the appropriate references in the Biblical text would

---

[46] *Sermons of Latimer*, ed. G.E. Corrie, PS (Cambridge, 1844), 383, 515; Corrie, *Sermons and Remains of Latimer*, 91, 117, 157–8; *An Answer to Sir Thomas More's Dialogue, the Supper of the Lord . . . and William Tracy's Testament expounded. By William Tyndale*, ed. H. Walter, PS (Cambridge, 1850), 207. Latimer was nevertheless equally prepared to use Mary's silence (Luke 2.51) as an example to other women to keep silent: Corrie, *Sermons and Remains of Latimer*, 91.

[47] C.W. Foster, *The State of the Church in the Reigns of Elizabeth and James I, as Illustrated by Documents Relating to the Diocese of Lincoln, Vol. 1*, Lincoln Record Society, 23 (1926), 370.

draw the conclusion that Jesus had brothers and sisters, and that is the conclusion that many readers did come to in the 1520s: so in May 1525 an unidentified radical, probably Conrad Grebel, scandalized the town leadership of St Gallen because he 'slandered Our Lady with seven children'.[48] This biblicism might in itself seem of minor significance; but as we will see, the Reformers unanimously resisted it, partly because it was soon allied with a profound challenge to the Chalcedonian package of doctrine. The challenge was to deny the Chalcedonian and Nicene conclusions about the Incarnation of Christ, and hence to downgrade the role of Mary in salvation.

Several trains of thought converged on such an agenda, both recent and ancient. For many radicals, as for humanist theologians like Zwingli, the starting-point was not so much Mary but that other focus of late medieval Western devotion, the Mass. Erasmus had habitually stressed the spiritual against the physical; one of his favourite texts was John 6.63. Zwingli had followed him in warming to this affirmation that the spirit gives life and the flesh profits nothing, and he had built on it his eucharistic doctrine of remembrance, denying the physical or corporal presence of Christ in the eucharist. It was not surprising that when such respected authorities distanced themselves from physicality, more adventurous spirits should combine that consideration with their loathing for the cultus surrounding both Mary and the Mass. If the body of Christ in the eucharist was a spiritual and not an earthbound flesh, that had implications for his incarnation on earth: it was logical to suppose that his flesh in his earthly life was created not of the Virgin but in heaven.

Besides this rooting in contemporary humanist scholarship, there were various older roots for this doctrinal departure. One strain within medieval mystical piety had affirmed and meditated on Christ's celestial flesh. A different medieval inheritance came from radicals like Lollards or Taborites who had been angered by the Marian cult and had sought to downgrade Mary; they often rationalized their anger by drawing on the ancient male fantasies about reproduction made respectable in Aristotelian biology, where a woman was considered merely as a vessel for the receptacle of male seed. If no male seed was

---

[48] *The Sources of Swiss Anabaptism: the Grebel Letters and Related Documents*, ed. L. Harder, Classics of the Radical Reformation, 4 (Scottdale, PA, 1985), 362 and n.1, p. 719: the number seven derives from Mk. 6.3, where the mention of four brothers and plural sisters of Jesus indicates a minimum of seven children in the Holy Family.

involved in Christ's incarnation, it was logical that he did not partake of human flesh. The eighth-century iconoclast Byzantine Emperor Constantine V had expressed the 'vessel' theory of Mary in a vivid metaphor: 'When she bore Christ within her womb, she was like a purse filled with gold. But after giving birth, she was no more than an empty purse.'[49] The Emperor's aphorism was destined to have a long history, although the many generations who repeated it over some eight centuries no doubt had little idea of its origin. In the Netherlands of Charles V, for instance, it could be heard on the lips of Pieter Floriszoon, a tailor in Gouda, who said that Our Lady was like 'a sack that had once held cinnamon, but now only retains the sweet savour'. In a rather less flavoursome version, Willem die Cuper said that she was like a flourbag from which the flour had been emptied.[50] The common variant motif among contemporary English radicals was the saffron bag, in which the smell of the precious contents would linger; Hugh Latimer was once accused of having used this metaphor, and true to form he did not entirely repudiate it but did his best to turn it into an orthodox sermon illustration.[51]

The first known developed celestial flesh doctrine of the Reformation came from Alsace in 1524, much at the same time as the images of Mallerbach and Riga were being put to the torch: here the lay preacher Clement Ziegler developed in a series of tracts on the sacraments a theory of the celestial body of Christ pre-existent before his acquisition of visible human flesh at the Incarnation.[52] On this foundation were built a number of more thoroughgoing doctrines of celestial flesh, first in the contrasting proposals of Caspar Schwenckfeld and Melchior Hofmann in Strasbourg. Hofmann produced an alternative metaphor for Mary to that of the bag, unconsciously echoing the ancient Gnostic Valentinus in describing Christ as passing through Mary 'as water through a pipe'.[53] Hofmann's ideas were taken up by Menno Simons

---

[49] Quoted in E. Mâle, *Religious Art* (1949), 167. On the medieval background to celestial flesh doctrine, see G.H. Williams, *The Radical Reformation* (1962), 325–35.

[50] A. Duke, 'The face of popular religious dissent in the Low Countries, 1520–1530', *JEH*, 26 (1975), 41–67, at 52, quoting Gouda, Gemeentearchief, Oud-rechterlijk archief 147, fol. 45v, and *Corpus documentorum inquisitionis haereticae pravitatis Neerlandicae*, ed. P. Fredericq, 5 vols (Ghent and The Hague, 1889–1902), 4:372.

[51] Corrie, *Sermons of Latimer*, 60.

[52] Williams, *Radical Reformation*, 245.

[53] Ibid., 329, 330–2. Hofmann may have been aware that one of Bernard of Clairvaux's best-known sermons on Mary employed the metaphor of an aqueduct to describe her role in mediating grace. See Donna Spivey Ellington, *From Sacred Body to Angelic Soul. Understanding Mary in Late Medieval and Early Modern Europe* (Washington, DC, 2001), 128.

later in the decade, among the quietist radicals of the Netherlands, and celestial flesh doctrine became characteristic of his followers, despite their own further disagreements as to its mechanics. It was Melchiorite or Mennonite Christology which led Joan Bocher to the stake in London in 1550, after the trial in which we have already met Archbishop Cranmer balancing on the Lady Altar of St Paul's.[54]

Almost as soon as this series of celestial flesh solutions to the Incarnation problem developed, they were being confronted by the opposite form of radicalism in unitarianism: Jesus was not God at all, but a human prophet. As much as any celestial flesh doctrine, this too would downgrade the role of Mary in salvation. The belief was first picked up by scandalized mainstream reformers at trials of radicals in Augsburg in 1527, and paradoxically it was given wider currency among radicals when official publication of statements from the trials deliberately or inadvertently ascribed the doctrine to the widely-respected radical leader Balthasar Hubmaier – entirely without foundation.[55] While celestial flesh doctrine found its refuge in the Netherlands, Simons kept his followers distanced from unitarianism or Arianism; these doctrines were instead to find a home among the persecuted evangelicals of mid-century Italy, before migrating for a long and tempestuous career in central and eastern Europe.[56]

So both main forms of surviving radicalism were means of downgrading Mary far more drastically than did mainstream Protestantism. Perhaps that is why the radical social message of the Magnificat rarely seems to have been an inspiration to the radicals, when one would think that this scriptural text would have been an obvious stimulus to social idealism and a sacred reordering of society. It is significant that radical thinking rarely took the opposite course, to give Mary more honour than the old Western Church had done, even although there was no absolute reason why this should not have happened.[57] The exception to the rule was that wayward and original genius Paracelsus.

[54] On Bocher's beliefs, and those of her contemporary English radicals, see I.B. Horst, *The Radical Brethren* (Nieuwkoop, 1972), 109–15. See Williams, *Radical Reformation*, 394–5, 490–2.

[55] Ibid., 176–8.

[56] Ibid., 490–3, 562, 610, 666–8, 745. For a late sixteenth-century echo of Italian unitarianism in Menocchio the Friulian millar, see A. del Col, tr. J. and A. Tedeschi, *Domenico Scandella known as Menocchio: his Trials before the Inquisition (1583–1599)* (Binghamton, NY, 1996), esp. liii–liv, 4, 6–8, 54.

[57] One notices, for instance, that when a group of Swiss radicals in Appenzell fell under the spell of a local woman, she proclaimed herself to be a new and female Messiah, but not

Particularly in a couple of stormy years in Salzburg in 1524 and 1525, Paracelsus turned his thoughts to a fundamental rethink on the nature of the Trinity, and the relationship of Our Lady to it, in a flurry of theological speculation, none of which was published till much later.[58] Paracelsus was concerned to find the female principle in God: in his *Liber de sancta trinitate*, he called this the 'Gottin'. Although in that work he did not identify the 'Gottin' with Mary, he did take this further step in the various tracts on the subject of Mary which he wrote at much the same time. So in *De virgine sancta theotoca*, probably of 1524, Paracelsus writes that Mary 'gehört in die gottheit' ('forms part of the Godhead').[59] It was not surprising, therefore, that he vigorously affirmed the immaculate conception and perpetual virginity of Mary. Equally remote from his Reformation contemporaries was Paracelsus's affirmation that Mary was of a different order of creation to other women, or his readiness to follow the traditional exegesis which identified her with the figure of Wisdom in Sirach 24. He considered that her earthly life was a tiny span compared with her pre-existence and her life in heaven; now she was the 'Fürstin der Himmelstadt' ('ruler of Heaven').[60]

In his later theological writings, Paracelsus became more cautious on the topic of Mary, and the theme of her mystical pre-existence receded. As much as his independent creativity could ever be categorized, after the 1520s he drew further away from the traditional Church and closer to the Reformers, which may have curbed his enthusiasm for the old devotional imagery and inclined him more to what magisterial Protestants were saying about Mary.[61] He might also have been somewhat chastened if he heard of the Marian antics of one of his south German contemporaries, the bigamous radical furrier Nicholas Frey, who may single-handedly have scandalized radicals out of interest in Mary. When Frey abandoned his first wife in Rottenburg and took up with an

---

[58] Biegger, 'De invocatione', provides an edition of the main Marian tract and invaluable general discussion; see also U. Gause, *Paracelsus (1493–1541): Genese und Entfaltung seiner frühen Theologie* (Tübingen, 1993). Biegger, 'De invocatione', 60–8, seeks to date the work at *c*.1527, but much is uncertain in Paracelsus chronology. The text of *De Trinitate* can be found in K. Goldammer, ed., *Paracelsus: sammtliche Werke: Abtl. II: theologische und religionsphilosophische Scriften, Band III: dogmatische und polemische Einzelschriften* (Wiesbaden, 1986), 233–66, and see discussion, ibid., xlii–xliv. I am much indebted to Charles Webster for pointing me to material on Paracelsus.

[59] Biegger, 'De invocatione', 26–38, 201.

[60] Ibid., 51, 163, 197, 254–5.

[61] Ibid., 238, 248, 262.

aristocratic widow, he saw his new relationship as a spiritual union with a new Mary and a new Eve, while he himself took the role of the Trinity. The territorial synod of Strasbourg in 1533 begged to differ, and eventually decreed that the unrepentant Frey should be drowned: he did not have a following.[62] What is certainly significant is how little impact Paracelsus's early speculations about Mary were to have in the many and varied circles, largely Protestant, which became fascinated by assorted aspects of Paracelsianism. Take, for instance, the mystic Jacob Boehme. Like Paracelsus a half-century before, he felt the absence of a female principle in God, and he sought to define what that principle might be. However, in one of his most important mystical writings, *The Way to Christ*, it is striking how Boehme distances from the Virgin Mary his figure of the Virgin Sophia, through whom the soul might experience mystical union with God. Mary is given a conventional functional role as the vessel of the incarnation, and in one long passage which is a detailed exposition of the Incarnation, Boehme emphasises the human flesh of Mary, that she was part of the corruption of human flesh which resulted the Fall. In this, Boehme remains true to his Lutheran roots, and there is no hint of Paracelsianism.[63]

* * *

In the face of the varied forms of radicalism which threatened the Chalcedonian synthesis, the magisterial Reformers were anxious to show themselves true to beliefs which the early Church had affirmed about Mary. Many Reformers were happy to affirm the title Theotokos with the ancient Church, regarding it as as much a defence against modern deviant Christology as it had been against Nestorianism.[64] They revealed different degrees of agnosticism towards the Assumption, with (as we have seen) Bullinger apparently more positive than most.[65] As to the doctrine of the Immaculate Conception, Protestants

[62] Williams, *Radical Reformation*, 286–8, 292.

[63] J. Boehme, *The Way to Christ* (New York, 1978), esp. 9, 44, 150. The English conformist polemicist Thomas Rogers claimed in the 1580s that the women of the radical sect the Family of Love believed that they were all Marys, 'and say, that Christ is come forth in their fleshe': P. Crawford, *Women and Reformation in England, 1500–1720* (1993), 122, qu. T. Rogers, *The Family of Love*, sigs kv, kii. The beliefs expressed by the Familists themselves contain no trace of this canard: cf. e.g. C. Marsh, *The Family of Love in English Society* (Cambridge, 1994), Ch. 2.

[64] Cf. e.g. *Zwingli and Bullinger*, ed. G.W. Bromiley (Philadelphia, PA, 1953), 256, Locher, *Zwingli's Thought*, 87, and Bullinger's use of 'Deipara', above, n.39; *A Disputation on Holy Scripture ... by William Whitaker*, ed. W. Fitzgerald, PS (Cambridge, 1849), 538, 603.

[65] Cf. e.g. *Doctrinal Treatises and Introductions to Different Portions of the Holy Scriptures. By*

could simply stand back and enjoy the continuing row within the Roman Church on this topic.[66] The issue was simple for them: the Immaculate Conception was a late and illegitimate development of doctrine which clashed directly with Luther's assertion of justification by faith alone. Luther's paradoxical soteriology was at its most dramatic on the subject of Mary's sinful flesh: he revelled in the Saviour's genealogical connection to the incest of Judah and Tamar. 'God allows [Christ] to be conceived in most disgraceful incest, in order that he may assume the truest flesh'. Christ was born of a flesh truly 'polluted by Judah and Tamar', which was equally truly sanctified by the Holy Spirit.[67] Perhaps the most hard-hitting statement of this evangelical paradox came from Roger Hutchinson, an Edwardian chaplain of Archbishop Cranmer, who emphasised that no dishonour came to Christ's divinity because his humanity filled the Virgin's womb: 'For his divinity is not defiled thereby, no more than the sun shining upon carrion and filthy jakes is dishonoured or defiled through their stinking scents.' This was a remarkable meditation on the mystery of the Incarnation, and it is worth noting that it arose directly out of Hutchinson's disputes with the Melchiorite radicals of Edwardian London.[68]

It was, however, on the perpetual virginity of Mary that the magisterial Reformers showed themselves unanimously and adamantly conservative. This was despite the fact that their stance left them ideologically vulnerable both to Roman Catholics and to radicals. Humanist Catholics like Thomas More could point to Erasmus's affirmation that the perpetual virginity was a matter of faith, yet still could not be found in scripture. If so, continued belief in it was a powerful argument for the validity of 'unwritten verities', the traditions of which the Church was a guardian, a doctrine which was roundly condemned

---

William Tyndale, ed. H. Walter, PS (Cambridge, 1848), 315; Walter, *Answer*, 28; Tappolet, *Marienlob*, 55 (Luther); H. Hackett, *Virgin Mother, Maiden Queen: Elizabeth I and the Cult of the Virgin Mary* (Houndmills, 1995), 204 (William Perkins; above, 203. It may be that some early Reformers saw the Assumption as a possible argument against the doctrine of psychopannichia (soul-sleep) held by some radicals.

[66] For some English examples, Walter, *Treatises by Tyndale*, 159; Walter, *Answer*, 131; H. Joliffe and R. Johnson, *Responsio venerabilium sacerdotum, Henrici Joliffi et Roberti Jonson* (Antwerp, 1564), fol. 165v (John Hooper); *The Works of John Jewel, Bishop of Salisbury*, ed. J. Ayre, 2 vols in 4, PS (Cambridge, 1845–50), 3:611, 4:1045–6, 4:1053; *A Defence of the Sincere and True Translations of the Holy Scriptures . . . by W. Fulke*, ed. C.H. Hartshorne, PS (Cambridge, 1843), 35; Fitzgerald, *Disputation by Whitaker*, 504–5.

[67] D. Steinmetz, *Calvin in Context* (New York and Oxford, 1995), 86, citing *WA*, 44:324: Luther's lectures on Genesis, 1545.

[68] *The Works of Roger Hutchinson*, ed. J. Bruce, PS (Cambridge, 1842), 148.

by the Reformers.[69] By no means all Catholics agreed with Erasmus, and Thomas Swynnerton, an English evangelical polemicist of the 1530s, had some fun pointing up their divisions on the matter; but the challenge was a serious one.[70] More serious still was the radical challenge on perpetual virginity, because it was a dialogue between two parties who were likely to be committed to *sola scriptura*. The radicals could combine with Catholics to accuse the reformers of stretching the biblical record in affirming the perpetual virginity; indeed radicals would say that the biblical evidence pointed in precisely the opposite direction.

If biblicism was to determine the argument, then there was only one convincing line of defence for the magisterials: to follow the tendentious exegesis of the relevant biblical passages which Jerome had pioneered back in the fourth century, when he had faced similar objections from Helvidius, and had answered them in characteristically acid tones. This is what the Reformers did: they reiterated Jerome's contention that contextually, the Synoptic Gospels' mention of Jesus's 'brothers' actually referred to his 'cousins', and that when Jesus was described in Matthew 1.24–5 as Mary's first-born son, it actually meant that he was her only son. Repeatedly and monotonously they sneered at the name of Helvidius, and took it as read that Jerome had demolished Helvidius's case.[71] Moreover, some Reformers could suddenly rediscover a taste for medieval allegorical interpretation and patristic exegesis which in other circumstances they would have regarded as distinctly suspect: they rejected the guidance of Erasmus and pointed confidently to the proof-texts Ezekiel 44.2 and Isaiah 7.14. Both Zwingli and Bullinger abandoned their humanism in this regard.[72] An alternative Protestant approach, useful against papists and radicals alike,

---

[69] On More, see Walter, *Answer*, 96; cf. *Remains of Myles Coverdale*, ed. G. Pearson, PS (Cambridge, 1846), 414.

[70] [T. Swynnerton], J. Roberts [pseud.], *A mustre of scismatyke bysshoppes of Rome* (1534), sigs Eviiir–Fir. For the importance of the argument over 'unwritten verities', see P. Marshall, 'The debate over "unwritten verities" in early Reformation England', in B. Gordon, ed., *Protestant History and Identity in 16th Century Europe* (Aldershot, 1996), 60–77.

[71] *Documents on the Continental Reformation*, ed. W.R. Naphy (Basingstoke, 1996), 97 (Zwingli); Tappolet, *Marienlob*, 227, 246 (Zwingli and Osiander); *The Decades of Henry Bullinger*, ed. T. Harding, 4 vols, PS (Cambridge, 1849–52), 4:437; Cadier, 'Vierge Marie', 47 (Calvin); *Works of Archbishop Cranmer*, ed. J.E. Cox, 2 vols, PS (Cambridge, 1844–6), 2:60; *The Examinations and Writings of John Philpot*, ed. R. Eden, PS (Cambridge, 1842), 426–7 (Caelius Curio and Philpot); Corrie, *Sermons and Remains of Latimer*, 104–6; *Early Writings of Bishop Hooper*, ed. S. Carr, PS (Cambridge, 1843), 161; Ayre, *Works of Jewel*, 3:440.

[72] Tappolet, *Marienlob*, 245, 280. More cautiously, Archbishop Cranmer's theological

was to express guarded agnosticism about the scriptural foundation of the doctrine, and then proceed to say that in any case it was a peripheral belief and not a matter of salvation.[73] But one never feels that the Reformers were very happy with this. Their doubts would only have been heightened if they were aware of a passage in the *Ecclesiastical Polity* by that Reformed Protestant gone to the bad, Richard Hooker: Hooker cited the doctrine of the perpetual virginity of Mary as an example that 'even in matters divine, concerning some things we may lawfully doubt and suspend our judgement'.[74]

Why this neurotic attachment to the perpetual virginity among the magisterial Reformers? At one level, one can ascribe it to the general worries about sexuality which have been especially pervasive within Western Christianity: Jesus Christ, however much one safeguarded his humanity along with Nicaea I and Chalcedon, needed to be distanced from the more messy realities of human reproduction, along with his mother, if one was to show true love and reverence for him. At a more conscious theological level, the debate about interpreting scripture on the perpetual virginity might have relevance to arguments among the Reformers themselves: thus at the Colloquy of Marburg in 1529, when Zwingli was lamenting what he saw as Luther's literalist obstinacy about Christ's words of eucharistic institution, he likened Luther's attitude to the wrong-headedness of Helvidius.[75] But the real impetus was the radical challenge: not merely because of radical views on the Incarnation which might bear on the perpetual virginity debate, but because of a different issue which was one of the other major concerns of radicals, the affirmation of adult against infant baptism. In both cases, the question of scriptural authority was the same. Beliefs which the magisterial reformers felt passionately were valid and important, the perpetual virginity of Mary and the necessity of infant baptism, had

common-place books noted that the allegorical argument from Ezek. 44 was a possible direction to take: Cox, *Works of Cranmer*, 2:60.

[73] Walter, *Answer*, 33; Bouwsma, *Calvin*, 267; *Fulke's Answers to Stapleton, Martiall and Sanders*, ed. R. Gibbings, PS (Cambridge, 1848), 272; Fitzgerald, *Disputation by Whitaker*, 538.

[74] *Ecclesiastical Polity*, I.7.5: *Folger Library Edition of the Works of Richard Hooker*, ed. W.R. Speed Hill *et al.*, 7 vols (Cambridge and Binghamton, NY, 1977–94), 1:179.27. On Catholic awareness of the Protestant problem in relation to the Perpetual Virginity, see [P. de la Place], *Commentaires de l'estat de la religion et Republique soubs les Rois Henry et Francois seconds et Charles neufieme* ([Paris], 1565), 291–4, and S.M. Manetsch, *Theodore Beza and the Quest for Peace in France 1572–1598* (Leiden and Boston, MA, 2000), 274–5. I am grateful to Philip Benedict for pointing me to these references.

[75] Naphy, *Documents*, 97.

distinctly shaky justification in scripture. Any admission of that meant toying unhappily with some notion of Church authority in addition to the authority of Scripture, and that meant vulnerability to radicals and conservatives alike. One Lutheran spokesman, Hermann Busche, innocently let the cat out of the bag when debating with Anabaptists at Münster, while debate was still possible there in 1533. After admitting that infant baptism was not explicitly found in the Bible, he said that there were many things 'not mentioned in the Bible which are still perfectly acceptable. For example the perpetual virginity of Mary or that the Bible nowhere mentions the baptism of the apostles'.[76] It was with such debates in mind that the perpetual virginity assumed the importance that it did. When Andreas Osiander wrote to Zwingli in 1527 that the sum total of religion consisted in the satisfactory proof of the virginity of Mary, or when in the same year Johannes Oecolampadius told Zwingli in strikingly similar terms that the whole of Christendom stood or fell on the acknowledgement of Mary's perpetual virginity, it was because they wrote in the aftermath of the first radical assertions at Augsburg that Jesus Christ was no more than a prophet.[77]

* * *

We have followed a tangled story, and it is not surprising that the tangles gradually led to a general Protestant silence falling over Mary. The aggressive promotion of Our Lady by Rome as a symbol of its mid-century recovery did not help matters. In England, where the last official Hail Mary was heard in the wake of the death of Queen Mary I, people were discouraged from singing about the Virgin as their ancestors had done. The ballads which were put into print from the London presses, which admittedly may not be identical with those which were actually sung, are notable for what they do not contain: it was God's providence, not our Lady's, which appeared in the lyrics.[78] Christmas carols, such as Luther loved and amplified, were controversial in England, associated with Catholic survival, and infrequently published in Elizabeth's reign, although they began making a comeback in the early seventeenth century; English publishers produced no picture of the Holy Family before 1637. One might even see the popular carol

---

[76] Ibid., 101.
[77] Tappolet, *Marienlob*, 246; see above, 208.
[78] A. Walsham, *Providence in Early Modern England* (Oxford, 1999), 80, 91–3.

'Righteous Joseph' as an attempt to take the spotlight off Our Lady and redirect it onto her husband.[79]

Even within the Lutheran world, Luther's continuing devotion and his permission for religious art did not lead after his death to any flourishing modified Marian devotion. New pictures of Mary ceased to be placed in Lutheran churches after mid-century, while images of the Crucifixion continued to be a staple of Lutheran church art. Luther's own promotion of one central image of the Crucifixion was symbolic of this silence: one of the most well-known title-pages designed by Lukas Cranach the Elder for Luther's translation of the Bible centres on a very medieval depiction of Christ on the cross – but the flanking figures are no longer Mary and John, but Luther himself and the Saxon Elector Johann Friedrich. For the Reformed world, Mary took her place in the scheme of salvation because she was there in the scripture and in the creeds. But those who learnt their catechism in the Reformed world were not encouraged to think further or more than functionally on the subject, any more than they were prompted to dally long with the communion of saints departed.[80] On the eve of the Church of England's stealthy tiptoeing away from Calvin and the Reformed world in the seventeenth century, it is noticeable that the forerunner of that movement, Richard Hooker, said almost as little about Mary as did John Calvin.

This silence is particularly striking among activist Protestant women, who might have been expected to look to the Church's archetypal woman for an example. Perhaps the problem was the limited range of models which Mary now offered. The few positively approving mentions of her in the staple of English official preaching, the *Homilies* of 1547 and 1563, pointed to scriptural references concerning her humility and her obedience to lawfully constituted authority.[81] In this, England was only following other parts of the

<hr>

[79] T. Watt, *Cheap Print and Popular Piety* (Cambridge, 1991), 120–1, and on Protestant attitudes to Joseph, cf. Hartshorne, *Defence by Fulke*, 535–6.

[80] Cf. *Calvin, Theological Treatises*, ed. J.K.S. Reid, Library of Christian Classics, 22 (1954), 97, the Latin catechism of Geneva, 27 Nov. 1545, almost certainly composed by Calvin; *A Catechism in Latin by Alexander Nowell . . . Together with the Same Catechism Translated into English by Thomas Norton*, ed. G.E. Corrie, PS (Cambridge, 1853), 150; I. Green, *The Christian's ABC: Catechisms and Catechizing in England c. 1530–1740* (Oxford, 1996), 336.

[81] *Certain Sermons or Homilies (1547) and A Homily against Disobedience and Wilful Rebellion (1570)*, ed. R.B. Bond (Toronto, 1987), 200, a 1547 reference where an allusion to Luke 1.52 in the Magnificat was made more explicit in 1563 (cf. *Certain Sermons or Homilies* (1852), 139); *Homilies*, ed. Bond, 169; *Certain Sermons or Homilies* (1852), 150.

Protestant world (and indeed, much Counter-Reformation spirituality) in picking up the theme of humility which Erasmus had highlighted; characteristically for the sixteenth century, official England also ignored the more radical messages contained in the Magnificat. A contemplative, passive model was not what the independent-minded Protestant woman was looking for; she needed stronger, more forceful biblical exemplars, and very often she found them in the Old Testament rather than in the stories of Mary. For instance, in the writings of the Strasbourg hymn-writer and lay theologian, Katharina Schütz, wife of the Reformer Matthias Zell, the women who stand out are Judith and Esther, or from the New Testament Anna the prophetess, passionate Mary Magdalene, or busy Martha. The Virgin Mary is hardly visible.[82] When, in London in 1582, Thomas Bentley edited a collection of descriptions and lives of biblical women as part of his proto-feminist anthology *The Monument of Matrones*, Mary came off badly. Old Testament women figure most, with Judith getting the longest entry at fifteen and a half pages, and even Sarah achieving five pages to the Blessed Virgin's four.[83] Nor was there any widespread impulse to draw on the traditional web of imagery around Mary for alternative Protestant purposes. There has been a good deal of exaggerated talk of Queen Elizabeth I of England taking on the attributes of the Virgin and becoming the centre of a substitute cult: such discussion has been effectively brought down to size by the research of Helen Hackett, who has shown how peripheral, gradual, and lacking in official encouragement was the development of any use of Marian imagery for the Queen.[84]

It is around the time of the passing of Elizabeth of England, as the nativity carols began finding their way back into print, and as cultured Protestant noblemen began risking pictures of scriptural scenes from the life of Our Lady in their private chapels, that one finds hints of a different voice within Protestantism.[85] With the passage of time, the

---

[82] E.A. McKee, *Katharina Schütz Zell*, 2 vols, Studies in Medieval and Reformation Thought, 69 (Leiden and Boston, MA, 1999). For similar comment, see P. Russell, *Lay Theology in the Reformation. Popular Pamphleteers in Southwest Germany 1521–1525* (Cambridge, 1985), 203, 201, 222. On Counter-Reformation discussion of the humility of Mary, see particularly Ellington, *From Sacred Body to Angelic Soul*, 182–4.

[83] C.B. and J.B. Atkinson, 'The identity and life of Thomas Bentley, compiler of *The Monument of Matrones*', *Sixteenth Century Journal*, 31 (2000), 323–47, at 328.

[84] Perhaps most telling is Hackett's balanced discussion of the much-exploited sermon of Dr John King preached immediately after Elizabeth's death: Hackett, *Virgin Mother*, 225.

[85] For the importance of the private chapel of the statesman Robert Cecil at Hatfield, begun in 1607, see P. Croft, 'The religion of Robert Cecil', *HistJ*, 34 (1991), 773–96, at 787–9.

heirs of the Reformation were better able to reflect on what might be missing in the Protestant devotional revolution. So, in the 1630s, the French Reformed pastor and popular devotional writer Charles Drelincourt was able to write a tract and a substantial follow-up book concerning the honour which was appropriate to the Blessed Virgin Mary, rather to the surprise of his Roman Catholic clerical contemporaries.[86] Above all, in England, the clerical party fostered by Lancelot Andrewes, the 'avant-garde conformists' who were being nicknamed 'Arminians' by the 1620s, gathered Mary up in their enterprise of rewriting the history and the theology of the English Church. But their devotional poetry, their liturgical adventures, or the statue of Our Lady on Oxford's University Church erected so controversially by the chaplain of Archbishop Laud, must remain another story. The last word is best given to John Jewel, a cosmopolitan champion of the whole European Reformation as well as defender of the English Church, in an aphorism generated by his long dialogue with the Catholic scholar Thomas Harding: 'Verily, M. Harding, to be the child of God it is a great deal greater grace than to be the mother of God.'[87]

St Cross College, Oxford

---

[86]   Cadier, 'Vierge Marie', 49–53: C. Drelincourt, *De l'honneur qui doit estre rendu a la saincte et bienheureuse Vierge Marie: Auec la response à Monsieur l'euesque de Belley sur la qualité de cét honneur* (Paris, 1642).

[87]   Ayre, *Works of Jewel*, 3:578.

MARIAN DEVOTION AND CONFESSIONAL IDENTITY IN SIXTEENTH-CENTURY GERMANY

by BRIDGET HEAL

THE Virgin Mary provided a powerful focal point for religious identity. During the early modern period Mary-worship marked out one Christian confession from another, rather than Christian from Jew, as in the Middle Ages, or Catholic from secularist, as in more modern times.[1] Intra-Christian disputes over Mary's status were particularly intense in Germany, the heartland of the Reformation, where Catholic and Protestant lived side by side. This paper will consider the fate of Marian imagery and devotion in three of Germany's key free cities: Nuremberg, Augsburg, and Cologne. Each city had a different confessional structure: Nuremberg adopted the Lutheran faith in 1525; Augsburg's council introduced wide-ranging and radical (Zwinglian-influenced) reforms in the 1530s but the city had religious parity imposed on it in 1548; Cologne remained Catholic, despite the presence of a considerable Protestant minority within its city walls and the attempts of two archbishops to introduce a synodal Reformation. These three cities therefore illustrate the spectrum of possible responses of traditional Marian veneration to the pressures of Protestant and Catholic reform. A comparison between them allows us to assess the impact of both doctrinal debate and local circumstance on the expression of Marian piety, and reveals the various ways in which Marian devotion might be used to create confessional consciousness and define religious allegiance.

* * *

Nuremberg was the first imperial free city to adopt the Lutheran faith. In 1530 Martin Luther wrote from the Coburg: 'Nuremberg verily shines on the whole German land, like a sun among moon and stars,

---

[1] On Marian devotion and anti-Jewish sentiment see Klaus Schreiner, *Maria: Jungfrau, Mutter, Herrscherin* (Munich and Vienna, 1994), 413–62. On Marian devotion and nineteenth- and twentieth-century Catholic identity see Barbara Colorado Pope, 'Immaculate and powerful: the Marian revival in the nineteenth century', in C.W. Atkinson, C.H. Buchanan and M.R. Miles, eds, *Immaculate and Powerful: the Female in Sacred Image and Social Reality* (Boston, MA, 1985), 173–200, and Ruth Harris, *Lourdes: Body and Spirit in a Secular Age* (1999).

strongly moving other cities by what is going on there'.[2] In Nuremberg Luther's desire to combine religious reform with social and political conservatism found perfect expression. Moderate in its confessional stance, the council never allowed radical Protestant or sectarian teaching to gain a foothold within the city. Zwingli's writings were proscribed in 1526 and local Anabaptists were expelled. Even more moderate in political terms, the city had, by the end of the 1520s, abandoned its role in the forefront of the campaign for empire-wide reform and was firmer than either Saxony or Luther himself in refraining from any kind of diplomatic initiative that might have resulted in it having to take up arms against its political overlord, the Catholic emperor.[3] Nuremberg was also the first city to recognize, albeit temporarily, the Interim issued by the imperial Diet in May 1548, which prescribed the reintroduction of various Catholic ceremonies.[4]

Given this religious and political moderation, it is scarcely surprising that there was little iconoclasm in Nuremberg. Nonetheless, it is remarkable that almost all of the city's pre-Reformation Marian imagery remained not only intact but also in situ, on public display.[5] An engraving of 1696 shows the interior of the Frauenkirche, the imperial chapel that stood (and stands) on Nuremberg's main market square. By then the church had been in use as a Protestant preaching hall for more than 150 years by the time it was made. Even so, it was still full of paintings and statues of the Virgin. An elaborate Marian retable stood behind the high altar, a rosary panel hung beneath the organ, and on the column opposite the pulpit was a panel showing the *Mater dolorosa* with a sculpture of St Anne with the Virgin and Child above it.[6] Similar images survived in Nuremberg's two parish churches: the Frauenkirche

2   Quoted in G. Seebass, 'The importance of the imperial city of Nuremberg in the Reformation', in J. Kirk, ed., *Humanism and Reform: The Church in Europe, England, and Scotland, 1400–1643: Essays in Honour of James K. Cameron*, SCH.S, 8 (Oxford, 1991), 113.

3   On Nuremberg's confessional history and relationship with its emperor see Hans Baron, 'Religion and politics in the German imperial cities during the Reformation', *EHR*, 52 (1937), 405–27, and Carl Christensen, 'Iconoclasm and the preservation of ecclesiastical art in Reformation Nuremberg', *Archiv für Reformationsgeschichte*, 61 (1970), 205–21.

4   B. Klaus, *Veit Dietrich: Leben and Werk* (Nuremberg, 1958), 222–7.

5   I know of only one image of the Virgin that was removed from one of the city's churches because of idolatry. See T. Hampe, ed., *Nürnberger Ratsverlässe über Kunst und Künstler im Zeitalter der Spätgotik und Renaissance*, 2 vols (Vienna and Leipzig, 1904), 1:254.

6   Parts of the retable survive today in the Frauenkirche, in St Jakob, and in the Germanisches Nationalmuseum (hereafter GNM). See GNM, ed., *Katalog der Veit Stoß-Ausstellung im Germanischen Museum* (Nuremberg, 1933), cat. no. 57. The rosary panel also survives in the GNM. See Heinz Stafski, 'Die Rosenkranztafel aus der Nürnberger Frauenkirche. Zu den angeblichen Entlehnungen aus der Graphik Dürers', in GNM and

was by no means exceptional. Moreover, Mary's continued presence was not confined to the ecclesiastical sphere. When, in the mid nineteenth century, a Nuremberg librarian drew up a list describing the city's medieval sculpted house signs there were forty of the Virgin Mary still surviving, a truly remarkable total more than 300 years after the introduction of the Reformation.[7]

Nuremberg's Lutheran citizens were not only exposed to numerous images of the Virgin, they also continued to celebrate some of her feast-days and they were still told that blasphemy against her was a punishable offence. Of the seven traditional Marian feast-days, three survived the council's reform of the liturgical calendar: the Annunciation, the Purification, and the Visitation. The latter two – the Purification and the Visitation – were retained against the advice of local theologians.[8] The council's attitude to Marian blasphemy was equally conservative: in a decree issued on 3 March 1526, a year after the official introduction of the Reformation, the council condemned blasphemy against God and against the sacrament of the altar, and added that whoever spoke malevolently of the Virgin Mary, 'impugned the doctrine of her perpetual virginity, and thereby harmed her in abuse or damage of the honour with which she is endowed by God', was to receive corporal punishment or a fine. This decree was repeated in blasphemy ordinances issued in 1529 and 1560.[9] It is difficult to say whether it was actively enforced, as very few of Nuremberg's trial records survive. One case does, however, suggest that even once Nuremberg's council was firmly committed to the Protestant cause it still felt the need to castigate those who spoke ill of the Virgin: during the first half of 1525, the very time at which the Reformation was being instituted, a knife-maker, Marx Plickner, was imprisoned because he had 'blasphemed much against the Virgin Mary'.[10]

Zentralinstitut für Kunstgeschichte, ed., *Veit Stoß: Die Vorträge des nürnberger Symposiums* (Munich, 1985), 245–59. The *Anna Selbdritt* is on display in St Jakob. See GNM, ed., *Veit Stoß in Nürnberg: Werke des Meisters und seiner Schule in Nürnberg und Umgebung* (Munich, 1983), 297–301.

[7]   G.W.K. Lochner, *Die noch vorhandenen Abzeichen nürnberger Häuser* (Nuremberg, 1855).

[8]   Gerhard Pfeiffer, ed., *Quellen zur nürnberger Reformationsgeschichte. Von der Duldung liturgischer Änderungen bis zur Ausübung des Kirchenregiments durch den Rat (Juni 1524–Juni 1525)* (Nuremberg, 1968), 236; E. Sehling, ed., *Die evangelischen Kirchenordnungen des XVI. Jahrhunderts*, 16 vols (Leipzig and Tübingen, 1902–77), 11:204.

[9]   Nuremberg, Stadtarchiv Nürnberg, Rep. A6, Sammlung der (gedruckten) Mandate, Urkunden and Verordnungen der Reichsstadt and Stadtverwaltung Nürnberg 1219 bis Gegenwart, 1526 März 3, fol. 2r; 1529, fol. 3v; B 31/1, fol. 100r.

[10]   Pfeiffer, ed., *Quellen*, 289, 311, 445.

Why did Nuremberg's council choose to preserve so many elements of pre-Reformation Marian devotion? And how could their survival be justified? There were good theological grounds for retaining some Marian images and feast-days, and for continuing to ensure that local citizens showed appropriate respect for the Mother of God. In Lutheran teaching Mary was denied any individual merit and was stripped of the salvific power that had, in the past, been attributed to her. She was also domesticated. It is impossible to imagine any Catholic author describing her as Luther did: 'She seeks not any glory, but goes about her meals and her usual household duties, milking the cows, cooking the meals, washing pots and kettles, sweeping out the rooms, and performing the work of a maidservant or housemother in lowly and despised tasks'.

Nonetheless, Mary remained important as an exemplary beneficiary of the plenitude of God's grace, and as one who, through her words at the Annunciation, showed Christians 'how to know, love and praise God'.[11] Lutherans were expected to abandon the traditional, superstitious elements of Marian veneration and to regard the Virgin not as an intercessor and protector, but as a model of right conduct and belief. Such efforts to transform popular belief often foundered, but evidence concerning devotional practice suggests that in Nuremberg most citizens did indeed exchange their idolatrous veneration of the Virgin for legitimate devotion.[12]

It has to be said, however, that the survival of Marian imagery and liturgy went beyond what could be justified in purely theological terms. The local reformer Andreas Osiander was adamant in his prescription that only images depicting biblical facts or true events from the lives of model Christians should be allowed to remain on display. He also advocated the abolition of all Marian feast-days except the Annunciation.[13] Yet in 1600 Nuremberg's churches still contained paintings and statues of the Holy Kindred, of the Coronation and Assumption of the Virgin, of the rosary and of the Virgin of Mercy, and

---

[11] Jaroslav Pelikan, ed., *Luther's Works*, 55 vols (St Louis, MO, and Philadelphia, PA, 1958–67), 21:323, 329.

[12] For a discussion of Marian devotional habits in Nuremberg and its surrounding territory see B. Heal, 'Images of the Virgin Mary and Marian devotion in Protestant Nuremberg', in H. Parish and W.G. Naphy, eds, *Religion and 'Superstition' in Reformation Europe* (Manchester, 2002), 25–46.

[13] G. Muller and G. Seebass, eds, *Andreas Osiander d. Ä.: Gesamtausgabe*, 10 vols (Gütersloh, 1975–97), 2:287. On the abolition of feast-days see n.8 above.

the festivals of the Visitation and the Purification were still being celebrated. The council's reluctance to follow the recommendations of its
leading theologian suggests that its decisions with regard to Marian art
and liturgy were shaped by something other than straightforward religious ideology.

Nuremberg's political conservatism has already been noted. The city
had no desire to disassociate itself more than necessary from its glorious
Catholic past and imperial present: economic interests, historic memories, and fresh political experience combined to make the city loyal to
its imperial overlord despite its religious transgression. It is difficult to
prove that this political conservatism helped determine the fate of
Marian imagery and liturgy, yet this may be surmised from the fact that
the council – the city's political body – pushed local preachers and
provosts – its religious advisors – to agree to the preservation of more
paintings, sculptures, and feast days than they would, of their own voli-
tion, have countenanced.

There is also some evidence to suggest that the council wished to
keep the city's main churches, the churches that were most likely to be
visited, looking and sounding as traditional as possible, but was
prepared to permit a greater degree of innovation elsewhere. The
images that filled the city's two parish churches and the Frauenkirche
were carefully preserved, while the images from the cloister churches
and chapels, which were no longer accessible and were therefore no
longer contributing to a public display of moderation, were mostly
dispersed (given as gifts or sold).[14] Furthermore, the liturgy of the two
parish churches retained more of its pre-Reformation elements than
the liturgy of the much less significant Spitalkirche, and in the case of
the Frauenkirche there is even evidence to suggest that the *Salve Regina*
was still being sung ten years after the introduction of the Reformation.[15] Behaviour towards the Virgin Mary was one of the criteria by
which religious identity was judged, and Nuremberg's council used this
criterion to its own advantage, in order to demonstrate for the benefit
of outside observers, amongst them the Catholic emperor, its religious
and political moderation.

---

14 G. Seebass, 'Mittelalterliche Kunstwerke in evangelisch gewordenen Kirchen
Nürnbergs', in Johann Michael Fritz, ed., *Die bewahrende Kraft des Luthertums: mittelalterliche
Kunstwerke in evangelischen Kirchen* (Regensburg, 1997), 43–8.

15 Oral communication from Dr Volker Schier. On the Frauenkirche see Nuremberg,
Staatsarchiv Nürnberg, Rep. 44e, Losungsamt, Akten, S. I. L. 113, Nr. 11, which mentions a
payment: 'Dem Cantor so das Salue singt'.

* * *

Augsburg's Reformation was, at least in its initial stages, distinctly Zwinglian in tone. Not surprisingly therefore, the city was more vehement in its rejection of pre-Reformation Marian imagery and liturgy than Lutheran Nuremberg. The local preacher Michael Keller asserted that Mary was 'a woman like another ordinary woman' and that her images, and those of other saints, were idols.[16] At the instigation of Keller, and other like-minded reformers, local churches were cleansed of most of their Marian images and the city's liturgical calendar was stripped of all Marian festivals except the Annunciation.[17] A decree against blasphemy and swearing that comprised part of the Discipline Ordinance issued by the Protestant city council in 1537 omitted all mention of the Virgin Mary and the saints: in Augsburg Marian blasphemy was no longer a punishable offence.[18]

Even after 1555, when Augsburg's Protestant church was Lutheran rather than Zwinglian and might therefore have been expected to display a more lenient attitude towards paintings and sculptures of the saints, Marian images remained too closely associated with Catholic culture to be assimilated into Protestant devotional life. Until the late seventeenth century Augsburg's Protestant churches were characterized by a complete absence of Marian imagery, to the extent that a local Jesuit who entered one in 1684 could comment that he 'saw with astonishment' a statue of the Virgin standing there (not something any Catholic familiar with Nuremberg's Lutheran milieu could possibly have been surprised by).[19]

After 1548, when the Edict of Restitution forcibly reintroduced the Catholic cult into the city, adherents of the old faith brought back images of the Virgin and Marian liturgy into the churches under their control. The first major post-Reformation Marian commissions were archaic in tone. Christoph Amberger's panel for the east choir of the cathedral, produced in 1554, followed the design of a previous panel by

[16] Friedrich Roth, *Augsburgs Reformationsgeschichte*, 4 vols (Munich, 1901–11), 1:305; *Die Chroniken der deutschen Städte vom 14. bis ins 16. Jahrhundert*, 36 vols (Leipzig, 1862–1931), 23:215–16.

[17] On Augsburg's iconoclasm see Jörg Rasmussen, 'Bildersturm und Restauration', in Städtische Kunstsammlung Augsburg und Zentralinstitut für Kunstgeschichte Munich, ed., *Welt im Umbruch: Augsburg zwischen Renaissance und Barock* (Augsburg, 1981), 95–114. On feast-days see Sehling, *Die evangelischen Kirchenordnungen*, 12:84.

[18] Augsburg, Stadtarchiv Augsburg, Reichsstadt, Ratserlasse, 1507–1599, 1537 14/8, fol. 3r.

[19] Ibid., E.W.A., Nr 941, Tom. 1, Nr 6, fol. 1v.

Hans Holbein the Elder that had been destroyed by the iconoclasts.[20] And Paulus Mayr's retable for the high altar of the Benedictine abbey church of SS Ulrich and Afra, dating from 1571, draws on the altar forms of the late Gothic period.[21] Conspicuously positioned on the high altars of the Catholic party's two flagship churches, these images made provocative allusion to a united Christian past, brazenly invoking the pre-Reformation cult of the Virgin in the face of Protestant criticism.

As confessional boundaries hardened during the late sixteenth century, the polemical element of Marian piety became even more pronounced. In his 1577 *De Maria Virgine incomparabile* the Jesuit Peter Canisius, who had served as cathedral preacher in Augsburg from 1559 to 1567, wrote:

> we Catholics should distinguish ourselves from the Protestants through eager Marian veneration, we should doggedly and with enthusiasm do everything that contributes to the greater honour of Mary, we should always study better why and how we can worship the most holy Virgin at home and in public.[22]

Augsburg's Catholic elite, dominated by the reforming bishop Otto Truchseß von Waldburg, the powerful Fugger family, and members of the Jesuit Order, took these instructions very much to heart. The Fuggers commissioned altarpieces showing Mary as Augsburg's special protectress from painters steeped in the visual aesthetics of the Counter-Reformation – Christoph Schwarz, Hans von Aachen, and Peter Candid – and placed them in the Jesuit church and in SS Ulrich and Afra.[23] Members of the Jesuits' proselytizing Marian sodalities pledged themselves to Mary's service and undertook to defend her honour.[24] And Mary was repeatedly invoked in liturgical rituals, for example in the much-publicized exorcism that Canisius performed on Markus Fugger's maidservant at Altötting in 1570.[25] In Augsburg Marian

---

[20] Freya Strecker, *Augsburger Altäre zwischen Reformation (1537) und 1635: Bildkritik, Repräsentation und Konfessionalisierung* (Münster, 1998), 178–91.

[21] Rasmussen, 'Bildersturm und Restauration', 106–8.

[22] Quoted in Reinhold Baumstark, ed., *Rom in Bayern: Kunst und Spiritualität der ersten Jesuiten: Katalog zur Ausstellung des Bayerischen Nationalmuseums München, 30. April bis 20. Juli 1997* (Munich, 1997), 483.

[23] See ibid., cat. no. 153, and Brigitte Volk-Knüttel, 'Candid nach Schwarz', *Münchner Jahrbuch der bildenden Kunst*, ser. 3, 39 (1988), 113–32.

[24] Theodor Rolle, *Heiligkeitsstreben und Apostolat. Geschichte der Marianischen Kongregation am Jesuitenkolleg St. Salvator und am Gymnasium der Benediktiner bei St. Stephan in Augsburg 1589–1989* (Augsburg, 1989).

[25] M. Eisengrein, *Vnser liebe Fraw zu Alten Oetting* (Ingolstadt, 1571), 273–90.

imagery and devotion became confessionally charged more quickly and more completely than in either Nuremberg or Cologne. The close juxtaposition of two competing confessions led to what Marc Forster has described as a 'mania for differentiation'.[26] Local Protestants rejected all manifestations of Mary's cult, and it thus became, as Canisius advocated in his 1577 text, a way in which Catholics distinguished themselves from their Protestant neighbours. Catholics made Mary their own: she became a symbol of militant recatholicization, and of the rejuvenation of the city's confessional minority. As a result even during the later sixteenth century, when Augsburg's Protestant population was predominantly Lutheran rather than Zwinglian, Mary was still too closely associated with Catholicism to play any role in Protestant piety.

* * *

The evidence from Cologne demonstrates the fallacy of assuming that the Jesuit-sponsored Virgin, who had, by the end of the sixteenth century, come to dominate the Marian piety of Augsburg's Catholic citizens, was the only prototype for post-Tridentine devotion to the Mother of God. Religious polemic did not inevitably become part of Marian piety. In Cologne, a bastion of the old faith, traditional usages persisted alongside modern innovations such as the Jesuits' Marian sodalities. There was very little iconographic innovation: in most of the city's churches the Marian images that had been donated during the fifteenth and early sixteenth centuries remained in place until well into the seventeenth.[27] There was a conspicuous absence of the kind of militant Marian imagery produced by Christoph Schwarz and Peter Candid for the Fuggers in Augsburg. Even in Cologne's Jesuit church the main focus for Marian veneration appears to have been an archaic alabaster Madonna that acquired a reputation as a grace-giving image.[28] Statues of the Virgin and Child also continued to be richly decorated with robes, crowns, and veils, despite Trent's decree that 'all sensual appeal must be avoided, so that images are not painted or adorned with seductive charm'.[29] And although various synods attempted to reform

---

[26] Marc Forster, *The Counter-Reformation in the Villages: Religion and Reform in the Bishopric of Speyer, 1560–1720* (Ithaca and London, 1992), 225.

[27] Bridget Heal, 'A woman like any other? Images of the Virgin Mary and Marian devotion in Nuremberg, Augsburg and Cologne c.1500–1600' (University of London Ph.D. thesis, 2001), 90–111.

[28] Paul Clemen, ed., *Die kirchlichen Denkmäler der Stadt Köln* (Düsseldorf, 1911), 144.

[29] Norman P. Tanner, ed., *Decrees of the Ecumenical Councils*, 2 vols (London and Washington DC, 1990), 2:775–6.

processional practice, cult images were still carried through the city amidst great festivities.[30]

Why was Cologne's Marian piety more traditional than Augsburg's? In Cologne, unlike in Augsburg, there was no hiatus to incite transformations in devotional practice. Cologne's Catholics never confronted a militant Protestantism that rejected Mary, and they therefore never had to adopt a militant affirmation of her in order to strengthen their own confessional solidarity. Partly because of this lack of disruption, and partly because of the diversity and strength of Cologne's numerous ecclesiastical institutions, the forces of the Counter-Reformation never established a monopoly over Marian imagery and devotion as they did in Augsburg. In Augsburg the alliance between Bishop Otto Truchseß von Waldburg, the Jesuits and their Fugger patrons decisively shaped the local Catholic cult. In Cologne there was no equivalent undisputed source of confessional authority. Cologne's archbishop-electors were conspicuously lacking in reforming zeal, and certainly did not provide suitable conduits for the transmission of the spirit of the post-Tridentine church.[31] The Jesuits, the other likely channel for the dissemination of new ideas, were welcomed by Cologne's reform-minded circle of clerics but were treated with suspicion by the council, reluctant to grant yet another order privileges within the city and anxious to avoid confessional conflict wherever possible.[32] Cologne's Jesuits apparently did not feel the need, or perhaps, lacking institutional support from either the archbishop or the council, did not have the opportunity, to turn Mary into militant symbol of Catholic renewal.

* * *

This article has sought to demonstrate the inadequacy of the crude, bipolar model frequently adopted by scholars when discussing the cult of the Virgin and its demise. We cannot simply assume two alternatives: rejection on the part of Protestants, and approbation on the part of Catholics. Sixteenth-century attitudes towards Marian imagery and devotion were complex and contingent, shaped as much by intellectual and political pressures as by the normative prescriptions of Protestant

---

[30] Heal, 'A woman like any other?', 235–7.

[31] K. Repgen, 'Der Bischof zwischen Reformation, katholischer Reform und Konfessionsbildung (1515–1650)', in P. Berglar, ed., *Der Bischof in seiner Zeit: Bischofstypus and Bischofsideal im Spiegel der Kölner Kirche* (Cologne, 1986), 245–314.

[32] Bernhard Duhr, *Geschichte der Jesuiten in den Ländern deutscher Zunge*, 4 vols (Freiburg im Breisgau, 1907–28), 1:35–6, 38–9, 42.

and Catholic reformers. Mary's role in the construction of confessional consciousness varied according to cultural context, not just according to religious environment. In Nuremberg a specifically Lutheran Virgin emerged, a Virgin who was stripped of her divine power but who nonetheless continued to provide a model of right conduct and belief. This demystified Mary served as a symbol of confessional moderation, distinguishing Nuremberg's Lutherans from adherents of the old faith on the one hand, and from more radical Protestants on the other.

In Augsburg the Virgin's status could not be so easily transformed. Local Protestants were much less ready than their Nuremberg counterparts to tolerate Marian art and liturgy: between 1534 and 1548 almost all reminders of the pre-Reformation cult of the Virgin were purged from the city's visual and devotional culture. Impelled by this caesura in the city's traditions of Marian piety, and pressured by the continued presence of a predominantly Protestant population, the leaders of Augsburg's Catholic cult placed the Virgin at the forefront of their campaign of reconquest. While Cologne's Catholics remained steeped in the Marian piety of the pre-Reformation period, Augsburg's turned, with great alacrity, to images and expressions of devotion characteristic of Counter-Reformation Mariology. In bi-confessional Augsburg, to a much greater extent than in Catholic Cologne, Mary became a symbol of Catholic solidarity, a role that she has continued to play in Catholic communities throughout the world ever since.

University of St Andrews

OFFENDING GOD: JOHN FOXE AND ENGLISH PROTESTANT REACTIONS TO THE CULT OF THE VIRGIN MARY

by THOMAS S. FREEMAN

ON 20 January 1574, at about 7.00 p.m., Alexander Nyndge, one of the sons of William Nyndge, a gentleman of Herringwell, Suffolk, suddenly went into violent paroxysms. Edward Nyndge, Alexander's brother, intervened. Edward was a Cambridge graduate and a former fellow of Gonville and Caius, and his University education had apparently prepared him for just such an emergency. He immediately declared that Alexander was possessed by an evil spirit and summoned the villagers to come and pray for his brother's recovery. As the praying continued, Alexander's convulsions grew worse; a half dozen men had to hold him in his chair. Meanwhile the onlookers were praying extemporaneously. Suddenly someone invoked both God and the Virgin Mary. Edward pounced on this remark and admonished the crowd that such prayers offended God. The evil spirit, in a voice 'much like Alexanders voice', chimed in, endorsing the propriety of the prayer. But 'Edward made answere and said thou lyest, for ther is no other name under Heaven, wherby we may challenge Salvacion, but thonly name of Ihesus Christe'. This point settled, Edward proceeded to organize his brother's exorcism.[1]

Perfectly preserved in this episode, like a fly in amber, is a generational conflict in Reformation England over the veneration of the Virgin Mary. The young Cambridge-educated Edward Nyndge reproving his neighbours for praying to Mary is paradigmatic of elite suppression of the traditional cult of the Virgin, indeed of the suppression of late medieval popular devotion in England.[2] If the altars remained stripped, if the towers of Walsingham never again pierced the

---

[1] Edward Nyndge, *A Booke declaring the Fearfull Vexation of one Alexander Nyndge* (?1574), sigs A2r–A4v. I would like to thank Professor Eamon Duffy for reading and commenting on an earlier version of this paper.

[2] See Eamon Duffy, *The Stripping of the Altars: Traditional Religion in England 1400–1580* (New Haven, CT, 1992), 379–593; for the suppression of various aspects of the cult of the Virgin Mary see 402–3, 415–18, 465, 490, 580–2, 585.

sky, the attacks of the educated elites upon traditional English religion are a significant part of the reason why.

But there must be more to it than this. The English people did not blindly obey the dictates of the godly elites; Christopher Durston has described the inability of the puritans to reform popular culture during the Interregnum despite their control over the most important organs of central government.[3] To understand why the English Protestants were largely successful in their attempts to eradicate the cult of the Virgin Mary, it is necessary to examine in detail the English Protestant attacks on the cult.

There is not the space here to discuss all of these assaults: instead I will focus on those made by John Foxe, the martyrologist. Foxe's perspective on the traditional veneration of the Virgin is of particular interest for two reasons. Foxe, who was born in 1517, saw the cult of the Virgin reach its final efflorescence in England and also saw its shrines overthrown; in fact, he personally suppressed one of these shrines when he was in his early thirties.[4] Moreover, although it is not often appreciated, the *Acts and Monuments* was the first history of the Middle Ages written in English since the Reformation and, as such, it dealt with many aspects of Marian devotion. The popularity of Foxe's work, and the authoritative status English Protestants accorded it, ensured that Foxe's opinions about the cult of the Virgin would be widely disseminated and credited.

There is, in fact, little extended discussion of Mary or her cult in Foxe's work. The closest that Foxe came to an extended critique of the cult of the Virgin Mary occurred when he reprinted extracts from the *Psalter of Our Lady*, a work which Foxe attributed to Bonaventure. (It is now believed to have been written by Conrad of Saxony in the thirteenth century.) Foxe printed several pages of the psalter and surrounded them with a series of scathing marginal notes which denounced the praise of the Virgin Mary as an intercessor for sinners and a mediator with her son on humanity's behalf as blasphemous because it negated, or at best minimized, the sufficiency of Christ's sacrifice.[5] So far, so straightforward; this appears to be a fairly represen-

---

[3]   Christopher Durston, 'Puritan rule and the failure of cultural revolution, 1645–1660', in Christopher Durston and Jacqueline Eales, eds, *The Culture of English Puritanism, 1560–1700* (Basingstoke, 1996), 210–33.

[4]   This episode is described in John Foxe, *Christ Jesus Triumphant*, trans. Richard Day (1607), sig. A4r.

[5]   John Foxe, *The Ecclesiasticall History, contaynyng the Actes and Monumentes*, 2nd edn (1570) [hereafter *1570*], 1774–7.

tative example of a conventional Protestant attack on traditional veneration of the Virgin Mary. A closer comparison, however, of Foxe's text
with his source (which Foxe cited very precisely, noting that he had
used the two-volume edition of Bonaventure's works printed in
Strasburg in 1495) suggests that Foxe had other, less obvious, motives in
printing, and damning, the psalter.

For one thing, while almost all of the material which Foxe extracted
from the psalter was accurately reprinted, on a few occasions he altered
its actual words. The psalter read: 'I will give to thanks to thee O Lady,
with my whole heart and sing thy praise and glory among the nations.
Sinners will find grace *in the Lord* through you the procurer of grace and
salvation'. Foxe reprinted this omitting the words 'apud Deum' with the
result that the second sentence now read 'Sinners will find grace
through you . . .'.[6] And where the psalter read: 'We magnify thee the
procurer of grace through whom the world is repaired. Exalted above
the choir of angels, you pray for us before the throne of God', Foxe
omitted the last sentence which had Mary praying before the throne of
God. He also tendentiously translated the words 'gratiae inventricem' as
'the finder *and author* of grace'.[7] If Foxe's goal was simply to attack the
psalter for its putative 'blasphemy' in extolling Mary as the intercessor
for humanity, why did he go beyond this and alter the text to make it
appear that the work hailed Mary as the source of grace?

The placement of the psalter in the *Acts and Monuments* sheds additional light on Foxe's objectives. On the page before the excerpts from
the psalter, Foxe printed a proclamation which Queen Mary had issued
on 13 June 1555, banning heretical books. Foxe urged his readers to
contrast the books banned by the Marian Catholics with a work
published under the auspices of Mary's government, the version of the
Sarum primer printed by John Wayland.[8] This work was popular
(accounting, in its various editions, for over half of all the primers
printed in England in Mary's reign), and it was also a potentially
powerful instrument of Catholic propaganda. Eamon Duffy has
observed that the Wayland primers

---

[6] Cf. *Egregium opus . . . doctoris seraphici sancti Bonaventure*, 2 vols (Strasburg, 1495), 2, fol.
84v with *1570*, 1775. All translations in this article are my own.

[7] Cf. *Opus . . . Bonaventure*, 2, fol. 84v with *1570*, 1775. The psalter read 'Assiste pro nobis
ante tribunalem dei. Suscipe in fine animas nostras, et introduc nos in requiem eternam' (fol.
88r); Foxe dropped the first of these sentences from his version of the psalter.

[8] *1570*, 1773. Eamon Duffy has observed that the Wayland primers 'clearly represent the
religion approved for lay use in Mary's reign' (Duffy, *Stripping*, 526–7, 538–9).

are a remarkable blend of the old and the new. In them both the traditional and reformed materials have been pressed into service to a Catholicism in which the ancient pieties, to Sacrament and saint, have their place, but where they are subordinated to a strong emphasis on the centrality of the Passion of Christ . . . the Wayland primers testify to the resilence, adaptability, and realism of the Marian attempt to restore Catholicism to the people.[9]

Their concessions to a changing religious climate made the Wayland primers attractive to a wide range of readers who were by no means ready to embrace traditional Catholicism.[10] They also made the work more dangerous to zealous Protestants.

Foxe reacted to the danger by printing carefully selected passages which, in their insistence on the miraculous or even salvific powers of the Virgin Mary and the saints, might be rebarbative to a generation of readers with a more Christocentric theology. Unfortunately for Foxe, such passages were few and far between; the editors of the primer had already purged much of this material from it.[11] So Foxe rewrote passages in the primer to suit his ends.[12] And, as with Bonaventure's psalter, Foxe rewrote passages from the Wayland primer to make them appear more 'blasphemous'. A prayer to the Virgin Mary in the psalter reads:

> Loose *the* prisoners from captivity
> Unto the blind give sight again
> *Repel our great iniquity*
> *All that is good, for us obtain.*[13]

Foxe's version reads:

> Loose *thy* prisoners from captivity
> Unto the blind give sight again

---

[9] Duffy, *Stripping*, 542–3.

[10] A copy of the 1555 edition of the primer, now in the BL (shelfmark C.35. c.22), has all the passages praising the Virgin Mary and the saints as intercessors lightly rased out. Clearly this is not a case of wanton vandalism, but is instead the work of a non-Catholic trying to retain the primer for use in personal devotions.

[11] Duffy, *Stripping*, 540.

[12] For an interesting example of this, outside the scope of this paper, compare Foxe's printing of the prayer to St Laurence (1570, 1773) with the version in the primer (*The Primer in Latin and English (after the Use of Sarum)* [1555], sig. F1v).

[13] *The Primer in Latin and English*, sig. M4r.

> *Deliver us from malignity*
> *To the end we may grace obtain.*[14]

But even this rewriting was not enough. So Foxe moved arbitrarily from the Wayland primer to Bonaventure's psalter, trusting his readers to make the natural but erroneous assumption that since both works were 'official' Catholic texts (Foxe was careful to point out that Bonaventure had been canonized in 1482), and since both praised the Virgin Mary, the views expressed in one work were the views contained in the other. Even though the psalter was less guarded and more extreme in its praise of the Virgin as an intercessor who persuaded her son to show mercy to humanity, Foxe still gilded the lily by rewriting passages from it. Lest any reader failed to associate the two texts, Foxe added his own commentary linking them and stating that the failure to recognize the sufficiency of Christ's Passion and death, and the reliance on the intercession of Mary, were 'not onely in this Primer *and* Psalter of Our Lady aforesayd, but also in all their [that is, Catholic] proceedings, teachings and preachinges'.[15]

In other words, Foxe printed extracts from Bonaventure's psalter not only to attack the cult of the Virgin Mary, but also to subvert the Wayland primers. He resurrected, and then ridiculed, medieval devotional works in order to discredit their all-too-popular sixteenth-century successors. This same tactic can be seen in Foxe's account of the creation of the Rosary.

The first edition of the *Acts and Monuments* contained a brief account of the pontificate of Sixtus IV in which it was stated that the pontiff built brothels catering to all sexual preferences, that he reduced the period between jubilees from fifty to twenty-five years, that he established the feast of the Immaculate Conception, that he canonized Francis of Assisi and Bonaventure, and that Sixtus, in return for a large payment, granted a cardinal an indulgence to practice sodomy. Every word of this account was translated from the *Catalogus* of Foxe's mentor John Bale, although Foxe arranged the events in a different order.[16] (In

---

[14] *1570*, 1774. Foxe underscored the polemical point he was making in rewriting these lines in a marginal note placed next to them: 'The office of Christ given to our Lady'.

[15] *1570*, 1777 (my emphasis).

[16] Cf. John Bale, *Scriptorum illustrium maioris Brytanniae . . . catalogus* (Basel, 1557), 624–5 and John Foxe, *Actes and Monuments of these Latter and Perillous Dayes* (1563) [hereafter *1563*], 388. For the close relationship between Bale and Foxe, and Foxe's use of Bale as a source, see Thomas S. Freeman, 'John Bale's book of martyrs?: the account of King John in *Acts and Monuments*', *Reformation*, 3 (1998), 175–223.

fact, although Foxe appears to present this material in random order, there is actually a pattern to it, a progression from pimping and prostitution to 'superstition' to spiritual prostitution and, in selling an indulgence to practice sodomy, back to pimping.) However, there was one story which Bale had related about the pontificate of Sixtus IV which Foxe did not repeat in the first edition of his martyrology.

Bale wrote that around the year 1470, Alanus de Rupe, a Dominican, 'after he had seen the illusions of evil demons, fabricated the Rosary ... preached it in place of the gospel and established a fraternity of it'. After declaring that Sixtus IV had championed both the devotion and the fraternity, Bale continued:

> A book was published concerning this matter, in the beginning of which one reads that the Blessed Virgin entered the cell of Alanus although it was shut and, fashioning a ring out of her hair for him, betrothed herself to the friar, that she kissed him, and gave him her breasts to be fondled and milked and, finally, that she gave herself to him as familiarly as a wife customarily does to her husband.[17]

Foxe reprinted the narrative of Sixtus IV from the first edition of his martyrology in its second edition. Eighteen pages later, Foxe began another narrative of Sixtus's misdeeds. In addition to repeating the story of Sixtus building brothels (obviously an anecdote the martyrologist favoured), Foxe printed Bale's narrative about Alanus de Rupe. He then continued:

> This fabulous figment when I read it in the centuries of Iohn Bale,[18] I began with me selfe to mistruste the credite therof, and had thought not to trouble the reader with such incredible forgeries. But as the providence of God worketh in all thyngs, so also it appeared in this, that the very same boke came to my handes at the wryting herof, wherin this self same narration is conteyned, wherin I founde ... this to bee true, whiche in Iohn Bale is expressed.[19]

Foxe's unusually detailed reference (undoubtedly made to reassure readers as sceptical as he had been that he had not invented the story) reveals that the book which came into his hands was a late fifteenth-century devotional work, Jodocus Beissel's *Rosacea augustissime*

---

[17] Bale, *Catalogus*, 624–5.
[18] Bale's *Catalogus* was divided into centuries.
[19] *1570*, 860.

christiferae Maria corona. Moreover, Foxe's version of the story of Alanus de Rupe's betrothal to the Virgin was an accurate rendition of Beissel's version of the story.[20] In this case, rewriting was unnecessary; the inability of Foxe's contemporaries to understand or empathize with devotional writings of the previous century did the martyrologist's work for him. Alanus de Rupe had claimed that the Virgin Mary had appeared to him and commissioned him to preach the Rosary and establish a confraternity dedicated to it.[21] Accounts of Alanus's 'betrothal' to the Virgin Mary very similar, if not identical, to Beissel's, were published by Alanus's admirers throughout Western Europe in the final decades of the fifteenth century. One even hailed Alanus in its title as 'the new bridegroom of the most blessed Virgin Mary'.[22] Claims of an intense spiritual relationship, couched in erotic terms, between Alanus and the Virgin, which seemed wonderful on the eve of the Reformation seemed manifestly ludicrous five or six decades later.

In fact, a generational divide is even apparent in the different responses of Bale and Foxe to the story of the celestial betrothal. Bale thought that the story was false and sinister, but he took it seriously, ascribing Alanus's visions to demons. Foxe, on the other hand, refused to believe that even Catholics related such a story and thought that it was a forgery. (It might be objected that Foxe's claims that he initially did not believe the story were merely rhetorical. The fact that he did not use this story in his first edition, but used it as soon as he had corroboration of Bale's accuracy, suggests that Foxe's incredulity was genuine.) When Foxe was satisfied that Alanus had claimed to have fondled and caressed the Virgin Mary, he regarded the story with contempt as the delusion of a dirty old man rather than a diabolic conspiracy. Foxe's derision was perfectly expressed in a marginal note he appended to the story: 'An old knave to suck his wifes breasts'.[23]

Yet Foxe did not use this story to discredit the Rosary or the veneration of the Virgin Mary; rather he related it to denigrate Sixtus IV, and

---

[20] Cf. *1570*, 860, with Jodocus Beissel, *Rosacea augustissime christiferae Maria corona* (Antwerp, 1495), sig. B5v.

[21] Gilles Gérard Meersseman, *Ordo fraternitatis: Confraternitie e pietà dei laici nel Medioevo*, 3 vols (Rome, 1977), 3:1157–8, 1164–5. For further background on Alanus de Rupe and the confraternity he established see Anne Winston-Allen, *Stories of the Rose: The Making of the Rosary in the Middle Ages* (University Park, PA, 1997), 24–5, 66–7, 77.

[22] *Magister Alanus de Rupe, sponsus novellus beatissime virginis Marie . . . de immensa et ineffabili dignitate et utilitate psaletrii . . . virginis Mariae* (Gripsholm, 1498). The story of Alanus's 'betrothal' to the Virgin, almost identical to Beissel's version, is on sigs S6v–S7r.

[23] *1570*, 860.

by extension the papacy, for believing in such outrageous stories and basing festivals and doctrines on them. Alanus's 'betrothal' underscored papal superstition and, with its erotic overtones, the carnality of Sixtus IV and other pontiffs. The link between papal carnality and doctrinal corruption, between spiritual venality and physical depravity, which was a fundamental theme of Foxe's treatment of the papacy was neatly epitomized in the story of Alanus and the Virgin Mary.

There is nothing mysterious about Foxe's targets when he discussed the debates over the Immaculate Conception. He began the discussion by describing the controversy as a quarrel between the Franciscans and the Dominicans. After summarizing the issues being debated, Foxe claimed that 'This frivolous question kindlyng and gendryng betweene these two sectes of Friers, brast out in such a flame of partes and sides taking, that it occupied the heades and wittes, scholes and universities, almost through the whole Church'.[24] After this blast of hyperbole, he described Sixtus IV's establishment of the feast of the Immaculate Conception and printed a summary of a bull of this pontiff defending the doctrine. Foxe took this material from a defence of the Immaculate Conception written by Jodocus Clichtoveus, a highly respected Paris theologian.[25] Foxe then printed nine statements about the Virgin Mary, declaring her exemption from Original Sin and her role in obtaining salvation for humanity, which he claimed were doctrines which Sixtus IV compelled all Christians to believe. Actually these points were gleaned from a list of debated propositions which opponents of the Immaculate Conception had challenged and which Clichtoveus defended.[26] Foxe took the most extreme of these propositions, which were already provocative statements on disputed issues, and presented them as official Catholic dogma. Clichtoveus had also penned counter-arguments to earlier Catholic theologians (such as Peter Lombard,

---

[24] *1570*, 924.

[25] Cf. *1570*, 924–5 with Jodocus Clichtoveus, *De puritate conceptionis beatae Mariae virginis: libri duo* (Paris, 1513), fol. 24r–v. Clichtoveus's work is itself an interesting attempt to present the arguments of Duns Scotus and other scholastics who championed the Immaculate Conception buttressed by humanist source criticism. For a discussion of *De puritate* see J.-P. Massaut, *Critique et tradition à la vielle de la Réforme en France* (Paris, 1974), 37–45.

[26] Cf. *1570*, 925–6 with Clichtoveus, *De puritate*, fols 27r–29v, 31v–32r, 33r, 35r–v, 38r–39r, 41r. Foxe was also misrepresenting Sixtus's bull which excommunicated anyone who denounced either the maculist or immaculist position as heretical. (See Rene Laurentin, 'The role of papal magisterum in the development of the dogma of the Immaculate Conception', in Edward D. O'Connor, ed., *The Dogma of the Immaculate Conception* (Notre Dame, IN, 1958), 265, 298–300).

Thomas Aquinas and Bernard of Clairvaux) who had rejected the Immaculate Conception; Foxe printed or summarized these in order to magnify the extent of dissension and controversy over the issue.[27]

Foxe followed this with a narrative of a series of a pious frauds committed by a group of Dominicans in Berne. By means of counterfeit miracles they had sought to demonstrate the supernatural support of the Virgin Mary for their denial of the Immaculate Conception; for this crime four were executed in Berne in 1509.[28] Foxe drew on a number of sources for his narrative of the scandal: Bale, Sebastian Munster, the chronicles of Caspar Peucer and Johann Stumpf, as well as Thomas Murner's scathing history of the episode.[29] Foxe's citations of the last two sources are both confusing and somewhat inaccurate; it is quite likely that he actually drew on a précis of Stumpf's and Murner's narratives prepared by a friend on the continent who had access to these works.[30] Whether the fault was Foxe's or that of an unknown redactor, the account of the scandal in the *Acts and Monuments* contains numerous inaccuracies. It was not an accident that many of these errors magnified the venality and strife among the mendicant orders.[31] Foxe appended the story of the Dominicans at Berne (which involved doctrinal debate only peripherally) to his account of the controversy over the Immaculate Conception because it highlighted the animosity between the mendicant orders. Concluding the account, Foxe emphasized the point yet again:

> And this much touchyng the begynnynge and ende of this tumultuous and Popishe tragedie; wherin evidently it may appeare to the

---

[27] Cf. *1570*, 926, with Clichtoveus, *De puritate*, fols 23r, 45rv–46r, 47v–51r.

[28] For details of the episode see R. Reuss, 'Le Procès des Dominicains de Berne en 1507–1509', *Revue de l'histoire des religions*, 52 (1905), 237–59; *Die Akten ders Jetzerprozesses nebst dem Defensorium*, ed. Rudolf Steck, Quellen zur Schweizergeschichte, 21 (Basel, 1904).

[29] *1570*, 926; also see Bale, *Catalogus*, 644; Sebastian Munster, *Cosmographiae universalis* (Basel, 1554), 424–5; Caspar Peucer, *Liber quintus chronici Carionis* (Frankfurt, 1566), 242–3; Johann Stumpf, *Gemeiner loblicher Eydgnoschafft Stetten, Landen und Vöckeren Chronikwirdiger Thaaten Beschreybung* (Zurich, 1548), fols 455r–459r; Thomas Murner, *De quattuor heresiarchis ordinis predicatorum de observantia nuncupatorum, apud Switenses in civitate Bernensi combustis* (Berne, 1509).

[30] Foxe cites the 'story of Ioan Stumsius' (note the error) and an unnamed history of the scandal published at Berne in German and Latin (*1570*, 926); this last must be Murner's treatise.

[31] E.g., Foxe states that the frauds were exposed by the Franciscans alarmed by the revenue they lost as the people of Berne no longer frequented their shrines (*1570*, 926). Actually the Franciscans played no role at all in unmasking the Dominicans; this was accomplished in an investigation initiated by the bishop of Lausanne and furthered by a papal commission.

reader, how neither these turbulent Friers could agree among themselves and yet in what frivolous trifles they wrangled together.[32]

Just as Foxe had used a thirteenth-century psalter to discredit the Wayland primers and the visions of Alanus de Rupe to embarrass the papacy, so he now used the disputes over the Immaculate Conception to attack the mendicant orders. Foxe attacked them for the same reason that he had subverted the Wayland primers; they were a potentially dangerous instrument of Catholic evangelization. As a bonus, the doctrinal disputes between the Dominicans and the Franciscans provided Foxe with a *tu quoque* defence against Catholic charges that Protestant disunity proved that the Protestants were not part of the True Church.

In all of the cases discussed, Foxe used aspects of the cult of the Virgin Mary to undermine other, more threatening, aspects of Catholicism. His use of Bonaventure's psalter, Beissel's book, and Clichtoveus's arguments indicate not only that Foxe regarded this material as risible and outlandish, but that he expected his readers to regard it in the same light. In this, Foxe was in sympathy with many contemporary Catholics as well as Protestants. Throughout the sixteenth century, Catholics would be recasting, rewriting, and redefining the traditional devotions for the Virgin Mary. Among the reforms which Guillaume Briçonnet, the Bishop of Meaux, launched in his diocese during the first two decades of the Reformation, were the removal of images of the Virgin Mary from the churches and the replacement of the *Ave Maria* with the *Pater Noster*.[33] Here, as in other of his reforms, Briçonnet anticipated the general spirit of Tridentine Catholicism; as one scholar has observed, 'One of the most important emphases at Trent was a renewed insistence upon the centrality of Christ as compared to the saints and Mary'.[34] It is very telling that while Pope Pius V's devotion to the Virgin Mary was made manifest in his revised Breviary (in which the Feast of the Immaculate Conception was elaborately observed), his revised missal pruned away much of the material extolling the Virgin Mary which had been present in its medieval predecessors.[35]

---

[32] *1570*, 926.

[33] Michael A. Mullett, *The Catholic Reformation* (1999), 21–2.

[34] Michael P. Carroll, *Madonnas that Maim: Popular Catholicism in Italy since the Fifteenth Century* (Baltimore, MD, 1992), 106.

[35] Mullett, *Catholic Reformation*, 115–16.

Eamon Duffy concludes the *Stripping of the Altars* with a description of the *Acts and Monuments*, along with the *Homilies* and Jewel's *Apology*, as 'a relentless torrent carrying away the landmarks of a thousand years'.[36] While Duffy's image is both apposite and striking, it should also be remembered that many of the landmarks which were swept away would probably not have survived unchanged even if the torrent of Reformation had never come. Even if Henry VIII had remained the defender of the Roman Catholic faith, many aspects of the cult of the Virgin Mary in England would have undergone change or become obsolete, as they did elsewhere in Europe. The fact that Foxe could use aspects of the traditional veneration of the Virgin Mary as an instrument to hack away at pillars of English Catholicism indicates the weakened hold of that veneration on at least some worshippers. In other countries, the atrophy of traditional devotion would lead to reform and renewal; in England official sanction and the ridicule of the Reformers destroyed the cult and its observances before reform and renewal could take place.

University of Sheffield

---

[36] Duffy, *Stripping*, 593.

THE VIRGIN MARY IN
THE REIGN OF MARY TUDOR

by WILLIAM WIZEMAN, SJ

EVIDENCE of devotion to the Virgin Mary in the restored Catholic Church of the reign of Mary Tudor survives in numerous religious texts published from 1553 to 1558. These sermons, catechetical texts, primers, and books of devotion and polemic were written to aid the restoration of early modern Catholicism in England after twenty years of religious tumult. By considering how these texts treat devotion to Mary, it is possible to answer two questions. First, was the cult of the saints in Marian England, particularly that of the Virgin, 'one of [t]he abiding casualties of the preceding reformations', as Ronald Hutton has argued from the few gilds and pilgrimage centres restored during this period?[1] Secondly, does devotion to the Virgin present any clues as to the nature of the Marian Church? Did it hark back to the Church of the 1520s? Did it embrace much evangelical belief and eschew much traditional religion, as Lucy Wooding argues in her recent monograph?[2] Or was it akin to the Catholic Reformation in Europe? In order to answer these questions, it would be useful to begin by evaluating two texts that possessed semi-official status in the Marian Church, the use and frequent printing of which were encouraged by the likes of Cardinal Pole: Bishop Edmund Bonner of London's catechetical work, *A Profitable Doctryne*, and the Wayland Primer, both printed in 1555.[3]

In the *Profitable Doctryne* Bonner, one of the most zealous traditionalists of the Marian regime, treated Mary's role in the Church by discussing the traditional prayer, the Ave Maria: 'Hayle Marye full of grace, our Lorde is with the[e], blessed art thou amongst all women.

---

[1] Ronald Hutton, 'The local impact of the Tudor Reformations', in C. Haigh, ed., *The English Reformation Revised* (Cambridge, 1987), 131.

[2] Lucy Wooding, *Rethinking Catholicism in Reformation England* (Oxford, 2000). I use the term 'evangelical' rather than 'Protestant', largely because the sharp distinctions between Catholics and Protestants were only beginning to be drawn during Mary's reign. See Diarmaid MacCulloch, 'Henry VIII and the early Reformation', in idem, ed., *The Reign of Henry VIII: Politics, Policy and Piety* (1995), 168–9.

[3] On the status of these works in the Marian church, see Eamon Duffy, *The Stripping of the Altars: Traditional Religion in England, 1400–1580* (New Haven and London, 1992), 534–9.

And blessed is the fruite of thy wombe'. Note that Jesus' name is not added to the prayer's end, despite thirteenth-century precedents; nor is the sixteenth-century phrase, 'Holy Mary, Mother of God, pray for us sinners now and at the hour of our death. Amen'. Hence the form of the Ave presented is very traditional. Yet Bonner's treatment of the text is much longer than that of the Catechism of the Council of Trent, which included these additions to the prayer. Moreover, both the *Profitable Doctryne* and the Tridentine Catechism considered the Ave in the context of the chief Christian prayer, the Pater Noster, and so underscored the former's importance in Christian belief. Bonner was quite explicit about the importance of the Ave. 'It is not without ... weightye considerations', he wrote

> that our forefathers, throughout the vniuersall, or catholike, churche haue next after the *Pater noster* set forth and commended the salutation of the Archaungell Gabryel ... called the Aue *Maria* ... to be frequently and deuoutly vsed, and sayd, of all chrysten people.

Indeed, in order to be 'true members of the catholyke churche', Christians must pray the Ave often; and if the Angel Gabriel and St Elizabeth had praised Mary with these words before Jesus' birth, Christians have all the more reason to praise Mary now.[4]

In his discussion, Bonner underlined God's unique presence to Mary as the Mother of Christ, exceeding God's presence to angels and other saints. He demonstrated the traditional doctrine of human freedom in Mary's voluntary consent to be Mother of God, in contrast to evangelical denial of free will.[5] For Bonner, this prayer was chiefly one of praising God for the gift of Christ's redeeming incarnation, yet Mary was also praised 'for her excellent, and singuler vertues, and chieflye, for that she beleued, and humbly consented'.[6] Lucy Wooding has stated that the stress on the prayer's aspect of thanksgiving rather than supplication was the result of a shift from traditional belief due to Henry VIII's religious polity.[7] Yet there is no supplicatory element in the text of the Ave as cited by Bonner. Moreover, the editors of the Tridentine Catechism concurred with Bonner's view that the Ave was a prayer of

---

[4] Edmund Bonner, *A Profitable and Necessarye Doctrine, with Certain Homilies adioyned therunto* (1555), sigs Aaa3r–Bbb2r.

[5] Ibid., sigs Aaa4r–v.

[6] Ibid., sigs Bbb1r–Bbb2r.

[7] Wooding, *Rethinking Catholicism*, 177.

thanksgiving to God, and they treated it under the heading of prayers of praise rather than prayers of petition, adding, like Bonner, that 'at the same time we congratulate the Virgin on her singular privileges'.[8] It therefore appears that Bonner's treatment of the Ave is rooted in England's traditional piety, but also in line with the Tridentine Catechism.

Bonner remarked further on Marian devotion when he discussed sacred images, and here he also described the intercessory role of saints. When Christians pray before an image of Mary, they should recall her miraculous conception of Christ, and so 'extoll her aboue all creatures, visible and inuisible'. But he reminded readers and listeners of the centrality of Christ in salvation; when Christians praise Mary they extoll 'in her, Chryst, whose mother she is'. As in his exposition of the Ave, Bonner's focus here is largely on Christ. Nevertheless, in praying before images of Mary and the saints, Christians should give thanks for their holiness, wish to emulate their example, and 'make prayer vnto almyghty God, that he wyllbe merciful . . . vnto vs, through the intercession and merytes of them'.[9] Thus Bonner advocated the traditional intercessory power of Mary, but insisted that such power was dependent upon Christ.

The main source of intercessory prayers associated with Mary was the primers, books of prayer which were printed in large numbers in Marian England.[10] In 1555 the frequently-printed Primer published by John Wayland first appeared, which possessed the sanction of Queen Mary and Cardinal Pole.[11] This Primer offered very traditional prayers that had been contained in books of devotion of the 1520s, including the Little Office of the Virgin with its Marian hymns and antiphons, as well as the usual series of prayers addressed to the Virgin after Compline. Mary also had her place in the collection of 'Godly Prayers' at the end of the primer, which were almost exclusively addressed to God. In the 'prayer of the .vii. wordes, that our lord spake hanging vpon the crosse', readers sought the 'pacience, loue, and charitie, in all aduersitie' that Jesus gave to Mary on Calvary.[12] In 'The comforte of all

---

[8] John McHugh and Charles Callan, tr., *Catechism of the Council of Trent for Parish Priests* (New York, 1956), 491.

[9] Bonner, *Profitable Doctryne*, sig. Ii3r–v.

[10] Jennifer Loach, 'The Marian establishment and the printing press', *EHR*, 101 (1986), 137.

[11] Duffy, *Stripping of the Altars*, 538–9.

[12] *The Primer in Latin and Englishe (after the vse of Sarum) with many Godlye and Deuoute Prayers* (1555), sig. Cc2r.

troubles and diseases is to praye to our Lorde Iesus Christe', readers prayed to God

> which diddest gyue health in the handes of the glorious vyrgin Marye, and mother of thy holye sonne iesus Christe. By the womb and by the deseruinge of her, and by thy most holie bodie, whiche Iesu oure redemer receaued of her, graciously heare my praier.

In some ways this prayer was akin to the traditional prayer to Mary 'agaynst the Pestilence' which appeared in the 1558 Primer as a lethal influenza epidemic was raging, but the former prayer also united the desire for physical health with devotion to the incarnate Christ.[13] Among the prayers for the dead, the 1555 primer contained the not-yet standard concluding petition of the Ave in Latin.[14] In terms of illustrations, the 1555 primer gave precedence to the Virgin's role in salvation history: the Annunciation, Visitation, Nativity, Mary at Calvary, Mary receiving the Spirit at Pentecost, and John's vision of the woman clothed with the sun, were all portrayed. One of the few illustrations in the 1558 edition was that of the coronation of the Virgin.[15] Mary therefore had a substantial place in the Marian primers, through the inclusion of numerous prayers seeking her intercession and illustrations reminding readers of her role in salvation. Yet they did not duplicate the Virgin's expansive place in earlier primers. Helen White has noted the reduction in the number and 'colourful' quality of prayers to saints in contrast to pre-1534 primers, illustrating what Eamon Duffy has described as 'the narrower devotional range of Marian Catholicism'.[16] Such reductions may have been a response to evangelical accusations of idolatry, but also a means of underscoring the centrality of Christ in salvation. Duffy has noted the Christocentric nature of the piety of the Marian Church which is apparent not only in Bonner's catechesis, but also in the prayers and illustrations cited above, for in all of them Mary is closely linked with Christ's redeeming power.[17]

Other Marian authors stressed Mary's traditional intercessory role and her Immaculate Conception, no doubt responding to evangelical attacks, but also in praise of the Virgin. Bishop John White made the

---

[13] Ibid., sigs P4v–P5v.

[14] Ibid., sig. &4r.

[15] Ibid., sigs G2v, A1r, C2v, G1v, I4r, H3v, L4v; *Primer*, sig. C7v.

[16] Helen White, *Tudor Books of Devotion* (Madison, WI, 1951), 122; Duffy, *Stripping of the Altars*, 563.

[17] Ibid., 564.

case for Mary's intercession by stating that to no woman 'of generous devotion does [Christ] close his heart', and added, '[o]f pious women whom has he turned away?' Christ especially listens to the prayers of Mary, 'the faithful Virgin' who had first heard the joyful news of the incarnation, cared for the infant Jesus, and 'carried him and covered him with swaddling clothes, him who at his will covers and uncovers all mortal things'.[18] John Gwynneth and the anonymous author of *A Plaine and Godlye Treatise, Concernynge the Masse* spoke well of traditional devotions such as praying the Ave and the Rosary.[19] In his *Agrement of the Holye Fathers . . . vpon the Cheifest Articles of the Christian Religion*, John Angel, Chaplain to Queen Mary, quoted that favourite Father of the Church of both evangelical and traditional theologians, John Chrysostom, in his exposition on the liturgy. Mary excelled all creation, Chrysostom wrote, yet was compassionate to sinners, and so Christians begged her to intercede with Jesus for their salvation.[20] The humanist bishop Cuthbert Tunstall, in the first of his eleven prayers printed in 1557, sought forgiveness of sins through Mary's intercession and merits, as well as the merits of Christ.[21] Another prayer in this collection was devoted to Mary. She was the 'most immaculate' Virgin, holy 'euen from the wombe' of St Anne; she possessed graces 'infused' in her 'by god very singularly'. Tunstall sought the intercession of Mary, 'whiche arte vnto vs a mercifull patronesse', so 'that our synnes may be forgeuen vs', enabling Christians to exult with her and acclaim her in heaven.[22] Tunstall not only attributed to Mary powerful intercession but also her Immaculate Conception, a notion also defended by traditionalists during Henry's reign. Among such defenders had been John Redman,

---

[18] John White, *Diacosio-Martyrion id est ducentum virorum testimonium, de veritatis Corporis, et Sanguinis Christi, in Eucharistia* (1553), fols 61v–62r: 'Nulli profusae pietatis uiscera clausit. / Quam non audiuit? Quam reppulit ille piarum[?]'. 'Prima incarnati loetissima nuncia Christi / Audijt angelicis uirgununcula credula uerbis. / Prima, recens nato, lac, & cunubula, prebet. / Atque parentalem implet sollicitudine curam. / Portat, & exigui tegit hunc uelime panni, / Omnia qui tegit, & retegit mortalia nutu'.

[19] John Gwynneth, *A Brief Declaration of the Notable Victory geuen of God to oure soueraygne Ladye Quene Marye* (1553), sigs D2v, D7v; idem, *A Declaracion of the State wherin all Heretikes dooe leade their Liues* (1554), sigs 46v–46r [*sic: recte* 47r]; *A Plaine and Godlye Treatise, Concernynge the Masse & Blessed Sacrament of the Aulter, for the Instruction of the Symple and Vnlearned People* (?1557), sig. G3r.

[20] John Angel, *Agrement of the Holye Fathers and Doctors of the Churche vpon the Cheifest Articles of the Christian Religion* (?1555), fol. 91r–v.

[21] Cuthbert Tunstall, *Certaine Godly and Deuout Prayers. Made in Latin by . . . Cuthbert Tunstall, . . . and Translated into Englishe by Thomas Paynell* (1558), sig. A6v.

[22] Ibid., sigs D2r–D3r.

President of Trinity College, Cambridge, whose work, *The Complaint of Grace*, was published in 1556 and dedicated to Queen Mary, in order to deny the recantations attributed to him on his deathbed in 1551. For Redman the Virgin Mary had been 'that euer immaculate and blessed virgin, a vessel singulerlie amonges all creatures, elected and prepared by [grace], to be the mother of Iesus'.[23] Mary was therefore unique in creation, yet she was also a most powerful advocate for sinful Christians. And so Marian theologians, like Roger Edgeworth in his 1557 sermons, proclaimed how '[g]reat was the prerogatiue of that virgine Mary, and the loue god had to her, in that his onely begotten son, by whom he made all the worlde, he gaue vnto her to be . . . her naturall sonne'.[24]

But despite her uniqueness, Mary was also viewed as both a companion and model of Christian living, views of sanctity with medieval antecedents, according to André Vauchez and John Bossy.[25] The 'blessed sayntes [are] our frendes, yea our brethrene', Leonard Pollard preached in one of his printed sermons.[26] The 1558 Wayland Primer contained the 'Euensonge of the compassion of our Ladye', in which readers prayed for the compassion of Mary and the mercy of Jesus on Calvary.[27] The English Dominican Superior, William Peryn, emphasised Mary as the Christian's companion. His *Spirituall Exercyses*, which was heavily indebted to that potent source of Counter-Reformation spirituality, the *Spiritual Exercises* of Ignatius Loyola, presented Mary as both an intercessor and a model of intimacy with God in Christ, especially in contemplating the focal point of early-modern piety, the Passion. Peryn encouraged the invocation of the 'mooste blessed and i[m]maculat mother marie' before commencing each period of prayer.[28] The reader sought the aid of the '[m]ost gloryus mother of mercy and ladye of grace, my syngular help and comfort in heauen and in earthe nexte vnto my lord god and sauyor Iesu', because of the 'most

[23] John Redman, *A Compendious Treatise called the Complaint of Grace* (?1556), sig. E3r.

[24] Roger Edgeworth (ed. Janet Wilson), *Sermons very Fruitfull, Godly and Learned by Roger Edgeworth: Preaching in the Reformation c.1535–c.1553* (Cambridge, 1993 [originally printed in 1557]), 173.

[25] André Vauchez, *Sainthood in the Later Middle Ages* (Cambridge, 1997), 388–90, 538; John Bossy, *Christianity in the West, 1400–1700* (Oxford, 1985), 11–12.

[26] Leonard Pollard, *Fyve Homilies of late, Made by a Ryght Good and Vertuous Clerke called Master Leonarde Pollarde* (1556), sig. H4r.

[27] *Primer in Englysh*, sig. K4r.

[28] William Peryn, *Spirituall Exercyses and Goostly Meditacions, and a Neare Waye to come to Perfection and Lyfe Contemplatiue* (1557), sigs I5v, A1v, D2v.

bitter compassion' that she endured 'for him and me', in witnessing the Crucifixion. Peryn further extolled the Virgin's merits in stating that Christ's suffering 'was a passyon mooste payneful vnto [the] mooste blessid and tender mother, more greuus & more bitter then euer was turment or martyrdom to any saint [that] euer sufferid'; and while Christ had been abandoned by his disciples on Calvary, Mary remained steadfast, for she 'dydest not regarde the pleasure or dyspleasure of any person'. Thus, Mary exemplified compassion, courage, and unyielding devotion to her son. For one who sought intimate union with Christ, therefore, Peryn valued reflection on 'the excedynge grate and moost ardent burning loue' between Jesus and Mary at Calvary.[29] Interestingly, Peryn's emphasis on the sorrowful Mary reflected not only the poverty, dearth, famine, and epidemic that the Marian Church underwent, but also the poverty of parochial religious art, due to past iconoclasm: the only image of Mary in most churches was 'the weeping figure standing under the Rood'.[30]

The accentuation of the cult of the Virgin in Marian England also found expression in the praise of Mary Tudor. These authors associated their Queen with the Queen of Heaven in language used otherwise exclusively for the latter, to underscore Queen Mary's essential role in England's re-Catholicization. As one Mary possessed an essential role in salvation, so the other possessed an essential role in England's participation in salvation. Both Marys were intercessors, acting for others' redemption. John Proctor marvelled that traditional religion had been 'newlye recouered and set furthe by oure heauenly and vertuous maiden Quene'.[31] To Bishop John Christopherson Mary Tudor was 'the humble handemayde of God, elected and chosen by him to rule and reforme this realme'.[32] It was not by chance that God had triumphed through a woman named Mary, wrote John Gwynneth, for 'nothynge escapethe his infinite prouidence'.[33] Gwynneth compared the Queen to 'the flower of al women, the mother of Iesus Christe' at great length in his *Brief Declaration of the Notable Victory geuen of God to . . . Quene Marye*.[34] He noted especially the great trust in God that both Marys

---

[29] Ibid., sigs D2v, K7r–v, F7v–F8r, I8r–v.

[30] Duffy, *Stripping of the Altars*, 563.

[31] John Proctor, *The Waie Home to Christ and Truth leadynge from Anticrist and Errour* (1556), sig. D1v, cf. sig. A3r.

[32] John Christopherson, *An Exhortation to all Menne to Take Heede agaynst Rebellion* (1554), sig. M1v; cf. sigs Ff5v–Ff6r.

[33] Gwynneth, *A Brief Declaration*, sigs C6v–D4r.

[34] Ibid., sigs A8v–B1v, B3v, B6v, C7v–D4r.

possessed.[35] Miles Hogarde claimed that as the Queen had restored Christ in the eucharist to England, so the Virgin had returned Jesus to Israel from Egyptian exile.[36] Hogarde also expressed his admiration for the Queen by interpolating the text of the Ave in one of his poems:

> Ave blessed lorde, to the[e] we may say,
> Praising thy goodnes in our Maria:
> Who gratia plena, did so to vs appeare,
> That dominus tecum to her we may say cleare,
> Benedicta to all men may thinke plaine,
> In mulieribus, that euer here did raigne . . .[37]

Leonard Stopes published a broadside in honour of Mary Tudor, with each of the twenty-three stanzas commencing with a word of the Ave in English, beginning with

> Haile Quene of England, of most worthy fame
> for vertue, for wisdome, for mercy & grace:
> Most firme in the fa[i]th: Defence of the same:
> Christ saue her and keepe her, in euery place.[38]

Moreover, it seems possible that Marian musicians also composed works devoted to the Virgin which also associated her with the Queen. Antiphons praising the Mother of God survive in large quantities, such as the *Regina coeli* composed by Robert Whyte, senior chorister at Trinity College, Cambridge, during Mary's reign. Mary had largely refounded Trinity as a bastion of early modern Catholicism in Cambridge with John Christopherson as head, complete with a chapel and choral foundation. According to Daniel Bennet Page, this *Regina coeli* and other works devoted to the Virgin, such as Thomas Tallis's *Gaude gloriosa mater dei*, William Mundy's *Vox patris caelestis ad sacram virginem Mariam*, and John Sheppard's *Gaude, gaude, gaude Maria*, 'attest to . . . the important symbolic value of Marian devotion during [Mary's] reign'.[39]

---

[35] Ibid., sigs B6r–v.

[36] Miles Hogarde, *A Treatise declaring howe Christ by Peruerse Preachyng was Banished out of this Realme: And howe it hath pleased God to brynge Christ home againe by Mary our Moost Gracious Quene* (1554), sig. A2v.

[37] Idem, *A new ABC paraphrasticallye applied, as the State of the Worlde dothe at this Daye require* (1557), sig. B1v.

[38] Leonard Stopes, *An Ave Maria in Commendation of our most Uertuous Queene* (1553).

[39] Daniel Bennet Page, 'Uniform and catholic: church music in the reign of Mary Tudor (1553–1558)' (Brandeis University, PhD thesis, 1996), 342, 180–3, 208–15, 236–7.

Marian authors relished portraying their Queen as most like the Virgin, by whose intercession God had redeemed England from heresy. The exaltation of the Virgin Queen Elizabeth, therefore, was not original, but the Virgin Mary was under no threat of near 'deletion' under Mary Tudor, as she would be under her half-sister, according to Helen Hackett.[40]

It is evident from these texts that devotion to the Virgin Mary in Marian England was not an abiding casualty of the preceding reformations, nor was interest in doctrine associated with the Virgin 'peripheral', as Lucy Wooding believes.[41] Rather, most Marian theologians, representing different generations and many of them leading members of the Church's hierarchy, emphasised Mary as the sinless virgin Mother of God, unique in creation yet approachable as a powerful intercessor for sinners, and as model and companion in the Christian life.[42] The frequently-printed primers also bear witness to Mary's prominent place in the Church's public worship, and attest to her enduring popularity in private prayer. Yet this devotion to the Virgin was not a return to the 1520s. These authors continually underscored the Virgin's close association with her son, and so demonstrated the Christocentric imperative of the Marian Church's spirituality. Bishop James Brooks implied that this imperative was a response to evangelical belief when he listed those elements of early modern Catholicism at which evangelicals had struck: 'at the cros of Christ, at the image of Christ, at the sainetes of Christ, at the mother of Christ, at the spouse of Christe, at the Sacrifice of Christ, at the Sacramentes of Christ, . . . at the body and bloud of Christ'.[43] And this imperative was in line with what H.O. Evennett held and Duffy described as the Counter-Reformation Church's attempt to bring the laity to an even greater focus on Christ's humanity and redemptive suffering, which should also be linked to the Church's efforts to redirect devotion to Christ since the fourteenth century, according to Ronald Finucane.[44] In this

---

[40] Helen Hackett, *Virgin Mother, Maiden Queen: Elizabeth I and the Cult of the Virgin Mary* (1995), 34–7, 237.

[41] Wooding, *Rethinking Catholicism*, 177.

[42] Regarding generational differences, Tunstall and Edgeworth were born between 1474 and 1488. Redman, Bonner, and Peryn were born about 1499–1500. White and Brooks were born between 1510 and 1512. Proctor, Christopherson, and Pollard seem to have been born about 1520. The dates of birth for Hogarde, Gwynneth, Angel, and Stopes remain uncertain.

[43] James Brooks, *A Sermon very Notable, Fruicteful, and Godlie* (1554), sig. E4r.

[44] H.O. Evennett, *The Spirit of the Counter-Reformation* (Notre Dame, IN, 1970), 41;

way the Marian theologians attempted to restore the cult of the Virgin, in response to evangelical assaults but also in uniformity with the renewal of popular devotion that the Church, both in the late medieval period and the Counter-Reformation, endeavoured to achieve.

Fordham University

Duffy, *Stripping of the Altars*, 364; Ronald Finucane, *Miracles and Pilgrims: Popular Beliefs in Medieval England*, 1st pbk edn (New York, 1995), 195–202.

WILLIAM PERKINS VERSUS WILLIAM BISHOP
ON THE ROLE OF MARY AS MEDIATOR

by W.B. PATTERSON

W ILLIAM Perkins and William Bishop, two of the leading
spokesmen for their respective religious traditions in late
sixteenth- and early seventeenth-century England, clashed
in print over the status of the Blessed Virgin Mary, as well as a number
of other issues. They were formidable adversaries. Perkins, the most
widely-read English Protestant theologian of the day, helped to make
Cambridge University a centre of Reformed thought and practice.
Bishop, an Oxford-trained theologian with extensive experience and
associations on the continent, eventually became the first Roman Catholic bishop in England since the death of the last surviving bishop of
Mary I's reign. Though discussions of the Virgin Mary were not major
themes in the books of either writer, their views on this subject are
significant in showing how the two traditions developed, in competition with each other, during this phase of the long English
Reformation.

Perkins, according to Ian Breward, was 'the first theologian of the
reformed Church of England to achieve an international reputation'.[1]
His influence can be seen, partly, in the number of foreign editions of
his books: fifty editions published in Switzerland, fifty in Germany, and
almost ninety in the Netherlands.[2] There was such a demand for his
writings that they were translated into Latin, Dutch, German, French,
Czech, Hungarian, and even, in the case of the book to be discussed
here, Spanish.[3] At home, he was, as a best-selling religious author, edged
out only by the popular preacher Henry Smith. After Perkins's death in
1602, at the early age of forty-four, new books by him, based on writings left in manuscript, continued to appear for several decades. His
collected *Workes* were published in three volumes in 1608–12, with
further editions up to 1635. His *Opera theologica* appeared in two

---

[1] Ian Breward, 'The significance of William Perkins', *Journal of Religious History*, 4
(1966), 113.
[2] Ian Breward, ed., *The Work of William Perkins* (Appleford, 1970), xi. For a discussion of
his career and writings, see the Introduction, 3–131.
[3] Ibid., 130. Perkins, *Catholico Reformando* (1599; Amsterdam, 1624).

volumes in Geneva in 1611 and in three volumes in 1624, with further editions of the latter in 1658 and 1668.[4] A native of Warwickshire, where he was born in 1558, Perkins entered Christ's College, Cambridge, in 1577, received his M.A. there in 1584, and became a Fellow of the college in the same year. He spent his entire career in Cambridge, at Christ's College and as a preacher at Great St Andrew's Church across the street.[5] He is usually referred to as a Puritan, though he was on the periphery of the Elizabethan Puritan movement if, indeed, he was a part of it at all.[6] Perkins's writings dealt with the fundamental principles of Christian belief, the calling of the ministry, social ethics, cases of conscience, predestination, and the errors of Roman Catholicism, an interest represented by *A Reformed Catholike* of 1597, which contains his views on Mary.[7]

Bishop, also a native of Warwickshire, was born a few years before Perkins, in 1553 or 1555, and educated at Oxford, though he did not take a degree there.[8] He studied further at Rheims and at Rome and returned to England as a Roman Catholic priest in 1581. Arrested soon

---

[4] For editions of his works, see Breward, *Work*, 613–32. For other treatments of Perkins's thought, see Paul R. Schaefer, 'Protestant "scholasticism" at Elizabethan Cambridge: William Perkins and a Reformed theology of the heart', in Carl R. Trueman and R. Scott Clark, eds., *Protestant Scholasticism: Essays in Reassessment* (Carlisle, 1999), 147–64; Bryan D. Spinks, *Two Faces of Elizabethan Anglican Theology: Sacraments and Salvation in the Thought of William Perkins and Richard Hooker* (Lanham, MD, 1999); Richard A. Muller, 'Perkins' *A Golden Chaine*: predestinarian system or schematized *Ordo salutis*?', *Sixteenth Century Journal*, 9 (1978), 69–81; Thomas F. Merrill, ed., *William Perkins, 1558–1602, English Puritanist: His Pioneer Works on Casuistry* (Nieuwkoop, 1966), Introduction, ix–xx; Louis B. Wright, 'William Perkins: Elizabethan apostle of "practical divinity" ', *Huntington Library Quarterly*, 3 (1939–40), 171–96.

[5] There are two contemporary lives: Thomas Fuller, 'The Life of Mr Perkins', in *The Holy State* (Cambridge, 1642), 88–93; Samuel Clark, 'The Life of William Perkins', in *The Marrow of Ecclesiastical History* (1650), 414–18 (an account heavily dependent on Fuller). See also J. Bass Mullinger's life of Perkins in *DNB*, 15:6–9.

[6] Patrick Collinson, *The Elizabethan Puritan Movement* (1967), 125, 127, 401, 426, 434–5. For the question of Perkins's relation to Puritanism, see Breward, 'Significance', 117–20, and *Work of William Perkins*, Introduction, 4–5, 10–13.

[7] Among Perkins's important works published during his lifetime were *Armilla aurea* (Cambridge, 1590) – English, *A Golden Chaine* (1591); *The Foundation of Christian Religion* (1591); *A Case of Conscience* (1592); *Prophetica* (Cambridge, 1592); *An Exposition of the Symbole* (Cambridge, 1595); *A Reformed Catholike* (Cambridge, 1597); *A Graine of Musterd-seede* (1597); and *De praedestinatione, modo et ordine* (Cambridge, 1598).

[8] For Bishop's career see Anthony à Wood, *Athenae Oxonienses*, 3rd edn, ed. Philip Bliss, 5 vols (1815–20), 2, cols 356–8, 862; Thompson Cooper in *DNB*, 2:558–9; Godfrey Anstruther, *The Seminary Priests: A Dictionary of the Secular Clergy of England and Wales, 1558–1850*, 4 vols (Durham, 1969–77), 1:36–9; A.F. Allison, 'Richard Smith, Richelieu and the French Marriage: the political context of Smith's appointment as Bishop for England in 1624', *Recusant History*, 7 (1964), 148–211, esp. 148–52; and Francis Edwards, *Robert Persons:*

after his arrival, he was condemned to death for allegedly plotting Elizabeth I's death, but he was banished instead in 1585. A few years later he returned to England, where he became a spokesman for priests who had grievances against the archpriest George Blackwell, alleged to be too much under Jesuit influence. On their behalf he journeyed to Rome to request the appointment of a bishop for England. Charged with disrupting the Catholic community in England he was confined for a time in the English College in Rome. He eventually returned to England in early 1603, where he signed a profession of allegiance to Elizabeth I. Despite being arrested in England in late 1603, he was able to pursue his ministry in Herefordshire and in Oxfordshire a few years later. After being imprisoned in London in 1611, he was released and went to Paris, where he became a member of Arras College, recently established as a centre of higher education for secular Catholic clergy. In 1623, on the death of the third English archpriest, Bishop was appointed by Pope Gregory XV as titular bishop of Chalcedon, with jurisdiction over his co-religionists in England. After being consecrated in Paris, he left for England in July 1623. His short episcopate, lasting less than a year, was conducted at a time of partial relaxation of the penal laws against Roman Catholics brought about by negotiations for a Spanish match for Prince Charles.[9] Bishop administered confirmation to Roman Catholics in the London area in the summer of 1623 and planned a wider visitation across the country, which he had divided into archdeaconries and deaneries. This work of reorganization had barely begun when he died in April 1624.[10] His writings centred on a refutation of Perkins's *A Reformed Catholike*, which Bishop entitled *A Reformation of a Catholike Deformed*.[11] This book, published in two parts in 1604 and 1607, after Perkins's death, subsequently involved Bishop in controversy with Robert Abbot, chaplain to King James VI and I. Abbot was to become Master of Balliol College and Regius Professor of Divinity at Oxford.[12]

The Biography of an Elizabethan Jesuit, 1546–1610 (St Louis, MO, 1995), 230–8, 248, 254, 256, 262, 265, 276, 354.

[9] W.B. Patterson, *King James VI and I and the Reunion of Christendom* (Cambridge, 1997), 314–37.

[10] Bishop was succeeded by Richard Smith, appointed by Pope Urban VIII in 1624. He crossed to England in 1625 but retired to France in 1631. It was not until 1685 that another bishop was appointed. See Allison, 'Richard Smith', 148, 164, 167–8, 188–9, 193.

[11] D.B.P. [William Bishop], *A Reformation of a Catholike Deformed* (n.p., 1604); *The Second Part of the Reformation of a Catholike Deformed* (n.p., 1607).

[12] Robert Abbot, *A Defence of the Reformed Catholicke* (1606); *The Second Part of the Defence*

Perkins's *A Reformed Catholike* acknowledged in its dedication to Sir William Bowes that many Englishmen thought that the religion of the Established Church and that of the Church of Rome 'are all one for substance'.[13] He noted that there were books written in French proposing that the Protestant and Roman Catholic Churches be reunited and that that these books were treated with respect by many Englishmen.[14] Perkins believed that such a project would be to unite 'light and darknes', and he had therefore set out to show the crucially important differences between the two traditions.[15] The role of Mary was important in this context. Though, he contended, Roman Catholics affirm that Christ is 'our Mediatour of Intercession vnto God', nevertheless, 'his Mother must be [made by them] the Queene of heauen, and by the right of a mother commaunde him there'.[16]

Despite the book's polemical intent, it is, in form, far more conciliatory than most English anti-Roman Catholic treatises of the time. As its subtitle says, it aimed to show 'how neere we may come to the present Church of Rome in sundrie points of religion, and wherein we must foreuer depart from them'.[17] On issue after issue – original sin, certainty of salvation, justification, sacrifice in the Lord's Supper, saving faith, and others – Perkins made a serious and well-informed attempt to state the relevant Roman Catholic teaching, show how far Protestant teaching was in accord with it, and then state the Protestant view and the reasons why it was, in his judgement, the right one. In making his case for Protestant teachings, Perkins relied heavily on biblical passages, as might be expected, but he also cited the views of the fathers of the Church in Christian antiquity. In his discussion of free will, for example, he disagreed with the Roman Catholic teaching, which he stated as 'mans will concurreth & worketh with gods grace in the first conversion of a sinner'.[18] But he concluded, a few pages later, 'For

---

of the Reformed Catholicke (1607). Bishop answered with *A Reproofe of M. D. Abbot's Defence of the Catholike Deformed* (n.p., 1608). Abbot's *The Trve Ancient Roman Catholike: Being an Apology or Covnterproofe against Doctor Bishops Reproofe of the Defence of the Reformed Catholike, The First Part* (1611) was answered by Bishop's *A Disproofe of D. Abbot's Counterproofe against D. Bishops Reproofe of the Defence of M. Perkins Reformed Catholike* (Paris, 1614).

[13] Perkins, *A Reformed Catholike*, Dedication.

[14] For reunion proposals in France in the late sixteenth century, see W.B. Patterson, 'Henry IV and the Huguenot appeal for a return to Poissy', *SCH*, 9 (1972), 247–57; idem, 'Jean de Serres and the politics of religious pacification, 1594–8', *SCH*, 12 (1975), 223–44.

[15] Perkins, *A Reformed Catholike*, Dedication.

[16] Ibid.

[17] Ibid., title-page.

[18] Ibid., 16.

though there be not in mans conuersion a naturall cooperation of his will with Gods spirit, yet is there a supernaturall cooperation of grace. . . . See I Cor. 15, where Paul says he has laboured in the faith. . . yet not I. . . but Gods grace in me'.[19] He cited Augustine, Fulgentius, and the medieval theologian Bernard of Clairvaux in support of this view.[20]

Perkins treated the subject of Mary mainly in his discussion of the saints, though he returned to the subject in the conclusion to the book. The 'true Saints of God', were 'Prophets, Apostles, and Martyrs, and such like', and they were to be 'worshipped and honoured' in three ways:

> by keeping a memorie of them in holy manner . . ., by giuing of thanks to God for them, and the benefits that God vouchsafed by them vnto his Church . . ., [and] by an imitation of their faith, humilitie, meeknes, repentance, the feare of God, & all good vertues wherein they excelled.[21]

He used Mary's example to illustrate the first way: 'Thus the Virgin Marie as a prophetesse foretelleth, that all nations shall call her blessed, Luk. I. 48.'[22] Their memories, even their relics if anyone could prove them to be authentic, were to be kept with 'due reverence'.[23] On the question of what kind of worship was to be directed to the saints, he stated the distinction made by Roman Catholics between *latria*, worship offered only to God, and *doulia*, worship offered to saints and angels whom God had chosen and glorified.[24] Protestants, he said, made a distinction between religious worship, offered to God, and civil worship, the honour paid to those 'set aboue vs by God himselfe, either in respect of their excellent gifts, or in respect of their offices'.[25] The worship of the saints ought in either case to be distinguished from the worship of God. He went on to assert that praying to the saints was

---

[19] Ibid., 23–4.

[20] Ibid., 24. For other citations from the fathers, see 89–90 (Ambrose, Augustine, Chrysostom, Basil, and Origen, on justification by faith), 190 (Augustine, on the nature of Christ's presence in the eucharist), 204 (Augustine, Ambrose, and Jerome, on sacrifice in the Lord's Supper), 326 (Augustine and Chrysostom, on confession).

[21] Ibid., 243–4.

[22] Ibid., 244.

[23] Ibid.

[24] Ibid., 245. The latter was offered in the bending of the knee, in invocations to them, in the dedication of churches to them, and 'in pilgrimages vnto their reliques & images' (245–6).

[25] Ibid., 246.

unacceptable. 'All true inuocation and praier made according to the will of God', Perkins said,

> must haue a double foundation: a command and a promise. . . . we may not pray to Saints departed: for in the Scripture there is no word, either commanding vs to praie vnto them, or assuring vs that we shall be heard when we praie.[26]

He rejected the argument that prayers to the saints were warranted by miracles and revelations, since miracles had performed their function as a means of establishing the truths of the gospel, and revelation had been accomplished through the 'writings of the Apostles and Prophets'.[27] To pray to the saints was to ascribe to them a knowledge of ourselves and of human affairs possessed only by God. They were, after all, created beings, not deities. He quoted Augustine as saying, 'Let Marie be in honour: let the Father, Sonne, and holy Ghost be adored'.[28] Although it was appropriate to ask for the prayers of friends or those who know us, to ask someone in the next life to offer prayers was to ask the departed soul to mediate between God and ourselves, whereas there was only one mediator and that was Christ.[29]

Perkins readily acknowledged that the saints departed prayed to God for 'the redemption of the whole Church of God vpon earth', and in this sense the saints prayed for sinners on earth.[30] But he denied that they could know the needs of individual human beings: 'neither Marie, nor Peter, nor any other of the Saints departed know vs and our estate; and consequently they cannot make any particular intercession for vs'.[31] Unlike Christ, who is sinless, the saints could not offer themselves as a propitiation for the sins of humanity.[32] In the conclusion of the work, after stating that Roman Catholics were not to be hated and that theirs was a Church within which God had always 'reserued a people vnto himself, that truly worshipped him', Perkins charged the Roman Catholic Church with seven sins.[33] Among them was idolatry, because of the Church's view of the saints. Roman Catholicism had, he asserted, transformed into 'detestable idols' some of the saints,

> making them in truth mediatours of redemption, specially the virgin Marie, whom they call a Ladie, a goddesse, a queene, whom

[26] Ibid., 248.
[27] Ibid., 250.
[28] Ibid., 253.
[29] Ibid., 256.
[30] Ibid., 256–7.
[31] Ibid., 258.
[32] Ibid., 260–1.
[33] Ibid., 328.

Christ her sonne obeyeth in heauen, a mediatresse, our life, hope, the medicine of the diseased: and they pray vnto her thus; Prepare thou glorie for us: defend vs from our enemies, and in the houre of death receive us.[34]

Bishop's *A Reformation of a Catholike Deformed* is dedicated to James I, whom he quoted as having said at the recent Hampton Court Conference that 'no Church ought farther to separate it self from the Church of Rome, either in doctrine or ceremonie, then shee hath departed from her self, when she was in her flourishing, and best estate'.[35] The aim of the book, said Bishop, was to show that Roman Catholics 'now holde in all points, the very same Doctrine, which the most approued auncient Doctors, and holy Fathers held and deliuered'.[36] If James proved unwilling to adopt the faith and practice of his mother and his forebears, Bishop hoped that he would lead England to a toleration of Roman Catholics similar to the Roman Catholic toleration of Protestants in France, Poland, Bohemia, and other areas where Protestants were numerous. He acknowledged that in Spain and Italy, where Protestants were a very small minority, they were not tolerated.[37] In his preface to the reader, Bishop commended Perkins for the clarity of his argument, method, and style: 'the pointes in controuersie, are set downe distinctly, and for the most part truely'.[38] But the degree of common ground Perkins found ought not, Bishop said, to mislead the reader: he 'counterfeiteth to come as neare vnto the Roman Church, as his tender conscience will permitte him, whereas in deede he walketh as wide from it, as any other noveller of this age'.[39] He expressed regret that his own work was being published after Perkins's death – it had been in the press when he heard that Perkins had died – since it would do the Cambridge theologian no good, but he hoped it would be a preservative against spiritual death for many others.[40]

In the second part of Bishop's book, published in 1607, in which he dealt with Mary and the saints, he showed that he was a talented satirist in his description of the Church of England. In place of the sacrifice of the mass, practised since the Church's beginning, the real presence of Christ in the eucharist, baptism as the cause of remission of sins and an infusion of grace, confession to cure the wounds of the soul, and

---

[34] Ibid., 340.
[35] Bishop, *A Reformation of a Catholike Deformed*, sig. *iv^r.
[36] Ibid.

[37] Ibid., sig. **iv^v.
[38] Ibid., sig. ***ii^r.
[39] Ibid.
[40] Ibid., sig. ***ii^v.

anointing with holy oil accompanied by the prayers of a priest at the point of death, what had been substituted by the reformers?[41]

> They haue yet remayning some poore short prayers . . . Mattins, Euensong, and other set houres they leave to the Priests, sauing that on the Sabbaoth they solemnely meete together at the Church, to say their seruice, which is a certayne mingle-mangle, translated out of the old portaise and Masse booke, patched vp together with some fewe of their owne inuentions.[42]

If the liturgy was bare, the church buildings were more so:

> Now as concerning the place where their diuine service is said; if goodly stately Churches, had not beene by men of our religion built to their handes, in which simple cotes (trowe you) would their key-cold deuotion haue beene content to serue their Lord? if one Church or great steeple, by any mishap fall into vtter ruine, a collection throughout all England for many yeares together, will not serue to build it vp againe.[43]

Where there had been altars and pictures, there were now 'bare walles, hanged with cob-webs except some of the better sort, which are daubed like Ale-houses, with some broken sentences of Scripture'.[44]

Bishop put the disappearance of devotion to Mary in the context of this loss to England of its historic spiritual heritage. Protestants showed scant respect for Christ himself by being

> so backward in his blessed Mother the holy Virgins praises, not hearing with patience, any body that would so much as salute her with the Haile Mary, which notwithstanding is recorded in the Gospell. . . if they would not reuerence [her] for her owne vertues, which were most rare and singular: yet for her Sonnes sake (who loued her tenderly) they should shewe themselues better affected.[45]

On the issue of idolatry, as raised by Perkins, Bishop asserted that the worship given to God and that given to saints or angels was distinct, and that it was not inappropriate to call that 'religious honour and worship that is exhibited vnto men for their excellency in religious qualities, and religious affaires'.[46] This was quite distinct from the

---

[41] Bishop, *The Second Part*, 20.
[42] Ibid., 21.
[43] Ibid.

[44] Ibid.
[45] Ibid., 12.
[46] Ibid., 110.

worship offered to God for his perfection in all things. On the issues of mediation and intercession, he made a similar distinction between the actions of the saints and the saving work of Christ:

> we attribute no point of Christes mediation to them; but only range and place the Saints intercession, with the prayers of other good men liuing on earth, and with our owne ... all are made in Christes name, and are effectuall through the merits of his Passion.[47]

There were, Bishop argued, two sorts of mediators: those who attempt to bring two parties together and those who, in order to effect a reconciliation, pay the debt and satisfy all the other 'damages and detriments' that stand between the parties. Moses, the prophets, and Paul were mediators in the first sense; Christ was the mediator for all human beings in the second sense.[48] Bernard, said Bishop, taught that we need a 'mediatour to the mediatour; and no one more for our profit and commodity, then the blessed Virgin Mary'.[49] Bishop was as skilled in the use of the fathers as was Perkins, and was able to show that Augustine, Chrysostom, Ambrose, Basil, and Gregory Nazianzus wrote approvingly of prayers to the saints and the prayers of the saints.[50] He quoted Ambrose as saying, 'I request the aid of the blessed Virgin Mary, of the Apostles, Martirs, and Confessors, the prayers of such personages thou (O Lord) doest neuer despise'.[51] The titles given to Mary, such as lady, queen, 'mediatresse of intercession, our hope, our life' may be used of her in a 'good sence; because we hope through the helpe of her most gratious prayers to obtayne the life of our soules'.[52]

Perkins and Bishop reflect the larger conflict in western Europe between the Protestant Reformation and the Catholic or Counter-Reformation. Perkins saw Mary as a model of faith as the Reformers understood it, but he insisted on Christ alone as the way to salvation.[53] Bishop called for a renewed devotion to Mary as mediator and intercessor and as the most important member of the company of the saints in heaven.[54] Both claimed the support of scripture and of the ancient

---

[47] Ibid., 111.
[48] Ibid., 122.
[49] Ibid., 123.
[50] Ibid., 129, 132.
[51] Ibid., 139.
[52] Ibid., 209.

[53] Jaroslav Pelikan, *Mary through the Centuries: Her Place in the History of Culture* (New Haven, CT, 1996), 153–63.

[54] A.D. Wright, *The Counter-Reformation: Catholic Europe and the Non-Christian World* (1982), 74, 183, 213, 235, 237, 243, 277.

Church. Perkins, indeed, left an unpublished Latin manuscript in which he attempted to trace, through ancient and medieval writers, the development of doctrines in the Roman Catholic tradition.[55] Patristic scholarship was to become an increasingly important activity at the English universities in the early seventeenth century, as it already was in many universities abroad. Perhaps the most striking impression left by this exchange is that of a remarkable religious fluidity in England itself. Historians are apt to think of the late sixteenth and early seventeenth centuries in denominational or confessional terms, and there can be little doubt where these two theologians stood. Perkins wanted to distinguish the beliefs and practices of the reformed Church of England from the Roman Catholic Church in order to show that the liturgy, articles of belief, and homilies of the Established Church constituted a coherent body of teaching superior to that which his countrymen had known a generation or so before and which still survived in some measure. He commented, in his discussion of traditions, that 'popish inclinations and dispositions be rife among vs'.[56] Bishop wanted to restore to England a heritage of faith and worship that was threatened with eclipse. Perkins's books sold well. Bishop's, published with much more difficulty, also found a market, and they provoked detailed answers from Robert Abbot, one of the Established Church's leading theologians. Where did the bulk of the English people stand? This exchange suggests that England's religious allegiance was far from settled: Catholicism in its traditional forms was still very much a part of the culture; English Protestantism was still taking shape; and the Established Church, very diverse in membership, had a less clear identity than was later to be the case.[57]

University of the South, Sewanee, Tennessee

---

[55] William Perkins, *Problema de Romanae fidei ementito Catholicismo*, ed. Samuel Ward (Cambridge, 1604). The section on Mary is at 229–31.

[56] Perkins, *Reformed Catholike*, 149.

[57] Cf. M.C. Questier, 'What happened to English Catholicism after the Reformation?', *History*, 85 (2000), 28–47; Alexandra Walsham, 'The Parochial Roots of Laudianism Revisited: Catholics, Anti-Calvinists and "Parish Anglicans" in Early Stuart England', *JEH*, 49 (1998), 620–51; Peter Lake and Michael Questier, eds, *Conformity and Orthodoxy in the English Church, c. 1560–1660* (Woodbridge, 2000), Introduction, ix–xx.

'THAT IN HER THE SEED OF THE SERPENT MAY HAVE NO PART': THE AGREDAN VISIONS AND THE IMMACULATE CONCEPTION OF THE VIRGIN IN EARLY MODERN SPAIN AND GERMANY

by TREVOR JOHNSON

IN the winter of 1755, Giacomo Casanova, doing time in the Venetian jail known as the 'Leads', spent a disturbing week absorbed in the only reading matter available, a volume which he judged a work of 'heated imagination' and of 'chimerical and monstruous visions dressed up as revelations'. It was enough to induce repeated nightmares. 'On sleeping', he recorded,

> I perceived the sickness that this book had communicated to my spirit, weakened by melancholy and undernourishment. My extravagant dreams made me laugh when I recalled them on waking; I had an urge to write them down, and had I had the means to do so I would perhaps have produced up there an even madder book than the one I had been given.[1]

The work which had an unsettling effect on the captive Casanova was *La Mística Ciudad de Dios* (*The Mystical City of God*), the product of a seventeenth-century Castilian convent visionary, Sor María de Jesús de Agreda (1602–65). An enormous book of some 200 chapters, astounding in its novelesque detail, the *Mystical City* purported to be a life of Mary as revealed by the Virgin herself in regular visions to Sor María over many years. By Casanova's time it had become a spiritual classic and, to some, an infallible witness to the doctrine of the Immaculate Conception. Although not solemnly defined until 1854, Immaculism had been largely accepted in Catholic Europe by the seventeenth century, when it was a dominant theme in what has been termed a 'second golden age' of Mariology.[2] Nevertheless, it was not without its critics, a measure of scepticism being understandable in the

---

[1] Giacomo Casanova, *Histoire de ma fuite des prisons de la Republique de Venise qu'on appelle les Plombs* (Paris, 1987), 45–8.

[2] Nazario Pérez, *Historia Mariana de España*, 2 vols, 2nd edn (Toledo, 1993–5), 2:13.

case of a dogma absent from early Christianity and lacking direct biblical warrant (for here, as Robert Bellarmine had once remarked to Paul V, 'Scripture tells us nothing'). In the Middle Ages the testimony of special or private revelations, such as those of St Bridget of Sweden (c.1303–73), had fed the growth of tradition and helped to fill the evidential gap.[3] However, noetic mysticism did not wane with the Middle Ages. During the Counter Reformation, as the visions of Sor María and the contentious afterlife of her book exemplify, the mystical experience of a few continued to crystallize the intuition of the Church.

* * *

Seventeenth-century Spain provided the key arena for post-Tridentine controversy between Maculists and Immaculists, and the most fertile ground for the latter. Expressions of Immaculist fervour included the mobilization of popular opinion in intimidatory public demonstrations, as occurred in Seville in the second decade of the seventeenth century, and the exploitation of the artistic genius of the peninsula to promote the dogma. As the Spanish Habsburgs became increasingly involved in the campaign to secure its papal definition, royal councils of prelates and theologians were formed under Philip III and Philip IV to consider the issue, and a series of embassies maintained the pressure on Rome.[4]

The revelations of Sor María de Jesús de Agreda came as timely and potentially triumphant vindications of the Immaculist cause. Sor María is known today in the Hispanic world for her role as confidante and unofficial spiritual adviser (a 'mother confessor' one might say) to King Philip IV, and for her alleged miraculous bilocations to the New World. However, her reputation is chiefly a literary one and rests on the astonishing text of the *Mystical City of God*, the fruit of decades of visionary experience in her convent in Agreda and penned at the behest of her confessors.[5] The 'Mystical City' of her title is the Virgin herself, and the work is both a paean to Mary's unique function in the economy of salvation and a loving portrait of this most perfect of creatures, a

---

[3] Stefano de Flores and Salvatore Meo, eds, *Nuevo diccionario de Mariología* (Madrid, 1988), 910–41.

[4] See Suzanne L. Stratton, *The Immaculate Conception in Spanish Art* (Cambridge, 1994), for a splendid analysis of the development of Immaculist iconography in sixteenth- and seventeenth-century Spain and an elegant summary of its theological and political context.

[5] T.D. Kendrick, *Mary of Ágreda: the Life and Legend of a Spanish Nun* (1967); Clark Colahan, *The Visions of Sor María de Agreda: Writing Knowledge and Power* (Tucson, AZ, and London, 1994).

being of supreme intellectual as well as spiritual accomplishment. From the *Mystical City* we learn that during the lifetime of her son Mary preached and performed numerous miracles alongside him and that after his death she governed the Church. By vicarious participation in her son's Passion she has become humanity's Co-Redemptrix. However, all her graces and privileges stem from and thus necessitate an immaculate conception, a point maintained so vigorously and pervasively in the book that Immaculism has been described as its 'paramount doctrine'.[6]

In the early chapters of the *Mystical City*, the circumstances and significance of Mary's conception are set out in detail, some clearly deriving from tradition, some novel. In a parallel with the Gospel birth-narratives of Christ, Saints Anne and Joachim ('the most holy and perfect parents of that century') are informed of the good news of Mary's conception by the Archangel Gabriel.[7] Meanwhile the divine plan is proclaimed in Heaven by the Trinity:

> let us make this creature in all holiness and perfection, so that in her the disorder of Original Sin may have no part . . . let her be the unique image and likeness of our divinity . . . let us direct our kindness towards our beloved and exempt her from the ordinary law of the formation of all mortals, so that in her the seed of the serpent may have no part.[8]

Like Mary's soul, her human flesh from which Christ is to be formed must also be free of sin. Moreover, the greatest possible equality must exist between the Father and Mary, lest the Devil boast that he is superior to the woman whom God himself obeyed as his mother. Although Mary's own generation has to be through the common order of natural reproduction, it is therefore attended by a totally different order of grace. A mystical gestation is revealed. Mary's body, created on a Sunday, is formed in a perfect balance of the four humours, producing a 'miraculous temperament' which accounts for her lifelong serenity. Whilst, in the Aristotelian physiology accepted by Sor María, eighty days are normally required for a female embryo to develop to the stage at which the soul can be infused into it, Mary's is ready after only six

---

[6] Ibid., 160.

[7] I have used the standard modern edition: Sor María de Jesús de Agreda, *Mística Ciudad de Dios. Vida de María. Texto conforme al autógrafo original*, ed. Celestino Solaguren (Madrid, 1970) [hereafter *MCD*], 88, 98.

[8] *MCD*, 92.

days. At the moment of this 'second conception', the infusion of Mary's soul, 'the Blessed Trinity uttered these words . . . let us make Mary in our image and likeness, our true daughter and bride, to be Mother of the only Son of the substance of the Father'. Saturday is thus the day of Our Lady, while in the feast of the Conception of Mary, Sor María claims, the Church celebrates this second moment, the infusion of the soul, which then lay for nine months inside the womb of St Anne, 'without an instant in which she was . . . deprived of the light, friendship and love of her creator'. This prenatal residence was not passive but dynamic, and during it Mary acquired spiritual wisdom to the extent that at birth she was as omniscient as it is possible for a creature to be, and 'filled with grace and gifts above the highest Seraphim of Heaven'. 'I see', gushes Sor María,

> the true Ark of the Covenant, fashioned, decorated and placed in the temple of a sterile mother . . . I see the altar in the Holy of Holies, where the first sacrifice is offered . . . and the making of a new Earth and a new Heaven, being the first the womb of a humble woman, attended by the Blessed Trinity and innumerable courtiers of the old Heaven with a thousand angels assigned to guard this treasure of a tiny body.[9]

Such passages convey something of the flavour of the book as a whole, with its strange mixture of dizzy spiritual panoramas and engaging detail. Although investigated by the Holy Office in her lifetime, the nun of Agreda managed to charm her inquisitors and was handled by them lightly.[10] The real controversy did not open until after her death. The *Mystical City* was published posthumously in 1670 and promptly placed on the Index by the Spanish Inquisition. Rome too imposed a ban, which was lifted only after the intervention of King Charles II of Spain in 1681. The Agredistas, Immaculist supporters of the nun and her book, were pitted against opponents who, if not necessarily Maculists, were suspicious of the role of private revelation in shaping doctrine. Yet given the current tide of Immaculist fervour, it is unsurprising that such a powerful validation of the dogma was enthusiastically promoted, even in the teeth of curial censure. By 1700 there

---

[9] MCD, 102.
[10] Clark Colahan, 'María de Jesús de Agreda. The Sweetheart of the Holy Office', in Mary E. Giles, ed., *Women in the Inquisition. Spain and the New World* (Baltimore, MD, and London, 1999), 155–170.

had been twenty editions of the *Mystical City*, by 1740 at least a further thirty-seven, including translations into Portuguese, Dutch, French, Italian, Latin, German, Polish, Greek, and even Arabic.[11] But the book's popularity also reflected its enmeshment in controversy, which outside Spain flared up chiefly in France and Germany. The first major clash was in Paris, where a French translation was condemned by the Sorbonne in 1696. In Spain the reaction to the French judgement was intense: direct complaints were made to Versailles and defences of Sor María's book were penned by outraged Agredistas. Four decades later the book provoked its second and last great controversy, renewing in turn the polemic over the Immaculate Conception, in Germany.

* * *

In Germany the loss of swathes of lands to the Protestant confessions had interrupted the pre-Reformation Conceptionist battles between Dominicans and Franciscans; but the issue revived with the beginnings of Catholic resurgence in the Empire in the decades after Trent, above all with the arrival of the Jesuits under the indefatigable leadership of St Peter Canisius. In the first major Mariological treatise to appear post-Trent, *De Maria virgine incomparabili* (1577), Canisius conceded that the Immaculate Conception was a difficult question, but defended the doctrine against both traditional Maculist arguments and the more recent critiques of German Protestant divines.[12] The seventeenth century saw in Catholic Germany, as in Spain, the promotion of Immaculism by ruling dynasties. Elector Maximilian I (ruled 1598–1651) and other Bavarian Wittelsbachs lobbied Rome for definition of the dogma, whilst Immaculism was integral to the devotional life of the Austrian Habsburgs, with Emperor Ferdinand III (ruled 1637–57) personally composing sacred music honouring the Immaculata.[13]

As in Spain, the dogma was also promoted at the popular level, but its advocacy bore a particular edge in Germany, where Catholics resided in close proximity to Protestant populations which rejected Immaculism as an egregious example of papist superstition. Among the

---

[11] *MCD*, Introduction, cii–civ.

[12] Peter Canisius, *De Maria virgine incomparabili, et Dei genitrice sacrosancta, libri quinque* (Ingolstadt, 1577), 33–58.

[13] Steven Saunders, 'Der Kaiser als Künstler: Ferdinand III and the politicization of sacred music at the Habsburg court', in Max Reinhart, ed., *Infinite Boundaries: Order, Disorder, and Reorder in Early Modern German Culture* (Kirksville, MO, 1998), 187–208.

causes célèbres which highlighted the conflict was a series of exorcisms in Straubing (Lower Bavaria) in the mid 1660s, during which the energumen's four indwelling devils were coaxed by their Jesuit exorcist into proclaiming the truth of the Immaculate Conception. The dogma also found a demonological context with the missionary tours of Catholic Germany undertaken by the Friulian Capuchin, Marco d'Aviano, two decades later. One Lutheran tract of 1680 lambasted d'Aviano's mass healing and exorcistic rallies as 'blatant trickery ... this evil fellow must have been sent into the world by the pope to confirm the doctrine of the Immaculate Conception with his confected wonders'.[14]

Sor María's *Mystical City* therefore fell on fertile ground when it appeared in several German translations after 1715. Pushed hard by the Franciscans, the book gave a spurt to Marian devotion.[15] But the fresh wave of feverish excitement around the *Mystical City*, and around the Immaculate Conception, now also provoked the sharpest Catholic anti-Agredista critique since the Sorbonne's denunciation.

The attack came from Eusebius Amort (1692–1777), canon of the Bavarian Augustinian house at Polling.[16] Author of the *Philosophia Pollingana* (Augsburg, 1730), an ambitious attempt to harmonize scholasticism with modern natural philosophy, Amort belonged to a number of learned societies and was co-founder of the Bavarian Academy of Sciences. An inveterate polemicist, he had already clashed with the Jesuits over the theology of 'disinterested love' and with the Benedictines over the disputed authorship of the *Imitatio Christi*, receiving support from Rome but making powerful local enemies. He now turned his attention to the *Mystical City*, appalled by its enthusi-

---

[14] Maria Heyret, *P. Marcus von Aviano O.M.Cap., apostolischer Missionar and päpstlicher Legat beim christlichen Heere* (Munich, 1931), 150. The use of exorcism to promote Immaculism persisted in Bavaria, where the notorious depossessions performed nearly a century later by Johann Joseph Gassner (1727–79) also invoked the Immaculate Conception: Manfred Eder, 'Teufelsglaube, "Besessenheit" und Exorzismus in Deggendorf (1785–1791)', *Beiträge zur Geschichte des Bistums Regensburg*, 26 (1992), 295–321.

[15] The book was used to promote Christocentric piety as well. In Bavaria, the new devotional topos of the 'Dominus in Carcere', focussing on the suffering of Christ in prison, received impetus from Sor María's detailed and dramatic narrative: Benno Hubensteiner, *Vom Geist des Barock. Kultur and Frömmigkeit im alten Bayern*, 2nd edn (Munich, 1978), 93.

[16] On Amort, his role in the Agredan controversy, and the immediate intellectual context, see Richard van Dülmen, *Propst Franziskus Töpsl (1711–1796) und das Augustiner-Chorherrenstift Polling: Ein Beitrag zur Geschichte der katholischen Aufklärung in Bayern* (Kallmünz Opf., 1967), 23–33, 145–160. A brief but lively attack on Amort by a twentieth-century Agredista can be found in Luis García Royo, *La Aristocracia Española y Sor María de Jesús de Ágreda* (Madrid, 1951), 166–73.

astic reception in Bavaria where, as his superior claimed, the book was so popular that 'no one dared even to whisper against it'.[17] In 1744, shortly after the appearance in Bavaria of yet another German edition of the *Mystical City*, the canon published his 870-page *De revelationibus, visionibus, et apparitionibus privatis regulae tutae*. This analysis of the phenomenon of private revelation immediately brought the controversy over the Agredan visions to unprecedented heights.

Amort proclaimed his intention that his book should serve 'for the easier discernment of mystical and pseudo-mystical phenomena in order to put a stop to uncritical practice'. Part One laid down rules for the judgment of private revelations, which in Part Two were applied to a number of historical cases.[18] Despite the façade of comprehensiveness, his primary target was clear: 369 pages of Part Two are devoted exclusively to an attack on the Mystical City. Amort subjected Sor María's revelations to harsh scrutiny and concluded that her putative visions were likely to have been the product either of demonic illusion or (more probably) of her own imagination, precisely the suspicion of the inquisitors who had first reviewed her life and writings in the 1640s. The relevant section opens with a reprise of the Sorbonne's charges of 1696, including censure of the proposition that all Mary's graces, attributes, prerogatives, and privileges derived from and were dependent upon her Immaculate Conception, of flagrantly fantastical details of the Virgin's life in the womb of St Anne, and of the attribution to Mary of such designations as Mediatrix of Grace, Co-Redemptrix, and Coadjutrix.[19] Amort then appends his own list of hundreds of dubious passages extracted from the *Mystical City*. Finally the most 'difficult' sections are discussed under eighteen heads.

---

[17] Van Dülmen, *Propst Töpsl*, 154.

[18] Amort lists twelve indicators of 'probable' revelations in historical cases: (I) such revelations lead to the conversion of the heart; (II) they are free from suspicion of demonic or human illusion; (III) they provide consolation in times of persecution; (IV) at such times they are granted to several people and not just one; (V) they are attended by miraculous cures; (VI) they strengthen the faith of Christians; (VII) they come unexpectedly to people unaccustomed to receive them; (VIII) they come in circumstances in which fantastical or diabolical illusions are unlikely; (IX) they are granted to people for a manifestly good end; (X) they disclose the secrets of the heart for the emendation of the soul or other holy purposes; (XI) they impart an extraordinary knowledge of sacred things; and (XII) they dispose one to a good death. For Amort, Sor María's visions would pass some of these tests, but principally fail to meet his second condition, for which additonal criteria for discernment were applied. Eusebius Amort, *De revelationibus, visionibus et apparitionibus privatis reaulae tutae ex scriptura, conciliis, ss. patribus, aliisque optimis authoribus collectae, explicatae et exemplis illustratae* (Augsburg, 1744), Pars II, 32–9.

[19] Ibid., II, 220–1, 223.

The originality of Amort's critique of the *Mystical City* lies in the microscopy of his reading of the text and the severity of his rationalist analysis. Whilst not denying the possibility of special grace, he assumes that the latter should operate according to natural laws. At the same time, he makes no allowance for mystical licence, or the rhetorical free play of metaphor and allegory in the Castilian nun's account. Rather, every line, including the most trivial anecdote, is to be taken in the literal sense and must pass the test of rationalist plausibility. Unsurprisingly, few passages survive such critique. With references to the work of 'modern chronologers', backed up by a series of tables and juxtaposed with a redacted 'Chronologia Agredana', Amort systematically discredits Sor María's dating of such key events as Mary's conception (Saturday, 8 December, 16 BC, according to the *Mystical City*) or death (Friday, 13 August, 55 AD).[20] The nun's inorance of geography is ruthlessly exposed, whilst her cosmology, with its references to crystalline spheres in the heavens, is shown to be contradicted by modern astronomy. Equally incredible on physiological grounds are Sor María's descriptions of sacred hosts ascending from communicants' stomachs to their hearts, and her notion that Mary possesses a perpetual tabernacle within her heart: 'modern philosophy's discovery of the circulation of the blood invalidates this whole system of eucharistic residence in the hearts of the Blessed Virgin and other communicants'.[21] If many of Sor María's assertions are flatly disproven by science, others are at the very least implausible, since they contradict the historical record.[22] Likewise, Sor María continually reports striking events, above all the deeds and miracles of the Virgin performed in her lifetime, which had they really occurred would surely have been recorded in Scripture or elsewhere: for Amort the absence of documentary corroboration is a telling indictment.

[20] Ibid., II, 498–516.

[21] 'Hoc totum difficile est, quia S. Hostia nondum resoluta in Chylum ordinarie non potest per venas lacteas transire in Ductum Pecqueticum, et exinde residere in corde. Circulatio sanguinis, quae a Neotericis Philosophis inventa est, evertit hoc totum Systema Residentiae Eucharisticae in corde B. Virginis et communicantium': ibid., II, 521. The same discovery also enables Amort to rubbish Sor María's claim that the compression of Mary's heart produced three drops of blood from which Christ's body was formed (p. 521). On the provenance of this last notion see Augustin Poulain, *The Graces of Interior Prayer*, 6th edn, trans. L. Smith (1950), 352.

[22] Amort's zeal could lead him onto shaky ground at times, as when he lambasts Sor María for asserting that the form and stature of Adam and Eve exactly matched that of Christ and Mary: 'it is common knowledge that men in the first age of the world were of greater stature than those of the fourth or fifth millennium. This is proven by the size of the bodies of the ancients, according to the historians': Amort, *De revelationibus*, II, 543.

In a separate line of attack, Amort lambasts the redundance and uselessness, the sheer triviality, of so many of the immense number of alleged revelations in the *Mystical City*. These distinguish it from other visionary reports and constitute additional evidence for its falsity. The revelations attribute to the Almighty, angels, and demons, improbable and absurd means of acting, including verbose and superfluous discourses. Casting further doubts on their plausibility, Amort demonstrates that the Agredan revelations contradict those of other visionaries on points of detail as well as doctrine. Thus Sor María writes that Mary and Joseph did not have servants in Bethlehem, but Blessed Veronica de Binasco had said that they did. Sor María claims that Joseph was in attendance during Christ's birth, but St Bridget had said that he was not. Sor María writes that Christ was crucified with three nails; St Bridget, however, had counted four; and so on: twenty-one discrepancies are cited.[23]

The revelations are shown to contradict Scripture in some places, in others to rest on questionable exegesis, and in dozens of instances to depart from accepted doctrinal interpretations. Various passages, it is argued, are heretical or at least incline towards heresy unless 'well explained'; others contain 'dangerous' promises, such as the pledge that whoever invokes the Virgin from the heart will have eternal life.[24] Like the doctors of the Sorbonne, Amort is suspicious of the premature and unwarranted attribution to Mary of such titles as 'Redemptrix Generis Humani', 'Mediatrix Universalis', and 'Co-Redemptrix'; or the claim that for the human race the Virgin suffered everything which Christ suffered: 'revelations which advocate an opinion which Scripture, tradition, the Fathers or Scholastic doctrine do not commend . . . must be rejected'.[25]

Amort concludes that since some of the revelations are clearly false, and that since Sor María claimed (ironically, from an alleged revelation) that her whole book had divine approval, then the whole must be suspect. Amort was not above adding a traditional misogynist swipe at female mystics in general, citing from varied authorities such maxims as 'a woman's revelation must not be accepted without definite external evidence'; 'women are naturally disposed to ecstasies and raptures'; or 'women's revelations are assumed to be suspect from the start'.[26] Nor

---

[23] Ibid., II, 575–80.
[24] Ibid., II, 561.
[25] Ibid., II, 583.
[26] Ibid., II, 581, 585–6. Limitations of space prohibit here a discussion of the gendered discourse of the Agredan debates. Clark Colahan makes a persuasive case for a reading of the

did he shrink from a criticism of Sor María's character: she actively sought her revelations, used them to question the Almighty from vain curiosity and, puffed up with pride, clung tenaciously to her own interpretations. However, she was also inconstant, repeatedly expressing her fears that some or all of her visions might be demonic illusions. That the nun had allegedly been given to 'excessive melancholy' seems to have clinched the argument for Amort. His parting shot was surely not without irony: 'I do not wish to impugn the holiness of the Venerable Maria, for not even the saints are immune from follies, defects and illusions.'[27]

Had Amort contented himself with laying down rules of spiritual discernment and urging caution in regard to private revelation (his stated intent), his book might have been received as a simple reworking of the treatises of Alvarez de Paz or Giovanni Bona, or as a sibling to the works of the contemporary Jesuit missioner and spiritual writer, Giovanni Battista Scaramelli.[28] However, his ruthless demolition of the *Mystical City* could not go unopposed from the Franciscans and other Agredistas who had invested so much effort in the promotion of the book and its doctrines. Above all, its potent vindication of the Immaculate Conception had to be defended. In the *Mystica civitas Dei vindicata ab observationibus R.D.E. Amort* (1747), Fray Gonzalez Matheo both questioned the accuracy of Amort's Latin translation of the text of the *Mystical City* and, more substantially, insisted that the content of private revelations lay beyond the scope of natural scientific inquiry. Perhaps his most telling point was a rejection of Amort's assumption that the life of the Virgin was not attended by miraculous events. The canon responded to this and another Agredista text by the former provincial of the Bavarian Franciscans with a lengthy counterblast, the *Controversia de revelationibus Agredanis explicita*, dedicated to Benedict XIV. His

---

Mystical City as feminist text (*Visions of Sor María*, esp. 147–65). Amort's defence of patriarchal restrictions on the female religious voice is evident from his scepticism about private revelation in general, from his specific attacks against female visionaries and from his critique of passages of the *Mystical City*, as when he questions Sor María's assertion that 'through the descent of the Holy Spirit the gift of miracles was even imparted to women . . . Why is St Luke silent about this in Acts?': Amort, *De revelationibus*, II, 541.

[27] Ibid., II, 587.

[28] Alvarez de Paz, *De inquisitione pacis sive de studio oratione* (Lyons, 1617); G. Bona, *De discretione spirituum liber unus* (Brussels, 1674); G.B. Scaramelli, *Discernimento degli spiriti* (Venice, 1753) and *Direttorio mistico* (Venice, 1754). On Scaramelli, see Leo A. Hogue, S.J., 'The Direttorio Mistico of J.B. Scaramelli S.I.', *Archivum historicum societatis Iesu*, 9 (1940), 1–39.

robust defence forced his opponents to change tactics, proceeding now to attacking the man rather than the message.[29]

Tipped off by one of Amort's own confrères at Polling, the Bavarian Franciscans laid a charge of Jansenism against the canon at Rome. They had little luck with Benedict XIV's curia, where irritation at the credence accorded to doctrinal novelties arising from alleged private revelations and scepticism about the *Mystical City* in particular were greater even than Amort's own.[30] At the court of Elector Max III Joseph of Bavaria, however, they succeeded with a second and even more explosive accusation: that Amort had attacked the doctrine of the Immaculate Conception. Certainly the canon had been critical of the excesses of the Marian cult, had tried to demythologize the life of Mary, and had advised caution regarding the still undefined dogma; but he had never openly opposed Immaculism. However, by enlisting powerful allies at court, the friars convinced the Elector to issue a decree accusing Amort of traducing the Virgin and causing scandal with 'erroneous doctrines published solely out of ostentatious vanity'. A third anti-Agredista work by Amort, the *Nova demonstratio de falsitate revelationum Agredanarum*, was banned by the Elector. Threatened with banishment if he continued to publish on the theme, the canon now reluctantly gave up the struggle. To his satisfaction, however, Benedict XIV had suspended Sor María's beatification cause; while in 1768 Amort succeeded in blocking a new German edition of the *Mystical City*: 'the Church', he argued, 'must not be prostituted and exposed to the ridicule of the Protestants'.[31]

* * *

That the charge against Amort of denying Immaculism could carry such weight is an indication of the inexpugnable status which, even without formal definition, the dogma had attained in the devotional life of Catholic Europe by the mid eighteenth century. It also reveals how the *Mystical City* had become such a canonical text in the Immaculist corpus that any assault on it could plausibly be construed as

---

[29] Van Dülmen, *Propst Töpsl*, 156.

[30] Benedict XIV's views were explicit: 'What is to be said of those private revelations which the Apostolic See has approved of, those of the Blessed Hildegard, of St Bridget and of St Catherine of Siena? We have already said that those revelations, although approved of, ought not to, and cannot, receive from us any assent of Catholic, but only of human faith, according to the rules of prudence, according to which the aforesaid revelations are probable, and piously to be believed' (cited in Poulain, *Graces*, 320).

[31] Van Dülmen, *Propst Töpsl*, 160.

a slight on the dogma itself. By extension, the influence of private revelation in the formation of devotional tradition and hence ultimately of doctrine was highlighted.

Both parties to the Agredan controversy in Bavaria had been bloodied by the struggle. Amort's attempt to debunk the *Mystical City* had certainly scored some points, as the tactic of his enemies in shifting the ground to *ad hominem* arguments and opening up a broader debate on Immaculism demonstrated. One might sympathize with Amort's fastidious outrage at the superstition and credulity of his contemporaries (an outrage he shared with Casanova), but in his pedantry he could revel in trivia every bit as much as the nun of Agreda, and without her poetry. Indeed, there was something very unmodern in his refusal to countenance a liberal exegesis of Sor María's text. Amort sought to enhance practical piety by rejecting any form of private revelation except that deriving from purely intellectual vision. There was wisdom in his maxim: 'taking private revelations into account has often damaged the Church, but disregarding them never'.[32] However, he surely erred in taking Sor María's claim for the integrity of the entire work as an excuse to throw out the whole and in not admitting that in the difficult area of mysticism divine and human actions might be commingled.[33] More fundamentally, he failed to see that his exercise in disenchantment might itself wound the pious faithful in their genuine search for spiritual enrichment and excitement. There, as so many argued, the nun of Agreda's work had a role to play. Her compelling portrait of a rounded, dynamic, intellectual, all powerful, and (not least) immaculate Mother of God contributed to the growth of those 'most pious desires of the Catholic world' which Pius IX would claim to satisfy with his proclamation of the Immaculate Conception in 1854.[34] The *sensus fidelium*, the intuition of the faithful developing over time, had now produced a *factum ecclesiae*, a living reality of ecclesial practice.

University of the West of England

---

[32] Ibid., 154–5.
[33] On this problem, Poulain, *Graces*, 330.
[34] Flores and Meo, *Nuevo diccionario de Mariología*, 910–41.

BÉRULLE AND OLIER:
CHRIST AND THE BLESSED VIRGIN MARY

by A.D. WRIGHT

AFTER the disruption of French Catholicism during the Wars of Religion of the second half of the sixteenth century, the Catholic revival of the seventeenth century famously involved a restoration of Marian piety. When the second monarch of the new Bourbon dynasty, Louis XIII, had dedicated the kingdom to the Blessed Virgin Mary in 1637, the long- and anxiously-looked-for male heir to the throne, the future Louis XIV, was finally born in 1638, easing a sense of crisis which was as much political and religious as purely familial. The widowed Queen Anne of Austria, regent for her son from 1643, subsequently ordered the building of the great Parisian shrine of Val-de-Grâce. Yet the conspicuous Marian devotion of the French Catholic revival did not emerge in isolation, but rather in relation to a new and intense Christocentric piety. Central to the latter was the leading figure of the revival, Pierre de Bérulle (1575–1629), founder of the French Oratory, and subsequently cardinal. The nature of his piety also led to concentration on the priesthood, seen as an essentially male imitation of Christ. In that further context a second major figure must also be considered, Jean-Jacques Olier (1608–57), who was certainly influenced by Bérulle. But in one historic interpretation that influence was altered, in the direction of a Christian pessimism, by the process of transmission via a third figure, Charles de Condren (1588–1641).[1] Yet the relations between these persons and their priestly and pastoral piety may be open to another interpretation, and one in which the place of a complementary Marian devotion has considerable implications for the much-debated history of seventeenth-century and subsequent French Catholicism.

* * *

The better training of the secular clergy, in a newly systematic way, was a central objective of the Catholic Reformation, from the innovative provisions of the Council of Trent onwards. The campaign to create

---

[1] L. Cognet, *La Spiritualité française au XVIIe siècle* (Paris, 1949), 86–92.

adequate seminaries was necessarily a long one, despite the detailed nature of the Tridentine decrees on the subject. Even if Italy in some senses, at least chronologically, took the lead, further initiatives were attempted elsewhere, at periods yet more distant from the closure of the Council. For example in 1643 the first edition in France of Charles Borromeo's *Acta ecclesiae mediolanensis*, including seminary regulations, was printed, prepared, and financed by Olier, the originator of the famous Parisian seminary of Saint-Sulpice, and his companions. But from the next year Bartholomew Holzhauser, after experiments elsewhere in German-speaking Europe, established a notable seminary at Salzburg, in the archiepiscopate of Prince Paris Lodron. In a refounded version, dating from 1686, this was last until 1783. Although this 'Bartholomite' Congregation of priests only received papal approval in 1680, some years after Holzhauser's death, the seminaries which it ran eventually spread beyond the Germanic lands.[2]

Bérulle founded the French Oratory in 1611, the same year in which Adrien Bourdoise was founding the community of Saint-Nicolas-du-Chardonnet, Paris, which came to establish the preparation of secular priests at the heart of its aims. Historiographic convention accepts that Olier was much influenced by Bérulle and the latter's distinctive spirituality, while noting the influence on Olier of Condren, Bérulle's successor as superior of the Oratory. One particular tradition, in the famously contested history of French Catholicism, would claim that by the time of his death Condren foresaw the eventual Saint-Sulpice of Olier as the true 'heir' of his own Oratory foundation, rather than its own subsequent members, in line with the pro-Roman loyalties of Bérulle himself. In 1642, a year after Condren's death, the Oratorian-run seminary of Saint-Magloire finally began to function as a training institute for non-Oratorian priests, after a complicated pre-history as an initially episcopal foundation and then an exclusively Oratorian institution. But in the same year Olier and his embryonic community moved to the Parisian church and parish of Saint-Sulpice, after initial experiments outside the city.[3]

---

[2] A.D. Wright, 'Introduction: Rome, the Papacy and the Foundation of National Colleges in the Sixteenth and Early Seventeenth Centuries', in R. McCluskey, ed., *The Scots College, Rome 1600–2000* (Edinburgh, 2000), 1–17; F. Ortner, *Reformation, katholische Reform und Gegenreformation im Erzstift Salzburg* (Salzburg, 1981), 132; L. Bertrand, *Bibliothèque Sulpicienne ou Histoire littéraire de la compagnie de Saint-Sulpice*, 3 vols (Paris, 1900), 1:7–8.

[3] H. Bremond, *Histoire littéraire du sentiment religieux en France depuis la fin des guerres de religion jusqu'à nos jours*, 12 vols (Paris, 1916–36), 3:419–507; E.H. Thompson, *The Life of M. Olier, Founder of the Seminary of S. Sulpice* (1861), 136–7.

The spirituality of Bérulle is well known for its Christological concentration, with great devotion to the human person of Christ and a correspondingly high regard for the priestly office. Bérulle's insistence on the mysteries of the Trinity and of the Incarnation thus includes a natural stress on the intrinsic role of the Blessed Virgin Mary in those mysteries. But it might be suggested here that Olier himself goes in a sense beyond that, flanking the stress on the priesthood of Christ with something approaching a precocious awareness of the priesthood of Mary. For Olier an initial 'conversion' to the devout life seems to have occurred on a youthful trip to Italy, at the Marian shrine of Loreto, central to Counter-Reformation piety and a focus, by definition, of pious reflection on the home life of Jesus and Mary. This thus preceded another influential moment, Olier's experience of a specifically Christocentric 'joy' while participating at Chartres, itself a centre of Marian devotion and pilgrimage, in a mission inspired by Condren. Bérulle's devotion to the Blessed Sacrament was paralleled by the similar devotion promoted by Olier at Saint-Sulpice, but in the latter case, in both parish and seminary, this was accompanied by conspicuous Marian devotions. Olier's emphasis on Christ revealed in Mary and in the lives of the saints therefore complemented the advances in French piety led by both Bérulle and Condren. From the time of his hesitant acceptance of the parish of Saint-Sulpice, Olier recorded dedicating his pastoral work to the Blessed Virgin Mary. The parochial piety to both the Blessed Sacrament and Mary was subsequently noted by Fénelon. Marian devotions were naturally central to provision for the children of the parish but, with properly theological reason, conspicuous in the ceremonies surrounding their first communion. Olier's clarity of vision could even be assessed more literally, since his experience at Loreto apparently involved cure for an eye problem contracted at Rome. His interest in the religious provisions for Montreal in Canada, moreover, dating back to at least 1640, involved a mission centre known to him as Villemarie.[4]

At Corpus Christi tide in 1642, as Olier struggled with the proposition that he accept the parish of Saint-Sulpice, he discerned in himself a vocation to be the Marian-modelled vessel of Christ Incarnate. It might

---

[4] Bremond, *Histoire littéraire*, 3:447, 494–6; G. Letourneau, *Le Ministère pastoral de Jean-Jacques Olier, curé de Saint-Sulpice 1642–1652* (Paris, 1905), 22, 57–64; J. Dagens, *Bérulle et les origines de la restauration catholique (1575–1611)* (Bruges, 1952), 357–9; M. Dupuy, *Se laisser à l'Esprit. L'itinéraire spirituel de Jean-Jacques Olier* (Paris, 1982), 30, 175–6, 389; J. Bellord, *Monsieur Olier (1608–1657)* (1899), 30.

be speculated that this compensated for his mother's disapproval, at the time, of his refusal of projects for an episcopal career in favour of pastoral work which was still widely disparaged. But he had taken initial possession of the cure by the feast of the Assumption, definitive possession on the feast of Charles Borromeo in November. The Presentation was chosen by Olier as the feast of title for his new seminary; the mystery of the Purification reflected the fact that priests, like Mary, offer by their hands the Son to the Father in the Temple. For the seminary a new, purpose-built chapel was created, with a Marian decorative scheme, entrusted to Le Brun. Olier's subsequent, famous if unsuccessful interviews with the exiled Charles II of England, with a view to effecting his conversion to Catholicism, were an undertaking which, perhaps understandably, he committed to the patronage of the Virgin Mary. The eucharistic piety encouraged by Olier at Saint-Sulpice, with appropriate confraternity devotions and processions, was in striking contrast to the effective (even if not ostensible) message of Arnauld's 1643 publication, *De la fréquente communion.*[5]

After his Loreto experience, on his return from Rome to France, Olier made pilgrimages to local Marian shrines and in 1632 preached a notable sermon in Paris on the feast of the Assumption. His First Mass in 1633 was celebrated on the feast of St John the Baptist, but at the Carmelite nuns' chapel of Notre Dame des Champs. To a prayer composed by Condren, 'Veni, Domine Jesu', Olier added, for its use at Saint-Sulpice, the amplification 'Veni, Domine Jesu, vivens in Maria'. He had himself been in some way affected, allegedly, even in his 'unconverted' state, prior to the Loreto pilgrimage, by a pious parishioner in the area of Paris in which he was later to minister, Marie Rousseau. The foundation where he celebrated his first mass had been due to the initiative of Mme Acarie, Marie de l'Incarnation in religion. After ordination he recovered while staying at Notre Dame de Bon-Secours at Tournon from a fever contracted while on mission in the Auvergne. When the new, purpose-built seminary at Saint-Sulpice was finally complete in 1651, Olier made another pilgrimage to Chartres to dedicate it to the Blessed Virgin Mary.[6] His letters demonstrate a conviction

---

[5] [Anon.], *Abrégé de la vie de M. Olier fondateur du séminaire de Saint-Sulpice et de la colonie de Montréal, en Canada* (Montreal, 1866), 44, 81, 89, 94, 100; Dupuy, *Se laisser à l'Esprit*, 188–9, 197; C. Hamel, *Histoire de l'église [de] Saint-Sulpice* (Paris, 1900), 60–4; P. Pourrat, P.S.S., *Jean-Jacques Olier, fondateur de Saint-Sulpice* ([Paris], 1932), 131–5, 148; [Anon.], *M. Olier, instituteur et fondateur de la Congrégation de Saint-Sulpice* (Lille, 1861), 59.

[6] Thompson, *Life of M. Olier*, 13, 26, 29, 54, 110; *M. Olier, instituteur et fondateur*, 18;

of the powerful mediation of Mary in the life of the whole Church. When, in the politically sensitive context of the Frondes in the early 1650s, he was anxious to exclude the French Oratorians from setting up their own establishment within his parish, he attributed eventual success to the efforts of important human patrons, including Premier Président Molé, but also explicitly to Jesus and Mary. His continued anxiety to maintain the Queen's support also reflected awareness of the Oratorians' increasingly uncertain loyalties in the ecclesiastical sphere, in their response to the arrival in Paris of the 1653 condemnation by Pope Innocent X of the Five Propositions attributed to Jansenius, and allegedly summarizing Jansenist belief, an uncertainty with its own political implications. In any case Olier seemed to be particularly sensitive to the influence, as one might say, of the feminine.[7]

Bérulle, by contrast, had managed to get very much at cross purposes with the reformed Carmelite nuns, when they were first introduced to France from Spain. Though, once again, there was a complicating political context to this, the dispute also suggested the lines of subsequent division, as Jesuits and future Jansenists, among others, clashed over the Christological and Marian devotion which Bérulle sought to impose on the French Carmelite nuns. At the time of Richelieu's death at the end of 1642, however, that cardinal's renewed interest in French seminary foundations was apparent against the known background of a resurgence in England of persecution of Catholic priests. The beginning of the 1640s indeed marked an important stage in the evolution of Marian piety in France. The death in 1641 of Ste Jeanne de Chantal, of the Order of the Visitation, followed the death in 1638 of Père Joseph, co-founder of the Daughters of Calvary, and that in 1640, in Lorraine, of St Pierre Fourier, founder of another Marian congregation.[8] Olier, on the other hand, followed a Jesuit style of caution, in prohibiting to his associates the spiritual direction of female religious communities, a rule subsequently adopted at all the Sulpician seminaries. The prohibition on women entering the presbytery at Saint-Sulpice was, though, more of a

---

G.-M. de Fruges, *J.-J. Olier (1608–1657) curé de Saint-Sulpice et fondateur des séminaires. Essai d'histoire religieuse sur le XVIIe siècle* (Paris, 1904), 16, 19, 33, 69, 112.

[7] Fruges, *J.-J. Olier*, 343, 391–3, 443–4; *Lettres de M. Olier, curé de la paroisse et fondateur du séminaire de Saint-Sulpice*, ed. E. Levesque, P.S.S., 2 vols (Paris, 1935), 1:xxi, 469–76, 2:38–9, 154–5; Hamel, *Histoire*, 83, 97–8; Thompson, *Life of M. Olier*, 355.

[8] S.-M. Morgain, *Pierre de Bérulle et les carmélites de France. La querelle du gouvernement 1583–1629* (Paris, 1995); Pourrat, *Olier*, 122–3, 126; cf. Hamel, *Histoire*, 91–2; Dupuy, *Se laisser à l'Esprit*, 175–6.

commonplace in Catholic reform circles, French or otherwise. The crucial initiative, nevertheless, of Olier himself in launching the Sulpician seminary movement in Counter-Reformation France is evident when it is remembered that Condren's death in 1641 not only left Olier without a spiritual director but prevented the former's completion of an eagerly awaited instruction on the foundation of seminaries.[9]

It is therefore important not to underestimate the continuity of Christocentric piety in Olier, following both Bérulle and Condren, despite Olier's extra emphasis on Marian devotion. In 1642, following Condren's death, Olier put himself under the direction of the Benedictines of Saint-Germain-des-Prés, within the jurisdiction of which, to the exclusion of that of the archbishop of Paris, lay the parish of Saint-Sulpice. The vital, if indirect advice to Olier to accept the parish came from his personal director, Dom Grégoire Tarisse, superior of the Congregation of Saint-Maur and presiding in 1642 at the General Chapter of his Congregation. For by the early 1640s the monastic community of Saint-Germain adhered to the Maurist Congregation, and Olier was also influenced by its Procurator General, Père Bataille. Such influence thus complemented the necessary jurisdictional and political support given to Olier and his foundation by the contrastingly *ancien régime* abbot of Saint-Germain, Henri de Bourbon, holder of the bishopric of Metz. Condren himself had joined at an early date the famous Compagnie du Saint-Sacrement, drawing in after him Olier and some of the latter's original associates. This element of a shared Christocentric piety was not to be obscured by subsequent tension and rivalry over membership of Saint-Sulpice or, alternatively, the French Oratory, by the end of the 1640s and the early 1650s.[10]

The ambiguous ecclesiology of Bérulle, exposed by the clash over the Carmelite nuns in France, offered an opportunity to St Cyran, the virtual founder of French Jansenism, for defence of the Oratory and its founder. St Cyran thereby sought to capitalize on the fact that Bérulle had shared with the subsequent Jansenists a negative judgement of Jesuit teaching on divine grace, teaching contested in Spain, Italy, and the Netherlands since the late sixteenth century. Bishop Zamet of Langres, favoured by Jeanne de Chantal for his care over female reli-

[9] Hamel, *Histoire*, 59, 68; Pourrat, *Olier*, 100, 103, 213.

[10] Dupuy, *Se laisser à l'Esprit*, 176; Hamel, *Histoire*, 60–6; Bertrand, *Bibliothèque Sulpicienne*, 1:3; Pourrat, *Olier*, 102, 129–35, 163; Thompson, *Life of M. Olier*, 115–16, 129, 352, 355; Fruges, *J.-J. Olier*, 111, 170, 297–302, 340, 342–5; Levesque, *Lettres de M. Olier*, 1:469–76, 2:38–9, 155.

gious communities, in turn similarly favoured the French Oratorians, as well as intervening in the evolution of the Port-Royal foundations. But his own pet project, a convent established at Paris in 1633 for perpetual adoration of the Blessed Sacrament, became entangled in the condemnation of a mysterious text issuing from the convent, the so-called 'Secret Rosary of the Blessed Sacrament'. When the convent was consequently suppressed, in 1647, its community was transferred to Port-Royal, which was to become the centre of anti-Jesuit French Jansenism. But Zamet had approved the text, and its composition had allegedly been influenced by Condren, before St Cyran sought to defend it. By this means St Cyran came to exercise his dominant authority over Port-Royal, eventually to the exclusion of Zamet. Episcopal rivals of the latter may have contributed to the condemnation of the suspect text, but the possible parallels of aspects of it to the spirituality of Olier, in line with that of Bérulle and Condren, do not affect the singular, eventual outcome, the substantial parting of the ways between the Oratory and Saint-Sulpice.[11]

That division, so symptomatic and so influential in the subsequent evolution of French Catholicism, was surely as real as any contrast between Port-Royal itself and the Jesuits' devotional tradition in France based on the latters' promotion of a conspicuous Marian devotion. The truly eminent historian Louis Châtellier has argued that conflict on these grounds, between an external piety and an interior spirituality, was foreshadowed by a similar 'difference of emphasis' between the Jesuits on the one hand and both the Oratory and Olier on the other. He has stressed that for both Bérulle and Bourgoing, also of the French Oratory, true religion was concerned with the inner life, and that for Olier too, as in his 'Christian catechism for the interior life', it called for intense personal union in Christ with God. That may certainly be agreed and yet, as has been seen, Olier's pastoral practice involved the supporting of such personal spirituality by public devotion to Christ precisely in the Blessed Sacrament and, furthermore, by conspicuous Marian devotion. In this sense, then, Olier led a movement within French Catholicism which, while in no way conflated with Jesuit tradition, emerged as something clearly opposed to the French Oratorians' increasing sympathy with Port-Royal.[12]

---

[11] L. von Pastor, *The History of the Popes, from the Close of the Middle Ages*, 40 vols (1891–1953), 29:77, 82–7; Bremond, *Histoire littéraire*, 4:202–11.

[12] L. Châtellier, *The Europe of the Devout. The Catholic Reformation and the Formation of a New Society* (Cambridge, 1989), 155–6.

For though Olier echoed Benalle's care for the episcopal office, seeing the bishop as 'king' among the clergy, he also stressed, pursuing the ideas of both Bérulle and Condren, that every priest's pastoral role centred on making present the incarnate Christ in the Mass. That this naturally evoked the relationship of Jesus and Mary was further emphasised by those specializing in internal mission in seventeenth-century France, both John Eudes, on whom the influence of the Oratory had initially been direct, and Grignion de Montfort, inspired by his Sulpician training. Olier himself was certainly open to the influence of female religious, but saw the (male) priest as taking by his vocation the sacrificial role of Christ, priest and king.[13] Condren, by contrast, seems to have specifically excluded the possibility of allowing a priesthood of Mary.[14] The dying Condren's fears about his Oratorians' links with the emerging French Jansenists allegedly touched specifically on St Cyran's disparagement of the Council of Trent, a matter much more fundamental to all traditions within French Catholicism than differences over possible Marian attributes. Nevertheless, this raises the major issue of whether Olier's piety, with its Marian approach to the sacramental presence of Christ, represented a moderation of Catholic rigorism, and of such rigorism's relationship to Jansenism.[15]

The case for a distinction between a properly Catholic rigorism of Borromean inspiration in the French Counter-Reformation on the one hand, and a potentially fatal appropriation of pastorally and doctrinally insensitive ultra-rigorism by the Jansenists on the other, has been bravely made by Marc Venard.[16] On this interpretation, the 'French exception', if that is to be identified with Jansenism, was very much not the great glory of the French Catholic revival, but quite the contrary: a dangerous deviation from the mainstream of Tridentine Catholicism. Yet an attempt has now been made to recategorize such Tridentine Catholicism, at least in the form promoted by the post-Conciliar papacy and central hierarchy of the Church, as alien to the true tradition of Gallican religion. This would seem to reclaim for Jansenism an honourable connotation as the 'French exception'.[17] This approach,

---

[13] M. Venard, ed., *L'Âge de raison (1620/30–1750)* [= J.-M. Mayer et al., eds, *Histoire du Christianisme*, 9] (Paris, 1997), 245, 271, 842–3, 850, 856.

[14] C.E. Williams, *The French Oratorians and Absolutism, 1611–1641* (New York, 1989), 293.

[15] T. Wanegffelen, *Une difficile fidélité. Catholiques malgré le Concile en France, XVIe–XVIIe siècles* (Paris, 1999), 210.

[16] M. Venard, *Réforme protestante, réforme catholique dans la province d'Avignon* (Paris, 1993).

[17] Wanegffelen, *Une difficile fidélité*, 213–16.

indeed, has been accompanied by the magisterial approbation of Pierre Chaunu, in his extended introduction to a volume where the crisis of pre-Revolutionary French Catholicism is investigated via the capital case of eighteenth-century Paris.[18] His identification of the 'spécificité gallicane' can embrace a reserve about the degree of rigorism adopted by the French Jansenists.[19] Indeed even where the propriety of the traditional term 'Jansenism' in the case of France is doubted, Port-Royal is nevertheless awarded an honourable centrality, the charge of a distorted or ultra-rigorism brought instead against its antagonists.[20]

A consideration of the spirituality of Bérulle and Olier might all the same leave room to doubt even so magisterial a judgement. A Christocentric devotion and an emphasis on the priestly office can obviously be traced as a continuity, transmitted via Condren. The famous or notorious case, within Olier's own lifetime, when the Duke of Liancourt was refused absolution at Saint-Sulpice for his relations with Port-Royal might at first sight seem to support a reading of French religious history in which the Jansenists and the Oratorians of the generations subsequent to Bérulle and Condren faced a dispropor-tionate and inequitable rigorism, claiming to be mainstream Catholi-cism. But when the parochial and seminary life of Olier's Saint-Sulpice is considered, with devotion to the sacramental presence of Christ and a high doctrine of the priesthood, both inherited from the original ethos of the Oratory, now modified and tempered by a Marian piety adjusted to lay needs, it is surely arguable that Saint-Sulpice offered a more universally accessible Catholicism than did the elitism of Port-Royal.[21]

University of Leeds

---

[18] P. Chaunu, M. Foisil, F. de Noirfontaine, *Le Basculement religieux de Paris au XVIIIe siècle* (Paris, 1998): P. Chaunu, 'Avant-propos', 15–18, and 'Livre premier. Les fondements de la crise', 19–149; cf. his 'Postface', 531–40.

[19] Chaunu, 'Livre premier', 63–7, 84–5.

[20] Chaunu, 'Postface', 537–8.

[21] W. Doyle, *Jansenism. Resistance to Authority from the Reformation to the French Revolution* (Basingstoke, 2000), 27, 89.

THE VIRGIN MARY AND THE PEOPLE OF LIGURIA: IMAGE AND CULT

by JANE GARNETT AND GERVASE ROSSER

W E begin with an image, and a story. Explanation will emerge from what follows. Figure 1 depicts a huge wooden statue of the Virgin Mary, once the figurehead on the prow of a ship, but now on the high altar of the church of Saints Vittore and Carlo in Genoa, and venerated as Nostra Signora della Fortuna. On the night of 16–17 January 1636 a violent storm struck the port of Genoa. Many ships were wrecked. Among them was one called the Madonna della Pietà, which had the Virgin as its figurehead. A group of Genoese sailors bought this image as part of the salvage washed up from the sea. First setting it up under a votive painting of the Virgin in the harbour, they repaired it, had it repainted, and on the eve of Corpus Christi brought it to the church of San Vittore, close by the port. A famous blind song-writer was commissioned to write a song in honour of the image. Sailors and groups of young girls went through the streets of the city singing and collecting gifts. The statue became at once the focus of an extraordinary popular cult, thousands of people arriving day and night with candles, silver crowns, necklaces, and crosses in gratitude for the graces which had immediately begun to be granted. Volleys of mortars were let off in celebration. The affair was managed by the sailors who, in the face of mounting criticism and anxiety from local church leaders, directed devotions and even conducted exorcisms before the image. To stem the gathering tide of visitors and claims of miracles, and to try to establish control, the higher clergy first questioned the identity of the statue (some held it to represent, not the Virgin, but the Queen of England); then the statue was walled up; finally the church was closed altogether. Still, devotees climbed into the church, and large-scale demonstrations of protest were held. The archbishop instituted a process of investigation, in the course of which many eye-witnesses and people who claimed to have experienced miracles were interviewed (giving, in the surviving manuscript, rich detail of their responses to the image). Eventually the prohibition was lifted, and from 1637 until well into the twentieth century devotion to Nostra Signora della Fortuna remained strong, with frequent miracles or

Fig. 1 'Nostra Signora della Fortuna', in the church of S. Vittore
and S. Carlo, Genoa. Painted and clothed wooden statue,
sixteenth-century.

graces being recorded. So here we have a cult focused on an image of
secular origin, transformed by the promotion of the sailors into a devotional object which roused the enthusiasm of thousands of lay people. It
was a cult which, significantly, sprang up at a time of unrest in the city
of Genoa, and which thus focused pressing issues of authority. The late
1630s witnessed growing tension between factions of 'old' and 'new'
nobility, the latter being marked by their hostility to the traditional

Genoese Spanish alliance. Hostilities were played out both within the Senate and in clashes in the streets of the city. The cult of Nostra Signora della Fortuna grew up in this context, but survived and developed in subsequent centuries, attracting devotion from all over Italy.[1]

The project to which this evidence relates concerns cults of images – statues and paintings – reputed to work miracles.[2] Medievalists, to whom the miraculous is quite familiar, may feel that the subject has a natural affinity with their period, and indeed the phenomenon of the holy image credited with extraordinary powers is documented throughout the medieval era. However, it is by no means confined to the Middle Ages. The larger project to which this paper contributes considers the *longue durée* of such image cults between the later Middle Ages and the present day. The advantage of taking the long view is that it becomes possible to appreciate that the assumptions which underlie such cults did not simply wither away with the arrival of urban life, or industrialization, or the modern secular state; they have simply manifested themselves in different ways. To make detailed research practicable over such a long time-span, our principal focus has been upon a single region, that of Liguria in north-west Italy, although in due course this material will be set in the wider context of the whole Mediterranean world. Liguria is an area characterized to this day by strong traditionalist elements, rooted in a naturally conservative society of mountain settlements and small coastal fishing towns. At the same time, the commerce generated through Liguria by its command of the sea and a number of passes over into Piemonte has, since the twelfth century, injected a dynamic quality into the economy and society of the area. The capital city, Genoa, was the cradle of modern banking in the twelfth century, the capital of a far-flung empire in the later Middle Ages, and the birthplace of Italian socialism in the nineteenth century. The result, throughout recorded history, has been a striking mixture of traditional and modernizing elements in Ligurian culture. The experi-

---

[1] *Breve narrazione storica degli avvenimenti riguardanti il miracoloso simulacro di Nostra Signora della Fortuna che si venera nella chiesa dei SS. Vittore e Carlo in Genova* (Genoa, 1898); Genoa, Archivio della Curia Arcivescovile di Genova, Fondo 'Grazie e miracoli', Processo per la statua di Nostra Signora (della Fortuna), documents of 1636 and 1735. For the political conflict of the 1630s, C. Bitossi, *Il governo dei magnifici: patriziato e politica a Genova fra cinque e seicento* (Genoa, 1990), 236–43, and further references and discussion in the work anticipated in the following note.

[2] We are preparing a full-length study of miracle-working images in Liguria and the Mediterranean world between the late Middle Ages and the present day, with the title *The Moving Image: Zones of the Miraculous in Italy and the Mediterranean, 1500–2000*.

ence of economic and social change in the region subverts any assumption that image cults are to be associated solely with 'simple', 'primitive', or 'traditional' societies.

One sometimes encounters also another assumption, which holds that in traditional or past societies the supernatural was perceived as all-pervading. On this view magical or divine properties might inhere in any object whatever. Yet in fact, it has only ever been a minority of images which has acquired such a particular reputation. Both in medieval and in post-medieval western societies, the miraculous has always been the exception, not the rule, and this applies as well to images as to other forms of supernatural intervention. But here we would argue that there is a further distinction to be drawn; and this is one of the themes upon which we shall concentrate here. In Christian culture, the material objects in which divine power has most commonly been officially acknowledged to reside are the relics of the saints. Medieval scholars have naturally devoted much attention to the cult of relics, and some of their conclusions apply as well to the veneration of particular images. But the similarity between relics and miraculous images is only partial, for they are also differentiated in significant ways, which have to do above all with their respective relationships to ecclesiastical authority. If we compare image and relic, the most striking distinction between the two, apart from the visual interest of the former, is that the relic typically depends for its potency upon its authentication by Church leaders and its preservation in an ecclesiastical treasury. Of course, certain individuals, usually royalty or aristocrats, have at all times managed to acquire relics as personal possessions; but this has been an elite exception, not the general rule. The image, by contrast, is more openly and indiscriminately available to devotees from different backgrounds. In the comparison between the two, therefore, we come close to a central motif in the history of popular Christianity, which is its often tense relations with the authority of the institutional Church. In the histories of particular image cults in Liguria, we shall see not only the commonly prominent role of popular lay promotion, but also the ways in which miraculous images could become the preferred medium for the expression of communal or local rivalries.

The case we shall turn to here is the comparative development of certain relic and miraculous image cults in late medieval and early modern Genoa. The points which stand out from this comparison are the susceptibility of particular saints' *relics* to be appropriated and manipulated by authorities anxious thereby to legitimize their own status and to promote feelings of solidarity, and at the same time the potential difficulty of maintaining popular interest in such relics. *Images*, meanwhile, might more readily be promoted by local interests and popular enthusiasm to the status of *palladia* of particular communities, capable of enabling those communities to confront the forces of higher authority. The vast majority of such images in Liguria are images of the Blessed Virgin Mary.

The context of this discussion is the city and hinterland of Genoa, capital of the province of Liguria. Since the end of the eleventh century, when the ashes of St John the Baptist were stolen from Myra during the First Crusade and brought in triumph to the city, St John has been the chief official patron saint of Genoa. However, notwithstanding governmental patronage and promotion of his cult in the city and its large dependent territories, the Baptist never seems to have 'taken off' as a popular hero to the subjects of the Genoese Republic.[3] Although officially adopted as the principal 'Patrone, Protettore e Padre del Comune' in 1327, a status confirmed in 1853, St John the Baptist does not appear to have penetrated so deeply into the culture of Genoa as has St Mark, for example, into that of Venice, or even, perhaps, the Baptist himself into that of Florence, which also boasts an ancient allegiance to the Precursor of Christ, together with important relics acquired in the later medieval period.[4] The Baptist's historical links with Genoa were nil, apart from the somewhat inglorious story of the theft of the relics. Nor have relics of the Baptist been credited with large numbers of miracles on behalf of the local population. The miracles recorded by the Genoese writers Stella, Giustiniani, and Calcagnino between the fifteenth and the seventeenth centuries are not numerous; are largely concentrated in the first 150 years of the relics' presence in Genoa; and are of limited types, relating almost entirely to storms at sea, urban fires, and earthquakes.[5]

[3] J. Garnett and G. Rosser, 'Reliquie o immagini? Culti e miracoli in Liguria', in C. Paolocci, ed., *San Giovanni nella vita sociale e religiosa a Genova e in Liguria tra medioevo ed età contemporanea* (Genoa, 2003); Iacopo da Varagine (ed. G. Vigna), *Istoria sive legenda translationis beatissimi Iohannis Baptiste, Atti della Società Ligure di Storia Patria*, 10/iv (1876), 457–91; idem (ed. S.B. Guidetti) *Cronaca della città di Genova dalle origini al 1297* (Genoa, 1995), 273, 300, 312; C. di Fabio, ed., *La cattedrale di Genova nel medioevo* (Genoa, 1998), 55, 126–9 (on the cathedral as an official, civic building), 201–2.

[4] For St Mark at Venice see E. Muir, *Civic Ritual in Renaissance Venice* (1981), passim. For St John at Florence see R. Trexler, *Public Life in Renaissance Florence* (1980), passim. In general see D. Webb, *Patrons and Protectors: the Saints in the Italian City-States* (1996).

[5] A. Calcagnino, *Historia del glorioso precursore di N.S. S. Giovanni Battista Protettore della Città di Genova* (Genoa, 1697), 100–3, 106–9, 112–16, 125, 129–33, 145–8, 158–61: he cites

Fig. 2   Reliquary of St John the Baptist belonging to the cathedral of Genoa.
Twelfth-century.

The annual civic procession with the relics on the feast of the
Baptist's Nativity was instituted in 1327 by the ruling élite of the
Comune as a festival of state (see fig. 2). Its ostensible inclusion of the
entire community has ever since, at least until very recently, been
compromised by an undisguised intention to glorify the regime. Here
again there is a parallel with Florence, where in the later Middle Ages
the annual procession on the feast of the Nativity of the Baptist allowed
only very limited participation by the townspeople. The Florentine
procession comprised only male citizens: women, children, recent
immigrants, and the poor were reduced to the status of mere spectators.
In contrast to Genoa, however, the Florentine Republic remained, at
least until the sixteenth century, a relatively open political society, such
that the image of the commonwealth presented by the elite in the John
the Baptist procession was always fragile. At Genoa the entrenchment
in power, from an earlier date, of a relatively narrowly defined aristoc-
racy put a firm constraint on the generation of alternative images of the
state. Yet the St John procession here, too, had only partial success in

the late medieval Stella and the early modern Giustiniani. See also L. Persoglio, *San Giovanni
Battista e i genovesi*, 2nd edn (Genoa, 1899), 210–12, 224–41; *La settimana religiosa*, 29 (1899),
248, 255.

generating a spirit of common identity. It is notable that the procession has suffered significant periods of neglect, as the evidence of occasional revivals clearly indicates. Proclaiming the ceremony in 1514, the Senate urged citizens to participate,

> in view of the fact that for some time devotion has been somewhat lacking, and few citizens, compared with the past, have followed the procession, contrary to the honour of so great a saint and that of the city.[6]

Enough Ligurian men, at all periods since the twelfth century, have been called Giovanni or Giovanni Battista to warn against too firm a generalization. And the saint's name has for centuries been on everyone's lips on Midsummer Eve, even if the bonfires on 23 June have at least as much to do with fertility and harvest as they do with the holy man whose festival has been overlaid upon them. Yet songs about John the Baptist are not numerous, and it may be significant, at least for the early period, that the manuscript of *c.*1300 which contains several dozen pious poems by the Anonimo Genovese, including many dedicated to individual saints, includes no reference to the Baptist.[7] Of the thousand *edicole* in the streets and piazzas of Genoa (fig. 3), which were catalogued by the Remondini a century ago, no more than one in eighteen showed the saint, and of these, half portrayed him not as an autonomous figure, but as an adjunct to Christ or the Virgin Mary.[8]

If the cult of the Baptist in Genoa has seemed to lack a certain element of popular spontaneity, this is surely due in part to the physical nature of the relics. The ashes of the saint are, of course, just that; their visual impact is low. Alessandro in the early eighteenth century made the best of it, proclaiming 'Genoa's glory, to have in the form of dust, as though in extract, the best of men'; but as objects, the remains were irredeemably unexciting.[9] Hence, it would appear, the repeated efforts

---

[6] 'Vedendosse da qualche tempo in qua essere alquanto mancato la devocione e poco numero di Citadini a camparatione del pasato seguire detta processione contra lo honore de tanto Santo e de la Cita.' D. Cambiaso, *La processione delle ceneri di San Giovanni Battista in Genova* (Genoa, 1914); Persoglio, *San Giovanni Battista*, 215–16; for Florence see Trexler, *Public Life.*

[7] L. Cocito, ed., *Le rime volgari dell'Anonimo genovese* (Genoa, 1966).

[8] A. and M. Remondini, *I santuari e le immagini di Maria Santissima nella città di Genova* (Genoa, 1865); Persoglio, *San Giovanni Battista*, 196–200.

[9] 'Gloria di Genova, avere in polvere, come in estratto, la cima degli Uomini': F. Alessandro, *Genova gloriosa. Discorso in lode delle sagre ceneri di S. Giovanni Battista* (Genoa, 1712), 8.

Fig. 3   Street shrine, Genoa. Eighteenth-century.

of civic and ecclesiastical authorities to acquire and display slightly more substantial relics, namely the arm bone 'rediscovered' in 1613 and the finger appropriated from a private owner at San Remo in 1641, each with some evocatively charred flesh attached. These new finds were provided with individual reliquaries deliberately pierced to allow some visibility of the contents, and from the early seventeenth century the arm bone significantly replaced the image of the saint on the top of the processional casket of the ashes when these were taken in procession.[10] An evident desire for visual testimony was also fed by the dish, supposedly that on which the Baptist's head had been brought to Herod, which was given to the cathedral in the late fifteenth century by Pope Innocent VIII, with the intention that it be displayed to popular devotion on feast days. It is a striking feature of this Late Antique plate that its owners around 1400, possibly the kings of France, added in the centre the carved image of the saint's head, turning the relic into an object of visual devotion.[11] But the popular hunger for contact with the sacred was not easily satisfied with these fragments. From an early date there was established a popular custom of kissing, or pressing to sick parts of the body, the iron chains which had secured the first container of the ashes; and the same faith came to be invested also in the baldachin which was carried over the relics during the civic procession on the feast day. In the thirteenth century we even hear of an aristocratic nun who was mysteriously impeded from rising from her bed to visit the shrine, but was allowed the privilege of having a curative powder made for her from a fragment of the marble box which had originally held the relics.[12] Such practices were viewed by churchmen with an unease which increased over time, especially after the Council of Trent. Archbishop Pallavicino of Genoa in 1567 directed that the laity should be discouraged from venerating objects which had merely contained, or been in contact with, holy relics.[13] Yet in the present case no more direct means of contact with the saint appeared, in the popular mind, to be available.

The relics of the Baptist, therefore, offered to popular devotion only very limited access to the divine. The appropriation and promotion of this prestigious cult by the ecclesiastical and civic authorities is understandable; but the control which they exercised was so thorough as severely to limit the scope for any more popular identification with the holy thaumaturge. Apart from the Baptist's official promotion as patron of the Republic in 1327, the employment of the cult by the regime was typified by a regulation imposed in 1202 on subject territories, that each of these should annually, on the feast day, bring to Genoa a candle weighing twenty-five pounds in honour of the saint.[14] We do not know

[10] Calcagnino, *Historia*, 162–3, 165, 167–8; Persoglio, *San Giovanni Battista*, 157–9.
[11] Ibid., 177; C. Marcenaro, *Il museo del tesoro della cattedrale di Genova* (Genoa, 1969).
[12] Persoglio, *San Giovanni Battista*, 237–8.
[13] *Synodi diocesanae et provinciales editae atque ineditae S. Genuensis ecclesiae* (Genoa, 1833), 58.
[14] Calcagnino, *Historia*, 107.

how faithfully this law was observed. But it is clear enough that, for many inhabitants of Liguria until the fall of the Republic, John the Baptist was identified with the heavy, and more or less unwelcome, hand of central government. Even the saint's appearance on the coinage of the Republic, by means of which the Superba collected her taxes, reinforced an alliance which could only too readily be seen in negative terms. This is not to say that a 'culto di stato' could not co-exist with a 'culto popolare'; yet the evidence for the latter is relatively slight, and there are a number of indications that the nature of official patronage in Genoa had a narrowing effect upon the image of the saint.

The relatively low visibility of John the Baptist, in the city which boasts his ashes, has until recently been further accentuated by yet another feature of the local cult: the large-scale exclusion of women. Only in the mid-twentieth century was the ban removed, which since the early 1300s had denied to any woman (other than the members of one rich family of benefactors) the right to enter the chapel in which the relics were kept. Luigi Persoglio, the Jesuit who a century ago published *San Giovanni Battista e i genovesi* as part of an attempt to kindle fresh enthusiasm for the cult, opined that the ban on women had been instituted 'out of special respect for the holy relics', and he believed that in the fifteenth century Innocent VIII, renewing the order, equally intended to enhance veneration by keeping women out.[15] The same denial to women of the right to participate came to apply also, as in Florence, to the annual festal procession. John the Baptist, the Precursor of Christ, whose brutal martyrdom had been brought about by the deviousness of women, was presented by the keepers of his relics as definitely and uncompromisingly male. Of course, the history of the cults of St Francis, or of Christ himself, show that masculinity need be no bar to the engagement of female devotion. And certainly there were Genoese women who were devoted to John the Baptist, most notably Maria Antonia Solimani, the eighteenth-century founder of the Orders of Battistini and Battistine.[16] But the prevalent image of the Baptist in Genoa remained that of the emphatically male ally of a patriarchal regime, in the fitting company of other masculine protectors of the Republic: St Laurence and St George and, from the seventeenth century, St Bernard and St Joseph. Of the holy patrons of the Superba, only St Catherine of Genoa and the Virgin Mary softened the dominant

---

[15] Persoglio, *San Giovanni Battista*, 164, 176–7: 'per ispeciale rispetto alle sante Reliquie'.
[16] *La settimana religiosa*, 29 (1899), 221; Persoglio, *San Giovanni Battista*, 207–10.

tone of chauvinism. And of these two, only Mary offered the undiscriminating accessibility, and the wide range of succour, which the Genoese appear not to have found in John the Baptist.

Unlike the other saints with local associations, the Virgin Mary was known to the Genoese, from the twelfth century onwards, primarily through her images. The cathedral treasury used, in the early modern period, to contain a curious relic of the Virgin's hair but, once again, there is no evidence that this enjoyed the popular cult which, by contrast, was frequently addressed to her in the form of pictures and statues.[17] These cults were differentiated in a number of ways from the cult of John the Baptist's relics in the territory of the Genoese Republic. We can observe both a similarity and a difference between the cult of relics and that of images. First, the similarity: the ostensible inferiority of a 'mere' picture or statue, by comparison with a bone from the very body of a holy man, turns out on closer inspection not to be, in the general view, an inferiority at all. For the idea that certain objects can, by a process of metamorphosis, acquire new qualities has always been widely held. Only a minority of intellectuals, probably beginning with Aristotle, has continued to insist on the distinctions between things. To most people, however, it has always seemed quite natural that, in certain circumstances, a new form should flow into a given object, changing its substance. Carved or painted images have therefore no less potential for transformation than do relics. The critical difference between relics and miraculous images, meanwhile, lies in their relation to authority. Whereas the first are always, and by definition, jealously guarded by official bodies which alone can guarantee their authenticity, by contrast the latter crop up most readily where authority is weak. Indeed, image cults have often been used by particular communities to reclaim sites in the landscape, or local spheres of influence, which have previously been marginalized or proscribed by either secular or religious rulers.[18]

On Sunday 15 September 1537, at Cicagna, in Fontanabuona near Chiavari, about twenty miles to the east of Genoa, something extraordinary happened in the course of the morning mass in the church. In the words of an eyewitness, interviewed a few days later by the archbishop's vicar general, his neighbour suddenly spoke to him, pointing to an old and blackened statue of the Virgin Mary:

[17] For the Virgin's hair see Calcagnino, *Historia*, 147.
[18] This theme will be developed in our book.

Do you see that the face of the Virgin Mary is changing? The witness looked again at the face of the image, and saw that it really was transforming itself, altering from a state of deformation to one of beauty, above all in the lips which, under his gaze, became red, while the head, formerly quite black and covered with dust, was without human interference cleaned of dirt and made beautiful, as it now is.

This wonder was witnessed by several others, and was followed by the first of a spate of miracles attributed to the now enlivened statue. It was characteristic that, although in this case the image cult began in an ecclesiastical setting, the object of devotion was not the patron saint of the church (this, reflecting Genoa's first seizure of political control of this region in the twelfth century, was John the Baptist) but an old and neglected representation of the Virgin. Also typical was the fact that this local population, which showed itself so ready to believe in the miracle of the statue, was at the time exposed to the hazards both of plague and of invading armies, generating a sense of insecurity which was evidently not assuaged by promises of protection from the ruling Senate of the Ligurian capital. In such circumstances, to turn to an image was apparently a natural response.[19]

More marginal still at the inception of its fame, and to this extent more typical of image cults in general, was the painting of Nostra Signora dell'Orto of Chiavari (fig. 4). Once again this was an older image, neglected over time, which had survived on a garden wall near the sea, outside the city defences. In 1609 this, too, began to work miracles. The first to report that the picture was performing wonders was a poor midwife, who had habitually paused to pray before it as she travelled about her work. The second was a lad who collected eggs to sell in the market at Genoa, who early one morning saw a vision of the Virgin Mary in the sky above the fresco in the garden. These were figures who lived, in every sense, on the edge of Chiavarese society. On the basis of

---

[19] 'Vedi che la faccia della Beata Vergine si trasfigura? Allora il detto testimone rimirò in faccia della medesima Immagine, e vide che ella cangiavasi infatti, e che di diforme qual era facevasi bella, massimamente nelle labbra, le quale, sotto di lui veggente, divennero rubiconde, e la faccia del tutto nera e ricoperta di polvere, senza intervento di opera humana, fu reduta purificarsi da detta polvere e rendersi bella come è adesso'. *La trasfigurazione di Maria Santissima ossia veridico racconto delle di Lei maraviglie in una sua antichissima statua operate la quale si venera nella chiesa arcipresbiterale e plebana di S. Giovanni Battista in Cicagna sotto il titolo di Madonna de' Miracoli* (Genoa, 1872); R. Leveroni, *Cicagna: appunti di storia religiosa e civile* (Chiavari, 1912).

Fig. 4 'Nostra Signora dell'Orto' in Chiavari cathedral. Fresco, c.1500.

their experiences there very rapidly developed, in the summer of 1610, an enormous cult of the Madonna dell'Orto. Resistance to this development came, significantly, from the local authorities in both the secular and the spiritual spheres. The captain of Chiavari, the representative of the Genoese government, sneered at the activities in the garden from the height of the city wall. The archpriest of Lavagna, the mother church of Chiavari, denounced the cult as lacking archiepiscopal approval; and amongst other clerics who watched with jealous eyes was the parish priest of Chiavari's own senior church, which again (and for the same reason as at Cicagna) was dedicated to John the Baptist. Many features of the affair troubled the authorities. The gathering of huge crowds close to a strategic citadel of the Republic was seen as a security risk. The prominent role of women, both as proclaimed recipients of graces and as providers of hospitality for growing numbers of pilgrims, was felt to be improper. The organization by laity of paraliturgical rituals of litanies, exorcisms, and touching of the image, was identified as heretical. And the amazing social mixture of those who crowded into the garden to experience miraculous cures appeared to the conservatively minded to be perhaps the most disturbing aspect of all.

Not surprisingly, the cult at first suffered official condemnation, and was suppressed. But after a carefully constructed justification was presented both to the archbishop and to the Senate, and supported by sympathetic aristocrats, it gained legitimacy and the right to continue. The price was an element of official control, which arrived in the form of the Carmelitani Scalzi, the custodians from 1626 of the new church built, largely from popular subscriptions, to house the now famous image.[20] Yet even today, when that church has become so respectable as to be a cathedral in its own right, the miraculous picture on the high altar still offers to some individuals who frequent it an extraordinary immediacy of access to the divine. Because the splendour of the setting has created some physical distance between the old fresco and the modern pilgrim, printed versions attached to *prie-dieux* in various parts of the building enable the visitor to commune vicariously yet intimately with Nostra Signora dell'Orto. A lady enters the church, blows a kiss to one of these reproductions and waves a greeting to the Virgin. 'Ciao', she says.

The case of Chiavari also illustrates the ways in which, within a particular local society, particular political and neighbourhood identities could be expressed through competitive devotions to rival images. For in addition to the Madonna dell'Orto, Chiavari in the early seventeenth century saw the promotion of a rival cult of another miraculous painted Madonna in the mother church of San Giovanni. Meanwhile the adjacent and older town of Lavagna, to which Chiavari was technically subordinate, had since at least the fourteenth century promoted its own claims through the cult of a miraculous painted Madonna in a chapel at a bridge on the very boundary between the two settlements. And on the western approach roads to Chiavari, but outside the town's jurisdiction, two additional cults centred on images are documented from about 1500, respectively that of the Madonna of Bacezza and that of the Madonna delle Grazie. The former, though undocumented before the sixteenth century, was alleged to be of tenth-century origin – and hence the oldest known miraculous image of the Virgin in Liguria.

---

[20] For the principal sources see L. Sanguineti, *Nostra Signora dell'Orto. Storia documentata del suo santuario in Chiavari e dell diffusione del culto*, 2nd edn (Rapallo, 1955); R. Spiazzi, *Nostra Signora dell'Orto in Chiavari. Storia documentata della devozione e del santuario* (Rapallo, 1994). For fuller treatment of this and the other Chiavarese image cults noted below, see our forthcoming book.

The latter is a late-medieval carving of the Madonna and Child, located in a small religious house situated on the Via Aurelia and consequently passed by countless travellers passing between France or Genoa itself and the cities of Tuscany. The co-existence and at times competition between these various cults located within one very small area bear witness to the infinite potential for miraculous images to provide a focus for local interests and to challenge rival forms of authority.

The image cult, therefore, typically begins as a localist movement, directed by laity, with a prominent element of female participation. Thus far, it is the opposite of the centrally managed veneration of a saint's relics in a major church. Yet in a number of places authority has learned that, if it cannot effectively suppress the cult of miraculous images, it can usefully appropriate them. An example is the adoption by the Signoria of Florence, in the mid-fourteenth century, of the painted Madonna of Orsanmichele. This had begun as a simple image in a grainstore, which in about 1290, a time of great anxiety about food supplies, began to work miracles, particularly for the poor who prayed there. The picture soon became the centre of a booming cult, inviting the attention of the city's rulers. Their decision to ally the government with this hugely popular image led to the conversion of the grainstore into a civic chapel and to the formal declaration, in 1364, that the Madonna of Orsanmichele was the official Protector of the city of Florence. In moments of political crisis thereafter, Florence's political leaders could turn to this image in the knowledge that, to very many private citizens, this would seem the naturally right thing to do. Nor was this the sole instance of the Signoria's alliance with a picture. For throughout the fifteenth and early sixteenth centuries, another such image of the Virgin and Christ Child was quite frequently brought into the city from the nearby town of Impruneta, and set up in the central piazza to intercede, on the city's behalf, for rain, or peace.[21]

The leaders of church and government in Genoa, on the other hand, have never been quite so wholehearted in their embrace of a miraculous image. At the end of the sixteenth century a rare gesture of this kind was made, when the clergy of San Lorenzo acquired a painting of the Virgin, formerly in the monastery of Nostra Signora del Soccorso outside the Sant'Andrea gate of the city, which had an old reputation

---

[21] Trexler, *Public Life*, 69–72 (Orsanmichele Madonna), 353–8 (Madonna of Impruneta); idem, 'Florentine religious experience: the sacred image', *Studies in the Renaissance*, 19 (1972), 7–41.

for miraculous powers. We know of no efforts, however, to promote a cult of this picture in the cathedral before 1682, when a petition was successfully submitted to Rome for the right to crown the image.[22] In 1741 a Confraternity of Nostra Signora del Soccorso was founded; but it was typical that the heavy hand of official sponsorship hijacked this organization, which by the 1750s had been reduced to raising money to pay for the state galleys. In the mid-nineteenth century the first Società di Mutuo Soccorso, or workers' benefit society, was established in Genoa, with the joint name of St John the Baptist and Nostra Signora del Soccorso; but the linkage of relic and miraculous image in this case does not appear to have gone beyond the title. Although many Genoese would still today be able to point out Nostra Signora del Soccorso in the southeast chapel of San Lorenzo, the picture cannot be said ever to have enjoyed particular prominence amongst the other miraculous images of the city and its immediate environs.[23] Within the context of devotions in the cathedral, it may be that this picture has enjoyed most attention from women, precisely because of their exclusion from other cults. On a feast day held in 1913 in honour of Mary Queen of Genoa and Liguria, the chapel of John the Baptist in the cathedral was full of men and boys, while the women and girls were concentrated in the chapel of the miraculous image of Nostra Signora del Soccorso.[24]

The secular government of the city and Republic of Genoa has at all times preferred to leave the acquisition and management of miraculous images to others. It is true that the coronation of the Virgin as Queen of Genoa in 1637 aligned the state with an ancient popular cult of Mary.[25] There is, moreover, some indication that the official crowning of the Virgin in 1637 was stimulated in part by the example of a successful image cult at the church of Santa Maria delle Vigne, launched in 1603 by a priest who displayed for popular veneration a fourteenth-century painting of the Virgin and Child.[26] In 1616 a statue was carved for the

[22] M. Remondini, 'Esame critico di alcuni documenti riguardanti l'origine del culto di N.S. del Soccorso nella Metropolitana di Genova', *Giornale ligustico*, 13 (1886), 241–74.

[23] A. Pitto, *La Liguria mariana. I santuari di Genova* (Genoa, 1884), 29–31; G. Remondini, *Maria nella Metropolitana dei genovesi* (Genoa, 1878), 9; Genoa, Archivio di Stato, MS AS 1231, fol. 152 n. 23; ibid., MS 553, fol. 244.

[24] *La settimana religiosa*, 43 (22 June 1913), 292.

[25] N. Lanzi, *Genova città di Maria Santissima. Storia e documenti della pietà mariana genovese* (Pisa, 1992), 15, 42; P.R. Ravecca, 'Così Genova divenne "Città di Maria Santissima"', *Studi genuensi*, n.s. 8 (1990), 33–58; C. Di Fabio, 'Un'iconografia regia per la Repubblica di Genova. La "Madonna della Città" e il ruolo di Domenico Fiasella', in P. Donati, ed., *Domenico Fiasella* (Genoa, 1990), 61–84.

[26] A. Pollinari, *Narrazione cronologica dell'antichissima chiesa parrocchiale e collegiate di Sta.*

same chapel, and was for a time promoted by the clergy of Santa Maria delle Vigne as a miraculous civic image; at a popular level, this image enjoyed great success as a cult focus. But despite the creation of copies of this statue for a number of churches in the hinterland, the connection was developed no further by the Senate. As, over the years, particular and local claims were made on behalf of other images that they had protected the city miraculously in moments of great danger, senators were despatched on annual visits to render the government's thanks to, amongst other shrines, the Madonna del Monte, the Madonnetta, and also to the sindone of Christ – half relic, half image – at San Bartolomeo degli Armeni. But at the centre, the rational rulers of the Republic found no use for image cults. Their potentially integrative force was left untapped by the regime.

For Genoa, therefore, a distinction has persisted between the centralized, official cult of the relics of the Baptist, and a series of more popular and localist cults of miraculous images in many particular corners of the city and of the Genovesato. It would be wrong to insist too strongly on the difference in the past between authority and community. None the less, the distinction is a real one. The cult of the state has continued over long periods to exist in uneasy tension with local identity. Established authority has persistently tended to be male; community initiatives have very often been female-directed. The appropriate image of the Precursor of Christ, within the past life of Genoa, is perhaps rightly to be understood as a written, central, and absolute authority. Meanwhile the Virgin Mary, as she has been represented in cult images at Cicagna, Chiavari, Nostra Signora delle Vigne and SS Vittore e Carlo in Genoa, and many other places in Liguria, has been perceived as a visible, infinitely compassionate, universally accessible mediatrix and intercessor on behalf of a local, and perennially anxious, population. In the history of lay devotion, images have never been incidental, but have always been crucial to that sense of the accessibility, and even of the tangibility, of the divine. The word of authority and the image of compassion are not only the rhetorical polarities around which this paper has been structured. They represent real differences of cultural emphasis. So it would appear that miraculous image cults have much to reveal to us about the ways in which lay society and local communities shaped and expressed their identities in the past.

Maria delle Vigne, primiera esaltazione della statua di Nostra Signora, e sua incoronazione fatta solonnemente l'anno 1616 (Parma, 1718).

To many Protestant observers, as also to most of those who in modern times would define themselves as secularists, the idea that the sight of a picture of the Virgin Mary could transform an individual's psychological state, or could give political courage to an oppressed community, seems absurd, or distasteful, or mildly threatening. Yet it is a historical and social fact that just such faith in the potential power of certain Christian images has shaped and continues to shape the lives of thousands of people, not only in Italy, Spain, and Greece, but also in rural Mexico and uptown New York, in Soviet and post-Soviet Russia, and in the diverse Christian communities of the Near East. In Syria and the Lebanon, one may find miracle-working images of the Virgin Mary before which Christian and Muslim devotees pray alongside one another.[27] Remarkable as this example may seem in the context of less tolerant western Christianity, the case is just one more instance of the ways in which an image cult can at times subvert or transcend the cultural or hierarchical distinctions drawn by established authority, and can help to create new bonds of community.

Wadham College, Oxford
St Catherine's College, Oxford

---

[27] W. Dalrymple, *From the Holy Mountain. A Journey in the Shadow of Byzantium* (1997), 168–71, 188–91, 340–1; also B. Hamilton, 'Our Lady of Saidnaya: an Orthodox shrine revered by Muslims and Knights Templar at the time of the Crusades', *SCH*, 36 (2000), 207–15.

MOTHER MARY AND VICTORIAN PROTESTANTS

by CAROL MARIE ENGELHARDT

ONE of the defining characteristics of Victorian culture was its insistence that women were naturally maternal. Marriage and motherhood were assumed to be the twin goals of every young woman. Those who did not bear children were termed 'redundant' (perhaps most famously in W.R. Greg's 1862 article, 'Why are women redundant?'),[1] yet were still assumed to have maternal instincts.[2] Equally significant to Victorian culture was its Christianity. Notwithstanding the fact that only about half of the English and Welsh actually attended religious services,[3] the presence of an established Church, the frequency with which political and religious questions coincided, and the certainty that England was (as one clergyman confidently expressed it) illuminated by the 'very sun-shine of Protestantism',[4] combined to make Victorian culture Christian, and moreover, Protestant.

These two strains of Victorian culture would seem to collide in the figure of the Virgin Mary. She is a pivotal figure in Christian history because she is the mother of Jesus, while Catholics have derived from Jesus' assigning his mother and his favourite disciple into each other's care (John 19.25–7) their belief that she is also the mother of all believers. The apparent correlation between the Virgin Mary and the Victorian idealization of motherhood has led Sally Cunneen, in her impressive survey of representations of Mary, to argue that nineteenth-century Protestants exhibited a greater acceptance of the Virgin Mary: 'In part because Mary seemed so much like the Victorian ideal,

---

[1] *National Review*, 28 (April 1862), 434–60.
[2] Even women who, by joining an Anglican sisterhood, signalled their intention to remain celibate, were assumed to have innately maternal instincts. See Susan Mumm, *Stolen Daughters, Virgin Mothers: Anglican Sisterhoods in Victorian Britain* (London and New York, 1999), 111, 112.
[3] 'Census of Great Britain, 1851: Religious Worship, England and Wales', Parliamentary Papers, 1852–3, LXXXIX (89), cited in D.G. Paz, *Popular Anti-Catholicism in Mid-Victorian England* (Stanford, CA, 1992), 154.
[4] George Croly, *The Church of England, Founded on Scripture, and Essential to the Constitution. A Sermon preached at the Visitation of the Venerable the Archdeacon of London, William Hale Hale, A.M., May 3, 1853* (1853), 25.

especially because of her maternity, she began to receive a curiously positive reception among some distinguished Protestant writers.'[5]

Cunneen's assessment is based primarily on the writings of a few American Protestants; she cites only one Protestant – Anna Jameson – who actually was one of Victoria's subjects. Her conclusion is worth examining, however, because it is only the most recent scholarly claim that the Virgin Mary received greater approbation from nineteenth-century Protestants than she had from their forebears. Claudia Nelson has argued that in some of her many guises the Angel in the House could 'expand into a semisecular Virgin Mary',[6] repeating the earlier conclusion of Elizabeth Helsinger, Robin Lauterbach, and William Veeder Sheets that in the Victorian era 'the Anglo-American attitude toward Mary herself is generally positive',[7] and even that 'This self-effacing, Mary-like ideal remains a female standard for the rest of the era.'[8] This essay examines the attitudes of Victorian Protestants – who comprise Dissenters as well as Anglicans who considered their Church to be partly or entirely Protestant – towards the Virgin Mary. The paper particularly focuses on the argument that the Virgin Mary's maternal identity made Protestants more appreciative of her than they had been in the past, and so its conclusions have implications for the broader assertion that Protestants began to develop a more positive view of her in the nineteenth century.

* * *

Mary's first gospel appearance, at the Annunciation, inspired both Protestant and Catholic approbation. The Tractarian leader and Roman Catholic convert John Henry Newman's belief that at the Annunciation Mary had 'displayed especially four graces, humility, faith, obedience, and purity'[9] was seconded by the Methodist minister Thomas Jackson's certainty that 'In early life Mary was an example of deep piety.'[10]

---

[5] Sally Cunneen, *In Search of Mary: The Woman and the Symbol* (New York, 1996), 256.

[6] Claudia Nelson, *Boys Will be Girls: The Feminine Ethic and British Children's Fiction, 1857–1917* (New Brunswick, NJ, and London, 1991), 4.

[7] Elizabeth Helsinger, Robin Lauder Sheets, William Veeder, *The Woman Question: Society and Literature in Britain and America, 1837–1883*, 3 vols (New York, 1983), 2:195.

[8] Ibid., 196.

[9] J.H. Newman, 'Our Lady in the Gospel', in *Faith and Prejudice, and other Unpublished Sermons of Cardinal Newman* (New York, 1956), 89.

[10] Thomas Jackson, *A Warning against Popery: Being an Exposure of a Stealthy Attempt to Promote the Worship of the Virgin Mary, by the Erection of her Effigy beside the Church and School of my Native Village* (1867), 9.

Drawing on legends from the early Church and the Middle Ages, the Nonconformist minister Henry Hamlet Dobney elaborated on this theme, describing the young woman whom the angel encountered as one whose 'youth had been consecrated to God. Her mind was familiar with the high and holy themes on which the psalmists and prophets of Israel had loved to dwell, and she nourished her heart with the sublime hopes that they inspired.'[11]

However, when considering the period immediately following Jesus' conception, Protestant attitudes towards Mary became more negative. While Catholics celebrated Mary's pregnancy – the advanced Anglican priest Frederick George Lee was typical in acknowledging 'the womb of the pure and ever-virgin mother',[12] which Newman elevated to 'that tabernacle from which He took flesh'[13] – Protestants rarely even mentioned Jesus' gestation. The Anglican clergyman and future bishop, Samuel Wilberforce, one of the few who did, airily assured Queen Victoria and her court in an 1842 sermon, 'At length the months of waiting passed away, and the gracious birth was come.'[14]

Likewise, Catholics enjoyed meditating on the Virgin Mary's relationship with the infant Jesus. They imagined that the physical bond formed between Jesus and Mary during those nine months continued after his birth, that the baby once 'hidden within the womb of Mary'[15] now 'play[ed] with Mary's hair'[16] with 'those tiny hands'[17] and 'clasp[ed] Mary's neck/ In timid tight embrace'.[18] Filling in Scriptural silences, Catholics assumed that Jesus 'was nursed and tended by her; He was suckled by her; He lay in her arms'.[19] Drawing on the Catholic tradition of depicting a lactating Mary, Christina Rossetti first described the Virgin Mary, in her poem 'A Christmas Carol', as 'A breastful of milk'.[20]

[11] H.H. Dobney, *The Virgin Mary* (London and Maidstone, 1859), 4.

[12] Frederick George Lee, *The Truth as it is in Jesus: A Sermon Preached at the Church of S. Martin, Leicester, on Monday, March 2, 1868, at the Opening of the Lent Assizes* (1868), 3.

[13] Newman, 'Our Lady in the Gospel', 88–9.

[14] Samuel Wilberforce, 'The character of the Virgin Mary', in idem, *Four Sermons Preached before her Most Gracious Majesty, Queen Victoria in 1841 and 1842* (1842), 30.

[15] William Lockhart, *The Communion of Saints; or the Catholic Doctrine concerning our Relation to the Blessed Virgin, the Angels, and the Saints*, 2nd edn (n.d.), 51.

[16] 'The Infant Jesus', in F.W. Faber, *Jesus and Mary: or, Catholic Hymns* (1849), 21.

[17] Ibid.

[18] Ibid.

[19] J.H. Newman, 'On the fitness of the glories of Mary', in his *Discourses Addressed to Mixed Congregations* (1897), 362.

[20] Christina Rossetti, 'A Christmas Carol', l.19: *The Complete Poems of Christina Rossetti*, ed. R.W. Crump (Baton Rouge, LA, and London, 1979), 217.

Protestants, however, envisioned a reduced maternal role for Mary. The poet and non-denominational Protestant Elizabeth Barrett described the Virgin Mary in her poem, 'The Virgin Mary to the Child Jesus' as watching her baby sleep, a physical separation that signified her inferiority to this 'baby-browed/ And speechless being' (ll. 12–13). In direct contradiction of the Catholic insistence that Mary's humility elevated her above all other humans, the lowliness of Barrett's Mary was not to be redeemed: 'over Him my head is bowed/ As others bow before Him, still mine heart/ Bows lower than their knees' (ll. 76–82). Jesus, asleep and unresponsive, emphasised his mother's lack of status by not deigning to acknowledge her submission. The Protestant Mary was isolated and uncertain, unlike the joyful Catholic Mary.

* * *

Protestants were even more uncomfortable with the Virgin Mary in her maternal role when Jesus reached adulthood. They described her as a failure, both as a mother and as a believer, and therefore they sharply limited her role in Jesus' life and rejected it altogether in their own lives. Their attitude was in sharp contrast to the Catholic certainty that Mary was, as Jesus' mother, 'the only one whom Christ revered on earth' and 'His only natural superior'.[21]

Instead, Protestants said that Jesus repeatedly addressed Mary as 'Woman' rather than 'Mother'; an address the Anglican clergyman William Thomas Maudson described as, 'to say the least, politely distant',[22] and the Anglican divine George Miller as 'cold'.[23] Protestants generally marked the end of Mary's maternal authority with the beginning of Jesus' public life at the wedding at Cana where, Wilberforce declared, 'our Lord rejects her interference with His miraculous working'.[24] Dobney insisted that Jesus, even as he performed the miracle, 'intimated that the time was come when maternal influence over him must cease'.[25] This repeated a point Maudson had made a few years

---

[21] Birmingham, Oratory, Newman papers: John Henry Newman, 'The Annunciation of the Blessed Virgin Mary – on the honor due to her', *Course of Sermons and Lectures on Saints Days & Holidays*, No. 291. Preached at St Mary the Virgin [Oxford], Friday March 25, 1831, and Wednesday March 25, 1835; preached at St Mary's, Littlemore, Wednesday March 25, 1840 and Sat. March 25, 1842, p. 15.

[22] W.T. Maudson, 'The dogma of the Virgin Mary's Immaculate Conception: a sermon', *The Pulpit*, 67, no. 1,784 (8 March 1855), 233–40.

[23] George Miller, *A Letter to the Rev. E.B. Pusey, D.D., in Reference to his Letter to the Lord Bishop of Oxford* (1840), 62.

[24] S. Wilberforce, *Rome – Her new Dogma and our Duties* (London and Oxford, 1855), 2.

[25] Dobney, *The Virgin Mary*, 9.

earlier: 'When He entered on His official career, the filial connexion seems to have comparatively ceased. At any rate, whenever we find Him with His mother, it appears almost as though the association had been recorded for the very purpose of showing us how little control over him she possessed.'[26]

Protestants described Mary as increasingly obstreperous as her son matured. Though few went as far as the Nonconformist William Marshall in describing Mary as an ignorant and neglectful mother,[27] many believed that she was guilty of 'assuming too much authority over him'[28] and attempting to interfere in his mission.[29] Therefore, they approved of what Maudson described as Jesus' 'harsh and unduteous' response[30] to Mary at the Temple, and his responding 'with apparent indifference and contempt'[31] when Mary tried to interrupt his preaching. In sum, as the Anglican clergyman Francis Merewether said, 'The Virgin Mother received more than once from the lips of her blessed Son, during his earthly ministry, words savouring strongly of reproof.'[32]

Because they minimized Mary's maternal role on earth, these Protestants vehemently denied any suggestion that she retained that role in heaven, which they assumed would allow her to interfere with the divine work. The Anglican cleric William Ford Vance was horrified to think that Roman Catholics 'entreat her to exercise her influence and authority over God, as a mother over her son, that he may save your souls: *"Jure matris, imperâ Redemptori:"* By the right of a mother, command the Redeemer!!!'.[33] Nor did Protestants consider Mary to be the mother of all Christians: Jesus had assigned Mary to John's care, the novelist Catherine Sinclair said, only because she was 'a mere woman, . . . unable even to succour herself'.[34] In his novel *Yeast: A Problem*, the Anglican clergyman and author Charles Kingsley (a prominent anti-Catholic) mocked the belief that Mary was the mother of all as a sign of

---

[26] Maudson, 'Dogma', 238.

[27] W. Marshall, *Madonna or Mary?*, 2nd edn (1896), 28, 33–4.

[28] William Ford Vance, *On the Invocation of Angels, Saints, and the Virgin Mary: Two Sermons Preached at Tavistock Chapel, Drury Lane, in the Course of Lectures on the Points in Controversy between Roman Catholics and Protestants* (1828), 40.

[29] Maudson, 'Dogma', 238.

[30] Ibid.

[31] Ibid.

[32] Francis Merewether, *Popery a New Religion, Compared with that of Christ and His Apostles: a Sermon*, 3rd edn (London and Ashby-de-la-Zouch, 1836), 8.

[33] Vance, *Invocation*, 54 (emphasis as in original).

[34] Catherine Sinclair, *Popish Legends, or Bible Truths* (1852), xxxv.

weakness and effeminacy through the character of Luke, a recent convert to Roman Catholicism. Confessing to his cousin Lancelot, the novel's Protestant hero, that 'I am weak', Luke further admits, 'I am longing to be once more an infant on a mother's breast. . . . I am a weary child.' And therefore he has sought the comfort of the Virgin Mary:

> when I see a soft cradle lying open for me. . . . *[sic]* with a Virgin Mother's face smiling down all woman['s] love above it. . . . *[sic]* I long to crawl into it, and sleep awhile[.] I want loving, indulgent sympathy. . . . *[sic]* I want detailed, explicit guidance.[35]

The Protestant rejection of an eternal infancy was provided by Lancelot's declaration, 'I am not a child, but a man; I want not a mother to pet, but a man to rule me.'[36]

* * *

Mary's maternal identity did not, then, inspire a greater affection for her among Victorian Protestants, who described her as an interfering woman who would obstruct men's path to adulthood. The most obvious reason for Protestants' refusal to consider the Virgin Mary a model, and the only motivation they acknowledged, was their desire for orthodoxy: they did not want to worship the creature instead of the Creator. They said they were following Jesus' lead in this: Wilberforce argued that Jesus' harsh responses to Mary offered 'specific cautions against the rise of that superstitious reverence which has since defaced so large a part of Christendom';[37] while Vance agreed that Jesus' words and actions were motivated by his desire 'to avoid every thing likely to excite a feeling of undue veneration for her in the minds of his disciples'.[38] Sinclair said that Jesus addressed Mary as 'woman' rather than 'mother' in order to prevent Marian adoration: 'Our Divine Saviour in his last hour of suffering guarded against any mistake in respect to the reverence due to Mary by calling her, not "Mother," but "Woman" '.[39]

Their explanations were clear but not complete. I would suggest, not that they were trying to deceive either themselves or their audiences, but that they could not acknowledge that attacking Mary served interests other than the stated one of preventing the corruption of Chris-

---

[35] Charles Kingsley, *Yeast: A Problem* (1851), 86.
[36] Ibid., 282.
[37] Wilberforce, *Rome*, 2.
[38] Vance, *Invocation*, 40.
[39] Sinclair, *Popish Legends*.

tianity by worshipping a woman. Two facts suggest this conclusion. First, anti-Marianism had not previously been a significant aspect of Protestant culture in England; and second, it became a factor in an age which said that women were naturally maternal. This coincidence suggests that attacking the Virgin Mary was a way for Victorian Protestants to express their ambivalence about the idealization of motherhood. The Virgin Mary demonstrated the power potentially available to all mothers: it was Catholics' belief that she was the ideal mother that led them to praise her and claim her as their own mother. It seemed to Protestants that the virtuous mother could overshadow the men who claimed a monopoly on the public sphere. Therefore, attacking the Virgin Mary as a mother undermined the feminine ideal. Those with the motive and means to do this were primarily clergymen, whose authority was being eroded during the nineteenth century. They were joined by women like Barrett and Sinclair whose participation in the public sphere encouraged them to identify with men. They were also supported by their fellow Protestants, virtually none of whom volunteered to defend the Virgin Mary from these attacks.

Victorian religion was, at the official level, largely a masculine enterprise. In neither church nor chapel (with a few exceptions) could women preach or hold positions of authority; their role in religious assemblies as in the home was to support male authority. The ideal nineteenth-century clergyman was to be married,[40] which meant, as Mary Daly has pointed out, that the religious ideal for Protestant women was the minister's wife.[41] However, although Christianity overtly reinforced masculine authority, in the nineteenth century that authority was particularly open to challenge as religion was increasingly perceived as falling under the feminine sphere, thanks to the fact that the majority of worshippers were women and the widespread assumption that women were more spiritual than men. Clergymen were further removed from the mainstream masculine model by the two religious movements, at opposite ends of the spectrum, that occurred before Victoria ascended the throne. The Evangelical revival, which began in the second half of the eighteenth century, and the Oxford Movement both emphasised personal holiness and discouraged cler-

---

[40] Leonore Davidoff and Catherine Hall, *Family Fortunes: Men and Women of the English Middle Class, 1780–1850* (Chicago, IN, 1987), 122–3.

[41] Mary Daly, *Beyond God the Father: toward a Philosophy of Women's Liberation* (Boston, MA, 1974), 85.

gymen from pursuits that were typically masculine (at least for the educated and property-owning classes) such as riding, shooting and hunting, dancing, and gambling. Clergymen who were concerned about the erosion of their masculinity could find in Jesus' apparent rebukes of Mary evidence that the public sphere, and especially the religious sphere, was masculine.

However, identifying themselves with Jesus did not entirely solve the problem for clergymen; for Jesus bore little resemblance to the ideal Victorian man. '[T]he meek and lowly Jesus',[42] as an anonymous female writer described him at mid-century, was born into poverty, lived in relative obscurity, and died one of the most disgraceful deaths the Roman Empire could impose. He was a far cry from the ideal Victorian man who was supposed to strive and win, first on the playing fields and then in the brutally competitive marketplace, in the military, or in Parliament.

Jesus' apparent celibacy placed him further at odds with the masculine ideal. The importance of the family meant that life-long celibacy was not a Victorian value. This was clear in the accusations that priestly celibacy – which was voluntary for advanced Anglicans and mandatory for Roman Catholics – was unnatural. Kingsley condemned Roman Catholic priests as 'prurient celibates' and scorned celibate men as 'not God's ideal of a man, but an effeminate shaveling's ideal'.[43] The vast majority of Victorian Christians who rejected vowed celibacy had to acknowledge, however, that Jesus was apparently a celibate. There is no suggestion in Scripture that he had a wife or children, which in any case would have enormously complicated Christian theology, for it would have posited a race of semi-divine descendants.

Not just the person of Jesus, but his message as well undid the carefully crafted bipolar divisions between the sexes in Victorian culture. From the beginning, Christianity had claimed to overlook distinctions among believers. As Paul famously declared, 'There is no such thing as Jew and Greek, slave and freeman, male and female; for you are all one person in Christ Jesus' (Galatians 3:28). Christian virtues like faith, constancy, and charity were ungendered and urged on all believers. Christian reformers such as Josephine Butler and J.E.C. Welldon spread this message when they urged men to 'embrace feminine standards of

---

[42] A Lady, *The Contented Widow: a Narrative Illustrative of the Importance and Necessity of Church Extension* (Bristol, 1849), 3.
[43] Kingsley, letter dated 1 May 1849: BL, MS Add. 41298, fol. 46.

purity'.[44] Protestants like Dobney, who found Jesus to be 'the compassionate Redeemer'[45] and assured Victorians that artists generally 'assume a predominance of the feminine in him',[46] further undermined his ability to be a masculine role model. Therefore, describing Jesus as rejecting a role for his mother in his public life enabled Protestants to defend a world in which sons followed their fathers into the public world, while women were to stay behind. This reinforced the idea that religion, at least in its public pursuit, was a man's responsibility, and that even the virtuous mother could not interfere.

That Protestants' discomfort with the Virgin Mary as a mother reflected more widespread cultural anxieties is clear when we examine novels, which were both prime purveyors of the notion that marriage and motherhood was a woman's destiny and are remarkable for their callous elimination of parents, especially mothers. Main characters in Victorian fiction are often, like Jane Eyre and David Copperfield, orphans. In fact, pairs of orphans are surprisingly common: in Charles Dickens' *Great Expectations*, both Pip and Estella are orphans who are brought up by unsatisfactory surrogate mothers; and in George Eliot's *Adam Bede* the cousins Hetty Poyser and Dinah Morris are orphans, although they are luckier in their choice of guardians.

While older mothers are not, by any means, completely absent from Victorian novels, the number of mothers who either are dead before the novel begins or die during its course is striking, particularly given the fact that almost all the heroines are progressing towards the supposedly universal goal of motherhood. Certainly the lack of models for what Victorian heroines were to become reinforced the assumption that women were naturally maternal, yet a sub-plot of these novels seems to be that parents, and especially the allegedly beloved mother, must be eliminated in the progress towards adulthood. Catherine Hall and Leonore Davidoff have concluded that the absence of mothers in many Victorian novels suggests that the mother of older children could be problematic.[47]

Davidoff and Hall's conclusion is supported by Victorian Protestants' negative responses to the Virgin Mary as a mother. In addition, their responses reveal that the older mother was problematic because

---

[44] Nelson, *Boys will be Girls*, 76. See also Josephine Butler, *The Constitution Violated. An Essay [advocating the repeal of the Contagious Diseases Acts]* (Edinburgh, 1871), 91.

[45] Dobney, *The Virgin Mary*, 49.

[46] Ibid., 55.

[47] Davidoff and Hall, *Family Fortunes*, 347–8.

she seemed to threaten men's independence. Finally, the knowledge that Victorian Protestants did not believe the Virgin Mary was an ideal mother must cause us to re-examine the assertions that she was congruous with the Victorian feminine ideal.

Wright State University

MARY AND ROMAN CATHOLICISM IN
MID NINETEENTH-CENTURY ENGLAND:
THE POETRY OF EDWARD CASWALL

by NANCY M. DE FLON

IN her article on the nineteenth-century Marian revival, Barbara Corrado Pope examines the significance of Mary in the Roman Catholic confrontation with modernity.[1] 'As nineteenth-century Catholics increasingly saw themselves in a state of siege against the modern world, they turned to those symbols that promised comfort', she writes.[2] Inevitably the chief symbol was Mary, whom the 'patriarchal Catholic theology' of the time held up as embodying the 'good' feminine qualities of chastity, humility, and maternal forgiveness.[3] But there is another side to Mary that emerged as even more important and effective in the struggle against what many Catholics perceived as contemporary errors, and this was the militant figure embodied by the Immaculate Conception. The miraculous medal, an icon of Catherine Labouré's vision of the Virgin treading on a snake, popularized this concept. The crushing of the snake not only had a connection to the doctrine of the Immaculate Conception; it also symbolized victory over sin, particularly the sins of the modern world. 'Thus while the outstretched arms of the Immaculate Conception promised mercy to the faithful, the iconography of this most widely distributed of Marian images also projected a militant and defiant message that through Mary the Church would defeat its enemies'.[4]

The proclamation of this dogma by Pius IX in 1854 anticipated the Syllabus of Errors by ten years in allying the Church with anti-modernism by promulgating a 'truth' that could not be proved by science, history, or critical analysis.[5] Pius referred to the Virgin as the conqueror of all heresies who would ultimately also uproot the

---

[1] Barbara Corrado Pope, 'Immaculate and Powerful: the Marian revival in the nineteenth century', in Clarissa W. Atkinson, Constance H. Buchanan, and Margaret R. Miles, eds, *Immaculate and Powerful: the Female in Sacred Image and Social Reality*, Harvard Women's Studies in Religion Series (Boston, MA, 1985), 173–200.
[2] Ibid., 175.
[3] Ibid.
[4] Ibid., 177.
[5] Ibid., 181.

'dangerous error of Rationalism'; thus the enthusiasm that followed the proclamation 'manifested a hope, the ultimate and inevitable triumph of the universal Church' against both religious heresy and the errors of modern secular thought.[6]

In England belief in the Immaculate Conception was also associated with the expectation that the country would revert to Roman Catholicism. Catholics had been looking forward to this day ever since the Reformation, but never did the time for its fulfillment appear as ripe as it did in the mid nineteenth century, after the restoration of the hierarchy. That this event was linked with the Immaculate Conception was probably due to the country's historic devotion to Mary, and to English and Spanish monks' diligence in promoting belief in this doctrine.[7] At any rate, it was undoubtedly England's historic reputation as 'Our Lady's dowry' that caused anticipation of the country's return to the 'true faith' to be associated in a general way with Marian devotion. Frederick William Faber's hymn 'Faith of Our Fathers' anticipates that 'Mary's prayers // Shall win our country unto thee', while in John Henry Newman's 'The Pilgrim Queen' Mary promises:

> I am coming to rescue
>   my home and my reign
> And Peter and Philip
>   are close in my train.

Philip is St Philip Neri. Newman regarded the Oratorian mission to be a key instrument in the (re)evangelizing of England for Roman Catholicism.[8]

Newman's fellow Oratorian, the hymn writer Edward Caswall, utilized poetry to voice his Catholic compatriots' anticipation of the country's reconversion. He attributed to Mary a key role in bringing this event about and thus had much to say regarding the historic significance of Mary as protectress of the English Church. This paper investigates two of Caswall's major Marian poems, the verse drama 'A May Pageant', and 'The Easter Ship', in the light of contemporary English Catholic attitudes toward Mary's key role in the Church's restoration to its place as the religion of their country.[9]

---

[6] Ibid.

[7] Caswall had pointed out in his notes for his poem 'The Easter Ship', see below.

[8] See, e.g., Newman's 'Remarks on the Oratorian vocation (1856): rough draft', in Placid Murray, O.S.B., *Newman the Oratorian* (Dublin, 1969), 299–313.

[9] The original material used here survives unlisted and without call numbers among

'A May Pageant' underwent several revisions before it was published under this title in 1865.[10] The central drama concerns a vision of Mary experienced by the protagonist, a holy Franciscan priest named Euthanase (that is, 'happy death'). Caswall undoubtedly made him a Franciscan because of that Order's tradition of promoting belief in the Immaculate Conception.[11] Euthanase has been summoned to a cottage in the depths of an ancient wood known as 'Our Lady's Wood'[12] to attend a deathbed, but he arrives too late: the young maiden has died before Euthanase could give her the Viaticum.

The priest begins to return home but, overwhelmed with remorse, he falls on his knees and becomes

> . . . rapt at once in ecstasy of prayer.

While he is in this state he hears and sees a solemn procession approaching. One member of the throng, a youth named Theodore (that is, 'gift of God'), ferries him down the River Severn past several ruined monasteries to Tintern Abbey.[13] Here a ceremony of homage to Our Lady is held, in which the participants are denizens of the invisible world,[14] saints and angels who come to this hallowed spot each May for this purpose. When the pageant ends Theodore transports Euthanase back to our Lady's Wood, where his monastic brothers

> find their Father dead,
> The form indeed erect, the spirit fled!

'A May Pageant' affirms the truth-claims of the Roman Catholic

---

the Caswall papers in the Birmingham Oratory archives. Some of the notes are therefore unavoidably unspecific in their referencing.

[10] Edward Caswall, *A May Pageant and Other Poems* (1865). An earlier version, *L'Incoronata*, had been published in Birmingham in 1860. A revised version, *A Tale of Tintern*, was issued separately in London in 1873.

[11] Duns Scotus was the leading Franciscan proponent of this belief. Caswall copied from *The Rambler* of August 1850 (p. 119) a quote titled 'notices of English Franciscan writers'. It refers to the English Franciscans' 'constant defence of [Mary's] immaculate conception' and cites an order given in 1632 that after Compline the brethren were always to 'recite Tota pulchra etc. in honorem Immaculatae Conceptionis', along with the fact that in 1643 the convent at York was named after the Immaculate Conception.

[12] Coincidentally(?), the area of Birmingham immediately to the north of Edgbaston, where the Oratory is located, is called Ladywood.

[13] Tintern was founded in 1131 and dedicated to Mary. Cf. Sir William Dugdale, *Monasticon anglicanum*, 5 (1846), 265, from which Caswall has copied this information.

[14] The invisible world and its relation to the visible world was an important theological and poetic theme for Caswall throughout his life. His *Sermons on the Seen and Unseen* (1846) was the last book he published as an Anglican.

Church: the true catholic Church on English soil is the Church of Rome, which enjoys unbroken continuity with the apostolic Church. After suffering persecution in England for three centuries the Roman Catholic Church is destined to reclaim its rightful place, thereby restoring England to its traditional identity as 'Mary's dowry'. Mary in her role as the Immaculate Conception is powerful symbol of and catalyst for the Church of Rome's coming victory over religious heresy and modern secular errors, including rationalism and complete faith in scientific knowledge.

To prepare for 'A May Pageant' Caswall kept a notebook, juxtaposing pages of facts from historical tomes with phrases obviously jotted down in the course of walks through the Severn Valley countryside. Thus it contains a page on Buildwas Abbey taken from a *History of Shropshire*,[15] along with names and descriptive phrases of such natural phenomena as birds, flowers, landscape features, and words connected with water. Several of these have been incorporated verbatim into the poem. His purpose was to get a sense of the history and topography of the Severn and the districts through which it flows, because he intended to establish a definite sense of place by depicting a quintessentially English landscape. Indeed, it is specifically a landscape typical of the Welsh Marches. Caswall's family were originally from Glamorgan;[16] thus this region was sacred ground for the poet on a deeply personal level.

In an important sense, then, 'A May Pageant' represents the 'sacred space' genre of poetry. On a general level England is the sacred space that would soon return to the 'faith of its fathers'. More specifically the sacred space is Tintern Abbey, the eponymous site of Wordsworth's poem, to which 'A May Pageant' owes much inspiration.[17] In both poems Tintern is the site of encounter with transcendent reality. Caswall Catholicizes that encounter by making it an event in which the protagonist shares in a ritual of homage to Mary.

Caswall expands on the salient aspects of the overall theme of 'A May Pageant' in several ways, the first of which is his emphasis on the unbroken continuity between the Roman Catholic Church in England

---

[15] Caswall gives 'p. 870' but does not identify the book further.

[16] 'The family of Caswall . . . is said to have come from the county of Glamorgan and settled in the town of Leominster, county Hereford, as early as the 16th century': *Memoirs of the Caswall Family* (Privately printed, n.d.), 7.

[17] Caswall's subtitle for the poem, 'A Tale of Tintern', reflects the poem's Wordsworthian roots.

and the apostolic Church. This defies the Erastian notion that the valid Church in England started at the Reformation and upholds Mary's significance in the Roman Church. Caswall immediately establishes the connection between the present-day Church of Rome and the apostolic Church, and also identifies the early Church in Britain with the Roman Church as founded on Peter. The action opens in 'the Holy Virgin's Month of May', specifically on 'our great Augustin's Day', the feast of Augustine of Canterbury (May 27), sent to England by the Pope.[18] On their way to Tintern Euthanase and Theodore pass abbeys and other hallowed sites, the names of which recall England's monastic heritage and their Marian connections. These include 'ancient Shrewsbury', 'fair Bildas Abbey' where they stop to chant Mary's litany, and Evesham, famous for an eighth-century Marian apparition.[19] Through the procession Caswall reviews English Catholic history by naming important personages and alluding to their significance. It is led by 'two Princes' – Augustine of Canterbury and St Philip Neri, 'our Isle's new guest', who then shared the same feast day.[20] This was a happy coincidence for Oratorians, who regarded St Philip as the new Augustine under whose patronage they would be instrumental in reintroducing the ancient faith to England.

Second, Caswall stresses the persecuted status of the Roman Catholic

---

[18] In asserting the English Church's descent from Augustine Caswall rejects the claim that the true English Church – the Protestant Church – descends not from Peter but from a 'Pauline Church' that existed in Britain almost since the apostolic era. This view was espoused by Caswall's great-uncle Bishop Thomas Burgess. S.J. Barnett has shown that claims for the antiquity of the Protestant Church thrived into the eighteenth century: 'Where was your Church before Luther? Claims for the antiquity of Protestantism examined', *ChH*, 68, (1999), 14–41. Burgess not only continued the tradition into the nineteenth century, he also fashioned new bases for this claim which he set forth in a series of tracts. In 'An address to the Roman Catholics of the United Kingdom on their subjection to a foreign jurisdiction' he rejected papal supremacy as 'unfounded and unscriptural' by arguing that St Peter never enjoyed supremacy over the other apostles: Thomas Burgess, *Tracts on the Origin and Independence of the Ancient British Church; or the Supremacy of the Pope; and the Inconsistency of All Foreign Jurisdiction with the British Constitution; and on the Differences between the Churches of England and Rome*, 2nd edn, with additions (1815). Without mentioning Burgess by name, Caswall rejected this view in the journal he kept during the period leading up to his conversion to Rome in 1846–7, calling it 'childish and absurd': *Journal*, 204.

[19] According to the founder's charter of endowment, dated 714, St Egwin, third bishop of Worcester and founder of Evesham Abbey, and one of his herdsmen, Eoves, each had a vision of the Virgin Mary on the future site of Evesham Abbey. The Virgin commanded Egwin to build a monastery there in her honour. 'Evesham Abbey', in *The Catholic Encyclopedia*, ed. Charles G. Herbermann et al. (New York, 1909), 5:648, col. 1.

[20] St Philip Neri and St Augustine of Canterbury both died on 26 May, and St Philip's feast is celebrated on that date. However, St Augustine is commemorated on 27 May.

Church in England since the Reformation by drawing a parallel between the post-Reformation persecutions and the 'Egyptian bondage' of the Israelites. Each year Mary visits England and receives a report from St Michael on the status of every ruin – 'the sad memorials of a former day'. In the procession are the priest-martyrs who lost their lives during the days of 'false Elizabeth'.

A third strand is Caswall's voicing of the confident expectation that the Roman Catholic Church is destined to reclaim its rightful place, thereby re-establishing England as 'Mary's dowry'. Euthanase mourns that England still 'lingers in heresy', but he is optimistic: a 'work of grace' has begun and is proceeding. Theodore too expresses a wistful hope for England's return to Rome: amid the discords of the present time he catches

> a tone sublime
> That seems the prelude of a better time!

To the saints he addresses a fervent plea:

> And you, dear Saints, forgive the long delay,
> Nor cease for your loved Albion to pray,
> Till every hill and vale, from shore to shore,
> Rings with the Angelus it heard of yore!

Among Roman Catholics in England the expectation of the country's conversion was bound up with a general belief in their Church's victory over religious heresy and modern secular errors. Mary in her role as the Immaculate Conception was a powerful symbol of and catalyst for these events. It was thanks to the prayers of Mary that the Roman Catholic Church in England, its hierarchy recently restored by 'Immortal Pius',[21]

> again uprose
> In order bright confronting all its foes,
> With serried ranks and every flag unfurl'd,
> Boldly confess'd before a trembling world.

The whole purpose of this festival is to celebrate the solemnity of the Immaculate Conception. Every May in Tintern 'the Saints of Britain's Isle' 'hold festival'

---

[21] This had occurred in 1850.

In her Immaculate Conception's praise,
The late-defined Belief of earlier days.

Here the poem establishes not only the key position of this dogma but also a connection from the present to the early Church: although the dogma had only recently been formally defined, belief in it was not something new but could be traced back to earlier centuries.[22]

An unusual symbol of the Church's history is provided by the prominent place accorded in the procession to Ananias, Azarias, and Misael, who were thrown into the fiery furnace in the Book of Daniel. They are singing their great hymn the *Benedicite*. Described as

> entoned of yore
> On Dura's plain by old Euphrates' shore,
> And since in Holy Church reëchoed on
> The breath of rolling centuries along

the great canticle is

> No more array'd, as when it first was sung
> In pomp of Hebrew or Chaldean tongue,
> but gravely flowing forth in accents clear
> Of limpid Latin on the listening ear.

Thus it manifests continuity from Old Testament times to the present-day Church, which now sings it in

> Latin, blest tongue in which the Faith is shrined ...

The three young men are significant not only as authors of this canticle, but because they refused to

> bend down adoring knee
> In homage of a vain idolatry.

Thus they are figures with whom contemporary Roman Catholics could identify as well as types of their ancestors who risked their lives in the Reformation for bearing witness to the truth. Caswall would have had in mind the rejection not only of religious heresy but also of

---

[22] In the notes he compiled for 'A May Pageant' and 'An Easter Ship' Caswall comments that Protestants would 'be surprized [*sic*] to find ... from how very early a period [the doctrine of the Immaculate Conception] has been, as at present understood, the constant belief of the Church anterior to any dogmatic definition': Birmingham, Oratory archives, Caswall Files, loose notes in a box of miscellaneous poetry MSS [hereafter 'Box P'].

modern secular errors: he had earlier used the *Benedicite* canticle as a means of confronting the dangers of modern thought, in a prose work based on it,[23] and by which he hoped to prevent a mechanistic view of creation from stamping itself on the minds of young people.

Thus Daniel's companions join the communion of Christian saints in affirming the worth of eternal religious truth against modern secular thought. But above all it is Mary who leads Church militant and Church triumphant toward this victory. At the climax of the great festival St Edward the Confessor presents to Mary 'the Sceptre of our Isle' in anticipation of the 'happy days to come', when she will once more rule as defender of the hierarchy and crusher of heresy.

Caswall's 'The Easter Ship' also stands squarely in the tradition of the prophecy or expectation that England would be restored to the Roman Catholic faith. In his notes for this poem, which indicate that he began work on it shortly after Pius IX had defined the dogma of the Immaculate Conception,[24] Caswall recounts a vision experienced by the sixteenth-century Spanish mystic Venerable Marina de Escobar, that England would lie in the grip of 'heresy' for three centuries, after which a pope would proclaim the dogma of the Immaculate Conception and Mary, in gratitude, would restore England to the 'true faith'.[25]

'The Easter Ship' was originally conceived as a grandiose work that would have featured the poem supplemented by immensely detailed explanatory notes and by illustrations.[26] Caswall consulted history books, religious works, poetry collections, and miscellaneous sources, intending to reproduce relevant excerpts from these works, along with his own comments, as notes illuminating selected verses in his poem. By demonstrating the antiquity of Roman Catholicism in the British Isles, the work would show it to be deeply rooted in British culture and thus refute claims that Roman Catholicism was a foreign element in England.

Caswall's material included historical, cultural, and religious sources. He demonstrates how vestiges of England's intense devotion to Mary

---

[23] *The Young Churchman's Book of All Creation* (Birmingham Oratory archives).

[24] In his notes compiled for 'An Easter Ship' Caswall refers to and quotes from the encyclical of proclamation 'which appeared last year': Birmingham, Oratory archives, Caswall Files, Box P.

[25] The visions of Marina de Escobar (1554–1633) fill many volumes and were written down by her spiritual guide, Ven. Luis de Ponte (1554–1624). They were translated into German in 1861. Caswall mentions a translation by 'Wordsworth' of the vision in question.

[26] Caswall's extant material includes his own sketches along with several signed 'MRG' – Newman's friend Maria Giberne: Birmingham, Oratory archives, Caswall Files, Box P.

survive as folk customs and culture, most strikingly in old ballad poetry and carols. From various collections of carols he copied out various texts that celebrate Mary's motherhood of Christ. One of them is a version of 'I saw three ships come sailing in'. Even culinary matters of a Marian nature did not escape Caswall's attention: he describes a ginger-bread cookie found at cake stalls at fairs in the north of England in the 'shape of a gilt crowned Lady with an excrescence on one side'. This represents the Virgin and her Child. 'How divine must be the Faith which could thus stamp itself for ever on so perishable and worthless a substance!'

For the benefit of Protestant readers Caswall provided a theological explanation of and history of belief in the dogma of the Immaculate Conception, and explained how the eventual reclamation of England for Roman Catholicism to which the current 'Catholic movement' was surely leading had been predicted for two centuries.

In the end Caswall abandoned this ambitious project and instead published the poem, minus the explanatory apparatus, in his collected works.[27] He originally titled it 'The Vision and Prophecy of the Hermit of Finisterre'. The definitive title 'The Easter Ship' highlights the rich ecclesiastical symbolism of the ship as the Church,[28] in conjunction with the resurrection motif pertaining to England's rescue from

> The black Satanic deep
> Of heresy's awful flood.

The Hermit occurs in writings of this period and is perhaps a mani-festation of the then current fascination with things medieval.[29] In 'The Easter Ship' he is the 'last of Tintern's exil'd sons', a Cistercian monk forced to flee from England when Henry VIII dissolved the monas-teries. 'In the reign of Queen Elizabeth' he has a vision 'concerning the Immaculate Conception and the Restoration of England to the Cath-

---

[27] In *The Masque of Mary* (1858) it appears between 'A Masque of Angels' and 'St Kenelm's Well'.

[28] Caswall's notes include source material on the ship as symbol of the Church (see n. 30); he indicates that in this context it is to be interpreted as the Catholic Church in England (Birmingham, Oratory archives, Caswall Files, Box P). Margaret Johnson refers to Tractarian use of the ship 'as an image of spiritual journeying': *Gerard Manley Hopkins and Tractarian Poetry* (Aldershot and Brookfield, VT, 1997), 209.

[29] A Hermit plays a key role in Part VII of Coleridge's 'Rime of the Ancient Mariner'. 'The Minster of Eld' is another Caswall poem with a hermit as a key person. The mysterious Stranger from the Middle Ages who appears in Faber's *Sights and Thoughts in Foreign Churches* (1842) is probably a version of this personage.

olic Faith', and it is this vision that supplies the main theme of Caswall's poem. One Easter morning the Hermit sees

> . . . a Ship in the misty dawn
> Becalm'd on the silent sea;
> Her sails all drooping – her helm unwatch'd –
> As though no crew had she!

A deadly storm 'from Satan's breath' quickly blows up and sinks the ship. Soon nothing of it is visible except

> The topmost spar! – whence gallantly still,
> In the face of the storm unfurl'd,
> Old England's Catholic ensign wav'd, –
> The Cross that rules the world!

Scarcely has the cross touched the waters when the ship begins gradually to rise again, whereupon it steers 'for England's shore'. The Hermit now sees that the ship's crew consists of England's native saints and that Mary, once beloved in the British Isles, is at the helm. This image of Mary at the helm of a ship is not without precedent. Commenting on some material on the ecclesiastical symbolism of the ship which states that St Peter is usually at the helm,[30] Caswall notes that the Blessed Virgin and Child are sometimes found instead. As an example he gives a reproduction of the coat of the arms of the city of Leith as printed on the masthead of the *Leith Commercial List*.[31]

The Hermit's vision inspires him to utter a prophecy: For three centuries the Catholic Church will languish in England, reduced to virtual lifelessness. In the fourth century, however, a pope will formally define the dogma of the Immaculate Conception and Our Lady, in gratitude, will 'restore . . . the Isle of the Saints' to the true faith. The abbeys and other 'long desecrated shrines' will be restored to their former glory and the true Roman worship will once more take its rightful place.

The 'Easter Ship' is obviously a nautical version of 'A May Pageant', incorporating the same themes but organizing them around the central

---

[30] Giovanni Perrone, *Praelectiones theologicae*, 2nd edn, 9 vols (Rome, 1840–4), 9: 316.

[31] Among Caswall's material for 'An Easter Ship' is the original masthead, cut from the actual newspaper. 'A singular homage this, paid by a maritime port of Protestant but once Catholic Scotland to her who is emphatically named the Star of the Sea!' is his comment in his prose explanatory notes originally intended to accompany the poem: Birmingham, Oratory archives, Caswall Files, Box P.

image of the ship – a clear symbol, in this context, of the barque of Peter – and indeed an *Easter* ship, one that typifies the resurrection of the English Catholic Church from the grave of oppression.

Commenting on the carol texts he had reproduced in his notes and on 'the fact that the books whence they are taken are in constant sale among the poor', Caswall asserted that

> it is apparent that a Catholic literary element of no small influence still survives in this country, especially as regards the Blessed Virgin, and it cannot be doubted but a day will come, when in the providence of God this element will be turned to account in the reconversion of [the English people] to the Faith of their Fathers.

Thus, not only the poems themselves but also the source material painstakingly copied out and never directly used reveal Caswall's conviction that England's coming conversion would not be to something new and unfamiliar, but would truly represent a return to something deeply embedded in the English psyche. That 'something' was a deep affection for and devotion to Mary Immaculate, mother of God.

Diocese of Ogdensburg, New York

THE IMMACULATE HEART OF MARY: VISIONS FOR THE WORLD

by SARAH JANE BOSS

IN the Catholic Church throughout the world, the cult of the Immaculate Heart of Mary is one of the most widespread forms of modern Marian devotion, expressing a dominant mood within contemporary Catholicism.[1] For its devotees, the heart of Mary is almost literally 'the heart of a heartless world', and indeed, the image of the world – the globe of the Earth – is central to the cult.

In Amsterdam, between 1945 and 1959, a woman called Ida Peerdeman had a series of visions of the Virgin Mary. The Virgin revealed herself standing on the globe of the world, immediately in front of a cross, and she identified herself as the Lady of All Nations. Drawing upon traditional Christian imagery of the shepherd and his flock, the people of the nations were represented by a large flock of sheep around the globe [Fig. 1]. During these apparitions, the Lady of All Nations prophesied that the pope would proclaim the dogma that she – the Virgin Mary – is Co-Redemptrix, Mediatrix of All Graces and Advocate of the Faithful People. This, she said, would be the final Marian dogma.[2]

In the 1990s an American Catholic theologian, Mark Miravalle, of the Franciscan University at Steubenville, Ohio, took up the cause of promoting the definition of this final dogma. Miravalle has associated this cause with a prophecy from another series of apparitions of the Virgin Mary in the twentieth century – that of Our Lady of Fatima, in Portugal. At Fatima, Our Lady is reported to have predicted a period of warfare and destruction across the world, if people did not repent and make reparation for sin. But she concluded by saying, 'In the end, my Immaculate Heart will triumph.' According to Miravalle, the triumph of Mary's Immaculate Heart is the pouring out of God's mercy upon the whole world. But for this to be effective, the world must be willing to receive the mercy which God offers; and since the pope is the

---

[1] Very little has been written on the subject of the cult of the Heart of Mary. The only published article I have found devoted entirely to the subject is J. Arragain, 'La Dévotion au Cœur de Marie', in Hubert du Manoir, ed., *Maria: Études sur la Sainte Vierge*, 5 (Paris, 1958), 1007–48.

[2] Roy Abraham Varghese, *God-Sent: a History of the Accredited Apparitions of Mary* (New York, 2000), 149–63.

Fig. 1   The Lady of All Nations (from a prayer card)

universal pontiff, it is he who can make that gesture on the world's
behalf. More specifically, what is required of him is the definition of the
final Marian dogma, since it is through Mary's co-operation, mediation,
and advocacy that Christ's mercy is dispensed to humanity.[3]

   Along with the image of the globe, the language of totality and
finality are typical of the cult of the Immaculate Heart of Mary in
Europe and North America. In much current devotion, strongly influenced by Fatima, the globe is seen as a site of conflict, where the forces
of evil attack the forces of good, symbolized by and embodied in the

[3]   Mark Miravalle, 'In battle array with the Co-Redemptrix', in Mark Miravalle, ed.,
Contemporary Insights on a Fifth Marian Dogma (Goleta, CA, 2000), 39–50.

Immaculate Heart. The forces of evil are identified as the forces of secularization, whilst the forces of good operate in the pope and so-called 'conservative' groups within the Catholic Church.

The argument of this paper is that promoters of Immaculate Heart devotion in Europe and North America have generally adopted a rhetoric of opposition to the secular world: rather than seeking a reconciliation or an alliance between religion and science or Church and state, they claim to seek the subordination of the latter to the former. In practice, however, the cult of the Immaculate Heart has often not only served to maintain the separation of these different spheres of human culture, but has also generally failed to present any effective challenge or opposition to the secular forces that it sees as its enemy. Yet, at the same time, there is a somewhat older strand of devotion to the Heart of Mary – one that dates back at least to the seventeenth century – which runs as a barely visible thread through the fabric of the later devotion. This older strand is also concerned with matters universal, but considers them in terms of peace, rather than conflict. Where more recent devotion focuses on the end of time and the Apocalypse, the older devotion is concerned with God's work of creation. If 'conservative' Catholics are serious about forming a critique of contemporary culture, then, it is suggested here, they could do worse than to allow this submerged strand to make a dominant contribution to the pattern and colour of Immaculate Heart devotion.

* * *

This more ancient devotion was expounded by the religious founder St John Eudes (1601–80), whose *The Admirable Heart of Mary* was published in the year of his death. He had previously published a book on *The Sacred Heart of Jesus*, and devotion to Jesus and Mary together, and in particular to their hearts, was central to his teaching. The English translation of *The Admirable Heart* was published in the United States in 1948, and includes a *Foreword* by the then Archbishop of Boston, Richard J. Cushing. Cushing writes:

> We live in times full of danger for the Church. Her enemies have rarely in history been so numerous or so organized. Her property is the object of avaricious designs; her prelates are increasingly under attack; her organization, resented by those who hate her, daily encounters fresh opposition and malicious interference.[4]

---

[4] Richard J. Cushing, 'Foreword', in St John Eudes (trans. Charles di Targiani and Ruth Hauser), *The Admirable Heart of Mary* (New York, 1948), vii–viii.

This language of being under siege is fairly typical of much twenti-eth-century devotion to the Heart of Mary, but, as we shall see, it in no way echoes the writing of Jean Eudes himself, who speaks in entirely positive terms about the mystical reality of Mary's heart and the bene-fits of devotion to it.

In art, the image of the heart had for several centuries been employed to stand for Mary's soul. Luke 2.35 recounts that at the time of Mary's purification, Simeon prophesied that a sword would pierce Mary's soul; and that motif was, and is, found in art in the form of a heart pierced by a sword. The soul and the heart each stand for the whole person, and this is the sense in which Jean Eudes writes of the Heart of Mary. But although the heart of Mary had been represented and written about in earlier centuries, it had not previously been an object of devotion. That was something new in the seventeenth century, and seems to be modeled in part upon devotion to the Sacred Heart of Jesus, which was already well established, being directed towards a deeper appreciation of the Incarnation.[5]

Eudes begins his work with chapters on Mary's heart under three main headings: her 'corporeal heart', her 'spiritual heart', and her 'divine heart'. The corporeal heart, he says, is not only the principle of her own earthly life, but also produced the blood of which Christ's body was formed. It is the source of the material life of Christ in the womb.[6] The spiritual heart is the noblest portion of the soul; it is made in the image of God, and by grace is able to participate in the divine nature.[7] In Mary, that image is untarnished, and the participation, or divinization, is as full as possible. And finally, the divine heart is that aspect of Mary which is concerned directly with her divine mother-hood – with the fact that she is the Mother of God. Christ, says Eudes, is the heart of God the Father, and he is also the Heart of his earthly mother. That is to say, the Word of God is not only the Son of both God the Father and the human Mary, but is also the Heart of both. He lives in every part of her, both physical and spiritual.[8] The divine Heart therefore ties Mary immediately to the life of the Blessed Trinity.

Now, one aspect of what Eudes is telling us in this is that the Heart

[5] For example, the sixteenth-century spiritual writer Lanspergius encouraged devotion to the Heart of Jesus. A quotation illustrating this is given in James Brodrick, *Saint Peter Canisius* (1938), 16.

[6] Eudes, *Admirable Heart*, 14.

[7] Ibid., 19–20.

[8] Ibid., 24.

of the Virgin Mary is a microcosm of the universe. He outlines an Aristotelian account of the three parts of the human soul: 'the vegetative soul, which is similar in nature to that of plants, . . . the sensitive life, which we have in common with animals . . . [and] the intellectual life, like that of angels'.[9] This is already an account of the human person – any human person – as a microcosm which bears the three orders of life. In the case of Mary, however, not only does her heart embody these three modes of life in a state of perfection, but that heart is also a microcosm of the whole inanimate universe. For example, her heart corresponds to the heavens, because God went forth from Heaven to dwell in his mother's heart, so that it too became a heaven.[10] Yet more significant than this is the claim that Mary's heart corresponds to the sun. Eudes writes:

> The infinite power of God has divided this great universe into three different states or orders, namely, the state of nature, the state of grace and the state of glory. . . . whatever is in the order of nature is an image of the things belonging to the order of grace, and whatever belongs to the order of nature and grace is a figure of what is to be seen in the state of glory. Hence, the sun, which is truly the heart of the visible world, and the most beautiful and glowing gem of nature, gives us only a very faint shadow of our heavenly Sun, the Heart of the Mother of God.[11]

Drawing on an ancient identification between the heart and the sun, Eudes contends that as the sun is the source of life for the earth, so the heart is the source of life for the human body, and Mary's heart for the world which is redeemed in her son. And it is not Mary who is a reflection of creation, but creation which is a reflection of Mary.[12] Thus, the first earth, from which Adam was made, is an imperfect image of the second earth, who is Mary, from whom Christ was made. Correspondingly, then, other aspects of creation are images of Mary's glory or virtues. The mountains of the earth, for example, in their prominence reflect the 'perfections of the Sovereign Lady of the Universe'.[13]

[9] Ibid., 19.

[10] Ibid., 34–5.

[11] Ibid., 38. Elsewhere Eudes writes of Christ as the sun, and Mary's heart as the mirror which reflects it (e.g., 105–11).

[12] This general line of thought is not unique to John Eudes. The Mexican nun, Sor Juana Inés de la Cruz (1648–95), makes similar connections between Mary and creation. See Pamela Kirk, *Sor Juana Inés de la Cruz: Religion, Art, and Feminism* (New York, 1999), 60–5.

[13] Eudes, *Admirable Heart*, 42–3.

Mary's heart also corresponds to the fountain of Genesis 2.6, which waters the earth; it is a 'fountain of light', because Christ, who is the Sun, is the fruit of Mary's heart.[14] The sea, which was formed on the third day of creation, is a figure for the vastness of Mary's purity and miracles.[15] And the Garden of Eden, the paradise of the first Adam, is of course a portrayal of the paradise of the second Adam, which is the Heart of Mary.[16] Eudes then enjoins the reader: imitate Mary and make your own heart a paradise of delights.[17]

So Jean Eudes understands the human person to be a figure that corresponds to the whole order of creation, and the Heart of Mary to be, as it were, the perfection of the microcosm and the archetype of the macrocosm: creation in the state of glory. In her, furthermore, God is fully united to creation, and the purpose of devotion to the Admirable Heart is articulated in words such as the following: 'I would have you realize, dear Reader, that Our Lord Jesus Christ, who is the Heart of the Eternal Father, willed to become the Heart or life-principle of His Most Blessed Mother, and He likewise wills to become the Heart of your own life.'[18]

Now, in 1680, this way of viewing the human person and the cosmos was soon to become distinctly old-fashioned. Writing of seventeenth-century science, the historian Amos Funkenstein says:

> No longer were natural phenomena to symbolize and reflect each other and that which is beyond them; the symbolic-allegorical perception of nature as a network of mutual references was discarded as a source for protracted equivocation. The image, say, of man as a microcosm that reflects and embodies the macrocosm lost much of its immediate heuristic force. Things ceased to refer to each other intrinsically, by virtue of their 'participation in' and 'imitation' of each other. Only language was henceforth to refer to things and to constellations of things in a system of artificial, univocal *signs*, such as mathematics.[19]

---

[14] Ibid., 47–8.
[15] Ibid., 55.
[16] Ibid., 60.
[17] Ibid., 68.
[18] Ibid., 27. 'The Admirable Heart of Mary is the perfect image of the most divine Heart of Jesus. It is the pattern and model for our own hearts; and all our happiness, perfection and glory consists in striving to transform them into so many living images of the sacred Heart of Mary, just as her holy Heart is a consummate likeness of the adorable Heart of Jesus' (ibid., 265).
[19] Amos Funkenstein, *Theology and the Scientific Imagination from the Middle Ages to the Seventeenth Century* (Princeton, NJ, 1986), 28.

The French sociologist David Le Breton has argued that medieval conceptions of the human body as mirroring or participating in other aspects of the created order were falling into decline in the early modern period as an aspect of the growth of individualism. People were now judged to be separate both from one another and from other aspects of the natural world.[20] It is not surprising, then, that Jean Eudes' splendid cosmic vision is not referred to in later devotion to the Heart of Mary, although we shall see that there may be some unacknowledged echoes of it.

With regard to the development of modern ideas about the human heart in particular, Milad Doueihi has pointed out that whereas writers of earlier centuries could compare Christ to the sun, which is at the centre of the planets, and also to the heart, which in its functions is at the centre of the human body, during the seventeenth century the notion of the heart's centrality was being challenged by the increasing attribution of importance to the role of the brain in the functioning of the human body.[21] A great deal of more recent devotion to the Heart of Mary has continued to assert the overwhelming importance of that which the heart has come to symbolize, and it is often set in opposition to 'head' functions such as rationality. But most mainstream Catholics are more likely to say, 'If Rome is the head of the Church, then Lourdes is its heart', thus indicating a certain acquiescence to the notion that there is more than one major organ maintaining bodily life, and that the heart has been displaced from its central position.

A further respect in which Jean Eudes' understanding of the significance of Mary's heart has been supplanted by more modern ideas can be seen by comparing *The Admirable Heart of Mary* with a twentieth-century French work on the same subject, namely, Jean Galot's *Le Coeur de Marie*, published in 1955. The chapter headings of the work make it appear that it might be rather similar to sections of Jean Eudes' book. For example, Galot's book has chapters on the three theological virtues – faith, hope, and charity – as they are found in the heart of the Virgin. And Eudes likewise provides meditations on the various virtues that reside there. But for Eudes, the point about the perfection of virtues in Mary's heart is an entirely spiritual one, in a theological sense of the word 'spiritual'. That is to say, he is concerned with the state of Mary's

[20] David Le Breton, *Anthropologie du corps et modernité* (Paris, 1990).
[21] Milad Doueihi, *A Perverse History of the Human Heart* (Cambridge, MA, and London, 1997), 126–8.

soul before God, and he writes about her virtues in symbolic language. For Galot, on the other hand, the virtues of Mary's heart are explicitly located in her mental and emotional life, and so he imagines how she would have felt and what she would have thought on particular occasions. Indeed, the opening sentence of Galot's book says, 'To describe the heart of the Virgin is a difficult thing to do, because the Gospel offers few indications about the intimate feelings of the Mother of God.' And the second paragraph begins: 'To know the thoughts and affections of the Virgin, we can . . . base ourselves broadly on the Old Testament, which reveals to us the cultural outlook within which Mary's religious education took place.'[22]

For Jean Eudes, Mary is a theological, not a psychological, figure. She is the Mother of God, and knowing that tells us pretty well all that we need to know in order to deduce information about the spiritual condition of her heart. For Jean Galot, by contrast, Mary is a historical and psychological figure, and knowledge of her heart is knowledge of her mental and emotional state.

So key aspects of Jean Eudes' thought have been abandoned in the subsequent development of devotion to the Heart of Mary. Yet his influence has perhaps continued in more subtle ways; and indeed, *The Admirable Heart of Mary* can be used to some extent as a manual to make sense of certain aspects of the more recent cult of the Immaculate Heart.

* * *

Eudes employs a large number of adjectives to describe Mary's heart: admirable, lovable, holy, sacred, and immaculate, for example; and the term 'Sacred Heart of Mary' was common in the late eighteenth and early nineteenth centuries. But in the middle decades of the nineteenth century, the cult of Mary's heart came to use the adjective 'immaculate' almost exclusively. There were probably a number of different factors influencing this. One, for instance, may have been the development of the cult of Our Lady of the Sacred Heart.[23] This was a devotion which focused upon Mary in relation to the Sacred Heart of Jesus; and it is easy to see that a confusion could have arisen between the Sacred Heart of Mary and Our Lady of the Sacred Heart, so that the use of a term rarely applied to the Heart of Jesus, namely, 'immaculate', would make

---

[22] Jean Galot, SJ, *Le Cœur de Marie* (Paris, 1955), 7.
[23] Jules Chevalier, *Notre-Dame du Sacré-Cœur* (Paris, 1895).

for ease of comprehension. The most important influence on the choice of the term 'immaculate', however, was certainly the campaign for a papal definition of the dogma of the Immaculate Conception and the Holy See's promulgation of that dogma in 1854. The Immaculate Conception is the doctrine that Mary was conceived without original sin in the womb of her mother, traditionally known as St Anne; and by the early nineteenth century the doctrine was almost universally accepted as a part of Catholic belief. Once the adjective 'immaculate' became ubiquitous in devotion to the Heart of Mary, the notion of her immaculacy – her spotlessness and moral purity – became almost as important within the cult as was the idea of the Heart itself. The association between devotion to Mary's heart and the doctrine of her immaculate conception can be seen already in the vision of the Miraculous Medal in 1830.

At this point, it is helpful to turn to visual imagery to understand how the cult of Mary's heart was developing, and to see what influences there were on the iconography of the Miraculous Medal.

A very early representation of the Immaculate Heart comes from a book printed in France in 1746, and shows an anatomically exact human heart, pierced by the sword, and surrounded by heavenly light and angels [Fig. 2]. The book in which it appears is a work on the subject of devotion to the Sacred Heart of Jesus, so although the image shows Mary's heart alone, its context ties it to devotion to the Heart of Christ. In this image, science and religion seem to be happily united, the anatomical drawing providing the focus for religious devotion. This, however, is entirely exceptional. A more common association of Mary with the image of the heart is found in the custom of giving stylized hearts, made of precious metals, as ex-voto offerings at Marian shrines.

Yet at least as important for understanding the cult of the Immaculate Heart as images of the Heart itself is the modern iconography of the Immaculate Conception, of which Diego Velázquez's *Virgin of the Immaculate Conception* is a particularly fine example [Fig. 3]. This iconography for the Immaculate Conception was developed by Spanish painters of the fifteenth and sixteenth centuries,[24] as part of the campaign for the papal definition of the dogma. The image spread rapidly, being widely used in Jesuit churches, and also in those churches

---

[24] Suzanne L. Stratton, *The Immaculate Conception in Spanish Art* (Cambridge, New York, and Melbourne, 1994).

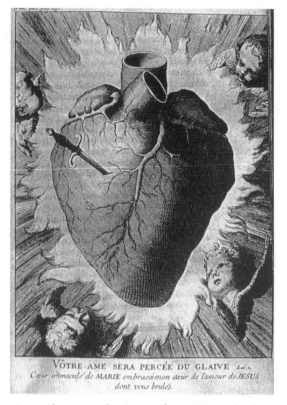

VÔTRE AME SERA PERCÉE DU GLAIVE *L.c.c.*
. *Cœur immaculé de MARIE embrasé mon cœur de l'amour de JESUS*
dont vous brûlés.

Fig. 2 The Immaculate Heart of Mary. From a book on
devotion to the Sacred Heart of Jesus, 1746.

which came under the influence of the French School, of whom Jean
Eudes is a representative figure. The image shows Mary as the woman
of the Apocalypse (Revelation 12): she is standing on the moon, clothed
with the sun, and crowned with twelve stars. The globe she is standing
on in this painting is definitely the moon. But Jean Eudes, in *The Admirable Heart*, refers to the artistic convention of showing Mary standing
on a globe, and he suggests that the globe should be interpreted as the
earth. That interpretation indeed became the more common, as we
shall see.

However, this type of iconography is not only concerned with an
image of the Apocalypse. It also associates Mary with Holy Wisdom,
and even identifies the two. Wisdom texts, such as Ecclesiasticus 24 and
Proverbs 8, representing Wisdom as present with God at the creation of

Fig. 3   Diego Velázquez: 'Virgin of the Immaculate
Conception' (Photo © The National Gallery, London)

the world, had been used in liturgies for Marian feast days since the
high Middle Ages. In preaching, these texts were initially interpreted as
being applied to Mary 'by accommodation'; but subsequently, the fact
that the Church had applied these texts to Mary was taken to indicate
that the scriptural imagery relating to Wisdom had an immediate
significance for the Blessed Virgin. The painting by Velázquez refers to
Wisdom being conceived in the mind of God before the foundations of
the world (e.g., Proverbs 8.22–31). It thus presents Mary's immaculate
conception as something intended by God from all eternity.[25]

---

[25] A discussion of the development of these ideas can be found in Sarah Jane Boss,
Empress and Handmaid: on Nature and Gender in the Cult of the Virgin Mary (2000), 123–55, esp.
140–51.

This is cosmic imagery, and it relates both to the first creation of the cosmos, by reference to the figure of Wisdom, and to its consummation at the end of time, in the Apocalypse. For Jean Eudes, the Heart of Mary is connected to the former: to the cosmos as the perfection of God's creation. For the later cult of the Immaculate Heart, on the other hand, it is connected to the cosmos as it falls into disarray in the catastrophe of the Apocalypse. And we shall go on now to see how that association of ideas gained precedence.

* * *

Fig. 4   The Miraculous Medal

In 1830, a young French woman called Catherine Labouré had a series of visions of the Virgin Mary. Catherine was a novice in the Daughters of Charity of St Vincent de Paul, in their house in the Rue du Bac in Paris. In one of these visions, which took place in the convent chapel, the Blessed Virgin showed her the image of a medal which she requested should be struck in order for people to wear it around their necks [Fig. 4]. The obverse side depicts the Virgin standing on a globe. Catherine was told that the globe represented the world, and France in particular, and that the rays emanating from the Virgin's hands were rays of God's grace coming down upon the earth, and upon France in particular. Around the edge of the medal are the words: 'O Mary, conceived without sin, pray for us who have recourse to thee'. On the reverse of the medal are the hearts of Jesus and Mary, the letter M surmounted by the Cross, and the twelve stars of the woman of the Apocalypse. So the heart of Mary and her immaculate conception are both indicated.

The then Archbishop of Paris, Monseigneur de Quélen, was a keen advocate for the cause of the pope's defining the Immaculate Conception as an article of faith, and when he was told of Sister Catherine's vision, he immediately saw it as a sign from God, and had the medal struck in 1832. It was officially called the Medal of the Immaculate Conception, but as soon as people started wearing it, they reported miracles being worked as a consequence, and so it acquired the popular name of the Miraculous Medal.[26] And the wearing of the Miraculous Medal has been a part of mainstream Catholic practice throughout the world ever since. In addition to the medal itself, the Virgin of the Miraculous Medal has gone on being represented in statues and on prayer cards ever since the medal was first produced. The Catholic Church is a global institution, and the miraculous medal is a global phenomenon.

When Catherine had the visionary sequence that included the showing of the medal, the Virgin's initial appearance was not that which appears on the actual medal: it was one in which she held the globe in her hands. And although there is a certain ambiguity in Catherine's account of the vision, it seems likely that it was this image, and not the one of the Virgin standing on the globe and with hands outstretched, which Catherine understood should appear on the medal. However, Church authorities seem to have been concerned about the orthodoxy of an image showing Mary alone holding the world in her hands, and so they opted for the more conventional representation of the immaculate conception when they had the image struck. A statue showing the Virgin holding the globe was put up in the chapel of the Sisters of Charity in the Rue du Bac after Catherine's death in 1870, and it stands over the altar which contains her body, in the chapel where the apparitions took place [Fig. 5].

At the time of Catherine's visions and of the initial production of the medal, the parish priest in the Rue du Bac was the Abbé Desgenettes, and he was a great enthusiast for the medal. But in 1832 he was moved

---

[26] Accounts of the origin of the Miraculous Medal are given in René Laurentin (trans. Paul Inwood), *The Life of Catherine Labouré* (1983), 52–105; and Joseph I. Dirvin, *Saint Catherine Labouré of the Miraculous Medal* (Rockford, IL, 1981), 80–123.

Fig. 5   The Virgin holding the globe. Statue in the chapel
of the Sisters of Charity, rue du Bac, Paris.

to the parish of Notre-Dame des Victoires, in the Place des Grands
Augustins, and there he found the parish in a run-down state, with few
church attenders. He worked hard to evangelize amongst the people of
the area, but all to no avail; and he started to wonder whether he should
not just leave the parish and go somewhere else where his ministry
would be more fruitful. However, in 1836, as he was celebrating Mass
one day, he heard a voice telling him to 'consecrate [his] parish to the
Most Holy and Immaculate Heart of Mary'. The standard accounts
narrate that he did this shortly afterwards, and that four or five
hundred people appeared, as it were, out of the blue, for the occasion.[27]

27   Louis Blond, *Notre-Dame des Victoires* (Paris, 1937), 10–13.

A confraternity of lay people was formed under the protection of the Heart of Mary, and in 1838, Pope Gregory XVI 'created and erected in perpetuity in the Church of Our Lady of Victories in Paris, the Archconfraternity of the Holy and Immaculate Heart of Mary for the conversion of sinners'. This was, and is, an association open to Catholics not just in France, but all over the world.[28]

* * *

So the Abbé Desgenettes found church attendance in inner city Paris in the 1830s to be very low, and consecration to the Heart of Mary seemed to be a means of acquiring supernatural help in the struggle to promote the faith and to save souls from sin and damnation. It is perhaps not surprising that the confraternity quickly became an international organization, since the events at Notre-Dame des Victoires took place in a broader cultural context of tension between religion and science, and a political context of threat to the Church as an institution.

In the last decades of the nineteenth century, the Italian rabbi Elijah Benamozegh wrote:

> Everyone agrees that we are in the midst of a great religious crisis. This reveals itself in three ways. The conflict between religion and science is in an acute state, and therefore occupies us the most; but to this must be added the antagonism among religions themselves, and the evolutionary changes which are occurring simultaneously at the heart of each religion.[29]

'[A]t bottom,' wrote Benamozegh, 'we are dealing with a single, identical crisis, which is nothing other than the struggle between faith and reason',[30] and he sought a means of reconciling the two.

The tension identified by Benamozegh had been widely felt amongst European intellectuals for almost a century before this, and many of those who wrote on the subject expressed some optimism for the possibility of a resolution to the conflict and division which they described. In 1844, the Catholic seminarian Alphonse Louis Constant published accounts of visions in which the Virgin Mary prophesied the marriage of Christianity and socialism, an event that would bring about the

---

[28] Ibid., 14–15.
[29] Elijah Benamozegh (trans. Maxwell Luria), *Israel and Humanity* (New York and Mahwah, NJ, 1995), 39.
[30] Ibid., 40.

millennium.[31] Constant subsequently abandoned his Catholic orders and became in effect the founder of modern magic and occult practice. Writing under the name of Eliphas Zaheed Lévi, he contended that the alliance of science and faith was already accomplished in the art of magic, and that it was this that he revealed in his own work on the history of the subject.[32]

This was the intellectual climate in which devotion to the Immaculate Heart of Mary was formed and in which the devotion took on many of the characteristics it has retained down to the present day. Devotion to the Immaculate Heart seems to represent emotion in the face of intellect, and religion in the face of Godless rationality.

The particular situation of the institutional Church, however, also needs to be taken into consideration. Events in France at this time are particularly significant, because it was in nineteenth-century France that a number of popular Catholic devotions which subsequently became universal enjoyed their infancy. Included amongst these are the Marian devotions already mentioned. The closing decades of the eighteenth century and the opening decades of the nineteenth were years in which the Papal States were lost and the Vatican attacked, and which saw the French Revolution, with its suppression of much Catholic practice and subsequently a large decline in the number of clergy. During the 1840s, matters got worse, with revolutions and famine spreading to several parts of Europe. And in this environment, visions and prophecies of an apocalyptic nature, predicting terrible disasters, became almost commonplace. Among the most notable of these were the predictions of the Virgin Mary in 1846 in an apparition at La Salette, in the diocese of Grenoble. Addressing two shepherd children, Mélanie and Maximin, she called for people to repent of their sins, to return to the practice of attending Mass, and to keep Sunday as a Sabbath. If they did not, she predicted, then there would be famine and war.[33]

The Marian revival, including its apocalyptic aspects, was further encouraged by a fortuitous event in 1842, namely, the discovery of the manuscript of a devotional work by Louis de Montfort (1673–1716), another religious founder to emerge from the French School. *The True*

[31] Cited in Thomas A. Kselman, *Miracles and Prophecies in Nineteenth-Century France* (New Brunswick, NJ, 1983), 80, 92.

[32] Eliphas Lévi (trans. A.E. Waite), *The History of Magic* (1969), 32.

[33] Sandra L. Zimdars-Swartz, *Encountering Mary: from La Salette to Medjugorje* (Princeton, NJ, 1991), 27–43.

Devotion to the Blessed Virgin[34] is a manual giving advice on how to live a devout Christian life by means of offering all things to God through Mary. It recommends consecrating oneself to Mary, and gives a prayer formula by which to make a formal act of consecration. Although the tone of *The True Devotion* is in no way alarming or apocalyptic, it was conducive to the ideas of those who were thinking along such lines in the nineteenth century, because it contains a clear doctrine that the Second Coming of Christ and the Kingdom of God will be preceded by an Age of Mary. Just as the first entry of Christ into the world was accomplished through Mary, so when he comes again to inaugurate the Kingdom, this last age will be preceded by an age in which Mary, by the grace of God, will reign supreme. In the nineteenth century, the upsurge of Marian devotion, combined with predictions of divine judgement, made it seem as though the Age of Mary, in preparation for the Second Coming, had indeed arrived.

Increasingly at this time, the Catholic Church was being put on the defensive, and many Catholics adopted a reactionary stance which attempted to protect and restore the institution. In 1864, the *Syllabus of Errors* declared its author, Pope Pius IX, to be irreconcilably opposed to 'progress, liberalism and recent civilization'.[35] The occasion for this formulation was specifically the closure of monasteries and church schools in Piedmont; but it was interpreted as a reaction against those Catholics who sought peaceful co-existence between the Church and the secular world, such as Count Montalembert, who had argued that the Church should simply be able to operate freely in a free, secular state. Opposition to so-called 'liberalism' within the Church has continued down to the present day to be a concern for so-called 'conservatives', including those promoting certain forms of devotion to the Virgin Mary.

Indeed, central to the process of Catholic retrenchment in the nineteenth century was a renewed emphasis on the Blessed Virgin Mary in both doctrine and devotion. In 1854, Pope Pius IX had promulgated the bull *Ineffabilis Deus*, making the doctrine of Mary's Immaculate Conception an article of faith for all Catholics. On 9 December 1854, the day after the bull's promulgation, the Pope concluded an address to

---

[34] St Louis Marie de Montfort, *True Devotion to the Blessed Virgin* (Liverpool, 1976).
[35] Barbara Corrado Pope, 'Immaculate and powerful: the Marian revival in the nineteenth century', in Clarissa Atkinson *et al.*, eds, *Immaculate and Powerful: the Female in Sacred Image and Social Reality* ([Wellingborough], 1985), 173–200.

a gathering of the faithful with the somewhat Augustinian reflection that the profession of this doctrine

> will be a powerful means of confuting those who deny that human nature was corrupted by the first sin and who exaggerate the forces of reason in order to deny or lessen the benefit of Revelation. Finally, may the Blessed Virgin, who conquered and destroyed all heresies, uproot and destroy this dangerous error of Rationalism, which in our unhappy times not only afflicts and torments civil society, but more deeply afflicts the Church.[36]

That the Virgin Mary was preserved from original sin by the grace of God was thus newly interpreted as a reminder of all humanity's dependence upon God's grace, and a pointer to the folly of those modern movements which attempted to reform the world through human effort alone. Symbolically, the cause of the heart was being championed against the ascendancy of the brain.

Catholic opposition to many aspects of modernity, however, was more rhetorical than practical. The Catholic revival was especially marked in France, as were a number of its characteristic features, including its strongly Marian focus. In 1858 a young girl named Bernadette Soubirous had a series of visions of the Virgin in a grotto close to the town of Lourdes, in the French Pyrenees. During these visions, the Virgin identified herself as the Immaculate Conception and directed Bernadette to find a spring of water in the ground, which turned out to have miraculous powers of healing. Bernadette's experience can be identified as an instance of the continuation of an ancient tradition of sacred grottos and healing springs in Pyrenean culture, and of a medieval tradition of Marian shrines in the region.[37] Furthermore, the highly successful efforts to promote pilgrimage to Lourdes were often associated with Catholic opposition to modernity. Healing should be sought from the grace of God, and not from human skill alone. Yet the promoters of those pilgrimages had no hesitation whatever in using every form of modern technology to accomplish their goal. Most notable in this regard were mass-circulation Catholic newspapers and the use, and even the building, of railways: indeed, it was the railway which enabled Lourdes to become the internationally important shrine

---

[36] Quoted ibid., 181–2.
[37] Kselman, *Miracles and Prophecies*, 12–36; Ruth Harris, *Lourdes: Body and Spirit in the Secular Age* (1999), 31, 33, 77–8.

which it has remained down to the present day. From the early days of pilgrimage, moreover, the taking of the waters at Lourdes was carried out alongside modern medical treatment, and not as an alternative to it. We should also note that, since the Church's rules for the discernment of miracles were formulated in the atmosphere of the eighteenth-century Enlightenment, by Cardinal Lambertini (later Pope Benedict XIV), all the officially-declared miracles at Lourdes were and are healings which medical scientists have investigated but have not been able to account for. That is the Catholic Church's definition of a healing miracle! So although the miracle is an act of pure grace, it is a grace that comes from a God of the gaps. This means that priority is given to the judgement of secular medicine before the Church allows itself to make any pronouncement on the matter. It is in effect doctors, not clergy or religious experts, who determine whether or not a healing is miraculous.

In one sense, the contradiction between the anti-modern rhetoric and the very modern practice of the Catholic revivalists of nineteenth-century France has now passed into history. For the Miraculous Medal, the shrine at Lourdes, and even the Archconfraternity of the Sacred and Immaculate Heart of Mary are all now a part of mainstream modern Catholicism – a Catholicism which no longer declares itself to be resolutely opposed to every aspect of the modern world. Yet the atmosphere of anti-modernism combined with the enthusiastic employment of all mod cons has survived in the cult of the Immaculate Heart, some of whose promoters are responsible for creating enormously elaborate videos and internet sites.[38]

* * *

The leading movement for devotion to the Immaculate Heart is the cult of Our Lady of Fatima. The history and practices of this cult are so ornate and complicated that there is no space for a thorough account of even the main features.[39] But attention can be drawn to at least one or two of them.

---

[38] See, for example, www.immaculateheart.com or www.archoftriumph.org. At the time of writing this article, the site www.fatima.org, devoted to promoting the cult of Our Lady of Fatima (see below), includes a page on which there is an article by Christopher A. Ferrara, entitled, 'A potential apocalypse?', the purpose of which is to point out that there is evidence from reputable scientists that the Earth is in danger of destruction. This evidence is interpreted as support for the Virgin's warning of a coming 'chastisement' upon the world.

[39] For a more detailed account, see Zimdars-Swartz, *Encountering Mary*, 67–91; for an account by a protagonist for the cult, see Francis Johnston, *Fatima: the Great Sign* (Chulmleigh, 1980).

In 1917, the Virgin appeared again to three children at Fatima in Portugal. In a series of visions between May and October, she addressed Lucia dos Santos and her cousins, Jacinta and Francisco Martos. Some of the things that Our Lady is reported to have said to the children were recorded at the time and subjected to scrutiny by the official commission of enquiry into the authenticity of the apparitions. Other things seem not to have been revealed until the late 1920s and the 1940s, when Lucia – who by this time had become a Carmelite nun – made them known.[40] There has been some dispute as to whether those matters that were told only later should really be counted as part of the visions that were authenticated by the Church; but for most devotees of Our Lady of Fatima, all Lucia's later pronouncements are deemed to be valid, so for the purposes of this paper, there will be no distinction between the different reports with regard to their authenticity.

The first apparition was inaugurated by a flash of lightning, which drew the children's attention to the brilliant figure of a 'lady' over a holm-oak tree in the Cova da Iria. During the sequence of monthly visions, the Lady asked the children to pray for the conversion of sinners and an end to the war. She called in particular for recitation of the rosary. In October, she said that if people would amend their lives, then the war would soon be over. 7 October is the feast of Our Lady of the Rosary, and October is the month specially dedicated to the rosary in popular Catholic devotion. It is therefore not surprising that it was during the October apparition that the lady identified herself as 'Our Lady of the Rosary'. What was most remarkable about the October apparition, however, was something experienced not only by the visionaries themselves, but also by the crowd that had gathered around them to witness their ecstasy. When the people arrived, it was pouring with rain, and they all stood with wet clothes and umbrellas. But then the sun came out and seemed to fall from the sky, so that the people were terrified and ran screaming for cover. This lasted for more than ten minutes, before the sun seemed to return to the sky, leaving everyone's clothes and umbrellas, and the ground around them, completely dry.

Some years later, Lucia had a vision in which she saw the Virgin holding her own heart encircled by thorns. The child who accompanied the Virgin told Lucia that the thorns were placed there by ungrateful people; he asked Lucia to have compassion on her Holy

---

[40] Zimdars-Swartz, *Encountering Mary*, 190–219.

Mother's heart, complaining that there was no-one to make the reparation that would remove the thorns. He then indicated a series of devotions to be undertaken on the first Saturdays of five consecutive months
in order to make this reparation. The devotions consisted principally of
confession, reception of holy communion and recitation of the rosary.[41]

At a later date, Lucia revealed that Our Lady of Fatima had spoken
against the errors of Communist Russia which, she said, were already
spreading across the globe. For this reason, devotion to Our Lady of
Fatima was especially adopted by Catholic organizations opposed to
Communism, such as the Blue Army in the United States.[42] In 1929
Lucia reported that Our Lady had called for the pope to consecrate
Russia to her Immaculate Heart in order to bring about its conversion.
Again, in the 1950s, Lucia said that if the Virgin's message of repentance was not heeded, then many nations in the world would be anni-
hilated, and – apparently following the model of Old Testament
prophecies such as those of Amos – she said that God would use Russia
as the instrument of his chastisement upon the world. But, Lucia said,
Our Lady had reassured her that 'in the end, my Immaculate Heart will
triumph', a phrase that is frequently repeated by Fatima devotees.

The question of what it means for a pope to consecrate the world to
anything – and whether, indeed, he can be deemed by Catholic
teaching to have the authority to do so – is one that we shall leave aside
here. But there is a certain precedent for such an act in Pope Leo XIII's
consecration of the entire human race to the Sacred Heart of Jesus in
1899.[43] Those who promote Fatima devotions have had some disagree-
ment as to when and whether a pope has actually accomplished the
consecration which Lucia said was demanded. In 1942, Pope Pius XII
consecrated the world to the Immaculate Heart of Mary. It is generally
asserted that the reason why this consecration did not mention Russia
by name was that it would have been politically unwise to do so –
which undoubtedly it would. This consecration of the world to the
Immaculate Heart was repeated in 1982 by Pope John Paul II. On both
these occasions, however, Lucia said that the act did not fulfill the

---

[41] This practice recalls that of a popular devotion to the Sacred Heart of Jesus, whereby
the devotee receives communion on the first Friday of each month for nine consecutive
months.

[42] Michael W. Cuneo, *The Smoke of Satan: Conservative and Traditionalist Dissent in Contemporary American Catholicism* (New York and Oxford, 1997), 134–7.

[43] René Laurentin (trans. Kenneth D. Whitehead), *The Meaning of Consecration Today: a
Marian Model for a Secularized Age* (San Francisco, CA, 1992), 56–9.

conditions requested by Our Lady, which were that the consecration should be made by the pope together with the Catholic bishops of the world. The fact that the bishops were not included rendered the consecration invalid. In 1983, however, Pope John Paul wrote to all the bishops of the world requesting that they should join him in making a further act of consecration of the world to the Immaculate Heart. After this further consecration was accomplished in 1984, Lucia said that the Virgin's request had now, at last, been fulfilled.

Now Lucia's claim had been that the consecration of Russia in particular would be to the benefit of the entire planet. Nonetheless, in the light of the global imagery associated with the Immaculate Heart, it is perhaps more in accordance with the logic of the symbols that the universal pontiff should have consecrated the whole world, rather than just one part of it. With the advent of *glasnost* and *perestroika*, and the fall of the Iron Curtain in 1989, many Fatima devotees claimed that it was because of Our Lady and the pope that these changes had at last come about.

* * *

Those who promote the cult of Our Lady of Fatima encourage, amongst other things, the recitation of the rosary, the devotions of the first five Saturdays, the wearing of the brown scapular (a practice whose origin lies in the Carmelite Order, to which Lucia belongs), and personal consecration to the Immaculate Heart of Mary. This consecration generally takes the form given by Louis de Montfort in his *True Devotion*. All these activities are carried out in reparation for sins and for the conversion of sinners, in the hope of ultimately averting the chastisement that will otherwise come upon the whole world.

Immaculate Heart devotion is strongly characterized by such bodily activities as ritual devotions and the wearing of holy objects. From this point of view, the work of Jean Galot cited earlier is not typical. Extensive meditations on the historical Mary are certainly characteristic of modern Marian devotion in general, but not of Immaculate Heart devotion in particular. And it could be argued that the practical devotions promoted by Fatima devotees are the sort of activities that would have been considered normal during the lifetime of Jean Eudes. Indeed, there may be a case for saying that these are the sorts of activities that constitute the fundamentals of human religion as such, and that the abandonment of them is an act or process of secularization. Certainly, devotion to the Immaculate Heart is strongest in Third World countries, such as

India, where what might loosely be termed 'traditional' religiosity is more prominent than in Europe and North America.

Amongst the Missionaries of Charity – Mother Teresa's sisters – devotion to the Immaculate Heart is a central activity; and when an Oxford student, Gaëlle Finlan, made a study of that devotion, she noted that the sisters generally spoke of the Immaculate Heart in terms of its purity.[44] Finlan argued that the devotion served the function of providing the sisters with a safe haven – a place of unsullied purity – to which they could retreat for sustenance in the midst of the dirt, disease, and death which surrounded them continually in their daily ministry to the poor. (Impressionistically, it seems that wherever devotion to the Immaculate Heart is a normal part of Catholic culture, rather than something exceptional, the motif of Mary's heart as a safe haven in a harsh world is an important aspect of it.) Thus, a contrast between the goodness of Mary's heart and the evils of the world is made here, as at Fatima, notwithstanding that the 'register' of the devotions is strikingly different.

The tone of the Fatima devotions is, however, markedly unlike that of the work of Jean Eudes on the Heart of Mary. Whereas Eudes sees the goodness of Mary's heart being reflected in the cosmos, and union with her heart as something that will enable Christ and paradise to be present in the devotee, the Immaculate Heart of Fatima is a weapon of combat against a Godless world and an object that stands in need of acts of reparation for sin.

Yet even at Fatima, traces of Eudes' vision of the Heart of Mary seem to remain. The miracle of the sun falling from the sky may recall apocalyptic imagery of a cosmos in chaos, but does it not also remind us of Eudes' vision of the sun as a reflection of the Heart of Mary? And if we were to imagine that the Heart of Mary was indeed at the heart of the world, then would the countless catastrophes of the twentieth century not give good grounds for supposing that that heart must indeed be in a state of great distress?

A postcard bought at Fatima shows the statue of Our Lady of Fatima with her heart encircled by thorns. In the caption, she requests devotion to her Immaculate Heart [Fig. 6]. The idea of Mary's heart being wounded and suffering is of course very old, and is tied initially to Simeon's prediction of a sword piercing her soul. Images are common

---

44   Gaëlle Finlan, 'Devotion to the Immaculate Heart of Mary among the Sisters of Charity' (undergraduate dissertation, University of Oxford Faculty of Theology, 1991).

Gosto
tanto do
Coração
Imaculado
de Maria!
Jacinta

Fig. 6   Our Lady of Fatima requests devotion to her
Immaculate Heart (from a postcard)

in which Mary's heart is pierced with seven swords [Fig. 7], representing the seven sorrows which, since the late Middle Ages, have been
a focus for pious meditation – a practice promoted especially by the
Servite Order.[45] The crown of thorns is of course an instrument of
Christ's Passion, and the placing of it around Mary's heart on Fatima
statues seems to suggest that it is she, rather than Christ, who is
wounded by the sins of the world. But if we bear in mind Jean Eudes'
understanding that Mary's heart is the prototype and heart of the

---

[45]   G.-M. Roschini, 'L'Ordre des Servites de Marie', in Hubert du Manoir, ed., *Maria:
Études sur la Sainte Vierge*, 2 vols (Paris, 1952), 883–907, at 886–7, 894, 896, 900, 904–6.

Fig. 7 Our Lady of Quito, Ecuador, 1906. Mary's heart is pierced by seven swords, and she holds the Crown of Thorns. Photo from Roy Abraham Varghese, *God-Sent* (New York, 2000), supplied by Ann Ball.

cosmos, then of course the sins of the world are also necessarily wounds upon her heart. A statue of this kind in the Italian town of Adrano is reputed to have wept tears of blood, as are numerous other, similar statues.

A video entitled *Marian Apparitions of the Twentieth Century* was made in the United States in 1985 to promote the cause of Mary's messages of repentance, and it shows a good deal of footage of visionaries in ecstasy and of weeping statues, and calls for repentance and for consecration to Mary's Immaculate Heart. The video emphasises the fact that Marian apparitions are occurring in every continent across the world. Interspersed amongst the scenes of statues and visions are views of the planet Earth taken from space, and other scenes of the horrific warfare that occurred in the twentieth century, including men being killed in trenches and the explosion of the atom bomb at Hiroshima. The linking of the Immaculate Heart with the images of the planet recalls several centuries of Marian iconography and Jean Eudes' association of the Heart of Mary with the cosmos. The linking of the Heart of Mary

Fig. 8   The Immaculate Heart of Mary. This type of
image is frequently found on prayer cards and religious
greetings cards.

with the violence of the past century reminds us also of the symbolism
of the heart in this culture.

The feminist writer Susan Griffin, in her brilliant critique of
pornography, argues that pornography is an attack upon the heart.[46]
Pornography depends upon and generates impersonal lust. A golden
rule in the construction of pornography is that the wishes of the victim
are not to be considered. If the pornographer allows himself to know
the real feelings of his victim, then he will be unable to use her as an
object, because he will see her as a person, and will feel compassion for

---

[46]   Susan Griffin, *Pornography and Silence* (1981), 81–154.

Fig. 9   Page from *Arena* magazine, April 1996

her. This refusal to see a human being as a person and to feel compassion is what Griffin identifies as the denial of the heart. Significantly for the present argument, Griffin sees this denial of the heart as part and parcel of a culture that has set itself against 'nature', and which constantly seeks to control and destroy the physical world. In support of Griffin's case, there is certainly evidence from the use that is made of the image and symbol of the Immaculate Heart.

The men's magazine *Arena*, in April 1996, took a standard representation of the Immaculate Heart of Mary [Fig. 8] and used it to head a page entitled, 'The world at once' [Fig. 9]. This is a page which ridicules religion, astrology, and belief in ghosts, all together. In effect, it says, 'Look what loony things people will believe in', and uses an image of the Immaculate Heart as its centrepiece.

The magazine in which that page occurred describes itself as an 'Italian' issue, and had as its front cover a picture of the model Monica Bellucci wearing only a bra, with the caption, 'Ciao Ragazzi!', making a little joke in reference to the well-known 'Wonderbra' advertisement. However, every article but one in the magazine is abusive about Italy and Italians. For example, one article is dedicated to arguing that Italian men are lousy lovers, unlike British men, who are, apparently, brilliant in bed. The only article which is not abusive is the article about Monica Bellucci (who, incidentally, has a rosary around her neck). And the article in praise of Monica Bellucci in fact consists of nothing other than an account of the author's liking for large breasts. On the evidence of this magazine, then, the ridiculing of the heart certainly does go alongside aggression and the viewing of women purely as sexual objects.

Now, even the sympathetic reader of this article may say that the iconography of the Immaculate Heart is so tasteless and absurd that it positively invites ridicule. But that only pushes the point one step further back: why is it that the *heart* should be represented so frequently in a form that many Europeans would regard as being at best sentimental and at worst tasteless? Does the iconography itself not speak of the low esteem in which this society holds the heart, or rather, that which it symbolizes?

A rather different mockery of the Immaculate Heart was made on the cover of the weekly science magazine, the *New Scientist*, in 1990. It shows Renaissance cherubs drawing back curtains as though to reveal a sacred mystery. Behind the curtains is a combination of images indicating the cosmos, and at the centre of those is a representation of the Virgin Mary, showing what should be her Immaculate Heart. But instead of a heart, there is model of a DNA double helix molecule. DNA, of course, is often referred to by means of a computing metaphor, as 'containing the programme for human life'. And as though to say that even in modern science the human person is a microcosm of the universe, the caption says, 'Is the universe a computer?' There is, it seems, a correspondence between the human person – exemplified by the Virgin Mary – and the universe, and that correspondence consists in the fact that both the human and the universe are programmed like computers. So at the heart of the universe there is no heart at all – only a computer programme.

Evidently, it is not only devotees of the Immaculate Heart who think there is a conflict between their view of the world and that of modernity. The *New Scientist* shares their opinion and agrees with them on precisely what that difference consists of.

It can be suggested, however, that Immaculate Heart devotees, and the Catholic Church in general, are not sufficiently thorough or radical in their critique of modernity for their views to have much effect. If you are calling for people to repent and to change their lives in order to bring about an end to suffering in the world, there is at least an inconsistency in transmitting your message by means of microtechnology that is built at the cost of severe human suffering and injustice in the Third World countries where the electronic components are made. The words and the actions seem to contradict one another. More fundamental, perhaps, is a conflict between the very character of much modern technology and the values which one might expect to be espoused by those calling for penitence and the preservation of an older worldview. This is partly because much of that technology is devoted to increasing the speed of work and communications, with a consequent tendency to reduce the amount of time that people spend in mental reflection or talking with other members of their families, for example. The mentality that looks for the 'technical fix' is essentially antagonistic to that which seeks what Catholics have traditionally understood by 'conversion'.

The Catholic Church is famous for its criticisms of research on embryos and of various forms of biotechnology relating to humans. But a Catholic woman who works for animal welfare recently commented, 'If experiments hadn't first been done on animals, we'd never have got to the stage at which they could be done on embryos.'[47] And she is of course quite correct. But we need to take the matter back a stage or two further. For it is a reasonable speculation that if the material world itself were held to be highly sacred, then the kind of science and technology that causes serious harm to both humans and animals would probably not exist, and humanity would have a very different relationship with other creatures from that which we have now. So Catholics who seek a starting-point from which to think in a genuinely radical and challenging way about how to approach the evils of the modern world, if they are serious about this, need to turn to fundamental questions

---

[47] Comment made at a meeting in Oxford, Jan. 1999, by Deborah Jones, editor of *The Ark*, the journal of the Catholic Study Centre for Animal Welfare.

concerning the theological status of the physical world as such. I suggest that they might find considerable mileage in recovering the kind of cosmic vision described by Jean Eudes, in which the world is an image of the Heart of Mary, which is itself a paradise and the dwelling-place of God. The consequences of that way of thinking would be so demanding that probably no more than a few Immaculate Heart devotees would be willing to follow it through. Yet without such a commitment, devotees of the Immaculate Heart have little chance of obtaining the kind of fundamental conversion which they seem to demand.

University of Wales, Lampeter

MARIAN REVIVALISM
IN MODERN ENGLISH CHRISTIANITY:
THE EXAMPLE OF WALSINGHAM

by SEAN GILL

O N 19 August 1897, a newly carved image of Our Lady of Walsingham, sent from Rome by Pope Leo XIII, was solemnly installed in the Roman Catholic Church in Kings Lynn. Since no plan of the original medieval shrine survived, the chapel that contained the image was modelled upon the Holy House of Loreto. The following day a pilgrimage led by the parish priest and by Fr Philip Fletcher, one of the prime movers behind the Marian revival, went from Lynn to the Slipper Chapel at Walsingham. This was an important focus of worship since it was the only building to have survived substantially intact near the great pilgrimage site destroyed at the Reformation. In 1934 the Archbishop of Westminster, Cardinal Bourne, led the first annual Roman Catholic pilgrimage to the Slipper Chapel, in which a new image of Our Lady of Walsingham based upon that of the seal of the medieval Priory had been placed.[1] In the intervening years, the Anglo-Catholic vicar of Little Walsingham, the Revd Arthur Hope Patten, had created a similar shrine in the Anglican parish church in 1922, and had gone on in 1931 to build a separate chapel with its own sanctuary of the Holy House of Nazareth.[2]

To both Fletcher and Patten, the recreation of Marian worship at Walsingham was not a radical new departure, but rather the restoration of an English Marian cult so intense and so widespread that England became famed in the middle ages as 'Mary's dower'. Said to have been built on the instructions of the Virgin Mary who appeared in 1061 to the lady of the manor, Richeldis, the Holy House known as 'England's Nazareth' became the premier shrine to Our Lady, visited by both poor pilgrims and by a succession of kings. Yet despite appeals to such a weighty historical and national pedigree, it was far from inevitable that Marian revivalism would find much resonance in either the English

---

[1] The best recent account of the medieval and modern Roman Catholic Marian cult of Walsingham is A. Williams, ed., *Walsingham: Pilgrimage and History* (1999).
[2] For the history of the Anglican shrine see Peter G. Cobb, ed., *Walsingham* (1990).

Roman Catholic Church, or amongst Anglo-Catholics, at the beginning of the twentieth century. In the case of the former, the ultramon-
tane baroque enthusiasms associated with the Marian devotions of the
Redemptorists and of Frederick Faber were not to the taste of the
majority of English Roman Catholics, brought up on the more
restrained piety typified by Richard Challoner's *The Garden of the Soul*.[3]
For their part Anglo-Catholics were the heirs of the leaders of the
Oxford Movement, such as Keble and Pusey, both of whom viewed the
practice of invocation of the saints, including the Virgin Mary, with
some distrust.[4] This paper examines the reasons for the successful and
somewhat surprising refoundation and development of the Marian
shrines at Walsingham. It also seeks to understand something of the
specifically English context of the revival in order to explain why its
subsequent development differed in important respects from that of
modern Marian cults elsewhere in Europe.[5]

In searching for the origins of Anglican Marian devotion at
Walsingham it is tempting to deal largely in personalities, and in
particular that of the Revd Arthur Hope Patten, Walsingham's vicar
from 1921 until his death in 1958. As both his admirers and detractors
have acknowledged, Patten had all the qualities needed to undertake
and sustain such an enterprise. He was single-minded, charismatic
when he wished to be, and had a gift for making use of the talents and
enthusiasms of others.[6] All the significant milestones in the development of Walsingham were the product of his vision, and he also
evinced a genius for organizational improvization. Thus his decision to
set up the College of Guardians, consisting of twelve priests and eight
laymen as a trust responsible for the overall management of the shrine,
was vital for its long-term survival. It was his ability to persuade
wealthy and titled Anglo-Catholic laymen to join that did much to
ensure the financial security of the shrine. As one of them, the Earl of

---

[3] Carol M. Engelhardt, 'Victorian masculinity and the Virgin Mary', in Andrew
Bradstock, Sean Gill, Anne Hogan and Sue Morgan, eds, *Masculinity and Spirituality in
Victorian Culture* (Basingstoke, 2000), 51–4.

[4] David Hole, *England's Nazareth: A History of the Holy Shrine of Our lady of Walsingham*
(1959), 34.

[5] I am grateful for help with sources and for advice to the Revd Peter Cobb, Master of
the College of Guardians of the Anglican shrine; also to the Revd Martin Warner, the shrine
administrator, for making available to me the only extant set of the publication *Our Lady's
Mirror*, kept in the archives at Walsingham. I would also like to thank Dom Philip Jebb for
allowing me to consult the archives of Downside Abbey.

[6] The most revealing assessment is in Colin Stephenson, *Walsingham Way* (1970).

Lauderdale, later recalled, 'Father Patten's gifts did not include those of chairmanship but they did include those of making sure that no matter what had been decided, *his* decision was final.'[7]

Vital though the force of Patten's personality was in the revival of Marian devotion at Walsingham, his contribution can only be fully understood in the context of broader changes in the Anglican spirituality of which he was a characteristic product. Whilst the original impetus behind the Oxford Movement's desire to reassert the Catholic heritage of the Church of England was a severely scholarly one, its early liturgical and architectural development was part of a much wider Victorian enthusiasm for the Middle Ages.[8] Representations of the Virgin Mary featured prominently in Victorian medievalism, an early controversial example being Rossetti's Pre-Raphaelite work *The Girlhood of Mary Virgin*. They also formed part of the iconography of many Gothic and Italianate churches erected from the 1840s onwards.[9] For example St Paul's church in Brighton, built in 1848, contained windows designed by Pugin depicting the Virgin and child, Mary at the foot of the cross, at Pentecost, and seated in glory at Christ's right hand. St Paul's was the work of the wealthy Tractarian vicar of Brighton, Arthur Douglas Wagner, and it was as a server at one of the other Brighton churches built by Wagner, St Bartholomew's, that Patten first acquired his passionate life-long interest in all things medieval.[10] In assessing the importance of this kind of religious background to the history of Marian revivalism at Walsingham, it is interesting to note that Fr Philip Fletcher, who had led the earlier Roman Catholic revival, was a convert who had also received his early religious upbringing in the heady atmosphere of Wagner's Brighton churches.[11]

Many features of the development of the Marian cult at Walsingham bear witness to Patten's own emotionally charged and highly romanticized view of the past. Thus members of the Society of Our Lady of Walsingham, set up in 1926, were to wear a form of monastic scapular, 'the Livery of Our Lady', recalling the age of chivalry in which the wearing of such a livery was 'a privilege, and a protection'. At the same time their names were to be entered in a richly

[7] Cobb, *Walsingham*, 90.

[8] John Milburn, 'The revival of Marian devotion in the Church of England', in *The Mariological Lectures of Fr John Milburn* (1998), 1–6.

[9] For this subject see June Osborne, *Stained Glass in England* (1997), 79–91.

[10] Stephenson, *Walsingham Way*, 90.

[11] Quoted in *The Ransomer* (Autumn 1958), 18.

illuminated manuscript book.[12] Patten's passion for heraldry was later evident in the insignia and elaborate dress worn by both priest and lay Guardians, and in the coats of arms emblazoned on their stalls in the shrine church.

Though it owed much to this kind of diffusive neo-medievalism, the Anglican Marian revival at Walsingham should not be seen exclusively in these terms. Patten's devotion to Our Lady was typical of a new generation of Anglo-Catholics for whom Marian doctrine and practice acquired a saliency that had not been true of the first generation of the Oxford Movement. Part of this change arose out of a revisionist interpretation of English Church history that had important if rather uncertain ecclesiological implications. As one of the new generation's leading protagonists, Dom Anselm Hughes, later explained, the aim was not simply to re-create the past – what he rather unkindly dubbed 'British Museum religion' – but something far more dynamic and, in the English context, controversial. It was 'to restore things as nearly as possible to the condition in which they would have been had Henry not severed relations with the Holy See and thereby with other countries in communion with it'.[13] For Anglo-Catholics who thought like this, it was the modern Roman Catholic Church, not its medieval predecessor, that provided the standard of liturgical practice and doctrine. Thus, in furtherance of his work at Walsingham, Patten frequently visited Marian sites in France and Belgium, returning home to adorn the shrine church with relics of the true Cross and of the saints and with an eclectic array of statues and images in high baroque style.

When, on 6 July 1922, a new image of Our Lady was enshrined in the parish church of Little Walsingham, Marian devotion had already become one of the hallmarks of advanced Anglo-Catholicism. An early indication of its growth, of which Patten later made use, was the creation in 1904 of the League of Our Lady which had the leading Anglo-Catholic layman, Lord Halifax, as its President. It was the League that organized the first Anglican pilgrimages to Walsingham in the years after 1922. More significantly, only two years before the enshrinement, the first of a series of Anglo-Catholic Congresses had been held in the Albert Hall. During this, one of the movement's leading theologians, Darwell Stone, the Principal of Pusey House, Oxford, had quoted Aquinas approvingly that it was 'through the veneration of the saints

---

[12]   *Our Lady's Mirror* (April 1926), 3.

[13]   Anselm Hughes, *The Rivers of the Flood. A Personal Account of the Catholic Revival in England in the Twentieth Century* (1961), 50.

and the high degree of veneration which we accord to the holy Mother of our Lord, [that] we mount upwards to the supreme worship of the Most High himself.[14] His audience did not need much persuasion, as the Congress organizer triumphantly reported:

> I am told that by 7.30 on Friday evening the queue of people waiting to get into Southwark Cathedral stretched from the Cathedral gates right across London Bridge to the Monument. It is the first time since the Reformation that London Bridge heard a great crowd singing to the honour of the Mother of our Lord, as the waiting multitude sang again and again, 'Hail Mary, Hail Mary, Hail Mary, full of grace'.[15]

Although it was within the Roman Catholic Church that the revival of devotion to Our Lady of Walsingham began, its subsequent development was less smooth than that driven forward by the autocratic Patten. The Slipper Chapel had been purchased in 1894 by a wealthy convert, Miss Charlotte Boyd, as part of her attempt to revive and develop the Benedictine religious life in England. For this reason she gave the chapel to the monastery of Downside without any initial intention of reviving Marian worship there.[16] When in 1900 it was suggested to the Bishop of Northampton that the pilgrimage to Walsingham might be revived, he made it clear that, having obtained papal permission for the creation of the pilgrimage shrine at Kings Lynn, he was not prepared to approve of any alternative, nor to sanction the saying of mass at the Slipper Chapel.[17] In 1922 the conventual Chapter at Downside proposed to lease the Chapel to the diocese, but the Bishop of Northampton declined, indicating that the diocese 'had an eye to the interests of Kings Lynn'.[18]

There were several reasons for the subsequent decision to move the Marian shrine to Walsingham, apart from its historical appropriateness. In 1897 Kings Lynn had been the nearest Roman Catholic parish to Walsingham, which was situated in an area with virtually no Roman Catholic families. In 1909 a new parish was created at Fakenham, only five miles from Walsingham and at the end of the railway line which

---

[14] *Report of the First Anglo-Catholic Congress, London 1920* (1920), 159.

[15] H.A. Wilson, *Received with Thanks* (1940), 89.

[16] Williams, *Walsingham*, 106.

[17] Downside Abbey: Bishop Riddell to Prior Ford, Downside, 28 May 1900. The Downside archive concerning Walsingham has not yet been catalogued.

[18] Ibid., Bishop Charles to the Abbot of Downside, 1 June 1922.

could bring pilgrims from London in little more than four hours. In the 1920s the parish priest, Fr Gray, made it clear that he regarded Patten's activities as an affront to the Roman Catholic Church, and the continued failure to make proper use of the Slipper Chapel as a lost opportunity to spread the faith both in the area and nationally. Gray's combative style of argument was tactfully described by the Bishop of Northampton as 'frolicksome',[19] but the case he made with reference to Patten's activities proved to be persuasive:

> His various pilgrimages, the Shrine of Our Lady in his Church, teaching and various thrusts at the 'Roman' & 'Italian' Church is all too irritating. It is jolly hard for me struggling to plant the Faith in these parts to withstand all this – then for the Slipper Chapel to be placed at his disposal on each of his pilgrimages. . . . WE doing absolutely NOTHING, but standing idly by & Slipper Chapel not being used.[20]

Following the national pilgrimage in 1934, Fr Bruno James was installed as the first shrine priest, and by 1939 he estimated that 50,000 Roman Catholic pilgrims a year were visiting the Slipper Chapel.[21] The establishment of Marian devotion centred upon Walsingham within English Roman Catholicism was reinforced by a series of high profile national events. Of these, the most notable were the national youth pilgrimage led by Cardinal Hinsley in 1938, and the celebrations surrounding the Marian Year of 1954 during which the Apostolic Delegate, Archbishop O'Hara, crowned a statue of Our Lady in the ruins of the medieval priory in the presence of some 15,000 pilgrims. O'Hara's involvement was a sign of Pope Pius XII's desire to foster Marian devotion within the Church following his promulgation in 1950 of the dogma of Mary's Assumption.[22]

In fact, as we have seen, in both the Anglican and Roman Catholic revivals at Walsingham the wider context of Marian cults in nineteenth- and twentieth-century Europe needs to be taken into account. In the English case there were a number of distinctive features. Whereas in France and Germany Marian revivalism has been interpreted by historians as in some measure a response to a prevailing cultural and political climate characterized by anticlericalism and scientific ration-

---

[19] Ibid., Bishop Charles to the Abbot of Downside, 26 April 1921.
[20] Ibid., Fr Gray to the Bishop of Northampton, 4 June 1930.
[21] Bruno James, *Asking for Trouble* (1962), 122.
[22] For this subject see Adrian Hastings, ed., *Modern Catholicism* (1991), 23.

alism, this appears to be much less evident at Walsingham.[23] Partly this was because the revival was based not on a recent, but on a very ancient series of apparitions. The only exception to this was an account in October 1931 of an appearance of Our Lady to a worshipper in the Anglican shrine 'clothed in a white robe and blue mantle with a golden crown at her head'. Patten chose to make nothing of this, merely noting – in what was for him a somewhat apologetic tone – that he knew the writer to be 'worthy of credit'.[24] References to the political context are equally rare. In mentioning the threat of Communism in 1951, Patten noted that the real danger to Christian belief, which devotion to Our Lady sought to counteract, lay in the growing indifference of the young. This was a far cry from the political apocalypticism of Fatima.[25]

The question of miraculous cures was more complex. In the first number of the Anglican shrine's quarterly paper, *Our Lady's Mirror*, Patten stated that one of its objects was to provide information about 'the good news of the favours wrought by Mary in answer to the petitions offered her'.[26] When the new shrine was being built in 1931, the finding of a well, which Patten claimed to be that of the original site, led to the drinking of its waters becoming an integral part of Anglican Marian worship at Walsingham. Nevertheless, his constant soliciting of accounts of answers to prayer did not produce the desired results. Surely, he asked plaintively in 1932, there were more than the forty-four recorded responses to the hundreds of petitions offered up at the shrine in that year? Those that were put forward were as likely to be accounts of the conversion of relatives and the finding of a job in the Great Depression as cases of healing. The development of the Roman Catholic shrine followed a similar pattern. Despite a letter in *The Tablet* describing Walsingham as 'the Lourdes of dear Catholic England',[27] the first shrine priest, Fr Bruno James, was more circumspect. During his years there from 1935 to 1943 he recalled that 'There were, indeed, any number of people who claimed to have been cured miraculously at the shrine, and although I did not doubt the good faith of these people, I was not in any case satisfied that the cures were truly miraculous.'[28]

[23] This approach is to be found in David Blackbourn, *Marpingen: Apparitions of the Virgin Mary in Bismarckian Germany* (Oxford, 1983); and John Delaney *A Woman Clothed with the Sun: Eight Great Apparitions of Our Lady in Modern Times* (New York, 1960).
[24] *Our Lady's Mirror* (Spring/Summer 1947), 8.
[25] Ibid. (Summer 1951), 3.
[26] Ibid. (Jan. 1926), 1.
[27] Ibid. (Winter 1928), 2.
[28] James, *Asking for Trouble*, 137.

Walsingham also differed from continental Marian shrines in the peculiarly English ecclesiological context in which it developed. Here Patten did battle on two fronts. On the one side, he faced opposition from sceptical liberal Anglicans such as the Bishop of Durham, Hensley Henson, as well as from the attentions of the Protestant Truth Society, whose protests against 'Popery' and 'Mariolatry' became a regular sight at the annual national pilgrimage.[29] Less intemperate in tone, but potentially more damaging, was the threat of episcopal disapproval. When the Bishop of Norwich, Bertram Pollock, visited the shrine in the parish church and asked pointedly 'do you teach your people to worship the virgin, Mr Patten?' he was fobbed off with the reply 'only in the sense that they worship their earthly mothers'.[30] Episcopal authority was not to be easily denied, and once the new shrine building was erected, Patten ignored Pollock's refusal to license it for Holy Communion, replying to all the bishop's subsequent letters on this subject with answers that might most charitably be described as equivocal.

On the other side, as we have already seen, relations with the Roman Catholic Church were also initially strained. Fr Gray's denunciations of Anglo-Catholicism were widely shared. In reporting on the first national pilgrimage in 1934 the editor of *The Tablet* concluded:

> What of the well-meaning Anglicans who of late years, have tried to reverence Our Lady at Walsingham? Surely the answer is that we owe sympathy to these right-hearted and wrong-headed men and women, and that we must ask Our Lady to reward them with the highest boon. Some she has rewarded already by opening their eyes and by giving them the priceless blessing of entrance into the One fold of her Divine and Blessed Son.[31]

For their part, Anglo-Catholics gave as good as they got. In 1928 Patten complained of the way in which the Roman Catholic Church studiously ignored his work at Walsingham. He went on to proffer a compliment with a sting in the tail to the way in which 'little by little

---

[29] Henson's biting attack on the 'pitiable rubbish of the Walsingham processional hymn', and on the dangers of bringing crowds of both sexes together in an atmosphere of 'hysterical excitement' appeared in *The Evening Standard*, 15 Sept. 1926. Patten regarded it, probably rightly, as something of an own goal, urging his readers to say a 'Hail Mary' for its author. See *Our Lady's Mirror* (April 1926), 2.

[30] Stephenson, *Walsingham Way*, 153.

[31] *The Tablet* (25 Aug. 1934), 234–8.

devotion to Mary under her old title, and at her National Shrine, is being revived by our fellow Catholics not living in visible communion with Canterbury'.[32]

There is always a danger in studying Marian cults of either a crude reductionism that fails to take religious experience seriously, or of an excessive concentration on those in authority to the exclusion of the meanings of such devotion for ordinary worshippers.[33] For this reason, it seems fitting to end with an account of Marian devotion at Walsingham which captures very well something of the, by continental standards, rather low-key but nevertheless genuine spirituality that has been its distinctive feature. In 1947 fifteen young men from Bolton visited the Anglican shrine. Unable to afford the cost of a 'chara' they made the trip in the back of a furniture van. One later wrote:

> I will not describe the details of the Greater Pilgrimage, familiar to you: daily Mass which we all attended; Sung Mass in the parish church; Evensong & Devotions at St Giles; the Stations of the Cross winding through the garden in brilliant sunlight; and finally the visit to the Holy Well, after offering our petitions in the Holy House. None of us had particular bodily ailments, but others have benefitted since, and all of us in different ways, known only to ourselves. . . . I think that we have learnt a new personal love and veneration for Our Lord's Mother, and to think of her as a real person actively helping us, and loving us.[34]

There is nothing here of the rather super-heated piety espoused by Patten, nor of the ecclesiological and administrative travails which took up so much of his time and energies. Also absent is any sense of the political and medicinal preoccupations associated with twenti-eth-century continental Marian shrines. What is revealed is a dimension of religious experience that does at least as much to explain the successful re-establishment of the Marian cult of Our Lady of Walsingham.

The University of Bristol

---

[32] *Our Lady's Mirror* (Winter 1928), 4.

[33] A particularly egregious example of a reductionist account of Marian cults is Michael Carroll, *The Cult of the Virgin Mary: Psychological Origins* (Princeton, NJ, 1986). An outstanding recent history that is sensitive to a wide range of interpretations is Ruth Harris, *Lourdes: Body and Spirit in the Secular Age* (Oxford, 1999).

[34] *Our Lady's Mirror* (Autumn/Winter 1947–8).

'AN INFALLIBLE FACT-FACTORY GOING FULL BLAST': AUSTIN FARRER, MARIAN DOCTRINE, AND THE TRAVAILS OF ANGLO-CATHOLICISM

by JEREMY MORRIS

IN 1960 the Anglican philosopher Austin Farrer preached a sermon 'On being an Anglican' in the chapel of Pusey House which must have amazed his hearers. It began gently enough; but halfway through, the tone changed. Human perversity had rent the unity of the Church with schisms and heresies. How could he, 'truly and with a good conscience', stay in the Church of God? 'Only by remaining in the Church of England'.[1] Farrer put down two markers for his Anglican identity. One was stated briefly and with restraint: 'I dare not dissociate myself from the apostolic ministry.' It was the other that must have startled his congregation:

> I dare not profess belief in the great Papal error. Christ did not found a Papacy . . . Its infallibilist claim is a blasphemy, and never has been accepted by the oriental part of Christendom. Its authority has been employed to establish as dogmas of faith, propositions utterly lacking in historical foundation. Nor is this an old or faded scandal – the papal fact-factory has been going full blast in our own time, manufacturing sacred history after the event.[2]

Written close to the convening of the Second Vatican Council, even in the context of today's 'ecumenical winter' Farrer's words have a harsh and polemical ring. They are all the more surprising, considering Farrer's seemingly impeccable Anglo-Catholic credentials.[3] If we are to take seriously Farrer's participation in the discussions and report on *Catholicity* published in 1947 by a group convened by Gregory Dix, it

---

[1] Farrer, 'On being an Anglican', in idem, *The End of Man* (1973), 50.
[2] Ibid., 50–1.
[3] See, for example, Farrer's participation in three of the most significant Anglo-Catholic publications of the mid-twentieth century: 'Eucharist and Church in the New Testament', in G. Hebert, ed., *The Parish Communion. A Book of Essays* (1954), 73–94; 'The ministry in the New Testament', in K.E. Kirk, ed., *The Apostolic Ministry. Essays on the History and the Doctrine of Episcopacy* (1946), 113–82; and co-authorship with E.S. Abbott, H.J. Carpenter, Gregory Dix, A.M. Ramsey et al., *Catholicity. A Study in the Conflict of Christian Traditions in the West* (Westminster, 1947).

cannot be the case that Farrer's objection to 'the great Papal error' involved objection to the concept of primacy *per se*.[4] Rather, there were two basic points of offence: the concept and declaration of infallibility itself, and of course the two Marian dogmas of the Immaculate Conception and the Assumption.

Farrer's hostility to these dogmas was symptomatic of the attitude of most leading Anglo-Catholic theologians until recently. Far from sharing enthusiastically in the swelling amplitude of Marian devotion, as Pickering seems to imply, the theological heirs of the Tractarians mostly were ambivalent about it.[5] This paper is an exploration of their ambivalence, through the lens of Farrer's attitude to the Marian dogmas. It will aim, first, to place Farrer's views in the context of the main streams of Anglo-Catholic theology after Pusey. Then it will return to Farrer, identifying points both of continuity and of development. Finally, it will contrast and examine the new perspective on Mary that began to emerge among Anglo-Catholic theologians in the 1950s and 1960s.

A survey of the broad history of Anglo-Catholic theologians' views of Mary must begin, not with the Tractarians, but with – of all people – Martin Luther, whose position conveniently highlights the limits and ambiguities of Protestant reflection on Mary.[6] Rejecting as he did the late medieval *cultus*, for Luther Mary had no soteriological function apart from her historical one. What could be said about her had to be evident from scripture. *Sola scriptura* left some latitude of interpretation in practice, but operated as a mechanism of doctrinal control, distinguishing between what may be held of Mary as a matter of private devotion, and what must be affirmed of her as a matter of holding to the catholic faith.

This remained the basic position even for most Anglo-Catholic theologians in the nineteenth century. Thus Keble, cited by Donald Allchin as one whose appreciation of Mary marked a significant enhancement of Anglican reflection, himself would not go further than scripture indicated.[7] Commenting on his unpublished poem of 1844,

[4] 'If such an institution as the 'universal Church' is to exist as more than a sentiment and an ideal . . . then some such central institution [as the Papacy] would seem to be more than just a convenience': Abbott *et al.*, *Catholicity*, 36.
[5] 'Anglo-Catholics made a great deal of the feast of the Assumption': W.S.F. Pickering, *Anglo-Catholicism* (1989), 39.
[6] See G. Maron, 'Mary in Protestant theology', in H. Küng and J. Moltmann, eds, *Mary in the Churches* (Edinburgh, 1983), 40–2.
[7] A.M. Allchin, *The Joy of all Creation. An Anglican Meditation on the Place of Mary*, 2nd edn (1993), Pt II, 'The Witness Continued', ch. 7, 'John Keble and B.F. Westcott'.

'Mother out of sight', he disavowed more extreme inferences: 'You see when I recommend the Ave, I mean merely the Scripture part.'[8]

Perhaps more significantly, it is not Keble who is the fountain-head of Anglo-Catholic theologians' views on Mary, but Pusey. In his first *Eirenicon*, Pusey surveyed the teaching and popular devotion of Roman Catholicism concerning Mary. The dogma of the immaculate conception had smuggled in a principle 'which made all evidence *as to fact* superfluous', namely that 'the Church, being incapable of erring, any thing taught throughout the Church . . . was necessarily true'.[9] To those who believed the Pope's personal infallibility, 'the fact that he pronounced any thing to be true was to be a proof that it had been always taught'.[10] For Pusey, like Luther, the only justification for Marian titles (such as the thoroughly orthodox *Theotokos*) was that they pointed to the central truth of Christian faith, the doctrine of the incarnation.[11]

Pusey's position was shared by the next generation of Anglo-Catholic theologians. Henry Liddon, for example, wrote that 'I never pass the Festival of the Assumption . . . without being thankful that I am not a Roman Catholic. For here you have an instance of a presumed fact, resting on no historical basis whatsoever, yet itself made the basis of a devotional system.'[12] The immaculate conception, he argued in his Bampton lectures, 'appears to presuppose a Church . . . which is empowered to make actual additions to the number of revealed certainties'.[13] Yet Liddon's position did not rule out a high estimate of Mary; he revered 'the unique prerogative and Perpetual Virginity of Mary, Mother of God'.[14]

Liddon's position was also almost identical with that of Charles Gore, whose 'Liberal Catholicism' is usually contrasted by historians with Liddon's conservatism.[15] Far apart though they may have been on the question of biblical inspiration, their conception of the *content* of

---

[8] A letter to J.T. Coleridge, dated 18 June 1845, cited in J.T. Coleridge, *A Memoir of the Rev. John Keble* (Oxford, 1869), 281. It is Coleridge who published the poem in full, at 305–9.

[9] E.B. Pusey, *The Church of England a Portion of Christ's One Holy Catholic Church, and a Means of Restoring Visible Unity. An Eirenicon* (Oxford, 1865), 148 [my italics].

[10] Ibid., 149.

[11] E.B. Pusey, *First Letter to the Very Rev. J.H. Newman* [Eirenicon II] (Oxford, 1869), 29.

[12] J.O. Johnston, *Life and Letters of Henry Parry Liddon* (1905), 93.

[13] H.P. Liddon, *The Divinity of Our Lord and Saviour Jesus Christ* (1869), 433.

[14] G.W.E. Russell, *Dr. Liddon* (1905), 135.

[15] See, for example, B.M.G. Reardon, *Religious Thought in the Victorian Age. A Survey from Coleridge to Gore* (1980), 430–1.

the apostolic faith was almost identical. The Church's dogmas, argued Gore, were justified on the basis of the dual appeal to primitive history and scripture.[16] Where doctrines lacked scriptural warrant, 'even without condemning them as positively heretical, we shall have no hesitation in declining them with emphatic decision'.[17]

Nor is it easy to find other Anglo-Catholic theologians who did substantially disagree with the position laid down by Pusey. Darwell Stone, the conservative Principal of Pusey House, could acknowledge the growing tide of Marian devotion, but in his *Outlines of Christian Dogma* he resisted the view that either the Immaculate Conception or the Assumption could ever be viewed as anything other than permissible opinions.[18]

Citing a string of authors – Pusey, Liddon, Gore, Stone – in this way can give the impression that there was a vigorous and lively debate amongst Anglo-Catholic theologians about Mary. But that was far from the case. There is little evidence of any strong interest in Marian doctrine amongst Anglo-Catholic writers even in the first half of the twentieth century. Surveying the work of Kenneth Kirk, Oliver Quick, Leonard Hodgson, Lionel Thornton, and Gregory Dix, to name but a few, one struggles to find more than a few passing references, and even then the broad continuity with Pusey is evident. Quick, for example, completely ignored Marian doctrine in his best-selling *Doctrines of the Creed*.[19] Nor did it feature in the influential essay collections *Essays Catholic and Critical*, *Essays Catholic and Missionary*, and *Northern Catholicism*.[20]

Yet this absence of theologians' interest before the middle of the twentieth century is certainly not reflected in the popular devotional culture and history of Anglo-Catholicism. The *Book of Common Prayer* had cut out from English devotion any sign of the medieval cult of the Blessed Virgin Mary. But Anglo-Catholics were increasingly susceptible to the influence of Roman Catholic practice. The formation of a number of Marian societies, such as the Confraternity of Our Lady in 1880, and later the Union of the Holy Rosary and the League of Our

---

[16] C. Gore, *The Creed of the Christian* (1895), 17.

[17] Idem, *Roman Catholic Claims*, 7th edn (1900), 70–1.

[18] D. Stone, *The Faith of an English Catholic* (1926), 82–8; idem, *Outline of Christian Dogma* (1903), 57–9.

[19] O.C. Quick, *Doctrines of the Creed* (1938), 160.

[20] E.G. Selwyn, ed., *Essays Catholic and Critical* (1926); E.R. Morgan, ed., *Essays Catholic and Missionary* (1928); N.P. Williams and C. Harris, eds, *Northern Catholicism* (1933).

Lady, reflected growing interest in Marian devotion.[21] The revival of Walsingham in the early twentieth century, encouraged by influential Anglo-Catholic laity such as Lord Halifax, though controversial, was to create a significant centre of Anglican Marian devotion.[22] Marian hymns appeared, such as those by Stuckey Coles, whose 'Ye who own the faith of Jesus', with its rousing chorus 'Hail Mary, full of grace', had already become something of an anthem for Anglo-Catholics by the time of the first Anglo-Catholic Congress in 1923.[23] In time, as Pickering points out, Anglo-Catholics and 'Anglo-Papalists', as he calls them, were to adopt Marian devotions such as the recitation of the rosary, the angelus, and the litany and the vespers of the Blessed Virgin.[24]

By the middle of the twentieth century a gap had opened up in Anglo-Catholicism. Laity and clergy were adopting a richness in Marian devotion which was perhaps bound, in time, to drag doctrinal reflection in its wake. Anglo-Catholic theologians, on the other hand, even conceding some space for the development of Marian devotion, neither considered the question of Marian doctrine to be of much significance, nor were prepared to countenance development beyond the scriptural and patristic norms.

Given this background, the provenance of Austin Farrer's views on Mary is clear. Yet the sermon 'On being an Anglican' is not by any means the most considered of his works on this. Instead, it is necessary to turn to two articles published some years later, after the Second Vatican Council had begun its work. These are 'Mary, Scripture and tradition', and 'Infallibility and historical revelation'.[25] In the latter, Farrer repeated his earlier charge: the two Marian decrees, he claimed, had the 'alarming appearance of an infallible fact-factory going full blast'.[26]

---

[21] J.S. Reed, *Glorious Battle. The Cultural Politics of Victorian Anglo-Catholicism* (1996), 89; P.G. Cobb, 'The development of modern day pilgrimage', in Anon., *Walsingham: Pilgrimage and History* (Walsingham, 1999), 157.

[22] C. Colven, 'The Anglican presence in Walsingham', in Guild of Our Lady of Ransom, *Walsingham 1061–1538, 1897–1997* (1998), 85–8.

[23] Pickering, *Anglo-Catholicism*, 50–2.

[24] Ibid., 38.

[25] E.L. Mascall and H.S. Box, eds, *The Blessed Virgin Mary* (1963); A.M.Farrer *et al., Infallibility in the Church: an Anglican-Catholic Dialogue* (1968).

[26] A.M. Farrer, 'Infallibility and historical revelation', repr. in idem, *Interpretation and Belief* (1976), 164.

In both, Farrer's broad continuity with Pusey is evident from his appeal to historical and scriptural fact:

> It is my special concern, as a reformed Christian, to emphasize the necessity of a constant overhaul of dogmatic development by the standard of Christian origins; and 'Christian origins' can only mean in practice the *evidences we have* for Christian origins; and they come down pretty nearly to the New Testament writings, and the primitive sacramental usage.[27]

For Farrer, then, revelation was 'the concordant testimony of Gospel fact and inspired Church'.[28] Scripture, reflected in the primitive *regulum fidei*, imposed a limit on authentic doctrinal decision-making: the Church could not definitively infer as presumed fact doctrines for which there was no historical testimony.[29] The Marian dogmas were a 'surely vicious' application of the principle that the Church could deduce what was theologically fitting, since not only was there no evidence that God had acted this way, but there was 'no possibility ever that there should be'.[30]

Farrer appeared to be pushing his argument further than Pusey. 'Mary, Scripture and tradition' contained an extended examination of the grounds of the virginal conception. Farrer noted that the scriptural evidence for the doctrine was both late (Matthew, Luke, and John, but not Paul or Mark) and not *prima facie* harmonious.[31] This was – in Farrer's terms – historical evidence, but not strong evidence. Consequently, the main prop of the doctrine was the Church's decision that it was 'absolutely fitting', from which it 'presumed the soundness' of the scriptural testimony.[32] In essence, Farrer said, the Church 'judged Christ to have been virginally conceived because they thought he must have been, not because they had evidence that he was'.[33]

Like his nineteenth-century forebears, Farrer was troubled by the relationship of scripture, history, and faith. Studying for a time under Emil Brunner at Zurich in the early 1930s, and noted as much for his forays into New Testament exegesis as for his philosophical theology, he was well equipped to probe the epistemological and hermeneutic

---

[27] Ibid., 158 [Farrer's italics].
[28] A.M. Farrer, 'Mary, Scripture and tradition', in Mascall and Box, *Blessed Virgin Mary*, 118.
[29] Ibid., 122.
[30] Ibid., 121–2.
[31] Ibid., 116.
[32] Ibid., 117.
[33] Ibid., 112.

conditions of Christian doctrine.[34] His defence of the virginal conception, and his criticism of the Marian dogmas, was not one more
instance of the lamentable history of liberal Protestantism's attempts to
trim Christian faith. Rather, it aimed to understand the inner rationale
of the Church's proclamation of truth. Farrer's approach did not give
priority to the independently-verified conclusions of historical scholarship over the traditional facts of revelation. Instead it insisted on the
presumed historicity of revealed fact itself.[35] The appearance of deviation from Pusey's position was just that – appearance. The basic ground
of Farrer's acknowledgement of the virginal conception and his rejection of the Marian dogmas was the same as that of Pusey – history and
text.

Farrer contended, then, not that the Marian dogmas were demonstrably untrue, but that there was nothing demonstrable about them.
The Church, Farrer insisted, is inspired 'to proclaim facts, and to inter-
pret facts; but not to create facts'.[36] For Farrer, infallibility was 'an
expression of the faith that God will effectively guide his Church in the
way of truth and salvation'.[37] But it had the status of a regulative idea; it
could not be 'spotted, pinned down, identified with an ecclesiastical
organ, or demanded on a given occasion'.[38] Like Pusey, Farrer implicitly
conceded two dimensions in Christian belief about Mary. In one,
authoritative teaching rested on the facts of scripture and primitive
faith, and constituted the essence of the Christian faith. In the other,
particular teachings about Mary rested on no such basis, could not be
required of Christians, and could not be regarded as essential.[39]

Yet even Farrer was not averse to Marian devotion. If generally
restrained in his language on Mary, still there is sufficient indication of

[34] On Farrer's studies in Germany and Switzerland, see P. Curtis, *A Hawk among Spar-
rows. A Biography of Austin Farrer* (1985), 75–80, 96–103.

[35] Farrer did nevertheless see as established without question in the nineteenth century
the view that scholarship is revisable, and that scholarship affects what we can conclude to be
the teaching of scripture: 'to admit primitivity as a judge or as a control is to submit to scholarship or historianship': Farrer, 'Infallibility', 158.

[36] Farrer, 'Mary', 113.

[37] Farrer, 'Infallibility', 162.

[38] Ibid., 163. This marks Farrer's position out clearly from that implied in the recent
ARCIC II report, *The Gift of Authority* (1999), in which the question 'What kind of statement
could be declared infallibly as fact?' is not dealt with at all.

[39] The dependence of this position on the Protestant tradition of 'fundamentals of faith'
is evident: see, for example, S.W. Sykes, 'The fundamentals of Christianity', in idem,
Unashamed Anglicanism (1995), 64–80. Though Sykes assumes here a general Tractarian
hostility to the use of the term, the use of the concept itself was, as I have indicated, more
widespread in Tractarian thought than he acknowledges.

a high regard for her: 'Her glory is that she is the virgin mother of God; what more can be added to it?'[40] Though Mary could not be regarded as the 'archetype, or universal matrix of the Church', still she was glorified 'by being taken up' into the Church's function of being mother to the children of God, and this in a 'unique way', through her motherhood of Christ.[41] In his preaching he rarely succumbed to an idealized portrait of Mary. He could even claim that the point of John's telling of the miracle at Cana was to show the foolishness of human beings (in this case Mary).[42] Yet he could also imaginatively explore the life and maternal feeling of Mary with immense sensitivity, as in his posthumously-published sermon, 'The friendship of Jesus', in which he describes Mary's faith growing through her separation from Jesus: 'Once he had been hers, now she was proud to be called his, and found her happiness in the bond with a son whose works and words were full of godhead.'[43] Five years before delivering the sermon with which this paper began, Farrer had already signalled a change of heart on the rosary by publishing his own commentary and prayers for it.[44]

Farrer himself, then, was a sign of a developing Marian sensibility within Anglo-Catholicism. What is striking now about his criticism of the evidential basis of the Marian dogmas is that it was expressed just at the time when other theologians were beginning to reflect a fundamental shift in Anglo-Catholic perceptions of them. Farrer's article on 'Mary, Scripture and tradition' was already somewhat at odds with other contributions to the collection in which it appeared. H.S. Box, for example, affirmed the immaculate conception of Mary on grounds opposed to Farrer, assuming it as fact: 'The Immaculate Conception was a privilege bestowed upon Mary . . . to the honour of the Second Person of the Blessed Trinity.'[45] In 1968, the year of Farrer's death, Eric Mascall tentatively affirmed the persuasiveness of the doctrine, attributing it to

---

[40] Farrer, 'Mary', 123.

[41] Ibid., 124.

[42] Farrer, *The End of Man*, 155. This is in a sermon preached in Keble College chapel in 1966.

[43] A.M. Farrer, *Words for Life* (1993), 13. Though undated, the sermon 'The friendship of Jesus' was probably preached in Trinity College chapel, Oxford, before Farrer left to go to Keble College as Warden in 1960: see Leslie Houlden's introduction, in Farrer, *Words for Life*, xi–xiii.

[44] In A.M. Farrer, *Lord I Believe* (1955), 80–95.

[45] H.S. Box, 'The Immaculate Conception', in Mascall and Box, *The Blessed Virgin Mary*, 88.

greater sophistication in our understanding of original sin.[46] By the late 1970s, John Macquarrie, in a bold side-stepping of Farrer's position, could insist that Christian truth was 'mutually implicate or coinherent', and that this removed the need for truths lower in the hierarchy of truth to be grounded explicitly on scripture and tradition.[47] For him, the immaculate conception was 'a clear implicate of basic Christian doctrines which we all accept'.[48] To Box, Mascall, and Macquarrie, we could add, amongst others, Donald Allchin, and other contributors to the Ecumenical Society of the Blessed Virgin Mary.[49]

Why – briefly – did the theological climate change towards the end of Farrer's life? Three possible reasons stand out. First, as the whole history of Anglo-Catholicism arguably indicates, theological development often follows rather than precedes popular devotion. The flowering of Marian devotion in Anglo-Catholicism perhaps subtly eroded the determination of its theologians to maintain a sharp distinction between the required truth of faith and permissible expressions of it. We may say, then, that the gradual acceptance of the Marian dogmas by many Anglo-Catholics was a classic instance of the *lex orandi, lex credendi*. Even so, it should be noted that this development marked a new and distinct phase in the theological history of Anglo-Catholicism. Much of the ritual development of the late nineteenth and early twentieth centuries was predicated on a common reinterpretation of eucharistic theology, placing the movement in what we can now see as a Europe-wide change in the ethos and shape of Christian worship and belief.[50] The same could not be said for Marian devotion: here was a dimension of Christian faith and practice which involved different and more contested grounds of appeal.

Second, the effect of Vatican II and the changes it initiated in Roman Catholicism on many Anglicans was paradoxical. The seeming readiness of Roman Catholics to acknowledge the weight of Protestant criticism, far from reinforcing wholeheartedly Anglican determination to maintain articulated grounds of objection to 'Romanist innovation',

[46]   E.L. Mascall, 'The Mother of God', in A. Stacpoole, ed., *Mary's Place in Ecumenical Dialogue* (Slough, 1982), 95.

[47]   J. Macquarrie, 'Immaculate Conception', in ibid., 100.

[48]   Ibid., 106.

[49]   Allchin, *Joy of All Creation*; Stacpoole, *Mary's Place*; McLoughlin Pinnock, *Mary is for Everyone* (Leominster, 1997).

[50]   See, for example, Y. Brilioth, *Eucharistic Faith and Practice Evangelical and Catholic* (1930); also, J. Fenwick and B. Spinks, *Worship in Transition. The Twentieth Century Liturgical Movement* (Edinburgh, 1995).

instead blunted it. It became harder to argue forcefully against infallibility, for example, and easier to countenance the possibility of agreement on matters such as the Petrine primacy. Correspondingly, more latitude opened up for Anglicans to acknowledge the Marian dogmas, albeit in largely unofficial ways. In this context, the recent restoration of the feast day of the Blessed Virgin Mary on 15 August (the feast day of the Assumption of Mary) to the Anglican calendar is surely significant.

Third, hand in hand with this greater openness to Roman Catholic views went the growing participation of Roman Catholics in the ecumenical movement. This opened up increasingly the possibility of joint study of Marian doctrine, and a greater freedom and sympathy of approach from Protestant theologians. In the Anglican-Roman Catholic ecumenical dialogue so far this has issued in just one paragraph on Marian doctrine, though even here the balance of the paragraph is to emphasise considerable areas of agreement on Mary's role and significance, before noting continuing differences on the status of the dogmas of the Immaculate Conception and Assumption.[51]

Farrer's position 'On being an Anglican', for all its force of language and argument, was already outmoded in tone, almost before the ink was dry. Anglicans – and particularly Anglo-Catholics – have continued to be troubled by the question of Anglican identity throughout the late twentieth century. Despite his strong defence of the plea of historical and revelatory fact, as we have seen Farrer himself was not immune to the attraction of Marian devotion. Yet his published work suggests that, had he lived, he would not have been impressed by the changing theological climate here sketched out, but would have maintained the critical responsibility of the Christian philosopher and theologian to point to the requirement that Church teaching should be authenticated by the united testimony of scripture and primitive tradition. In Farrer's words, 'the Catholic historian, however Catholic, is as much an historian as any other. He has Catholic expectations, he cannot force facts.'[52]

Trinity Hall, Cambridge

[51] ARCIC I, *The Final Report* (1982), 93–4.
[52] Farrer, 'Infallibility', 162.

MARY IN CONTEMPORARY ETHIOPIAN
ORTHODOX DEVOTION

by MARTA CAMILLA WRIGHT

IN a double monastery located near the important pilgrimage place of Lalibela,[1] two nuns I had been interviewing suddenly asked me, 'Why don't you ask us about Mary?' They wanted to tell me about how she cared for them, loved them, and answered their prayers. 'Whatever we ask her she will give us', they stated. Mary was important for the Ethiopian Orthodox believers I worked with; it became obvious that Mary has an exclusive place in Ethiopian devotion in general. Most of the time, Ethiopian Christians relate to Christ as a distant saviour and turn to Mary in dealing with their daily lives. Mary is pure in both body and soul, a human being without sin, so that Christ becomes the union of divinity and humanity.

Mary's role in popular Ethiopian piety, and also in Ethiopian orthodoxy, is that of mediatrix and healer, and even glides into that of co-redemptrix. It is highly important to venerate her. As an Ethiopian theologian and priest puts it, 'We can conclude that those who do not venerate her or ask her intercession and do not bow to her will lose the kingdom of God'.[2] In the introductory text of one of the most important books in the Ethiopian Christian tradition, *The Miracles of Mary* (*Ta'amre Mariam*), Mary is addressed in this manner:

> Oh my Lady, mother of salvation, mother of light, mother of incense, mother of offering, mother of fire, thou only mother, mother of the king, mother of Christ the Messiah. Oh mother, divine and awe-inspiring, through the compassion of thy son look thou upon our supplications and be thou graciously pleased with our entreaties, and by thy prayer do thou cool the wrath of thy son. Amen.[3]

This article presents something of the historical evolution of the

---

[1] Double monasteries are common in Ethiopia, with nuns and monks living in the same area.

[2] Kesis Merahi Kefjalew, *The Covenant of Holy Mary Zion with Ethiopia* (Addis Ababa, 1997), 46–7.

[3] Sir E.A.T. Wallis Budge, *One Hundred and Ten Miracles of Our Lady Mary* (1923), 3.

Marian Cult, and offers some examples of the extraordinary importance Marian devotion has in contemporary Ethiopia.[4] The cult's importance can be explained by its being rooted in two main characteristics of Ethiopian Christianity: the Ethiopian Orthodox understanding of the relationship between Mary and Christ *qua* female and male, human and divine; and the idea of Christology from above.

* * *

Christianity was resolutely introduced into Ethiopia from Syria during the fourth century CE by two Syrians, Frumentius and Aedesius, who became acquainted with the King of Axum.[5] The Axumite empire had earlier been exposed to Christianity via travelling merchants using the Red Sea route; Christianity was, however, not institutionalized until the arrival of the Syrians. The King of Axum is understood by scholars to have accepted the Christian religion *c*.340 CE. Later the Tsadkans and the Nine Saints, Unionites from Syria, established monasteries, some of them containing schools. These institutions became important for the spread and rooting of Christianity in Ethiopia.

Mary became an important object of veneration in Ethiopia when King Zara Yaqob (1434–68) made Marian veneration official.[6] Pictures of Mary were worn by people as a symbol of piety and were understood to have a protective function for believers.[7] According to Getachew one reason for King Zara Yaqob's focus on Mary rests upon the way the King was conceived and born. The King's mother had suffered a miscarriage before she conceived him, and had made a promise to Mary that if the next baby was born safely she would dedicate him to the service of Mary. Consequently, Zara Yaqob was trained in monasteries, so that by the time he succeeded to the throne he was an able theologian. During his reign, the kingdom was challenged by heretical groups and dogged with theological and political controversies. Zara Yaqob used Mary as a focus around which to unite the church and kingdom. During his reign he introduced thirty-three feasts of Mary into the

---

[4] The paper is based on field research conducted in Ethiopia during 1998–2000.

[5] One of them was in fact crowned after a series of coincidences.

[6] Getachew Haile, *The Mariology of Emperor Zara Yaqob of Ethiopia*, Orientalia Christiana Analecta, 242 (Rome, 1992); Marilyn E. Heldman, 'Maryam Seyon: Mary of Zion', in R. Grierson, ed., *African Zion. The Sacred Art of Ethiopia* (New Haven, CT, and London, 1993), 153.

[7] David L. Elias, 'Our Lady Mary with Her Beloved Son: protective prayer aid?', in Katsuyoshi Fukui, Eisei Kurimoto, and Masayoshi Shigeta, eds, *Papers of the 13th International Conference of Ethiopian Studies* (Kyoto, 1997), 222.

Ethiopian calendar, and promoted the production of icons.[8] Reading
from the *Miracles of Mary* was introduced into the liturgy in 1441.[9]

Contemporary official teaching of the significance of Mary is
described thus:

> The Virgin Mother of God has a very special place in the Ethiopian
> cult, and devotion to our Mother holds the highest place. Ethiopia
> is known as the country of Mary, her protectress.... She is loved by
> her Son so dearly that He will grant her every prayer. Because of
> the mission she received from God, her life is most closely linked
> with the mysteries of Jesus Christ, and there is no one who has
> followed in the footsteps of the Incarnate Word more closely and
> with more merit than she; and no one had more grace and power
> over the heart of the Son of God, and through him with the heav-
> enly father.[10]

* * *

Several books in Ethiopian Orthodox literature are dedicated to Mary,
among those are *The Visions of the Virgin*, *The Book of the Birth of Mary*,
The Book of the Passing of Mary, the *Praises of Mary*, and the *Miracles of
Mary*.[11] The *Miracles of Mary*, which originated in twelfth-century
France, consists of stories of miracles conducted by Mary.[12] In the thirteenth century the text was translated from Latin into Arabic in Egypt
and then into Ethiopic during the reign of King Dawit (1382–1413).
According to Wallis Budge, the Ethiopian collection consists of at least
366 miracles, but there is evidence that there are as many as 600,
including those that originate in Ethiopia.[13] This high number indicates
the importance of Mary and her miraculous power to Ethiopian
Christians.

The introductory text of the *Miracles of Mary* describes the position

---

[8] Heldman, 'Maryam Seyon', 72.

[9] Ibid., 73.

[10] A. Wondmagegnehu and J. Motovu, eds, *The Ethiopian Orthodox Church* (Addis Ababa, 1970), 106.

[11] To my knowledge, *The Miracles of Mary* is the only text which has been translated into English. The titles used in this text are translations from Amharic made by Fisseha Tadesse. *The Book of the Passing of Mary* is translated as *De transitu Mariae apocrypha aethiopice*, ed. Victor Arras, Corpus Scriptorum Christianorum Orientalium, 342: Scriptores Aethiopici, 66 (Louvain, 1973).

[12] E. Cerulli, *Il libro etiopico dei Miracoli di Maria e le sue fonti nelle letterature del medio evo latino* (Rome, 1943).

[13] Budge, *One Hundred and Ten Miracles.*

which, some Ethiopians argue, Mary has in Ethiopia. She is called the 'redeemer' and the one who brings salvation. Moreover, the world was created for her sake, a statement which is made about Christ in the New Testament (Colossians 1.1). This standpoint is debated within the Church, but because this is a text known to the laity who listen to recitals from the *Miracles of Mary* every Sunday, this is how many Ethiopian believers understand Mary's role, and they venerate her accordingly. Mary can almost be said to have taken over the role of Christ:

> Our Lady Mary existed before the world [was created] in the mind of God. For the sake of Mary, Adam and Eve were made, and Adam called his wife 'Life' because he knew that Mary would go forth from his loins and from the womb of his wife. What book can contain the majesty of Mary? For the sake of Mary the whole world was made. . . . Honour ye Our Lady Mary, oh children of this Church, for Our Lady Mary is the redemption for sinners, and Our Lady Mary giveth gracious gifts unto those who minister unto her with good service. Put your confidence in Our Lady Mary with all your hearts, and have no doubt whatsoever but that it is she who bringeth you salvation.[14]

The *Miracles of Mary* are normally recited every morning before prayer (*kidan*) and every Sunday after Mass (*qidase*) outside the church. Afterwards there will usually be preaching on a topic from the Gospels, but in parish churches in the countryside the priests, who are normally not theologically trained, often preach on the *Miracles of Mary* instead of the Gospels. Consequently, Mary gains a very important place.

For the many Christians who do not receive communion, hearing the *Miracles of Mary* becomes a substitute for it. Among the laity it is usual for only children and old people to take holy communion, because Ethiopian Christians rarely participate during their sexually active years. If married people take holy communion they have to be sexually abstinent for twenty-four hours before they go to church, they have to fast and be generally clean. Priests and deacons also have to observe a rule of abstinence for twenty-four hours before the Mass. Monks and nuns, however, who live in perpetual celibacy, may take communion, unless they have a bleeding wound or are menstruating. Many Ethiopian Orthodox nuns pray that Mary will terminate their

---

14 Ibid., 2.

menses so that they can maintain the rhythm of their spiritual practices without hindrance to their spiritual progress.

Ethiopian Christians face a strong conflict between purity and sex. Ethiopian Orthodox anthropology holds that human beings may achieve a state of holiness. For instance, Ethiopian ascetics who have reached the tenth and last step of their spiritual process sometimes turn into purely spiritual beings; their soul is no longer embodied. The methods of achieving this height of spirituality are ascetic practices which aim at purifying both the body and the soul. The main aim is to weaken the body so that one may not experience lust in either body or mind, and so become like both Mary and Christ.

Mary's miracles have achieved a soteriological status; she has the ability to heal those who listen to her miracles after Mass and believe in her. A nun confirms this perspective:

> Mary is pure and holy. She is necessary for the union with God, therefore she is a redeemer. Mary is our saviour; the female saviour of the world. Before you give birth to a child you will prepare everything for him. God also prepared for Adam. Before the world was created Mary was in God's thought. He had a council with the angels before he created the world. God showed both Adam and Mary to the angels and asked: shall I create Adam? The angels said: he is very sinful, but because of Mary, create Adam. So Adam was created because of Mary. When Jesus came he took her flesh and her soul, and became a human being in which he could keep his holiness.

The thirty-three Marian feasts that were introduced by King Zara Yaqob are still an official part of the liturgical year; they remain popular and are still widely observed. Among the fourteen *anaphora* of the Church, one is dedicated to Mary, and is performed on all the feasts of Mary, and on a number of other days. Ethiopians believe that Ethiopia has a special covenant in Mary's name and that she protects the country, since Ethiopia was given to her by her son when the holy family traveled through the country.[15] The feast of the Covenant of Mercy is celebrated every month, and is mainly connected to Mary. According to Kefjalew, 'The Lord gave the Covenant of Mercy so that

---

[15] Kefjalew, *Covenant of Holy Mary*; Wondmagegnehu and Motovu, *Ethiopian Orthodox Church*, 105–8.

all who plead in the name of the Mother of God will inherit blessing on earth and the everlasting kingdom and life in heaven.'[16]

Before a Marian feast, Ethiopian women prepare beer and the traditional bread, and they bring fresh grass to decorate the floor of their huts and houses. On the day of the feast people light a candle in front of their Marian icon, dress in white traditional dresses, and go to church in order to attend the 6 a.m. mass. After mass, at about 9 a.m., the neighbourhood of a Marian church is crowded with people heading towards their houses to celebrate with their relatives and friends. Certain traditions are connected to particular feasts. On the celebration of the birth of Mary, for instance, people eat cooked cereals and drink coffee outside their houses in memory of the birth of Mary. The birth of Mary is believed to have taken place in the open air on Mount Lebanon. Mary's mother lacked food, and the only food they had was cereals cooked in water.

The Marian fast (*filseta*), the two-week fast preceding the celebration of Mary's Assumption, is one of three important fasts in the Ethiopian Orthodox calendar, observed by both lay people (including children as young as seven years old) and clergy. The two other important fasts are the fast every Wednesday and Friday (*arbrob*) and the fifty-five days of fast preceding Easter.

Mary is important in people's daily prayers. The *Praises of Mary* are recited by most pious people every day. These hymns are attributed to Ephrem the Syrian. The *Praises of Mary* are perhaps the most common prayer in the Ethiopian Church, important for both lay people and priests. The rosary is often to be seen, and is an important method of prayer for the illiterate. In particular elderly widows,[17] who often become nuns during their last years in order to prepare for heavenly life and secure themselves a way of surviving, may be seen praying with their rosaries in the compounds of churches. Another prayer, the Image of Mary (*melke maryam*) is also widely used, and is a prayer honouring the beauty of the image of Mary.

There are some aspects of the Ethiopian Marian cult that are more strongly associated with women than with men. Some scholars have even interpreted the Marian cult in general as being of greater importance to women than to men. Helen Pankhurst describes the spiritual

---

[16] Kefjalew, *Covenant of Holy Mary*, 30.
[17] Widowers also choose this way of life in their last years, but possibly the number of elderly nuns is higher.

associations, the *mehaber*, as an example of this difference.[18] The members of the associations gather monthly, have mutual meals, make prayers, and help each other.[19] The male associations are often dedicated to St George, St Michael, or Jesus, whereas those of women are usually dedicated to Mary. Cressida Miller identifies the *Praises of Mary* as more widely sung by women than by men.[20] This indicates that Mary, although being important for all Ethiopian Christians, represents a female ideal.

There seems to be a close connection between the understanding Ethiopians have of Christ and their emphasis on Mary as mediatrix. The divine nature of Christ is emphasised in popular devotion. Even though Christ is the saviour, and he is understood as both fully God and fully human, his humanity is emphasised over his divinity. Alois Grillmeier argues that the Christology of the Ethiopian Orthodox Church is a Christology from above.[21] He says that Christianity was established in a culture strongly influenced by Jewish religion and introduced to Ethiopia from a pre-Chalcedonian environment. The Council of Nicaea (325) insisted that the Son was of one essence with the Father. The Ethiopian Orthodox Church rejects the Council of Chalcedon and does not accept the doctrine of the two natures. These are the historical roots of the contemporary popular understanding of Christ.

The strong emphasis placed upon Mary as intercessor is often explained by Ethiopians as the result of Christ's not being as empathetic as Mary. Mary's importance to Ethiopians witnesses to a more distant Christ. Mary is ascribed many of the qualities that are usually considered female among Ethiopian Orthodox Christians. On icons and in miracles Mary is often presented as the empathetic, sensitive mother, while Jesus is hard, just, and condemning. Some informants explain that Christ saved human beings once and for all, while Mary ministers the daily repeated forgiveness that the faithful require throughout their lives. It is Mary who begs Jesus to show mercy, on behalf of the sinners who call upon her, by reminding Jesus of the nurture she gave him as a child. From this perspective Mary and Jesus are stereotypes of female and male: the sensitive woman begging the strong man. Nevertheless,

---

[18] Helen Pankhurst, *Gender, Development and Identity: an Ethiopian Study* (1992).

[19] Eleonora Lvova, 'Forms of Marriage and the status of Women in Ethiopia', in Fukui, Kurimoto, and Shigeta, *Papers*, 583.

[20] Cressida Miller, 'Wedasse: Orality and Female Worship in the Ethiopian Orthodox Church', *Journal of Ethiopian Studies* (forthcoming).

[21] Alois Grillmeier, *Christ in Christian Tradition*, 2 vols (1996), 2:369.

even though Mary has such a pre-eminent position in the Church, she is not divine, but human, and has a subordinate position matching that of other women in relation to men. Mary represents the female, and in Judaeo-Christian tradition femaleness often represents humanity, subordinated to the male, which represents the divine. In Ethiopia only men can imitate Christ as priests, and women are subordinated to men in the spiritual hierarchy.

Among Ethiopian Orthodox Christians women are generally believed to be responsible for sin; this is because Eve seduced Adam to commit sin. Because Eve was a woman, all women are now responsible for sin. This, however, leaves contemporary women with the capability to help men to avoid committing (sexual) sin, unlike their foremother Eve. A nun stated that, 'Eve is responsible for our sin. Adam sinned through Eve. Women are more sinful than men because of Eve. We are now saved because of Mary, because she gave birth to Christ.'[22] Grillmeier argues that 'the anti-thesis Adam : Christ becomes here [in Ethiopian tradition] the juxtaposition between Adam : Eve and Mary'.[23] This is formulated by Kefjalew in this way, 'Because of our mother – Eve, all women were considered the source of sin. But since it is through Our Lady Mary we get salvation from sin. The early Eve gave us all sin and death. The second Eve, the Mother of God, Our Lady Mary gave us life eternal.'[24] In the commentary of the *Praise of Mary* (*Wuddase Mariam*) the relationship between Christ and Mary is described thus:

> Previously men were too proud of themselves because of the fact that a woman was taken of man. But now women are proud of themselves because of Mary, for even if Eve was taken from Adam, our Lord was also born from our Lady Mary. For this reason it has been said that 'just as man brings forth a woman without the help of any other woman, so also a woman brought forth a man without the help of any other man'.[25]

Mary can thus be understood as a source of the female and human spiritual ideal, and to represent the humanity of Christ. Her role in Ethiopian Orthodox contemporary devotion can partly be explained

---

[22] Interview, Waldebit Mariam, July 1999.
[23] Grillmeier, *Christ in Christian Tradition*, 2:368.
[24] Kefjalew, *Covenant of Holy Mary*, 15.
[25] Translation by Fisseha Tadesse, unpublished.

within the framework of the relationship between male and female, between Christ and Mary. Mary is the counterpart of Eve, who committed the initial sin, and is considered the redeemer of women and humanity. Moreover Christ is, to Ethiopian believers, a more distant figure, whereas Mary brings forth the prayers, and persuades Christ to fulfill the wishes. Mary has the role of the human-but-pure, almost divine, bridge between sinful, impure humans (particularly women, because they are more sinful than men) and the distant, sacred God. A nun stated, 'Everything we ask from Mary, she will give us. She will tell us good things. We meet her in dreams. We see her and hear her. She has a very nice and different smell.'[26]

---

[26] Interview, Waldebit Mariam, July 1999.